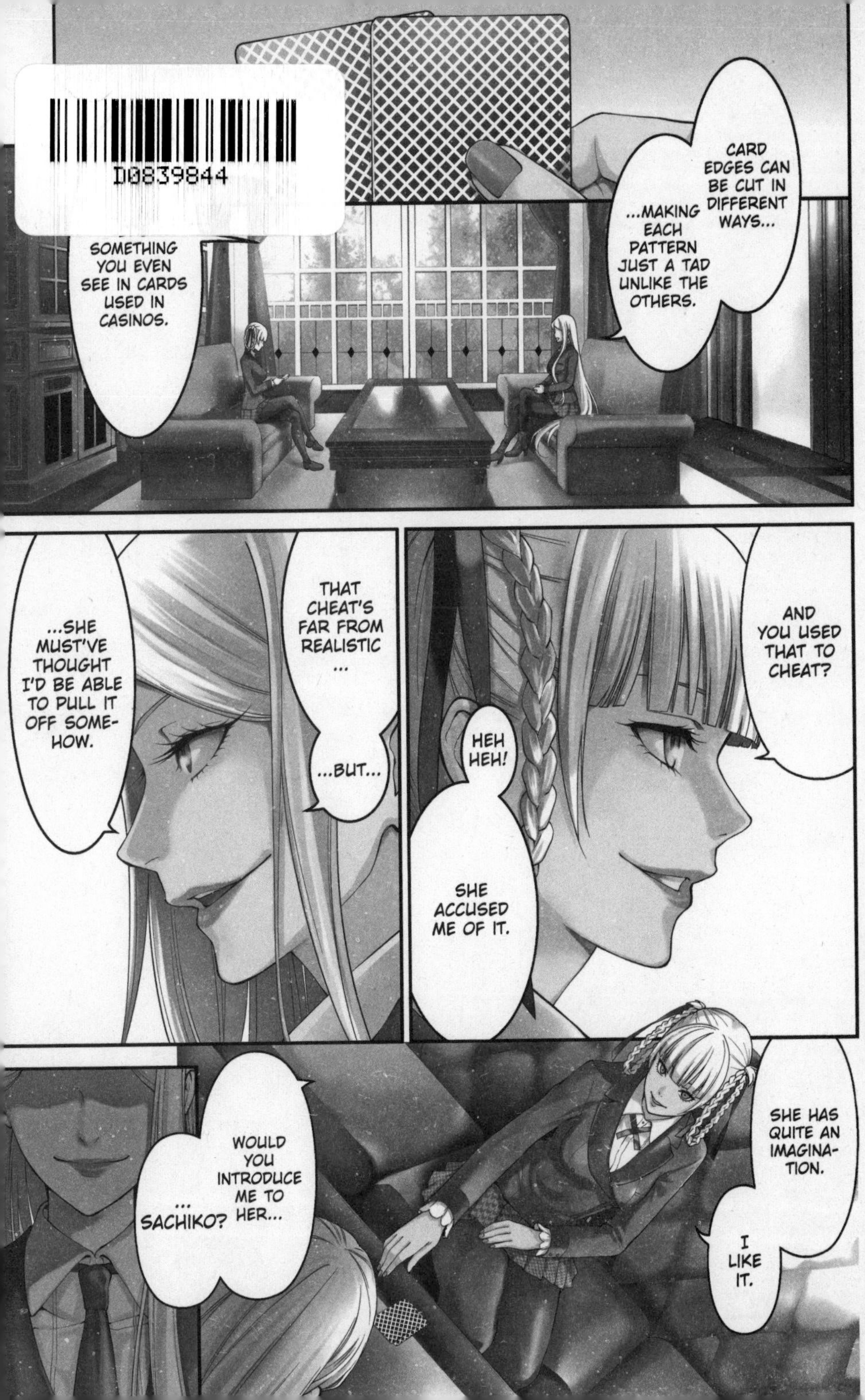
CARD EDGES CAN BE CUT IN DIFFERENT WAYS...
...MAKING EACH PATTERN JUST A TAD UNLIKE THE OTHERS.
SOMETHING YOU EVEN SEE IN CARDS USED IN CASINOS.
AND YOU USED THAT TO CHEAT?
HEH HEH!
SHE ACCUSED ME OF IT.
THAT CHEAT'S FAR FROM REALISTIC ...
...BUT...
...SHE MUST'VE THOUGHT I'D BE ABLE TO PULL IT OFF SOME-HOW.
SHE HAS QUITE AN IMAGINA-TION.
I LIKE IT.
WOULD YOU INTRODUCE ME TO HER...
...SACHIKO?

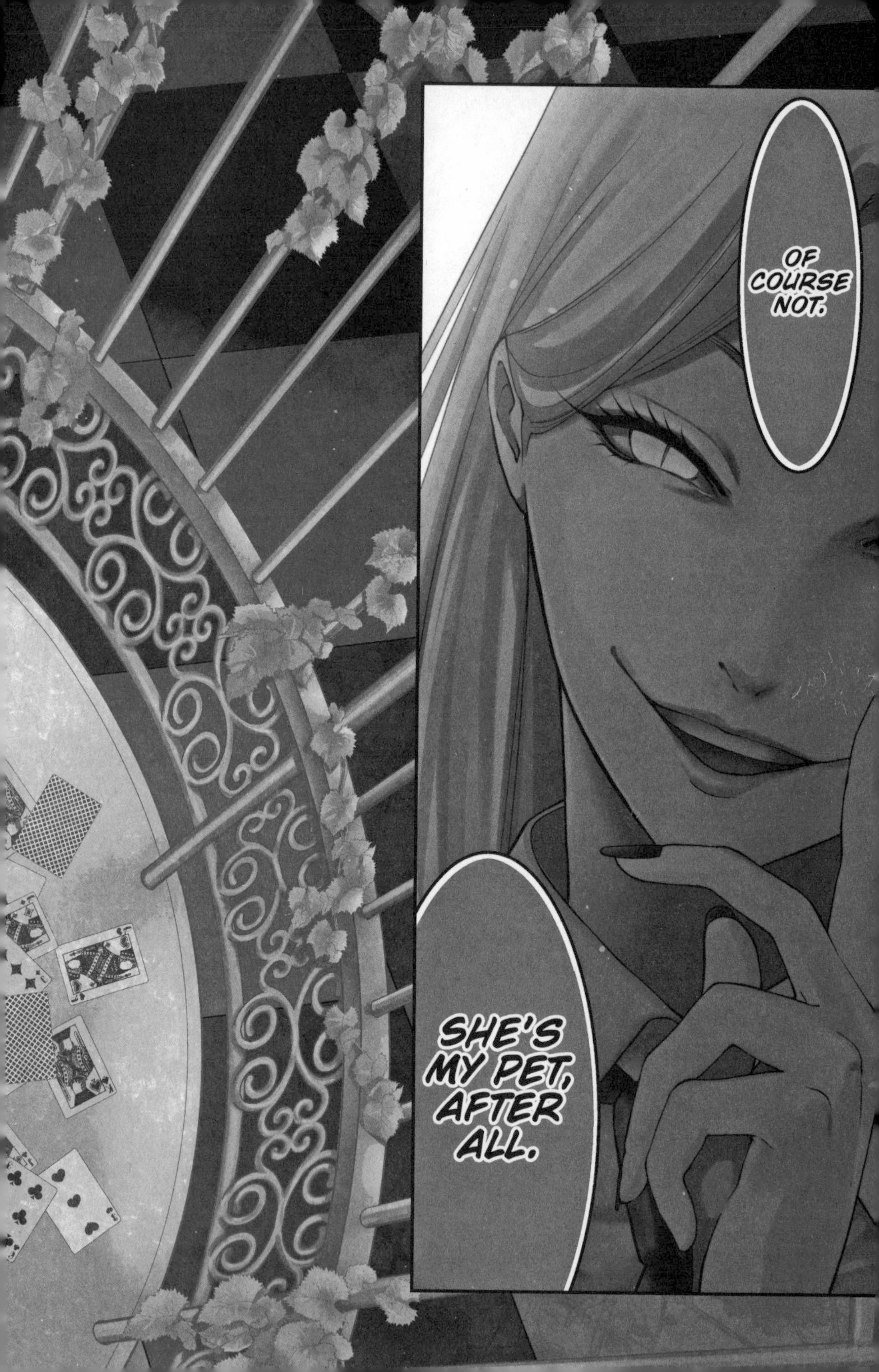
OF COURSE NOT.
SHE'S MY PET, AFTER ALL.

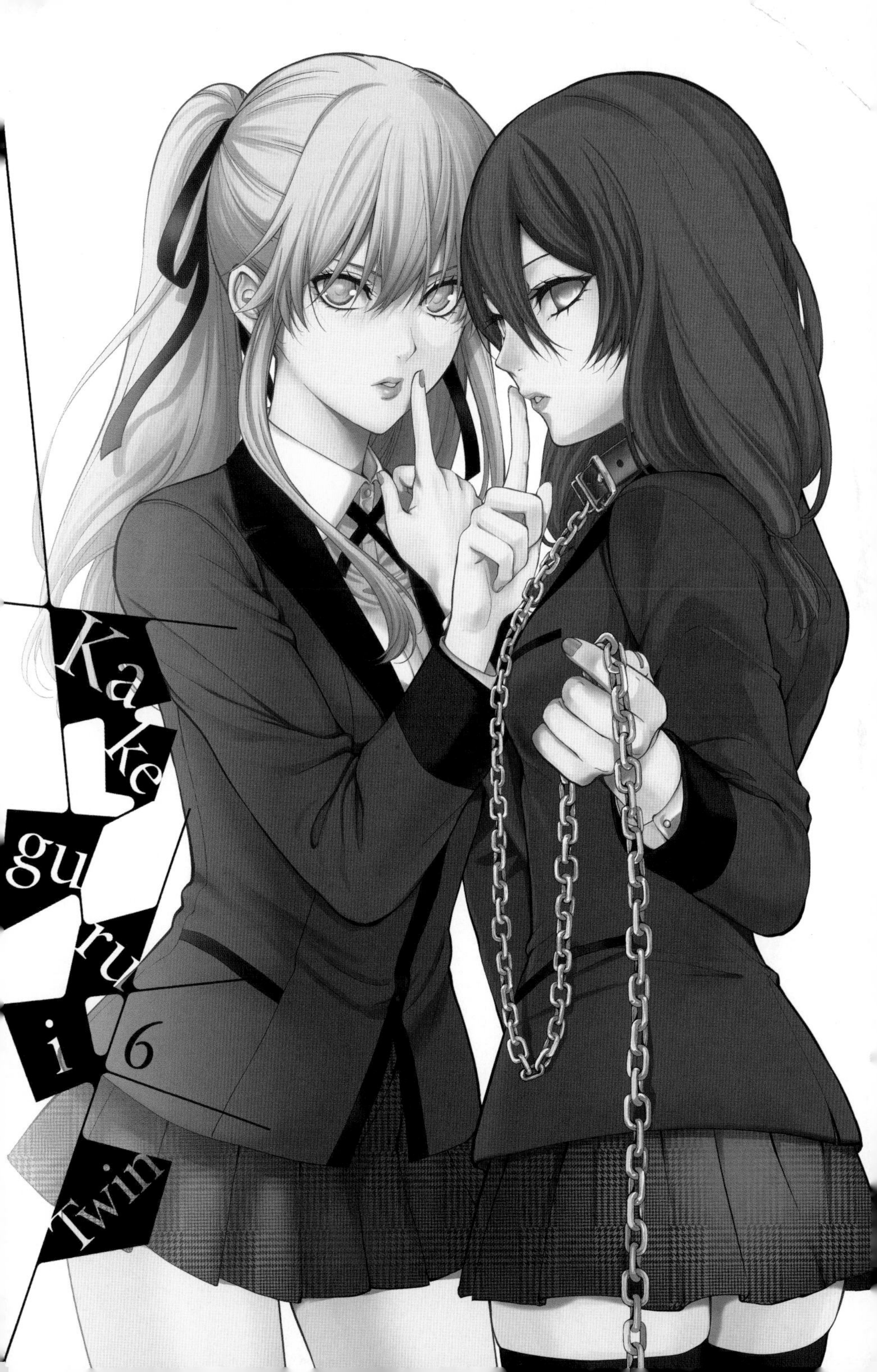
Kakegurui Twin 6

⑥

K
A
K
E
G
U
R
U
I

T
W
I
N

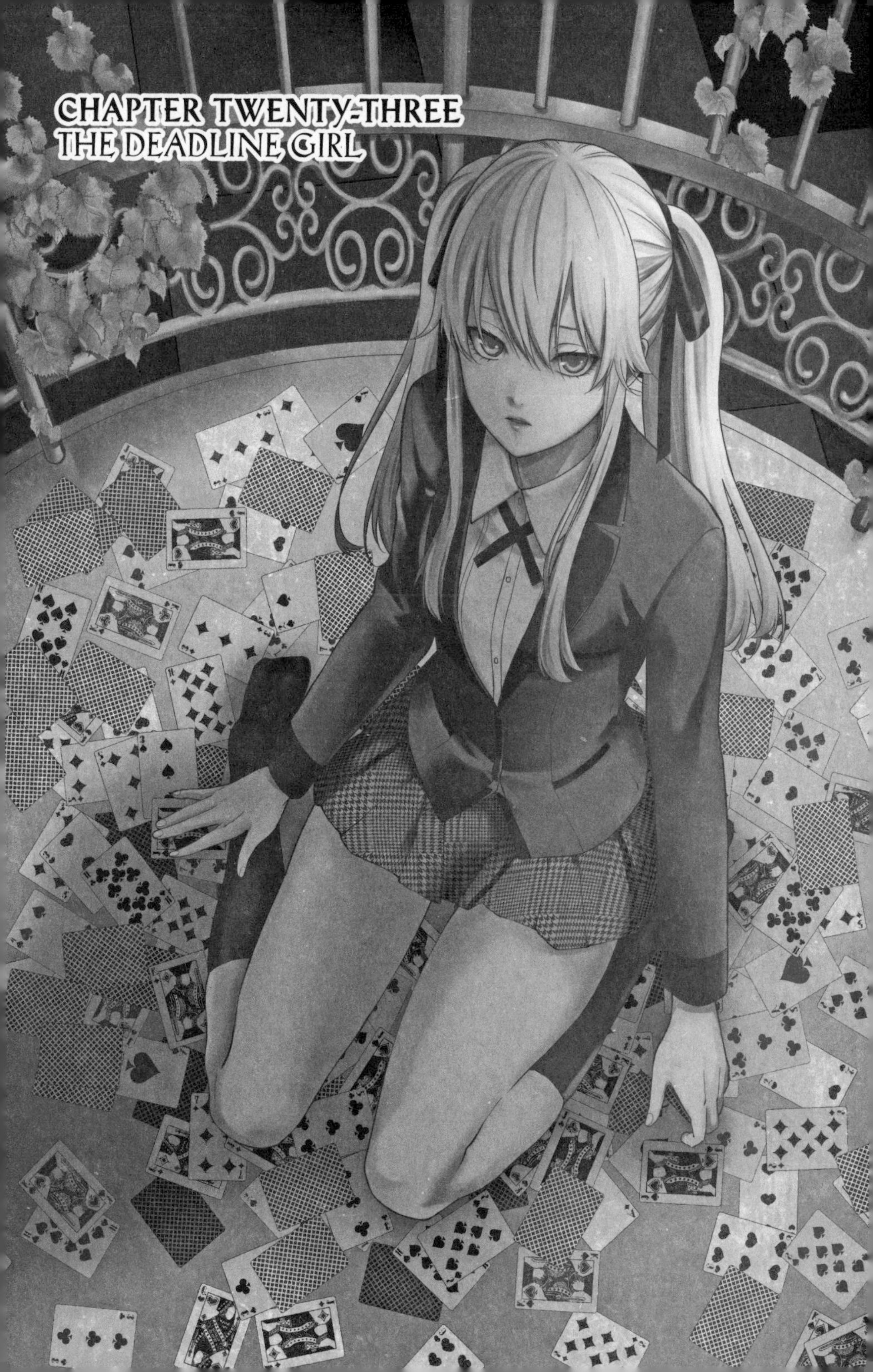
CHAPTER TWENTY-THREE
THE DEADLINE GIRL

Kakegurui Twin

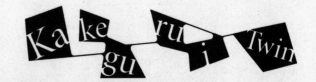

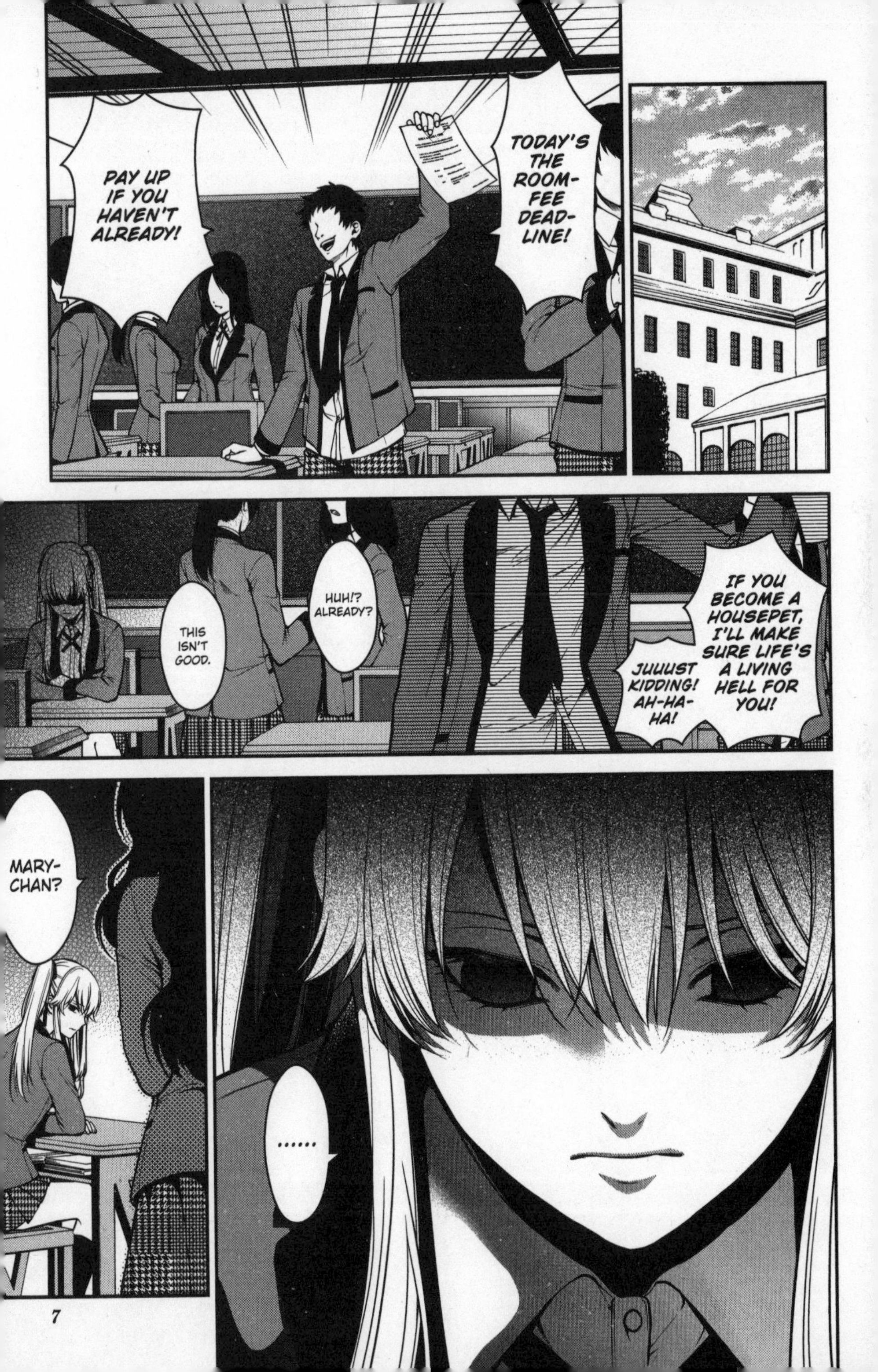
TODAY'S THE ROOM-FEE DEAD-LINE!
PAY UP IF YOU HAVEN'T ALREADY!
IF YOU BECOME A HOUSEPET, I'LL MAKE SURE LIFE'S A LIVING HELL FOR YOU!
JUUUST KIDDING! AH-HA-HA!
HUH!? ALREADY?
THIS ISN'T GOOD.
......
MARY-CHAN?

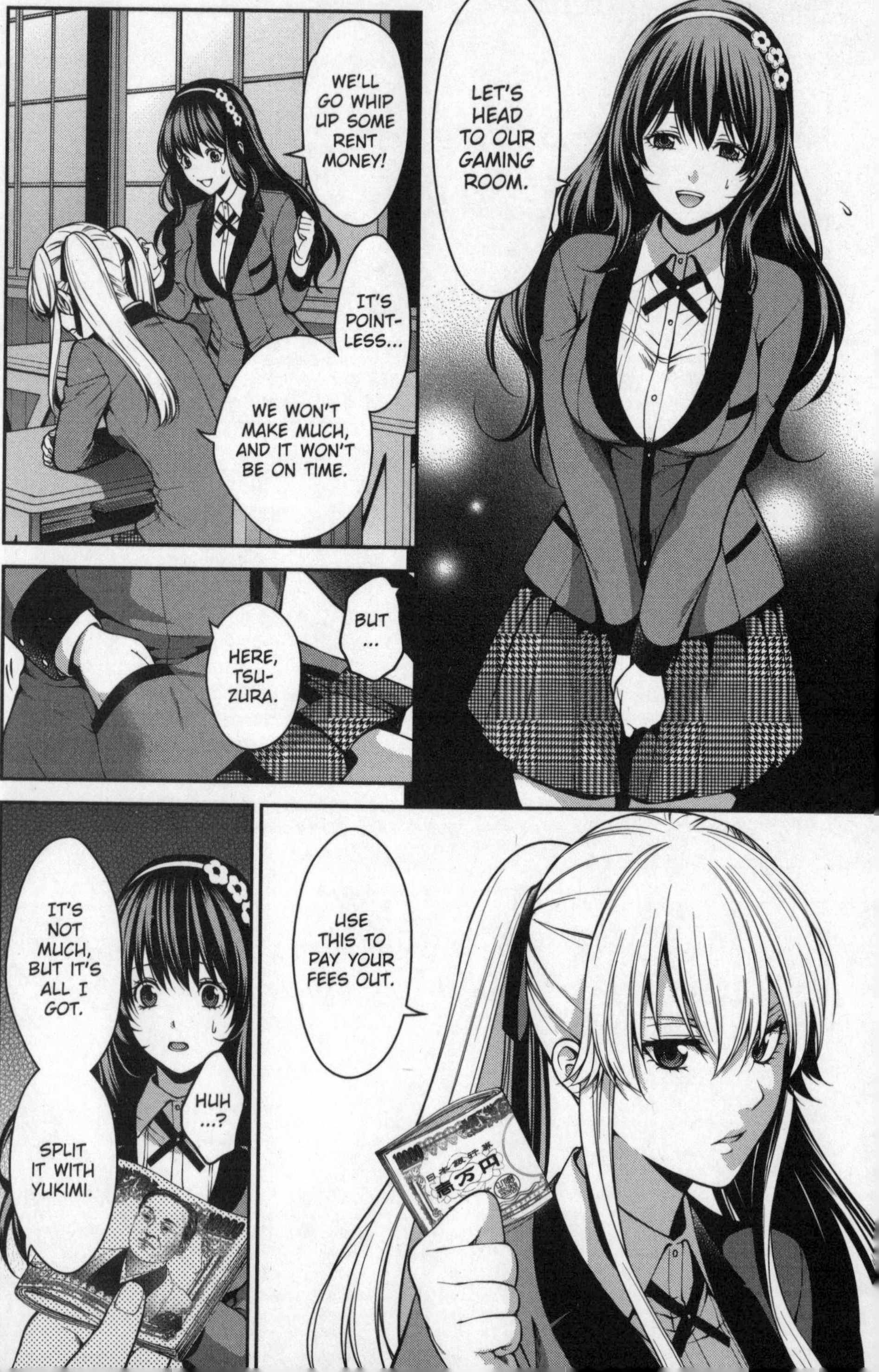
LET'S HEAD TO OUR GAMING ROOM.
WE'LL GO WHIP UP SOME RENT MONEY!
IT'S POINTLESS...
WE WON'T MAKE MUCH, AND IT WON'T BE ON TIME.
BUT...
HERE, TSUZURA.
USE THIS TO PAY YOUR FEES OUT.
IT'S NOT MUCH, BUT IT'S ALL I GOT.
HUH...?
SPLIT IT WITH YUKIMI.

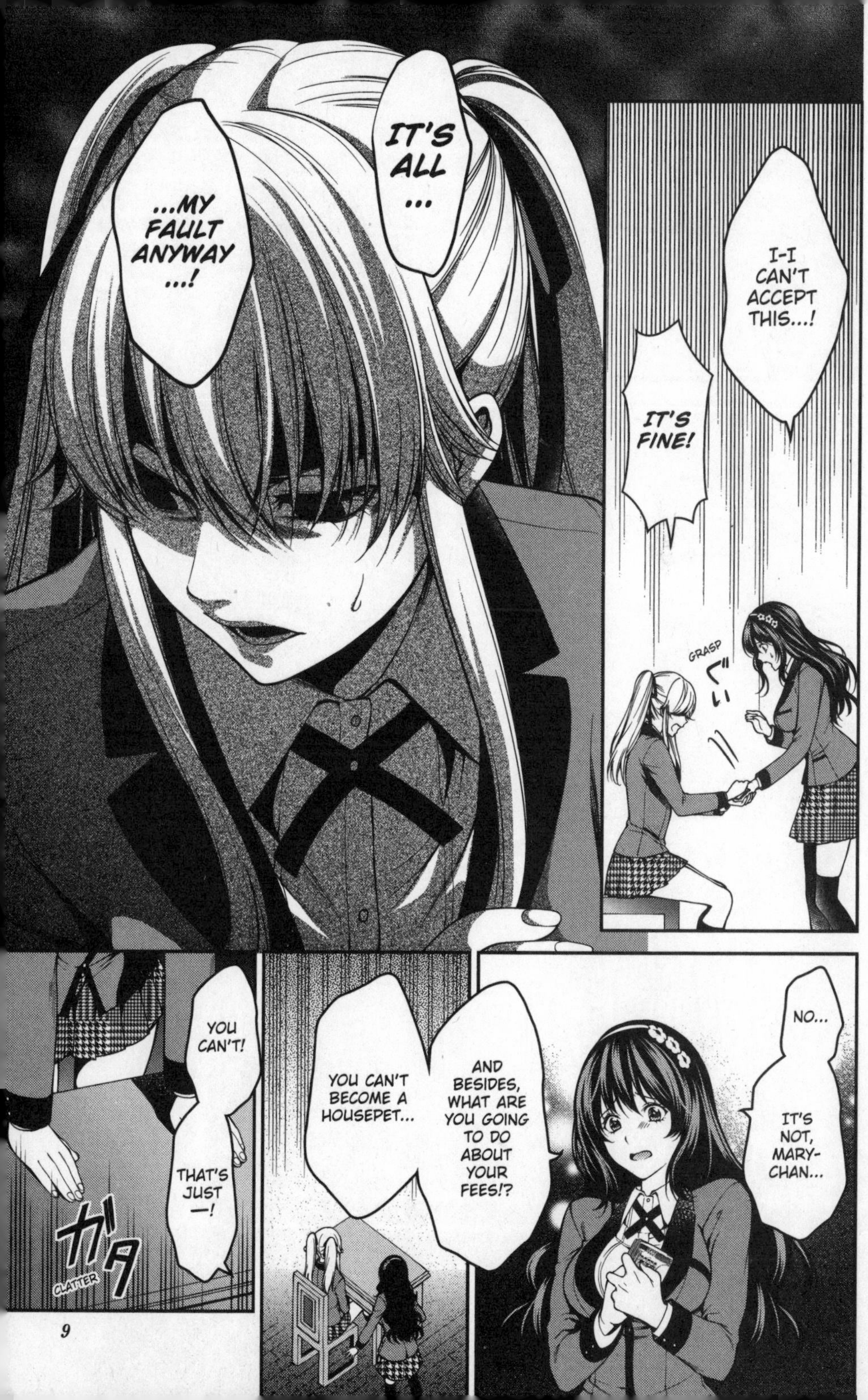

I-I CAN'T ACCEPT THIS...!
IT'S FINE!
GRASP
IT'S ALL...
...MY FAULT ANYWAY...!
NO...
IT'S NOT, MARY-CHAN...
YOU CAN'T BECOME A HOUSEPET...
AND BESIDES, WHAT ARE YOU GOING TO DO ABOUT YOUR FEES!?
YOU CAN'T!
THAT'S JUST—!
ガタ
CLATTER

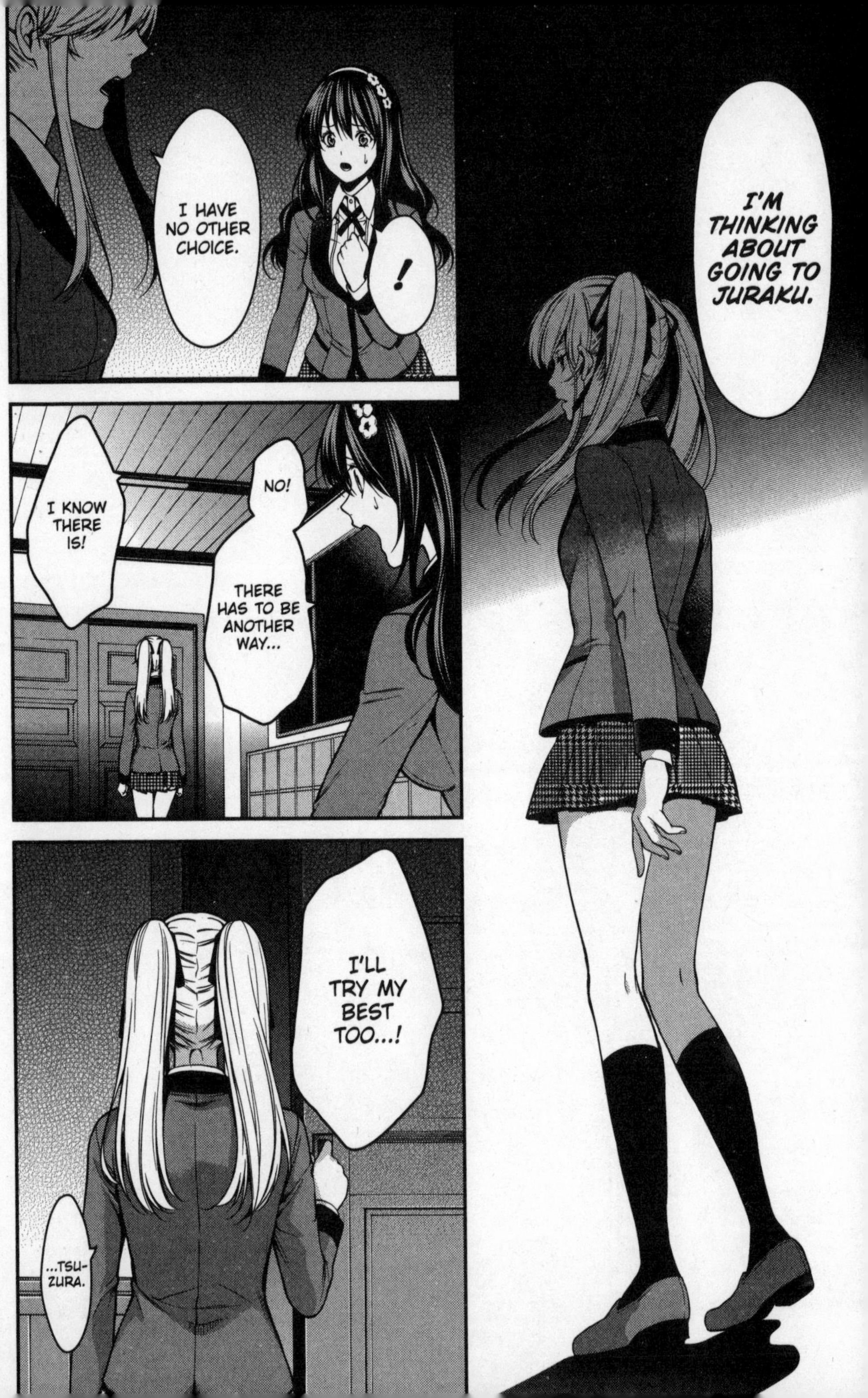
I'M THINKING ABOUT GOING TO JURAKU.
I HAVE NO OTHER CHOICE.
!
NO!
THERE HAS TO BE ANOTHER WAY...
I KNOW THERE IS!
I'LL TRY MY BEST TOO...!
...TSU-ZURA.

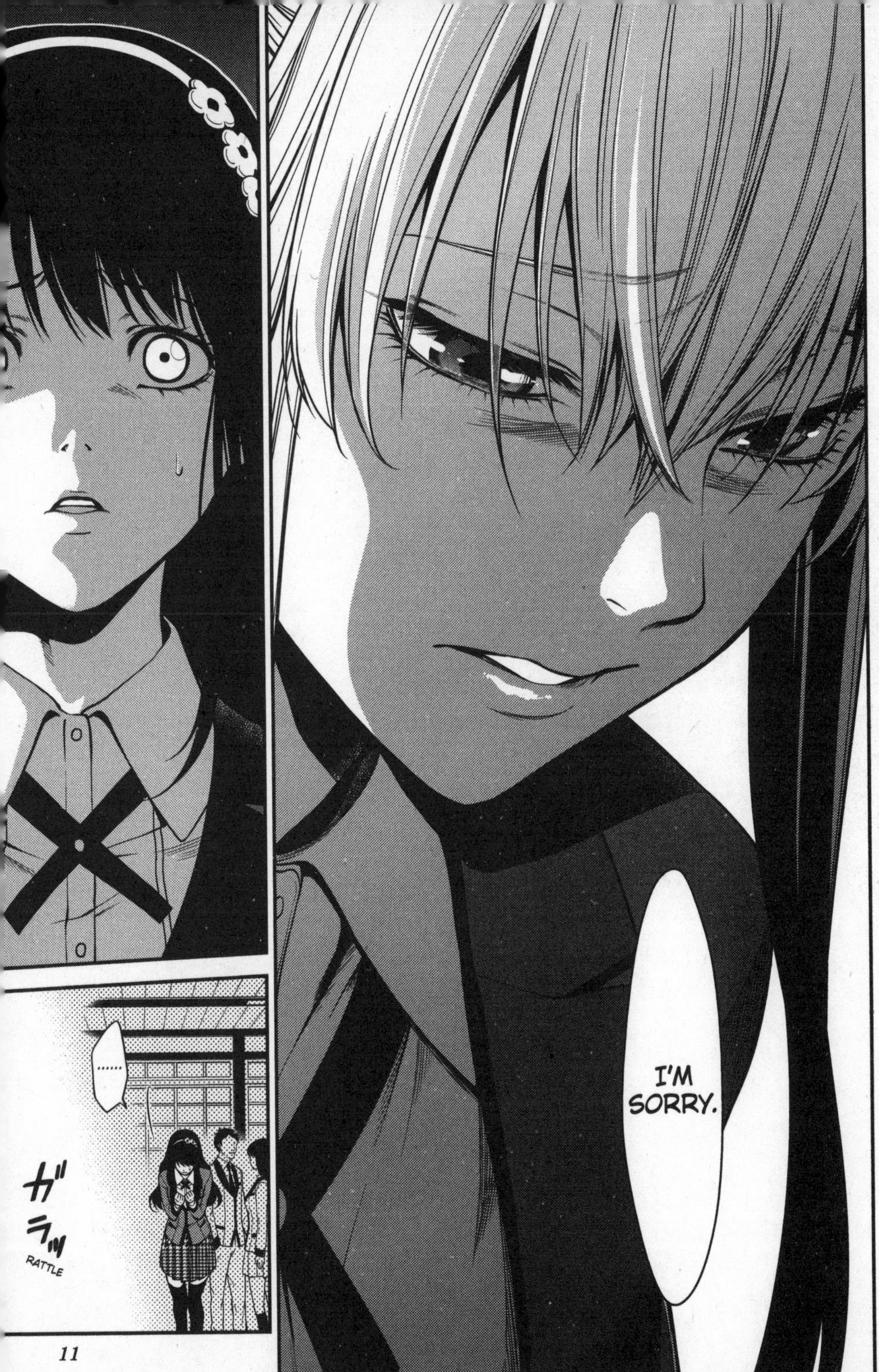
I'M SORRY.
......
ガラッ
RATTLE

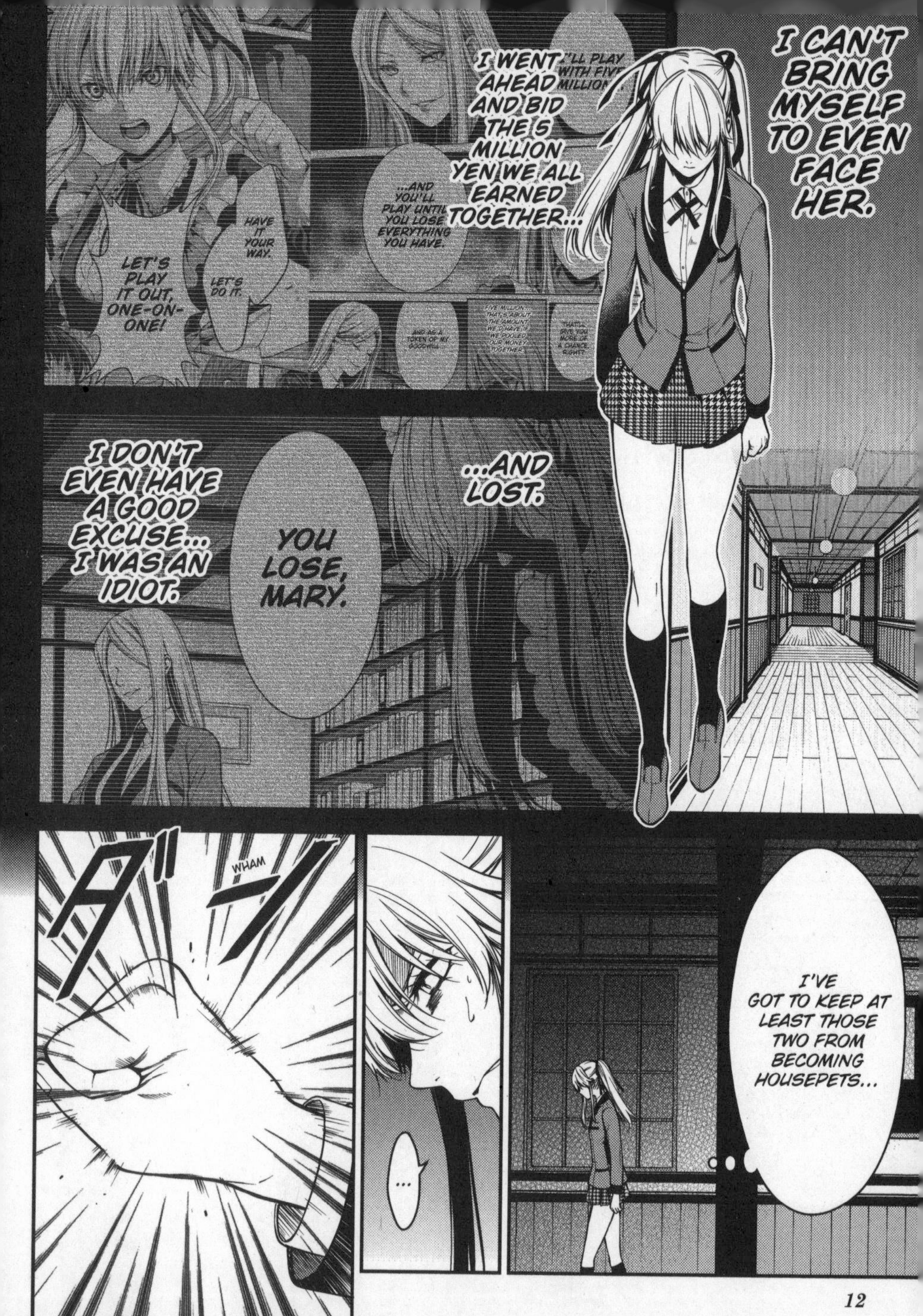
I CAN'T BRING MYSELF TO EVEN FACE HER.
I'LL PLAY WITH FIVE MILLION.
I WENT AHEAD AND BID THE 5 MILLION YEN WE ALL EARNED TOGETHER...
...AND YOU'LL PLAY UNTIL YOU LOSE EVERYTHING YOU HAVE.
HAVE IT YOUR WAY.
LET'S DO IT.
LET'S PLAY IT OUT, ONE-ON-ONE!
THAT'LL GIVE YOU MORE OF A CHANCE, RIGHT?
FIVE MILLION... THAT'S ABOUT THE AMOUNT WE'D HAVE IF WE POOLED OUR MONEY TOGETHER.
AND AS A TOKEN OF MY GOODWILL...
...AND LOST.
YOU LOSE, MARY.
I DON'T EVEN HAVE A GOOD EXCUSE... I WAS AN IDIOT.
I'VE GOT TO KEEP AT LEAST THOSE TWO FROM BECOMING HOUSEPETS...
...
...
WHAM

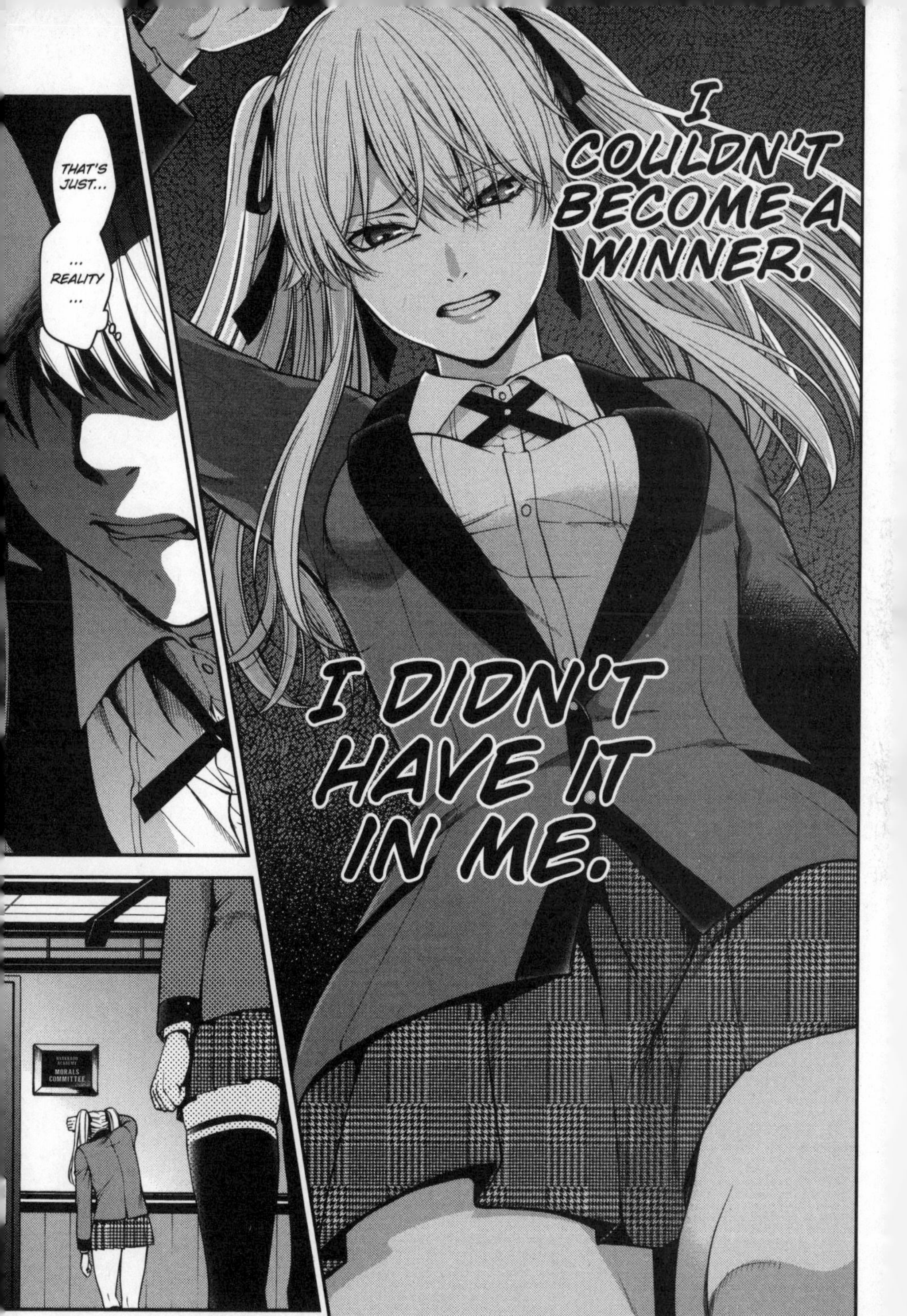
I COULDN'T BECOME A WINNER.
I DIDN'T HAVE IT IN ME.
THAT'S JUST... ...REALITY...
MORALS COMMITTEE

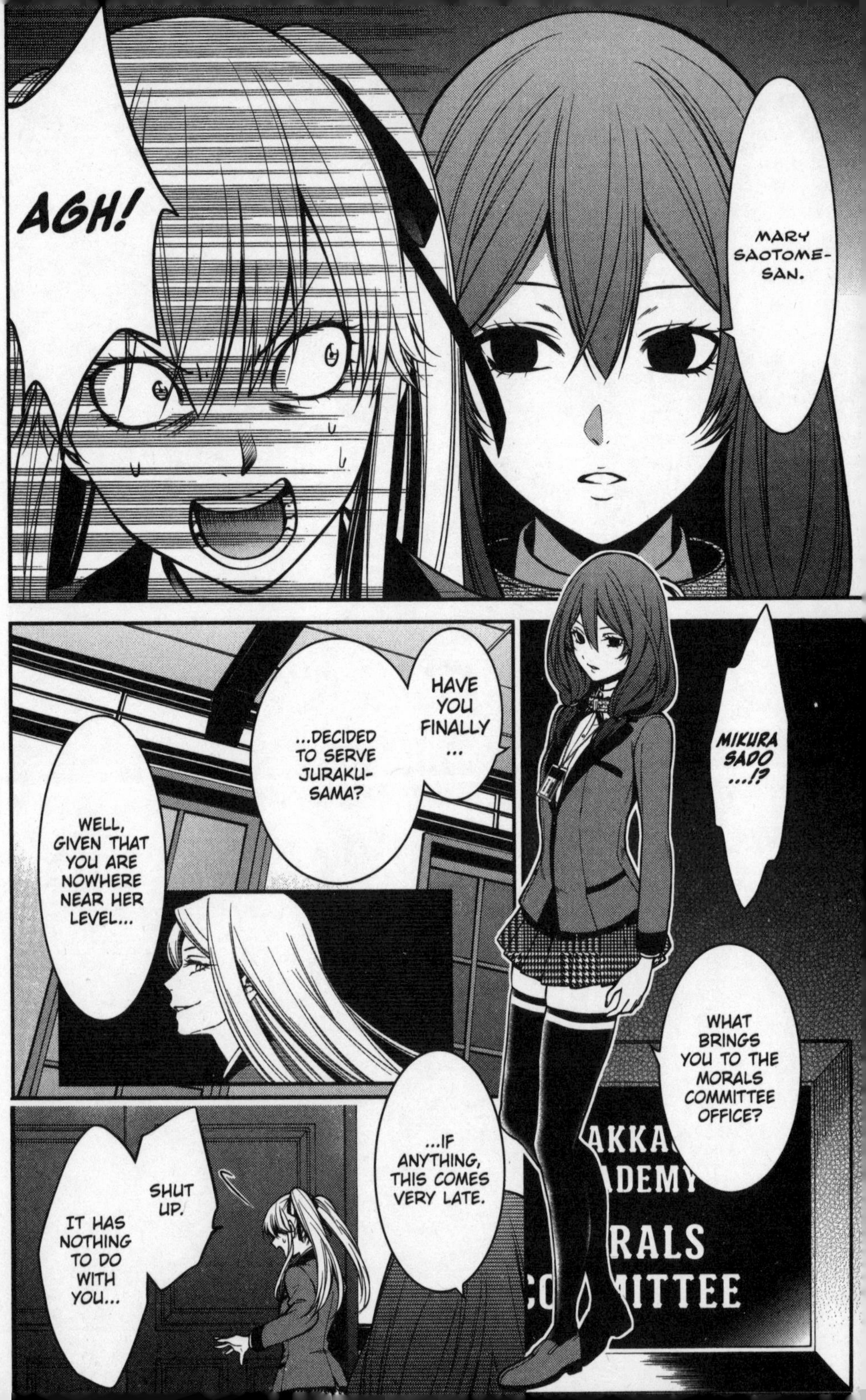
MARY SAOTOME-SAN.
AGH!
MIKURA SADO ...!?
WHAT BRINGS YOU TO THE MORALS COMMITTEE OFFICE?
HAVE YOU FINALLY ...
...DECIDED TO SERVE JURAKU-SAMA?
WELL, GIVEN THAT YOU ARE NOWHERE NEAR HER LEVEL...
...IF ANYTHING, THIS COMES VERY LATE.
SHUT UP.
IT HAS NOTHING TO DO WITH YOU...

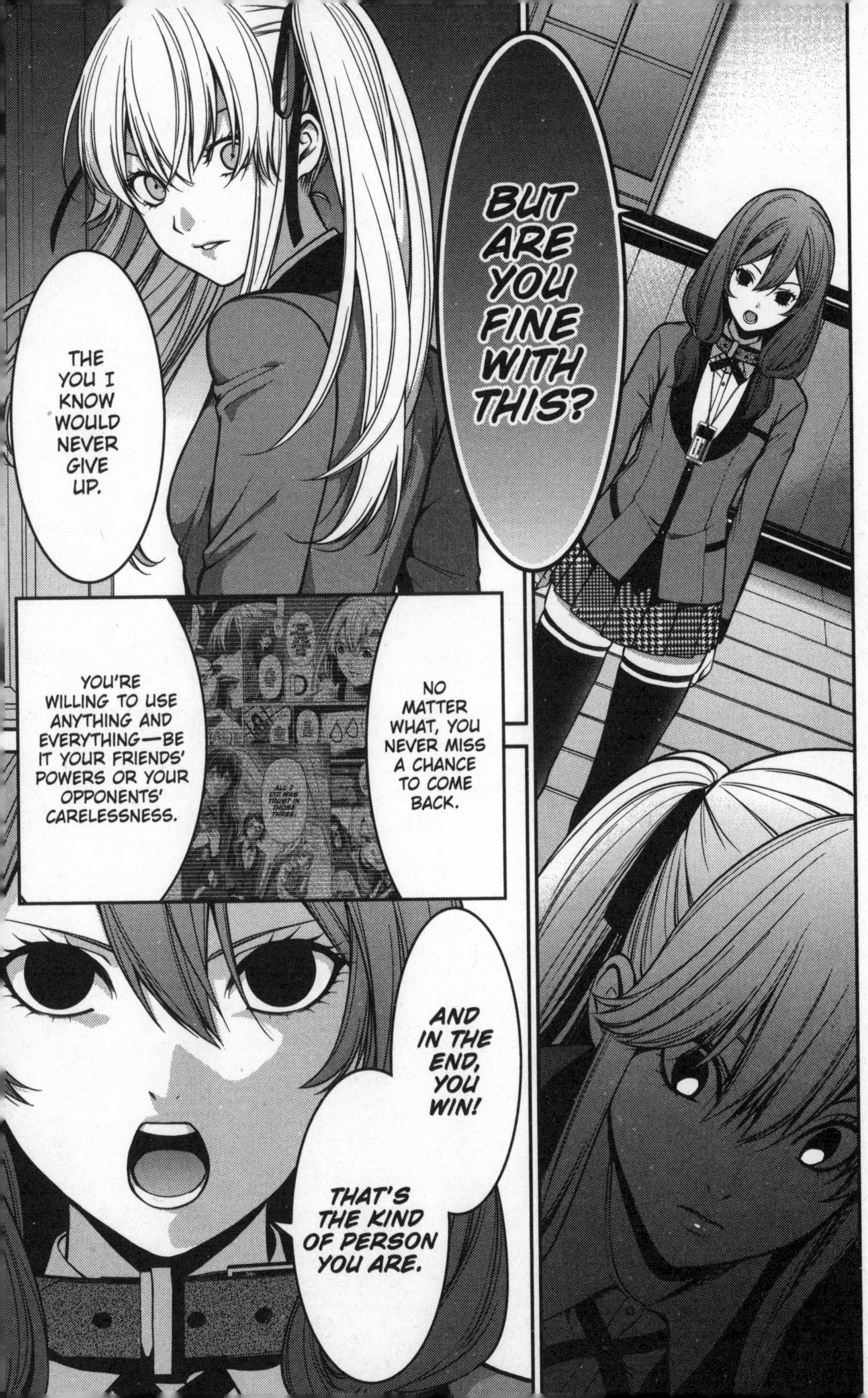
BUT ARE YOU FINE WITH THIS?
THE YOU I KNOW WOULD NEVER GIVE UP.
NO MATTER WHAT, YOU NEVER MISS A CHANCE TO COME BACK.
YOU'RE WILLING TO USE ANYTHING AND EVERYTHING—BE IT YOUR FRIENDS' POWERS OR YOUR OPPONENTS' CARELESSNESS.
AND IN THE END, YOU WIN!
THAT'S THE KIND OF PERSON YOU ARE.

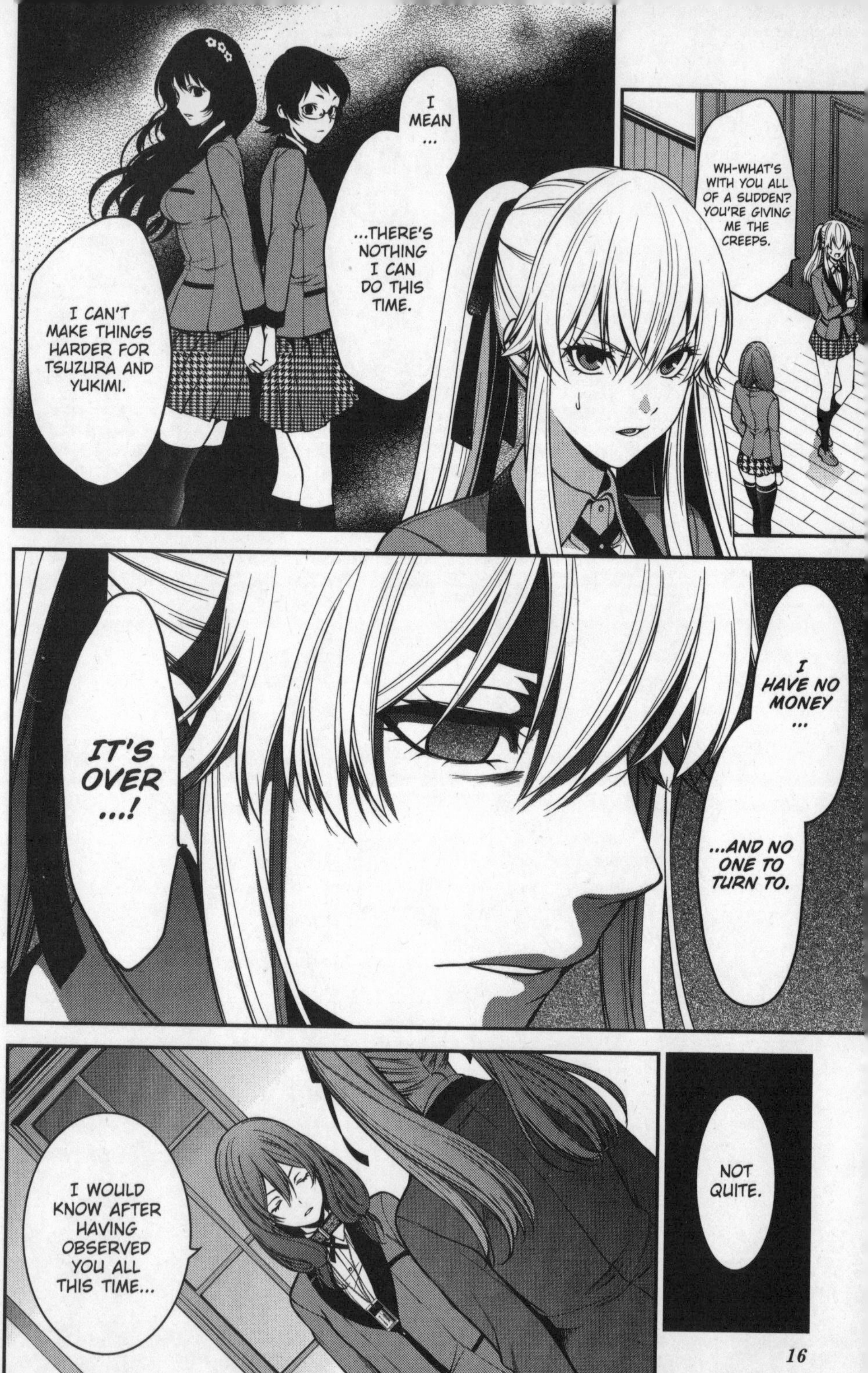
WH-WHAT'S WITH YOU ALL OF A SUDDEN? YOU'RE GIVING ME THE CREEPS.
I MEAN ...
...THERE'S NOTHING I CAN DO THIS TIME.
I CAN'T MAKE THINGS HARDER FOR TSUZURA AND YUKIMI.
I HAVE NO MONEY ...
...AND NO ONE TO TURN TO.
IT'S OVER ...!
NOT QUITE.
I WOULD KNOW AFTER HAVING OBSERVED YOU ALL THIS TIME...

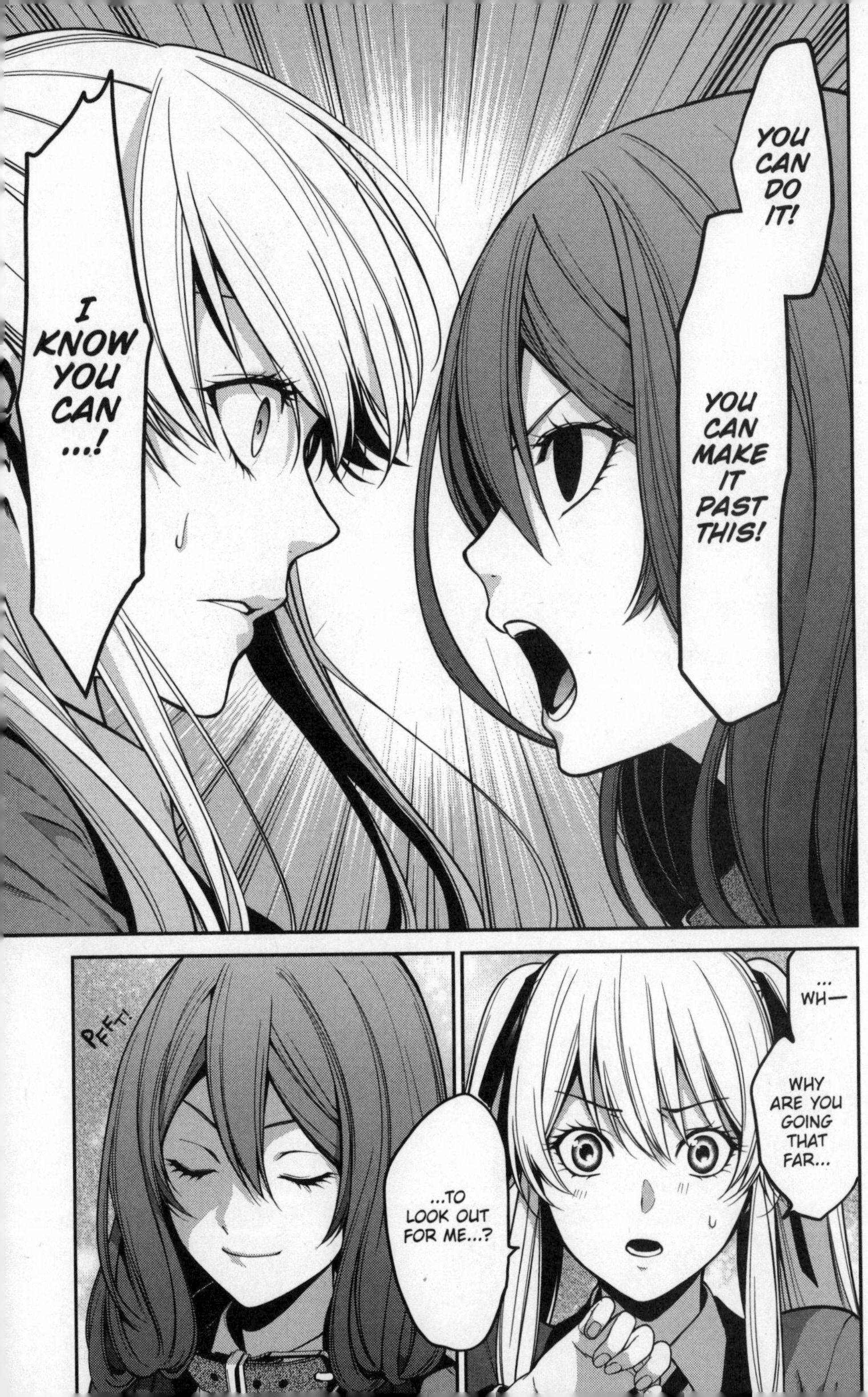
YOU CAN DO IT!
YOU CAN MAKE IT PAST THIS!
I KNOW YOU CAN ...!
...WH—
WHY ARE YOU GOING THAT FAR...
...TO LOOK OUT FOR ME...?
PFFT!

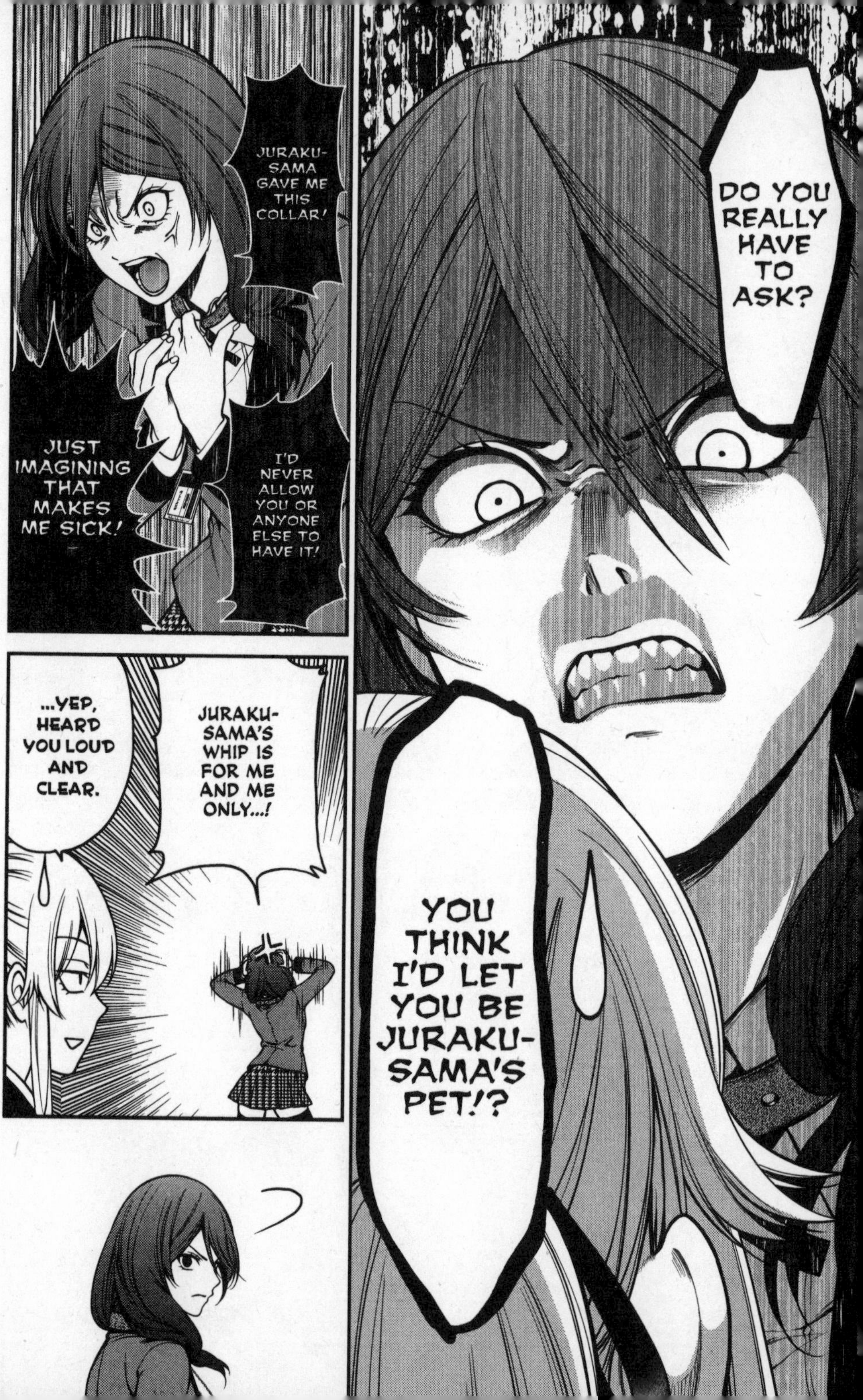
DO YOU REALLY HAVE TO ASK?
YOU THINK I'D LET YOU BE JURAKU-SAMA'S PET!?
JURAKU-SAMA GAVE ME THIS COLLAR!
I'D NEVER ALLOW YOU OR ANYONE ELSE TO HAVE IT!
JUST IMAGINING THAT MAKES ME SICK!
JURAKU-SAMA'S WHIP IS FOR ME AND ME ONLY...!
...YEP, HEARD YOU LOUD AND CLEAR.

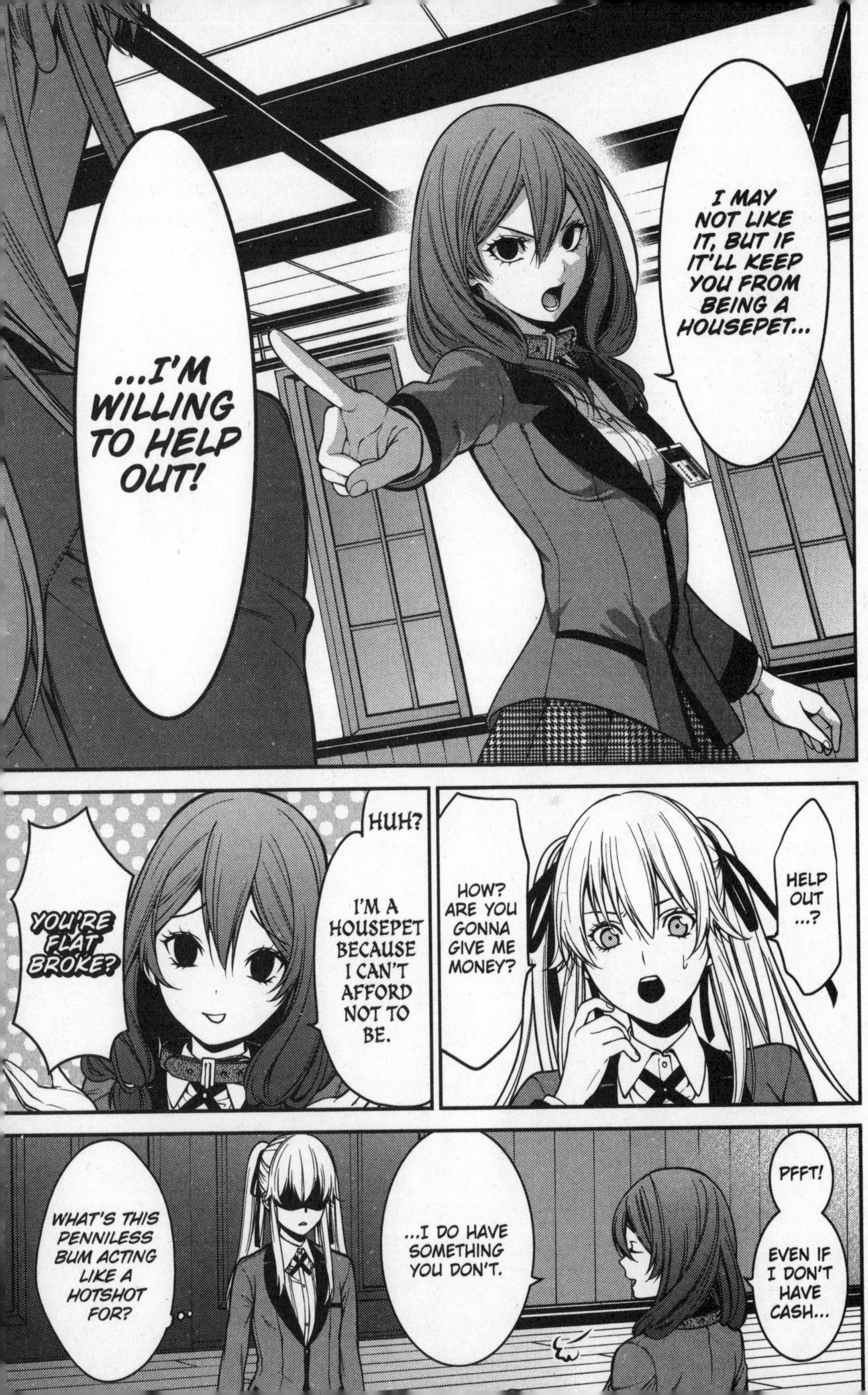
I MAY NOT LIKE IT, BUT IF IT'LL KEEP YOU FROM BEING A HOUSEPET...
...I'M WILLING TO HELP OUT!
HELP OUT ...?
HOW? ARE YOU GONNA GIVE ME MONEY?
HUH?
I'M A HOUSEPET BECAUSE I CAN'T AFFORD NOT TO BE.
YOU'RE FLAT BROKE?
PFFT!
EVEN IF I DON'T HAVE CASH...
...I DO HAVE SOMETHING YOU DON'T.
WHAT'S THIS PENNILESS BUM ACTING LIKE A HOTSHOT FOR?

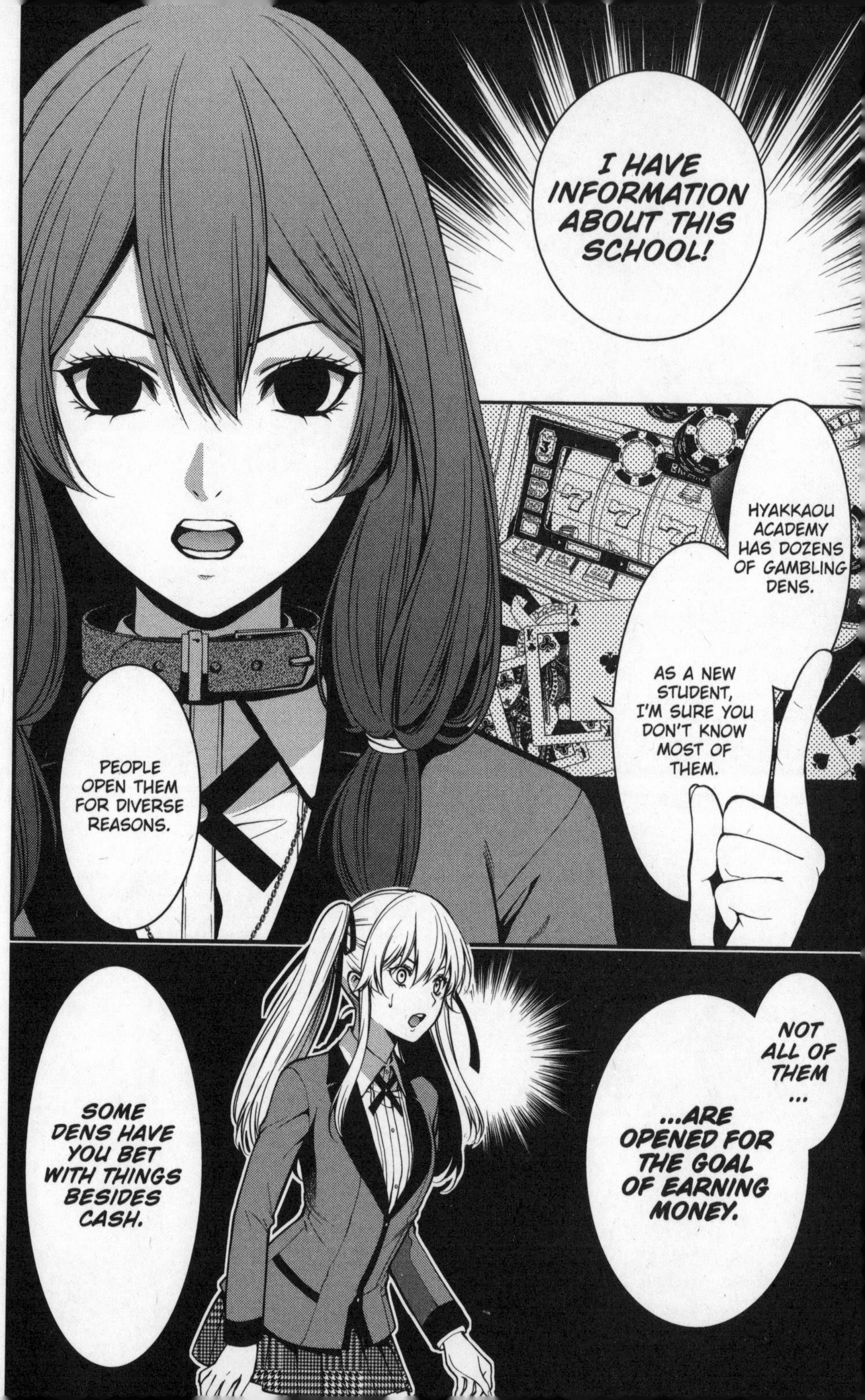
I HAVE INFORMATION ABOUT THIS SCHOOL!
HYAKKAOU ACADEMY HAS DOZENS OF GAMBLING DENS.
AS A NEW STUDENT, I'M SURE YOU DON'T KNOW MOST OF THEM.
PEOPLE OPEN THEM FOR DIVERSE REASONS.
NOT ALL OF THEM ...
...ARE OPENED FOR THE GOAL OF EARNING MONEY.
SOME DENS HAVE YOU BET WITH THINGS BESIDES CASH.

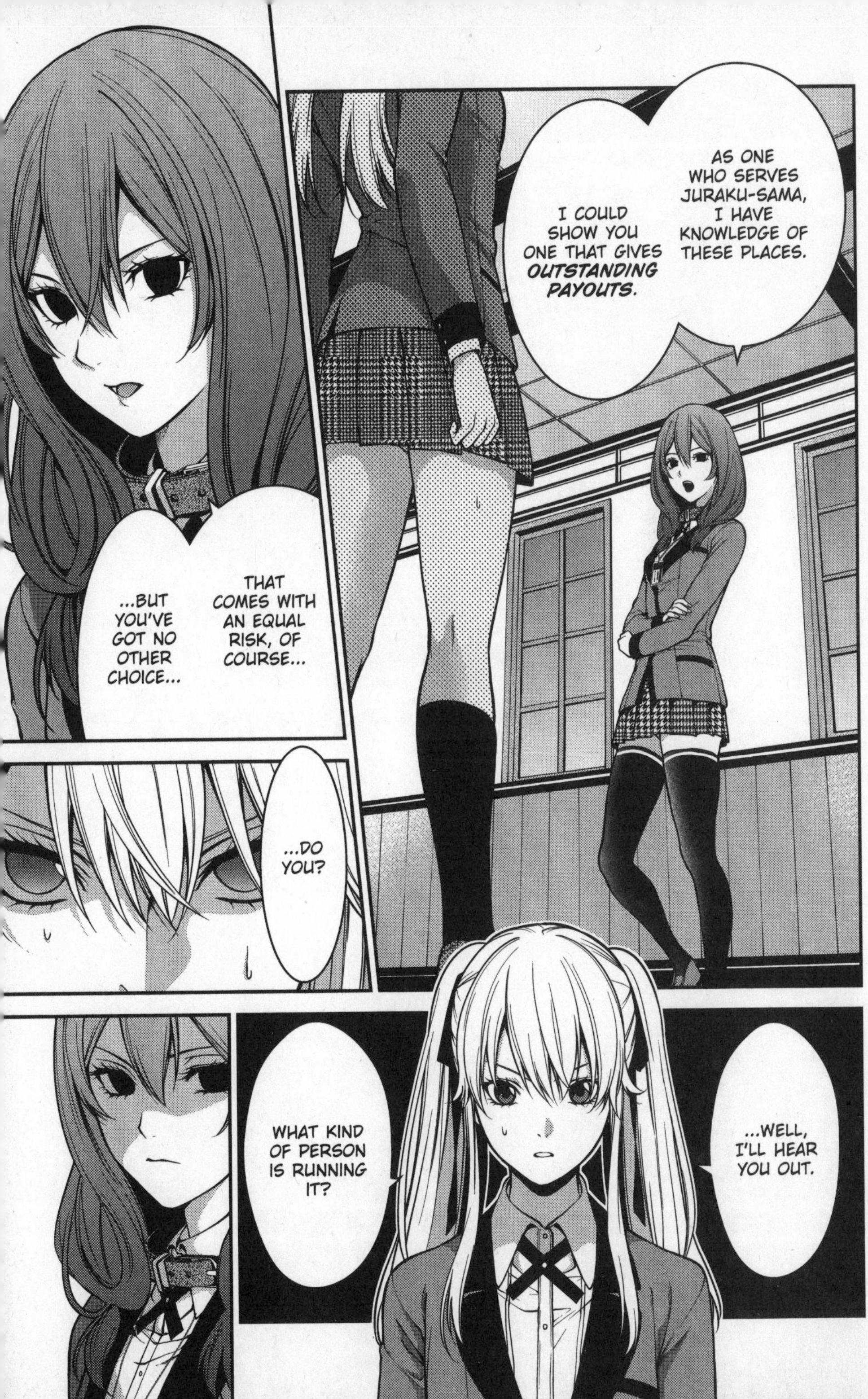
AS ONE WHO SERVES JURAKU-SAMA, I HAVE KNOWLEDGE OF THESE PLACES.
I COULD SHOW YOU ONE THAT GIVES **OUTSTANDING PAYOUTS.**
THAT COMES WITH AN EQUAL RISK, OF COURSE...
...BUT YOU'VE GOT NO OTHER CHOICE...
...DO YOU?
...WELL, I'LL HEAR YOU OUT.
WHAT KIND OF PERSON IS RUNNING IT?

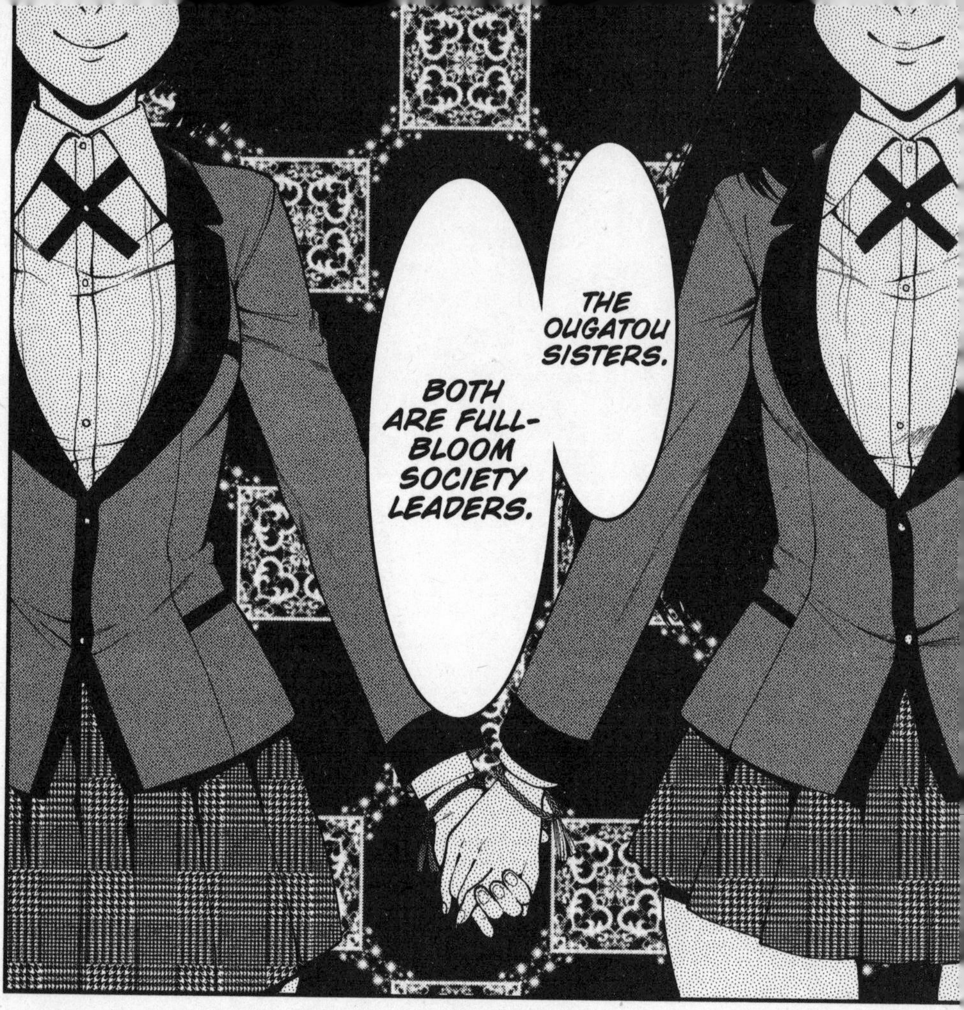
THE OUGATOU SISTERS.
BOTH ARE FULL-BLOOM SOCIETY LEADERS.

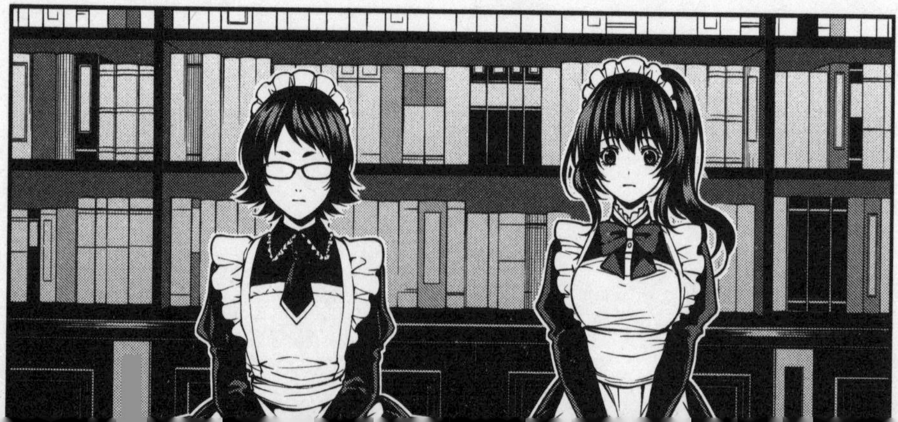

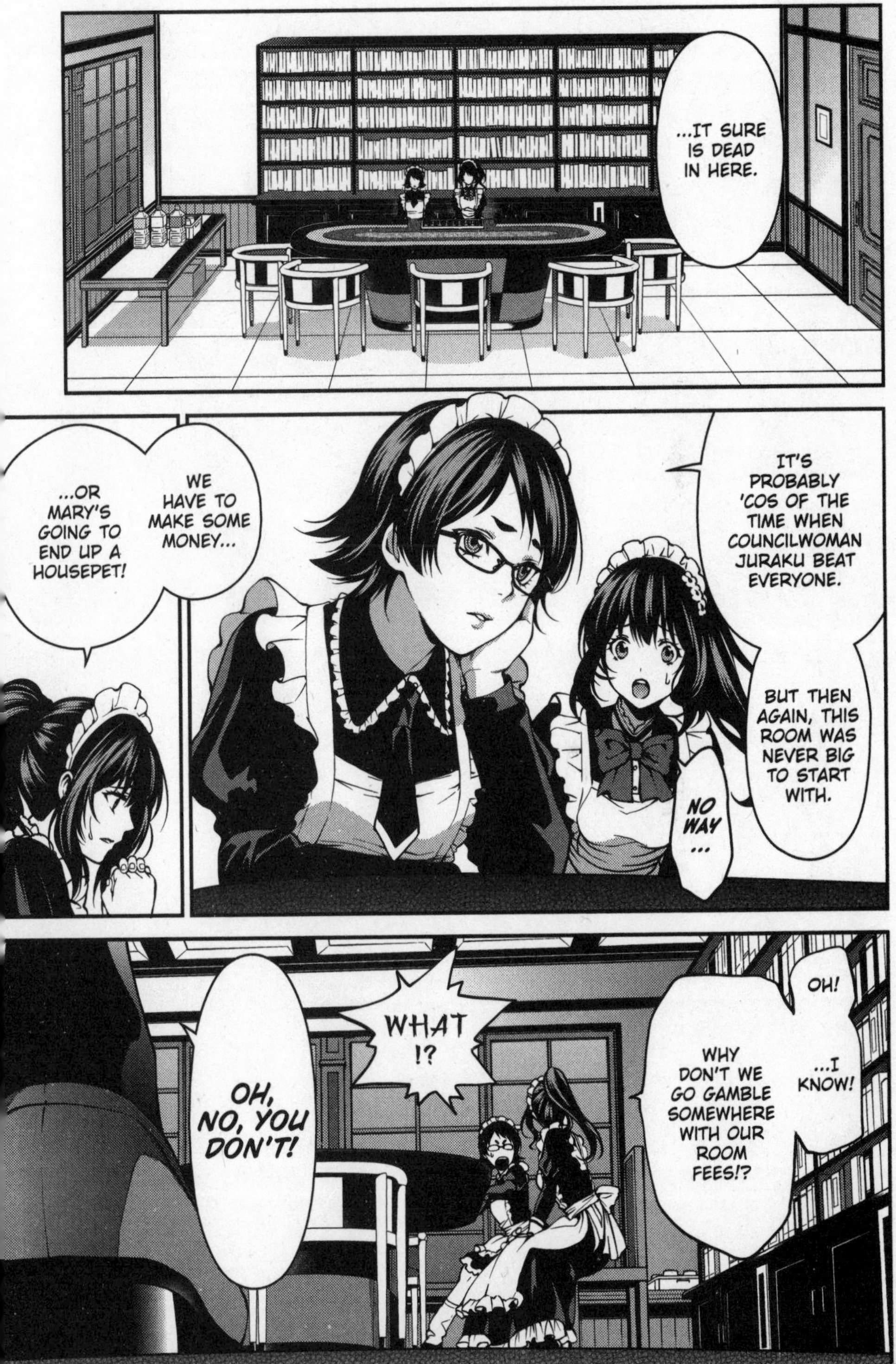
...IT SURE IS DEAD IN HERE.
IT'S PROBABLY 'COS OF THE TIME WHEN COUNCILWOMAN JURAKU BEAT EVERYONE.
BUT THEN AGAIN, THIS ROOM WAS NEVER BIG TO START WITH.
NO WAY...
WE HAVE TO MAKE SOME MONEY...
...OR MARY'S GOING TO END UP A HOUSEPET!
OH!
...I KNOW!
WHY DON'T WE GO GAMBLE SOMEWHERE WITH OUR ROOM FEES!?
WHAT!?
OH, NO, YOU DON'T!

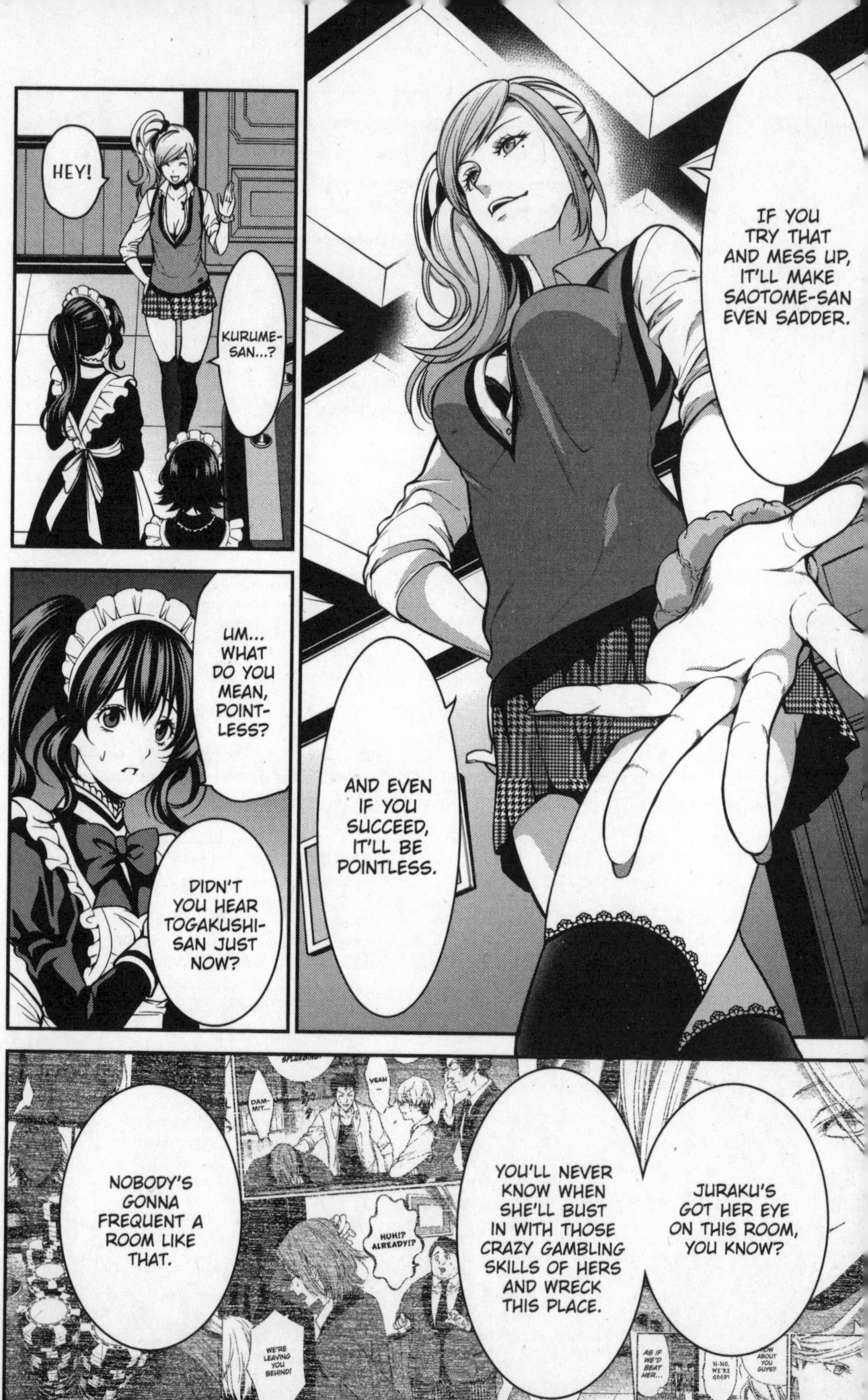
IF YOU TRY THAT AND MESS UP, IT'LL MAKE SAOTOME-SAN EVEN SADDER.
AND EVEN IF YOU SUCCEED, IT'LL BE POINTLESS.
HEY!
KURUME-SAN...?
UM... WHAT DO YOU MEAN, POINTLESS?
DIDN'T YOU HEAR TOGAKUSHI-SAN JUST NOW?
JURAKU'S GOT HER EYE ON THIS ROOM, YOU KNOW?
YOU'LL NEVER KNOW WHEN SHE'LL BUST IN WITH THOSE CRAZY GAMBLING SKILLS OF HERS AND WRECK THIS PLACE.
NOBODY'S GONNA FREQUENT A ROOM LIKE THAT.
HOW ABOUT YOU GUYS?
N-NO. WE'RE GOOD!
AS IF WE'D BEAT HER...
YEAH...
DAM-MIT...
HUH!? ALREADY!?
WE'RE LEAVING YOU BEHIND!

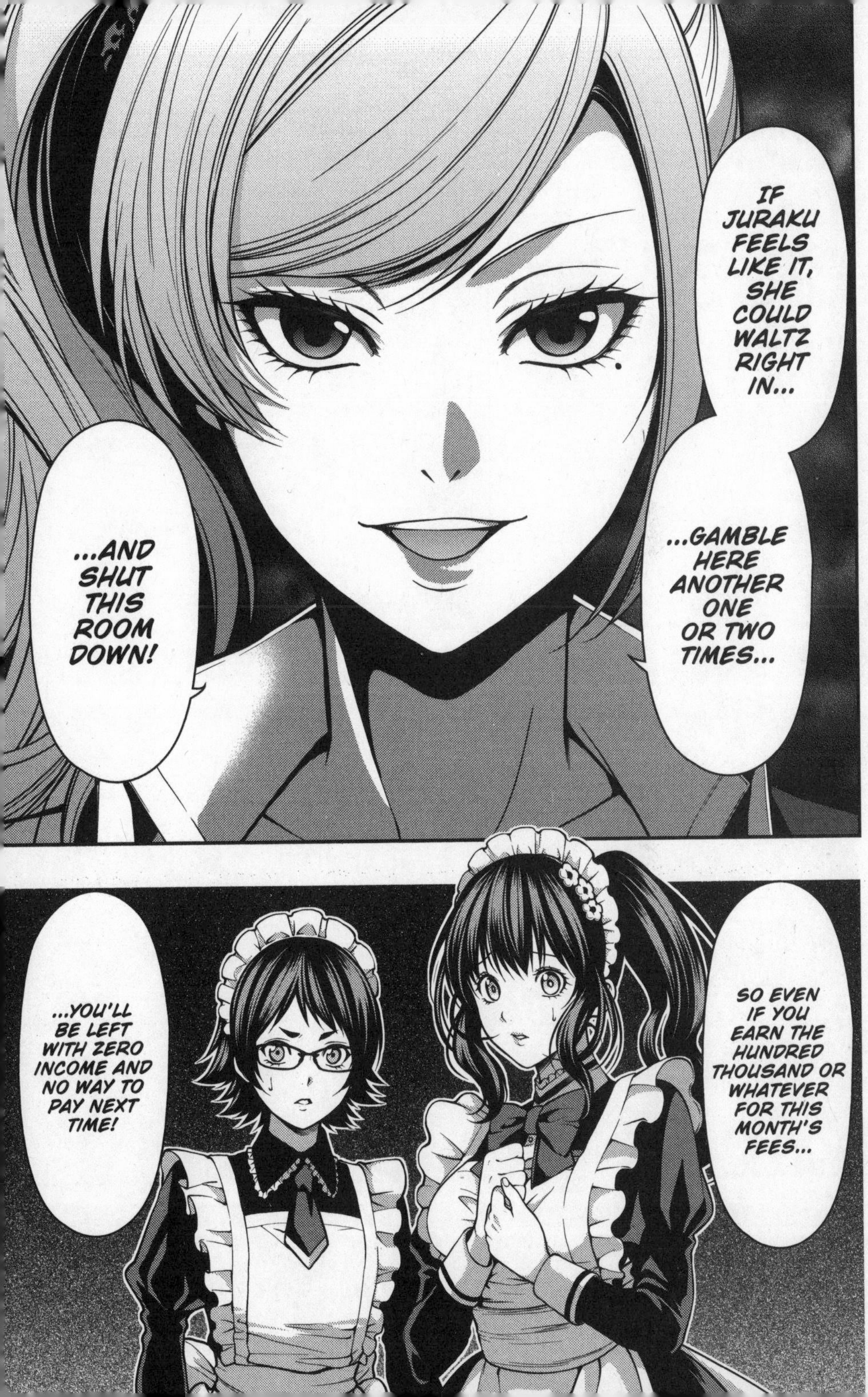
IF JURAKU FEELS LIKE IT, SHE COULD WALTZ RIGHT IN...
...GAMBLE HERE ANOTHER ONE OR TWO TIMES...
...AND SHUT THIS ROOM DOWN!
SO EVEN IF YOU EARN THE HUNDRED THOUSAND OR WHATEVER FOR THIS MONTH'S FEES...
...YOU'LL BE LEFT WITH ZERO INCOME AND NO WAY TO PAY NEXT TIME!

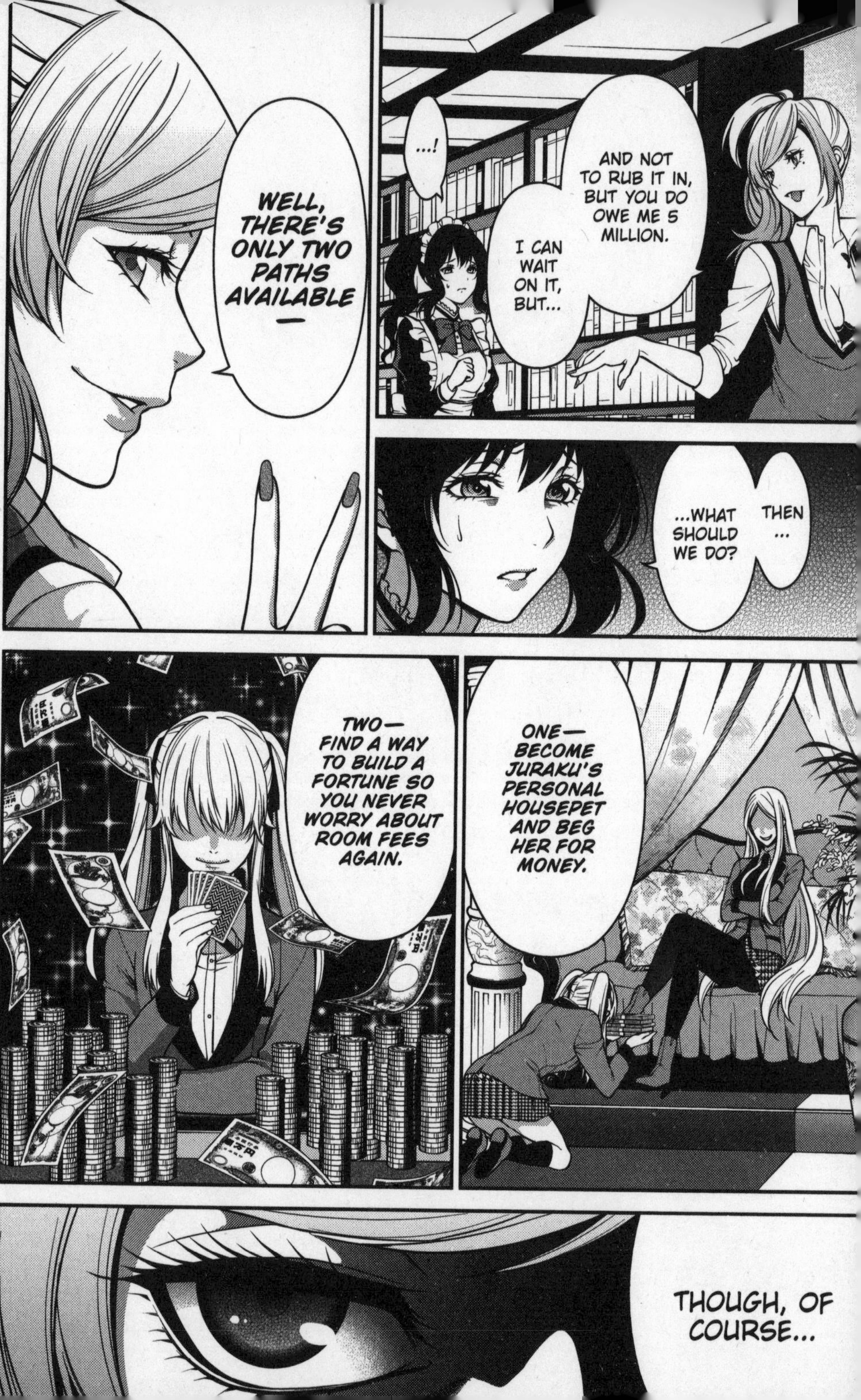
AND NOT TO RUB IT IN, BUT YOU DO OWE ME 5 MILLION.
I CAN WAIT ON IT, BUT...
...!
THEN ...
...WHAT SHOULD WE DO?
WELL, THERE'S ONLY TWO PATHS AVAILABLE —
ONE— BECOME JURAKU'S PERSONAL HOUSEPET AND BEG HER FOR MONEY.
TWO— FIND A WAY TO BUILD A FORTUNE SO YOU NEVER WORRY ABOUT ROOM FEES AGAIN.
THOUGH, OF COURSE...

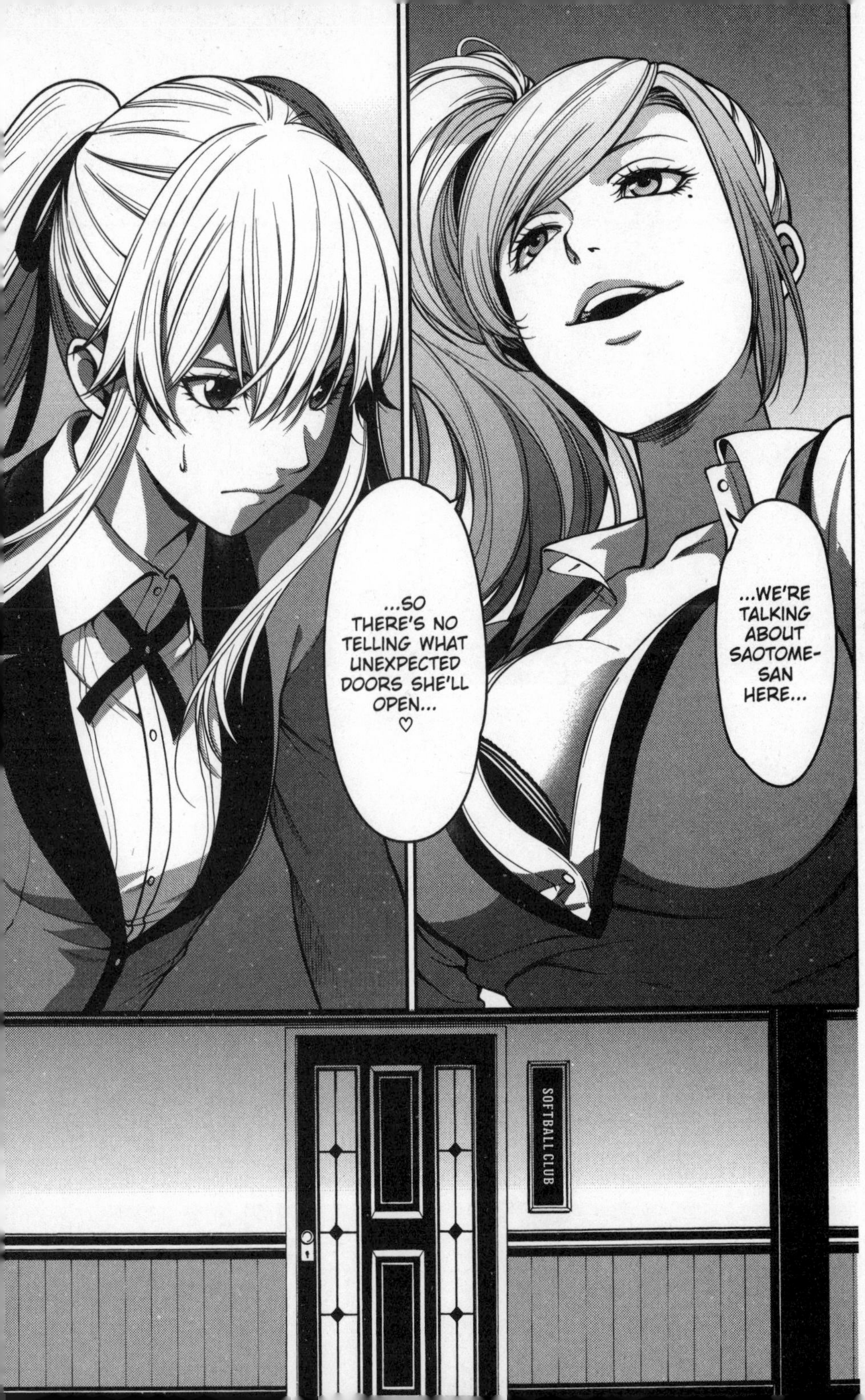
...WE'RE TALKING ABOUT SAOTOME-SAN HERE...
...SO THERE'S NO TELLING WHAT UNEXPECTED DOORS SHE'LL OPEN... ♡
SOFTBALL CLUB

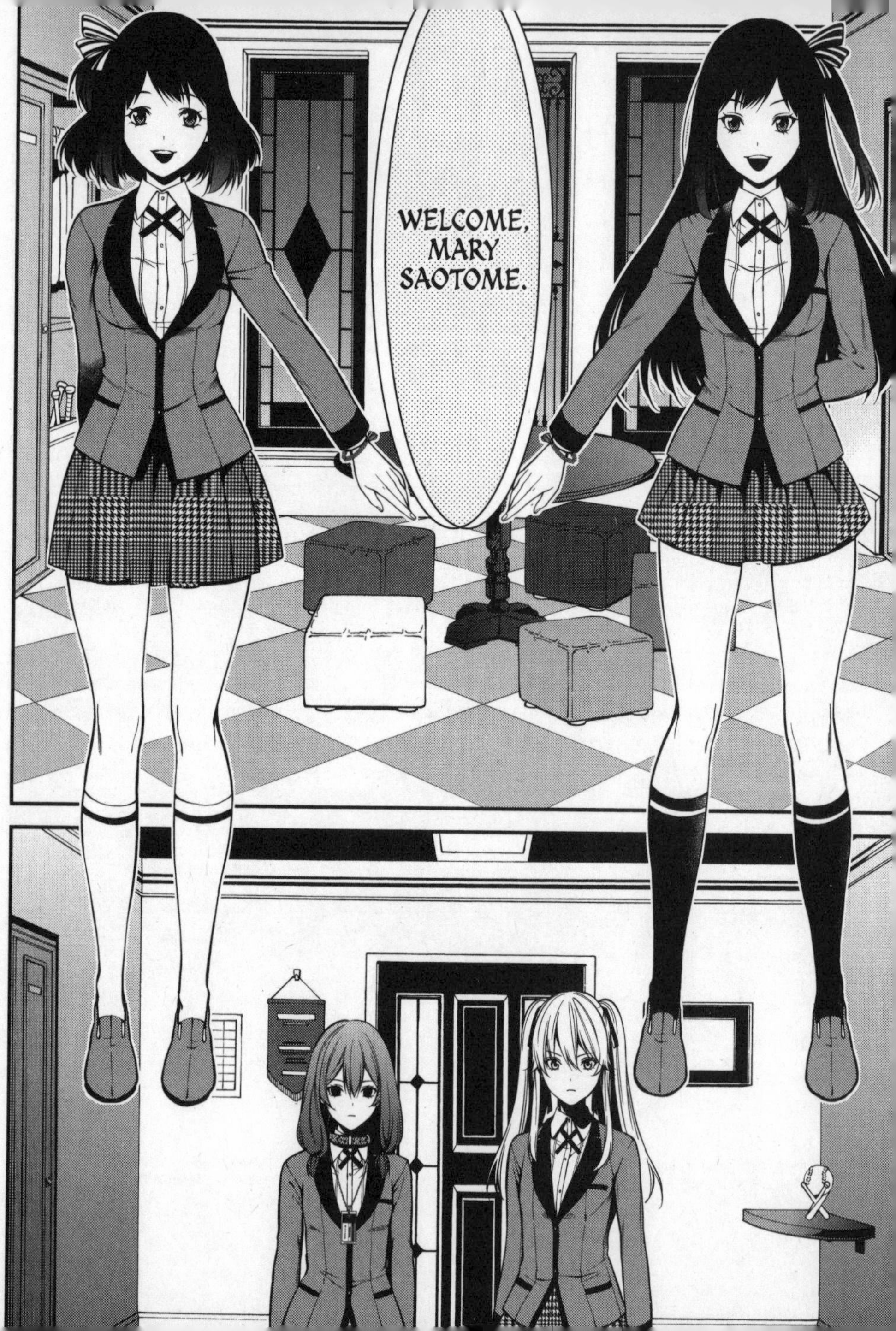
WELCOME, MARY SAOTOME.

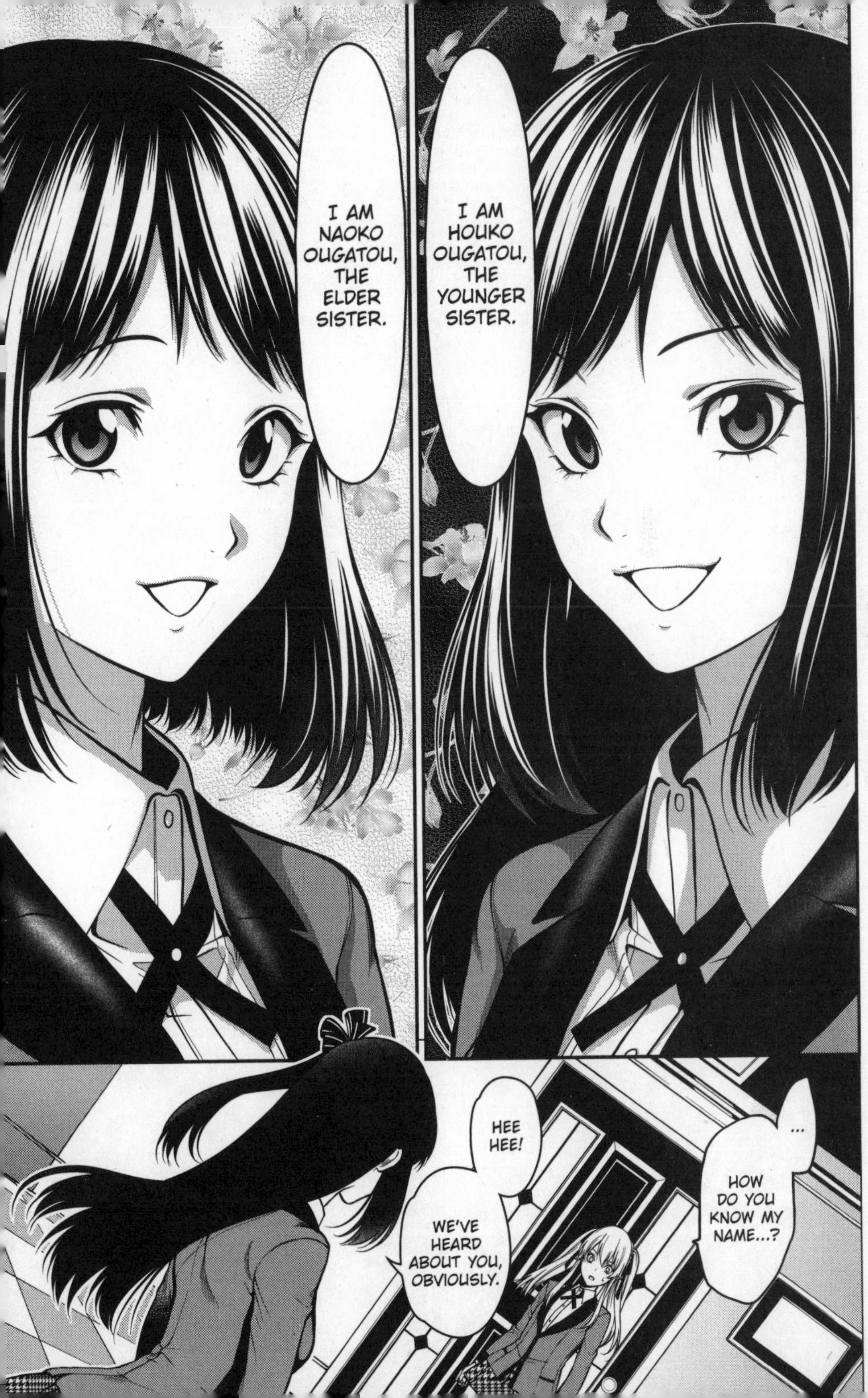
I AM HOUKO OUGATOU, THE YOUNGER SISTER.
I AM NAOKO OUGATOU, THE ELDER SISTER.
... HOW DO YOU KNOW MY NAME...?
HEE HEE!
WE'VE HEARD ABOUT YOU, OBVIOUSLY.

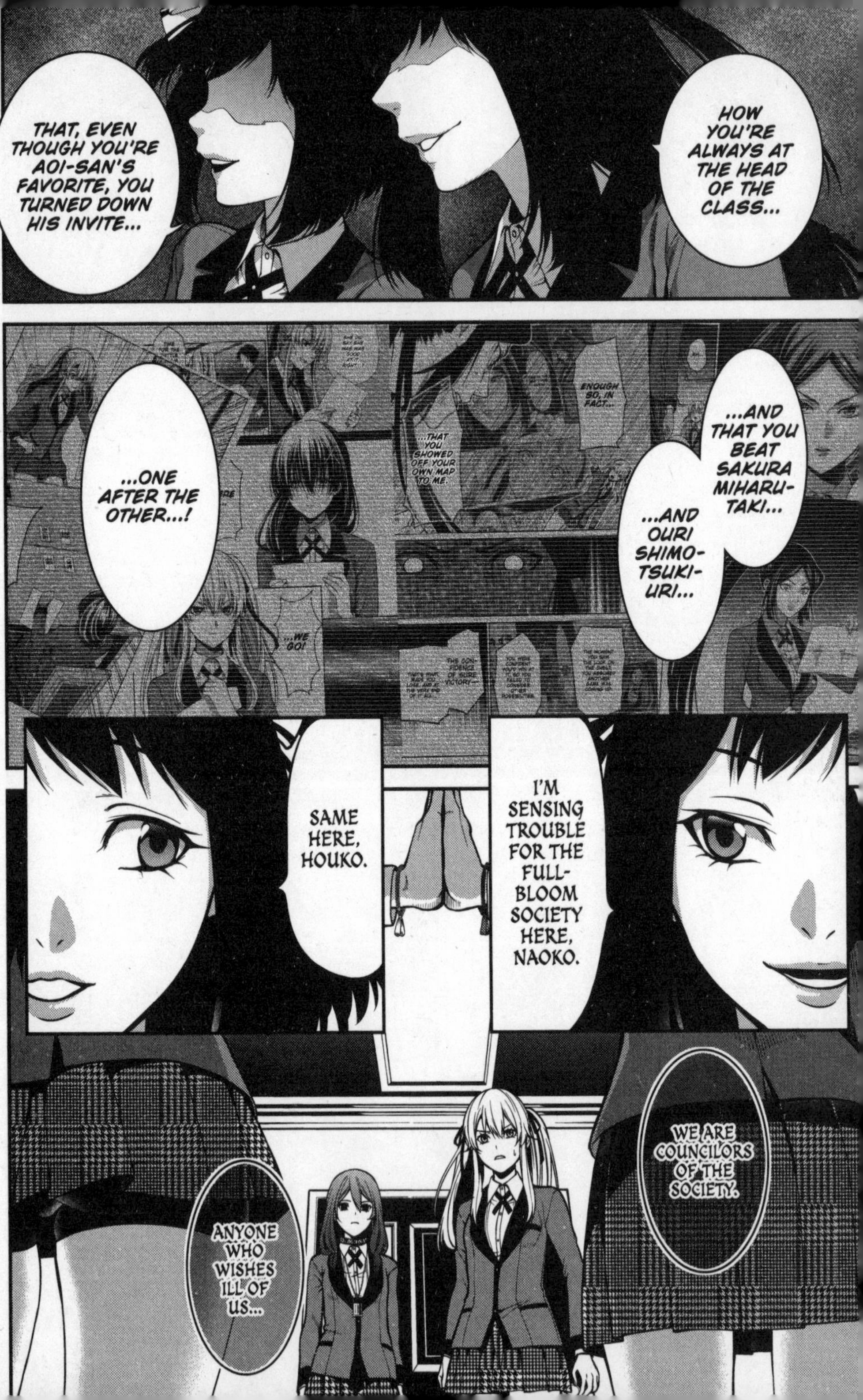
HOW YOU'RE ALWAYS AT THE HEAD OF THE CLASS...
THAT, EVEN THOUGH YOU'RE AOI-SAN'S FAVORITE, YOU TURNED DOWN HIS INVITE...
...AND THAT YOU BEAT SAKURA MIHARU-TAKI...
...AND OURI SHIMO-TSUKI-URI...
ENOUGH SO, IN FACT...
...THAT YOU SHOWED OFF YOUR OWN MAP TO ME.
...ONE AFTER THE OTHER...!
...WE GO!
I'M SENSING TROUBLE FOR THE FULL-BLOOM SOCIETY HERE, NAOKO.
SAME HERE, HOUKO.
WE ARE COUNCILORS OF THE SOCIETY.
ANYONE WHO WISHES ILL OF US...

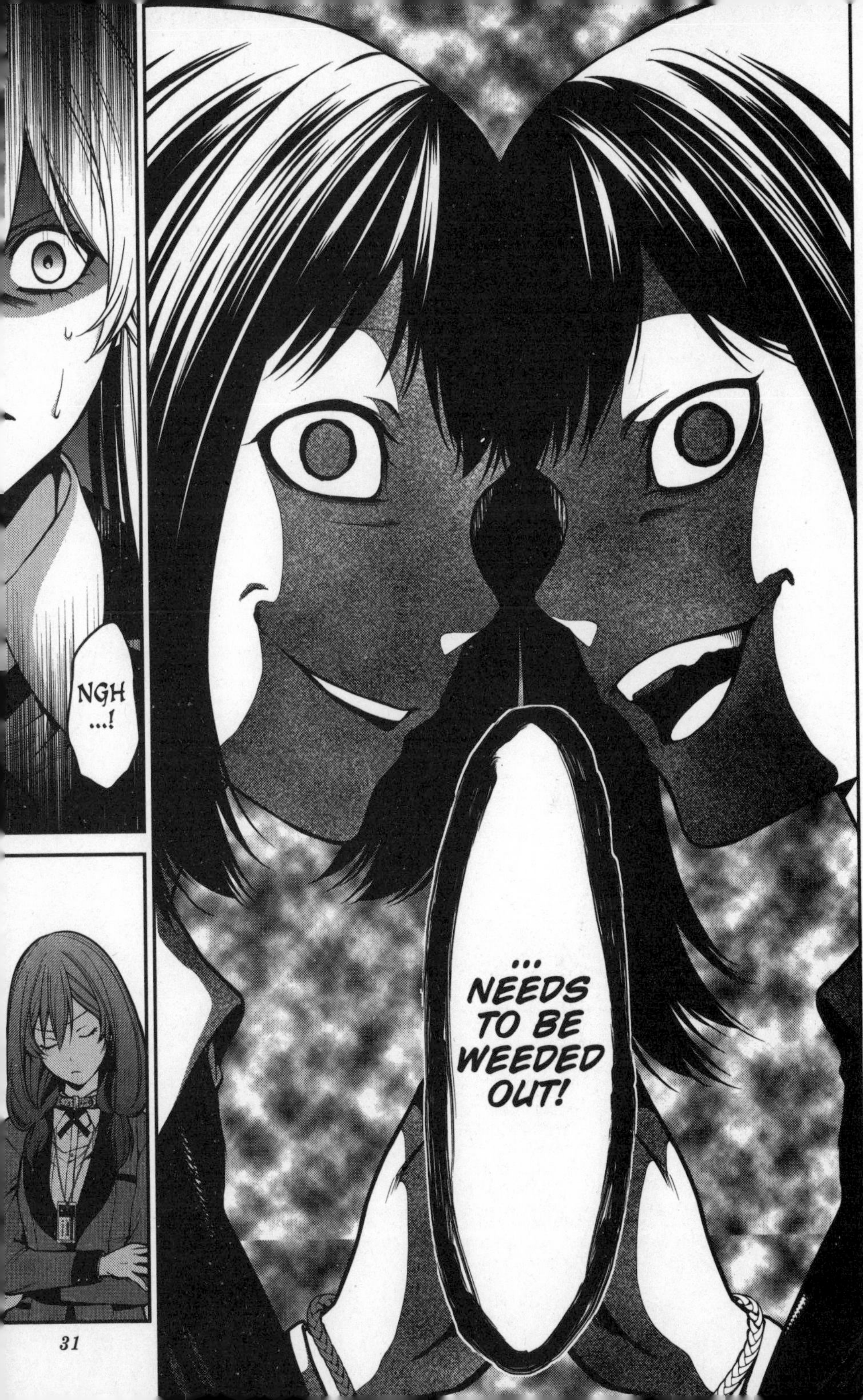

... NEEDS TO BE WEEDED OUT!
NGH ...!

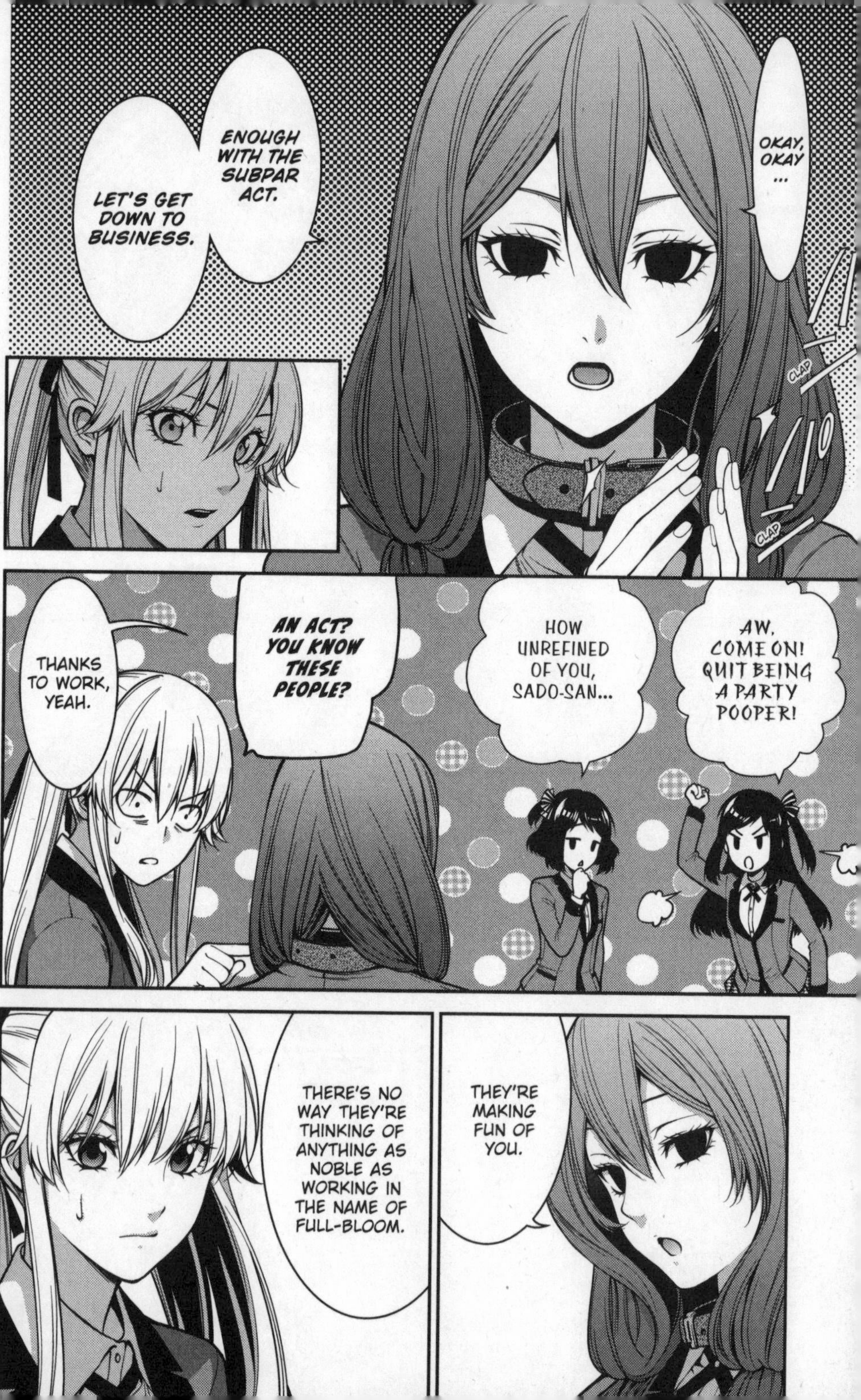
OKAY, OKAY ...
ENOUGH WITH THE SUBPAR ACT.
LET'S GET DOWN TO BUSINESS.
CLAP
CLAP
AW, COME ON! QUIT BEING A PARTY POOPER!
HOW UNREFINED OF YOU, SADO-SAN...
AN ACT? YOU KNOW THESE PEOPLE?
THANKS TO WORK, YEAH.
THEY'RE MAKING FUN OF YOU.
THERE'S NO WAY THEY'RE THINKING OF ANYTHING AS NOBLE AS WORKING IN THE NAME OF FULL-BLOOM.

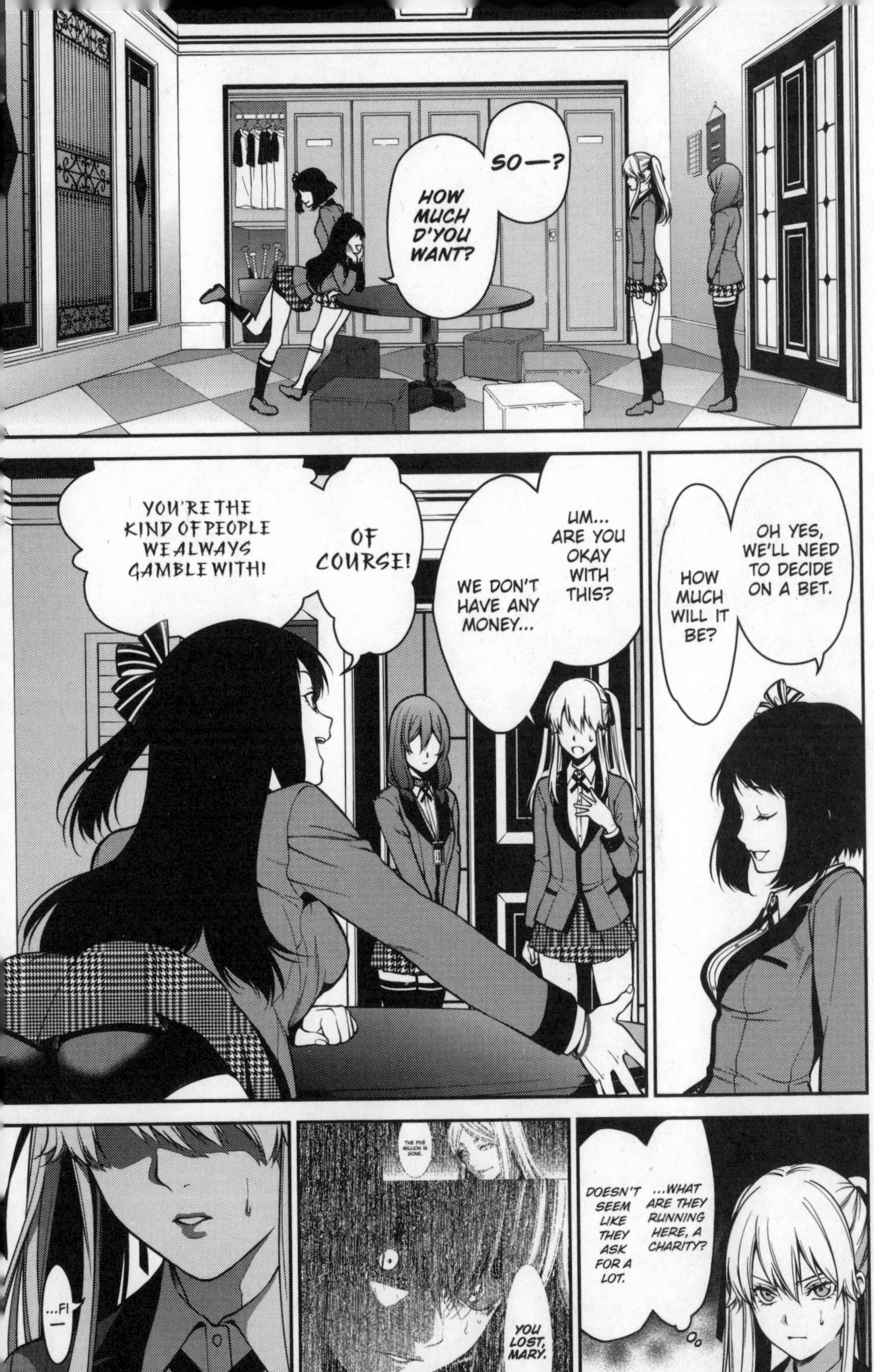
SO—?
HOW MUCH D'YOU WANT?
OH YES, WE'LL NEED TO DECIDE ON A BET.
HOW MUCH WILL IT BE?
UM... ARE YOU OKAY WITH THIS?
WE DON'T HAVE ANY MONEY...
OF COURSE!
YOU'RE THE KIND OF PEOPLE WE ALWAYS GAMBLE WITH!
...WHAT ARE THEY RUNNING HERE, A CHARITY?
DOESN'T SEEM LIKE THEY ASK FOR A LOT.
THE FIVE MILLION IS GONE.
YOU LOST, MARY.
...FI—

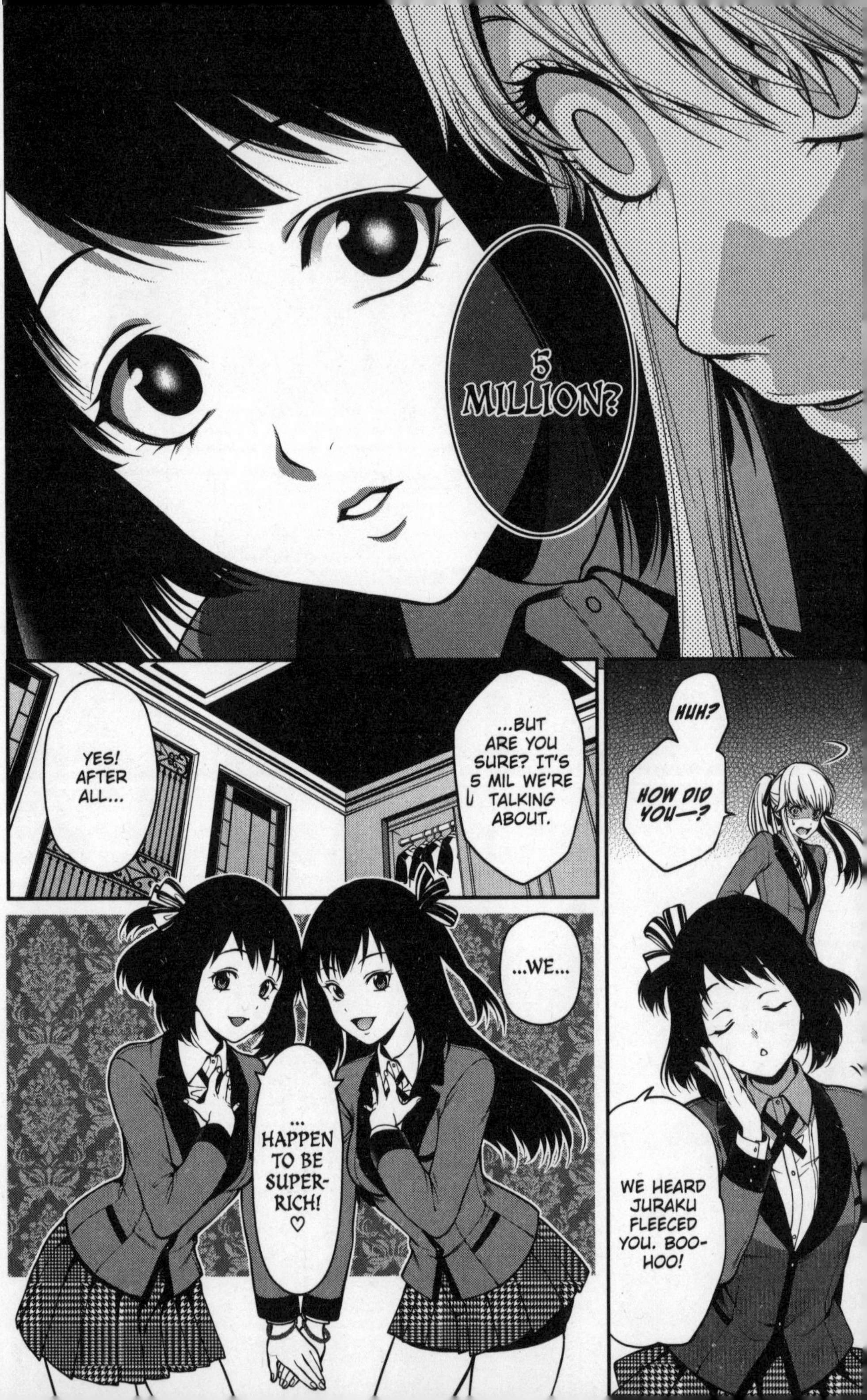
5 MILLION?
HUH?
HOW DID YOU—?
...BUT ARE YOU SURE? IT'S 5 MIL WE'RE TALKING ABOUT.
YES! AFTER ALL...
WE HEARD JURAKU FLEECED YOU. BOO-HOO!
...WE...
...HAPPEN TO BE SUPER-RICH! ♡

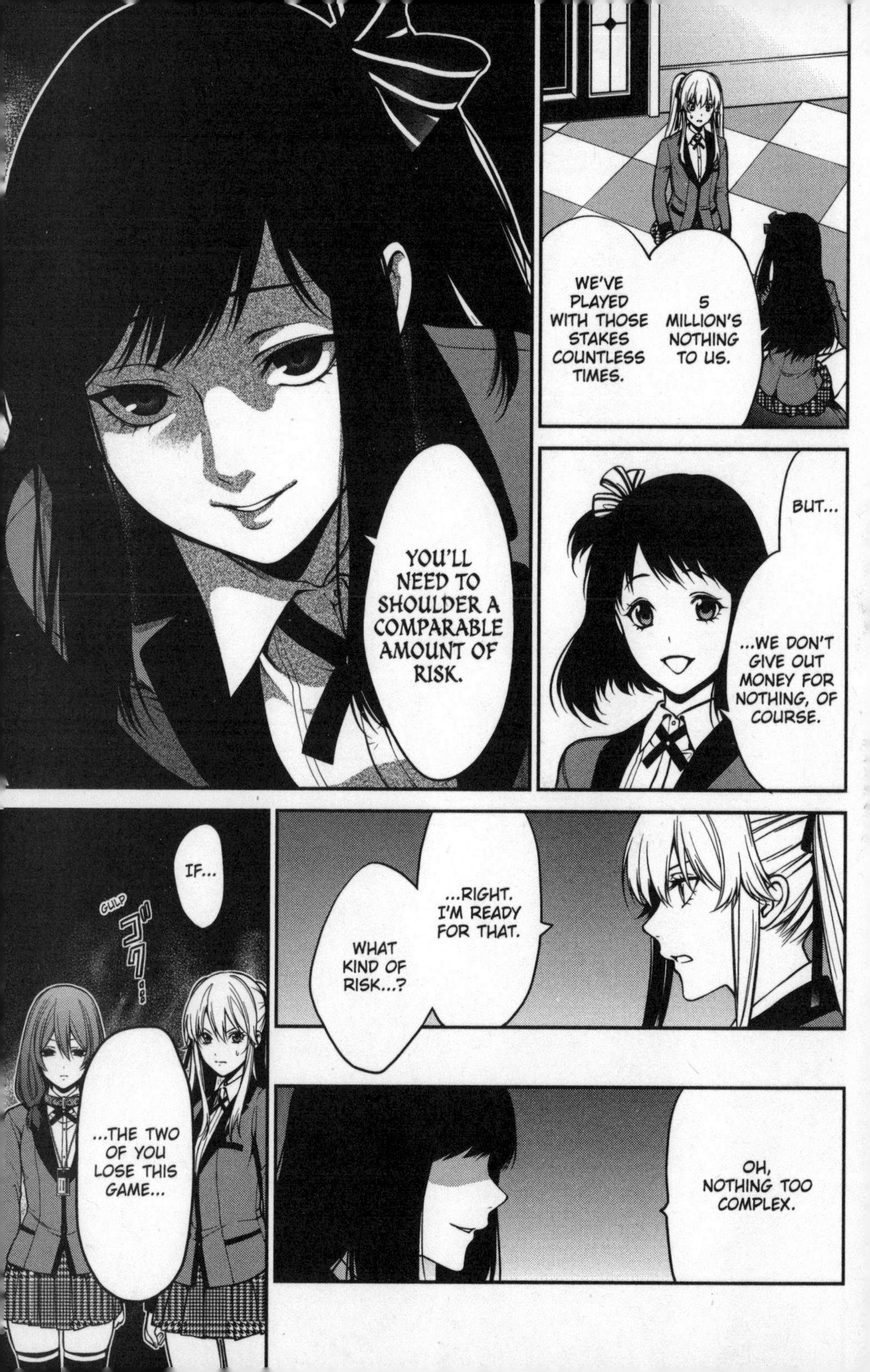
5 MILLION'S NOTHING TO US.
WE'VE PLAYED WITH THOSE STAKES COUNTLESS TIMES.
BUT...
...WE DON'T GIVE OUT MONEY FOR NOTHING, OF COURSE.
YOU'LL NEED TO SHOULDER A COMPARABLE AMOUNT OF RISK.
...RIGHT. I'M READY FOR THAT.
WHAT KIND OF RISK...?
OH, NOTHING TOO COMPLEX.
IF...
GULP
...THE TWO OF YOU LOSE THIS GAME...

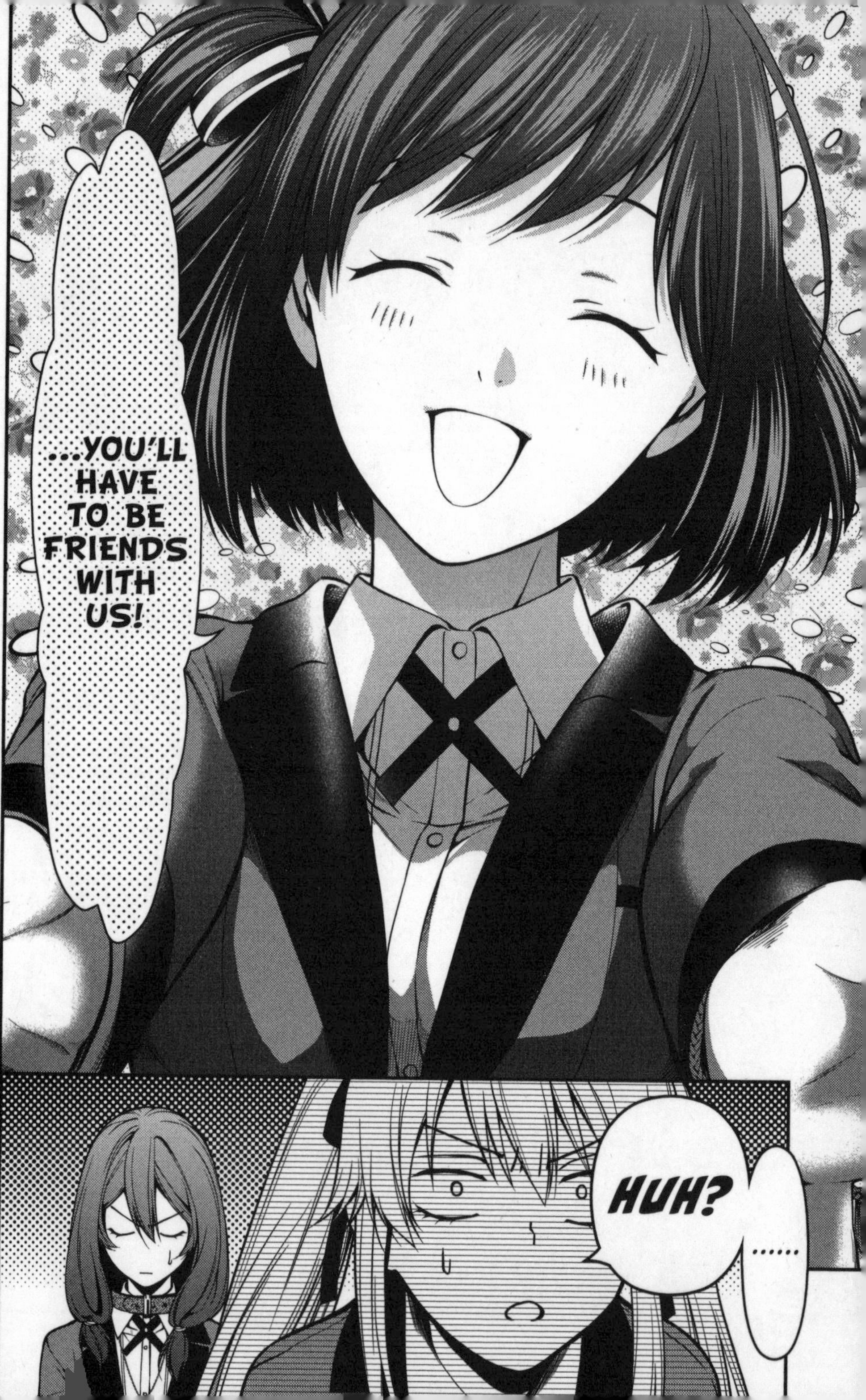
...YOU'LL HAVE TO BE FRIENDS WITH US!
......
HUH?

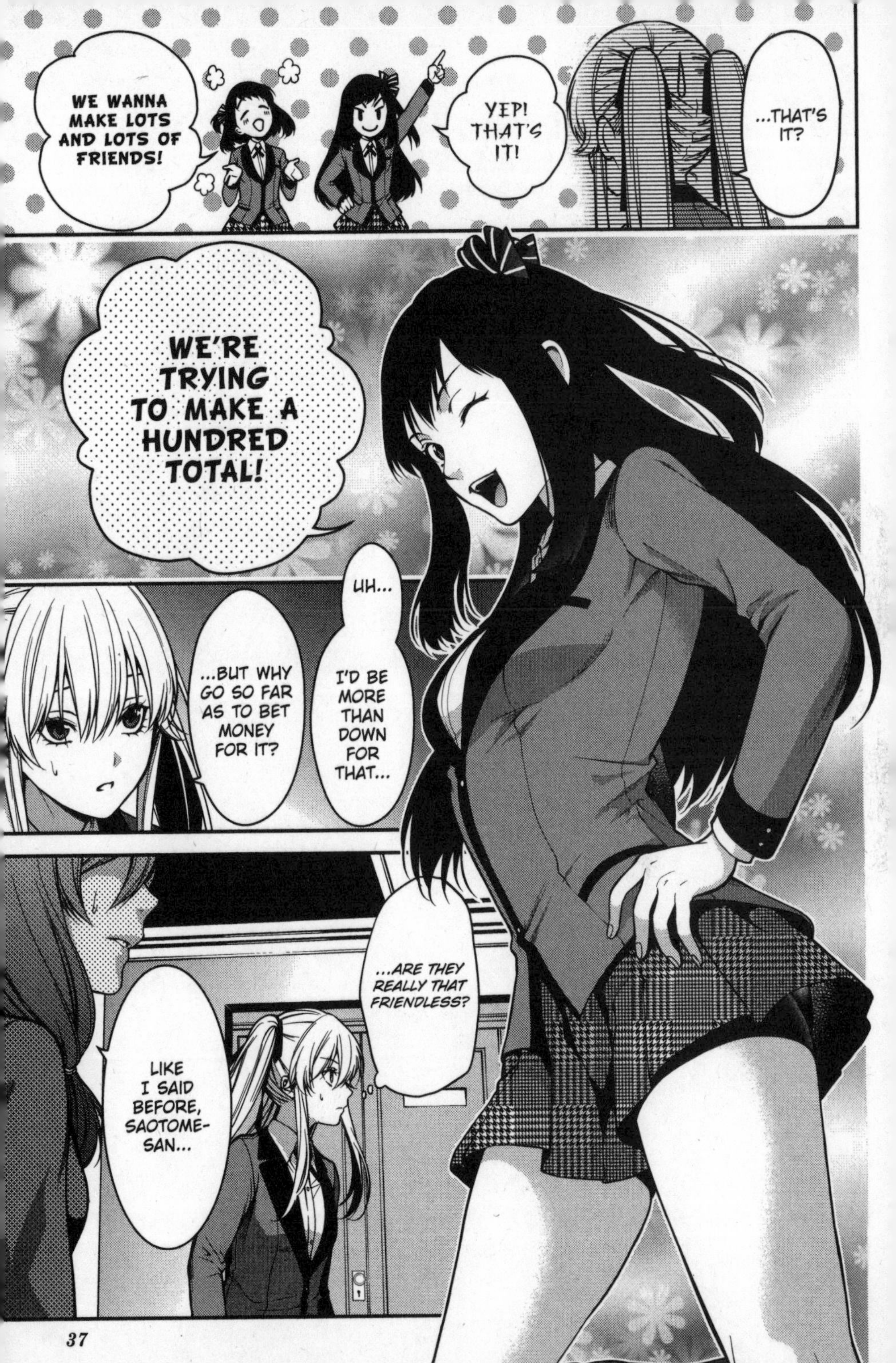
...THAT'S IT?
YEP! THAT'S IT!
WE WANNA MAKE LOTS AND LOTS OF FRIENDS!
WE'RE TRYING TO MAKE A HUNDRED TOTAL!
UH...
I'D BE MORE THAN DOWN FOR THAT...
...BUT WHY GO SO FAR AS TO BET MONEY FOR IT?
...ARE THEY REALLY THAT FRIENDLESS?
LIKE I SAID BEFORE, SAOTOME-SAN...

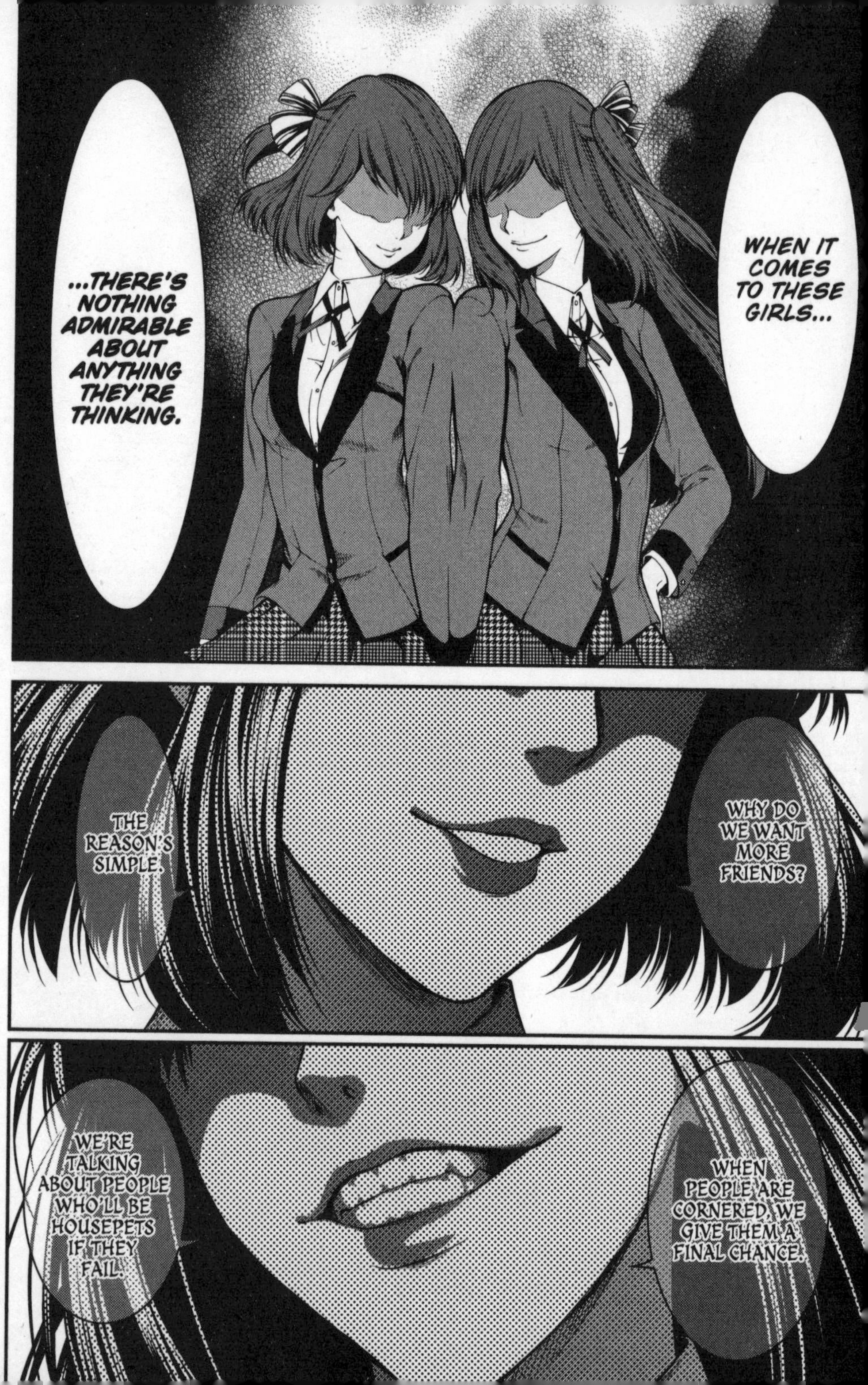
WHEN IT COMES TO THESE GIRLS...
...THERE'S NOTHING ADMIRABLE ABOUT ANYTHING THEY'RE THINKING.
WHY DO WE WANT MORE FRIENDS?
THE REASON'S SIMPLE.
WHEN PEOPLE ARE CORNERED, WE GIVE THEM A FINAL CHANCE.
WE'RE TALKING ABOUT PEOPLE WHO'LL BE HOUSEPETS IF THEY FAIL.

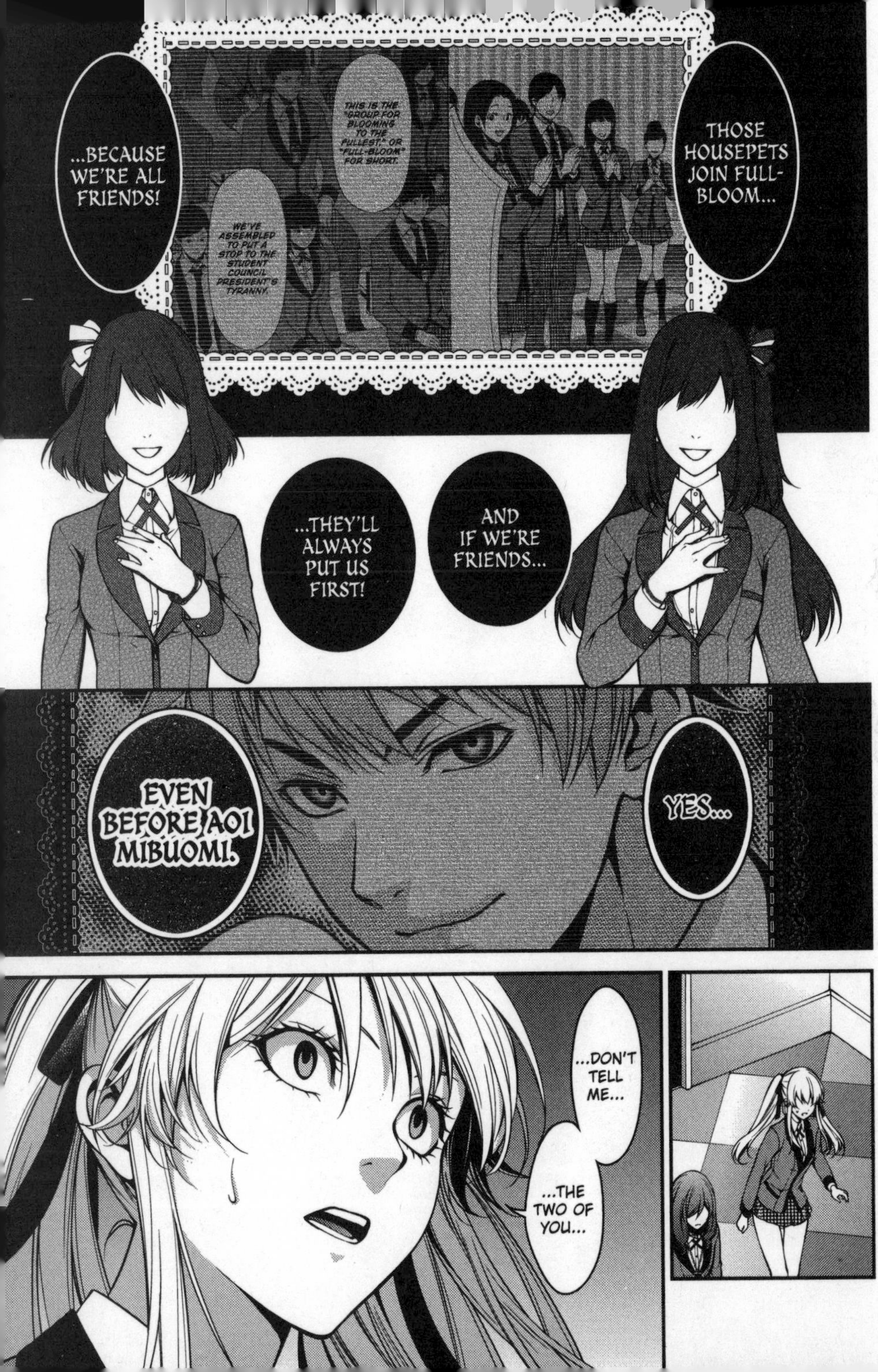
THOSE HOUSEPETS JOIN FULL-BLOOM...
THIS IS THE "GROUP FOR BLOOMING TO THE FULLEST," OR "FULL-BLOOM" FOR SHORT.
WE'VE ASSEMBLED TO PUT A STOP TO THE STUDENT COUNCIL PRESIDENT'S TYRANNY.
...BECAUSE WE'RE ALL FRIENDS!
AND IF WE'RE FRIENDS...
...THEY'LL ALWAYS PUT US FIRST!
YES...
EVEN BEFORE AOI MIBUOMI.
...DON'T TELL ME...
...THE TWO OF YOU...

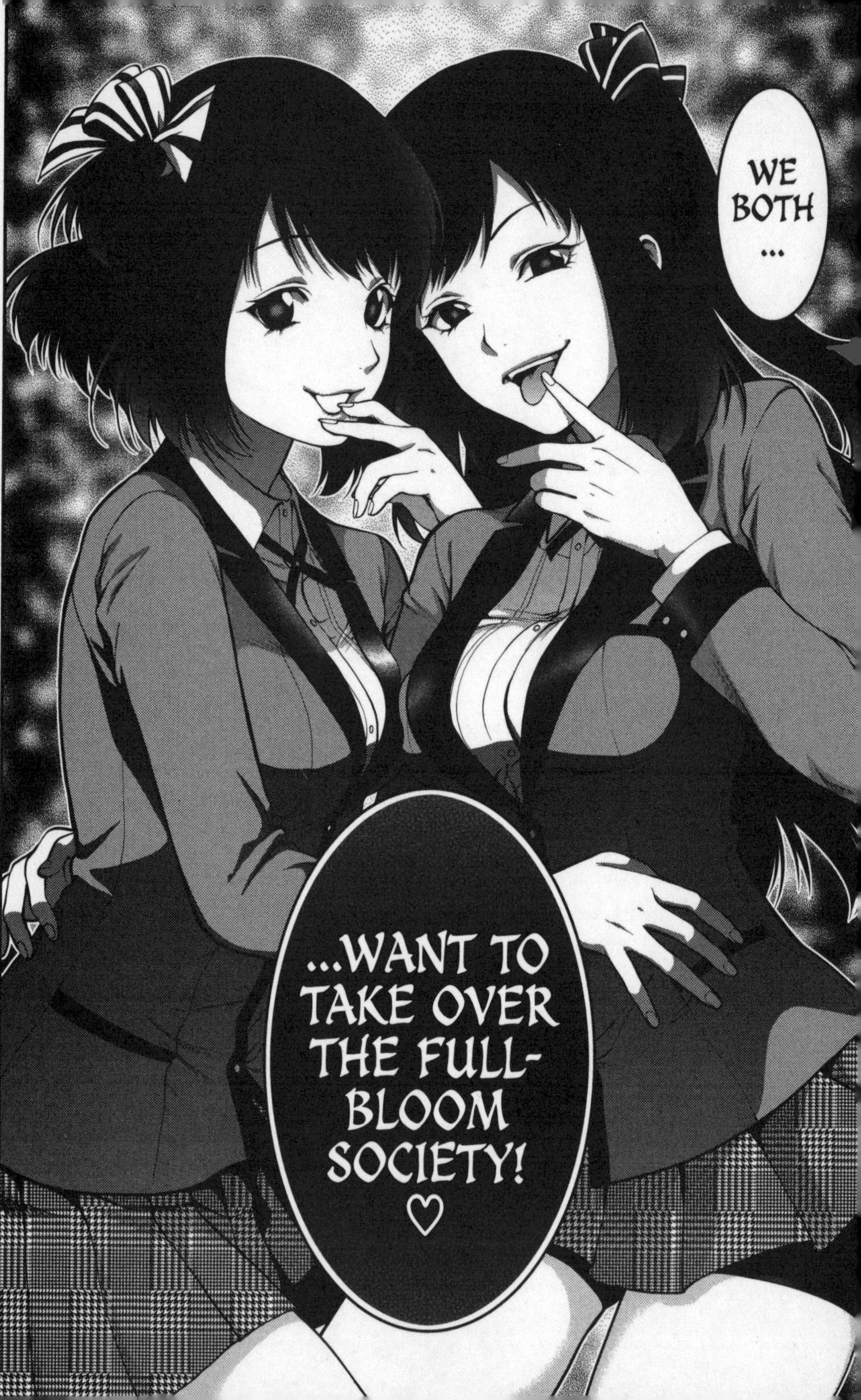
WE BOTH ...
...WANT TO TAKE OVER THE FULL-BLOOM SOCIETY! ♡

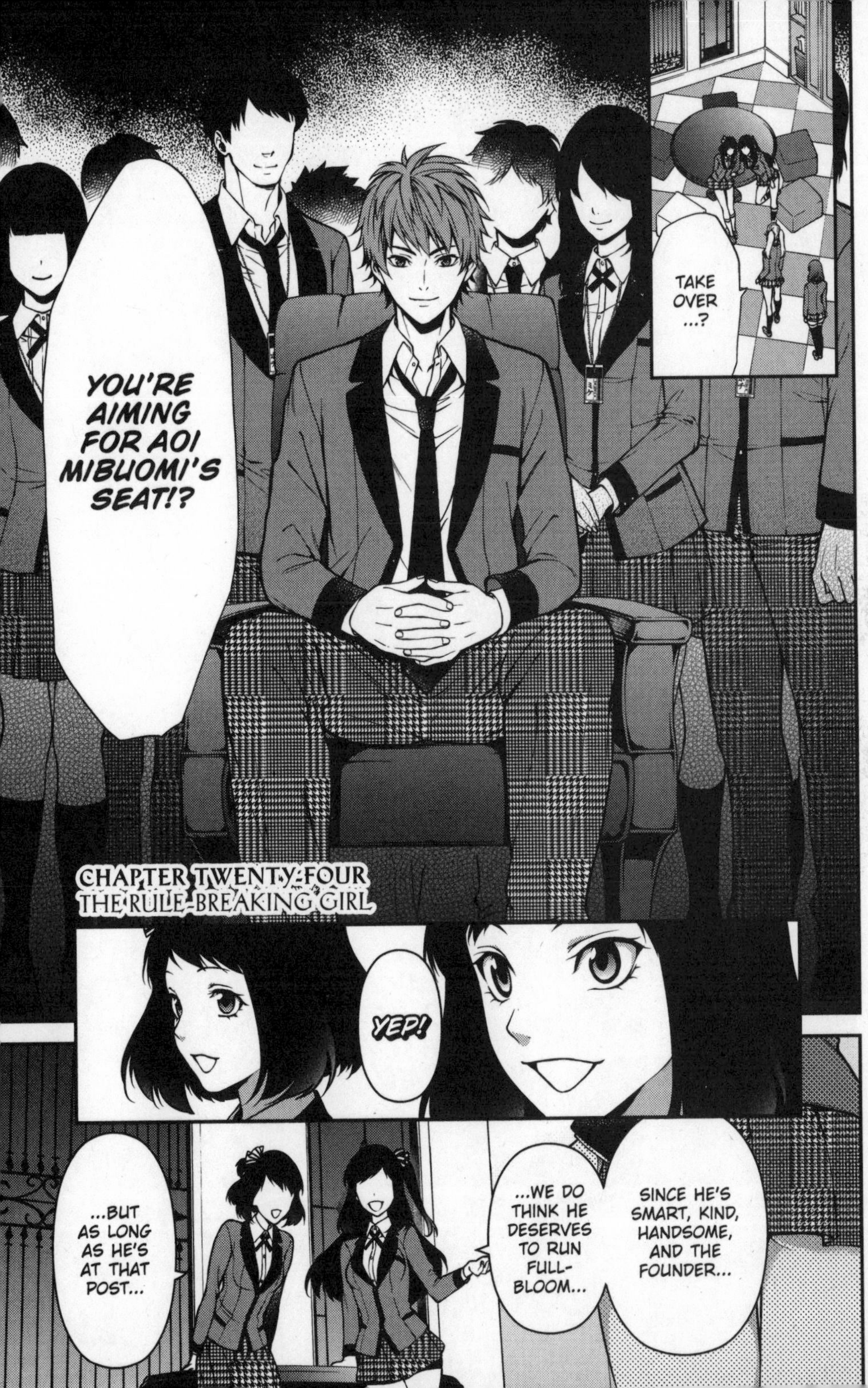
TAKE OVER ...?
YOU'RE AIMING FOR AOI MIBUOMI'S SEAT!?
CHAPTER TWENTY-FOUR
THE RULE-BREAKING GIRL
YEP!
SINCE HE'S SMART, KIND, HANDSOME, AND THE FOUNDER...
...WE DO THINK HE DESERVES TO RUN FULL-BLOOM...
...BUT AS LONG AS HE'S AT THAT POST...

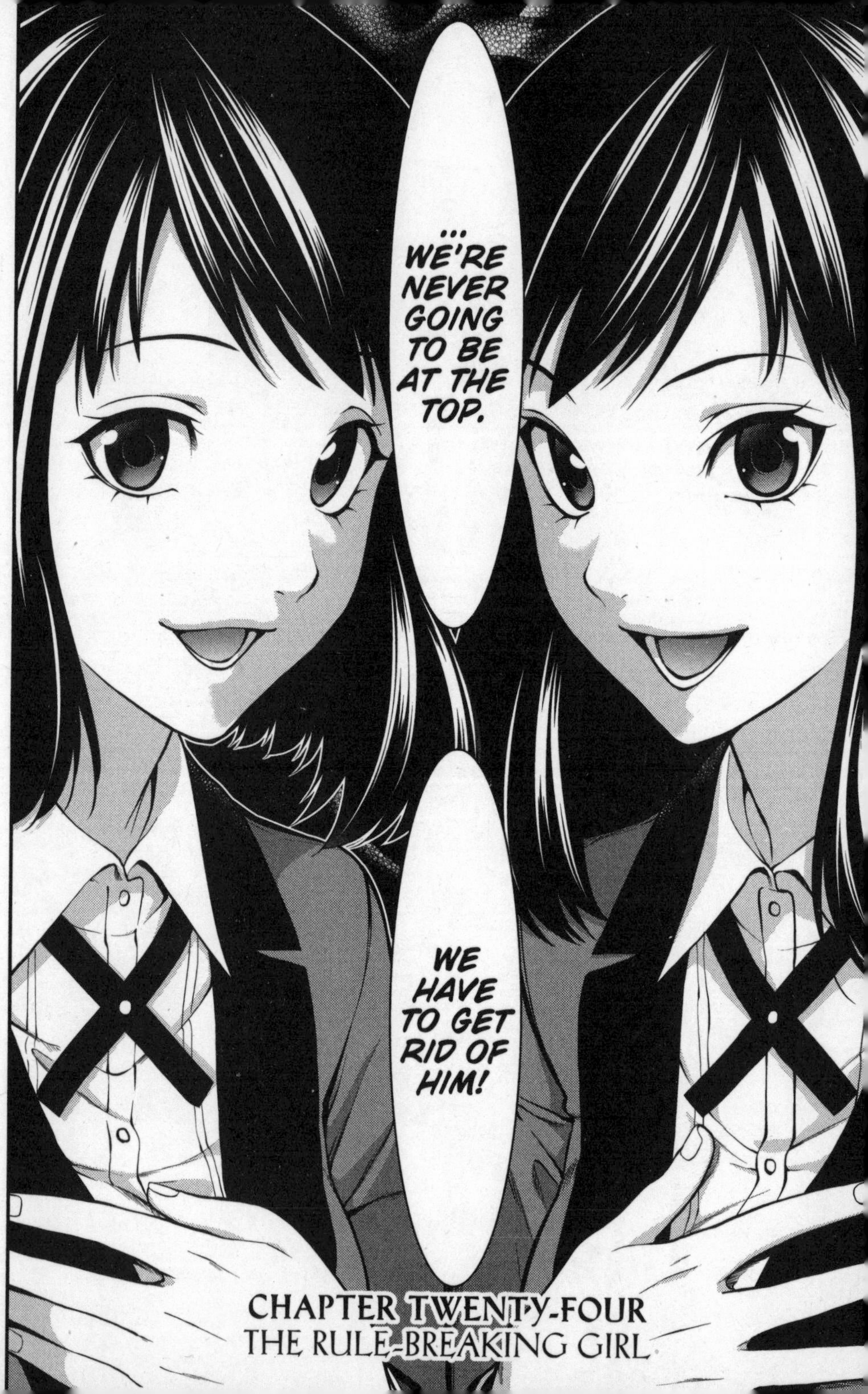
...WE'RE NEVER GOING TO BE AT THE TOP.
WE HAVE TO GET RID OF HIM!

CHAPTER TWENTY-FOUR
THE RULE-BREAKING GIRL

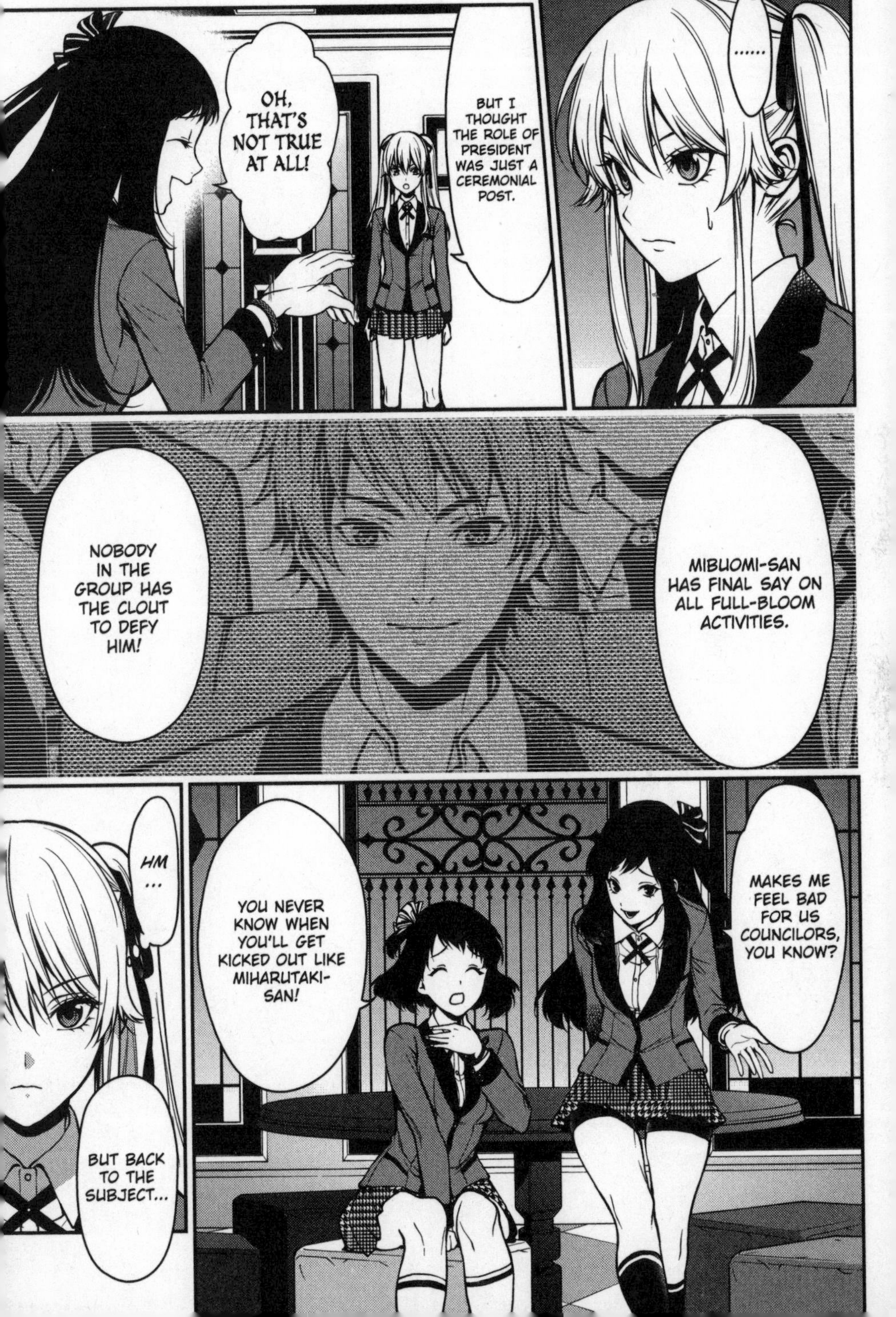
......
BUT I THOUGHT THE ROLE OF PRESIDENT WAS JUST A CEREMONIAL POST.
OH, THAT'S NOT TRUE AT ALL!
MIBUOMI-SAN HAS FINAL SAY ON ALL FULL-BLOOM ACTIVITIES.
NOBODY IN THE GROUP HAS THE CLOUT TO DEFY HIM!
MAKES ME FEEL BAD FOR US COUNCILORS, YOU KNOW?
YOU NEVER KNOW WHEN YOU'LL GET KICKED OUT LIKE MIHARUTAKI-SAN!
HM ...
BUT BACK TO THE SUBJECT...

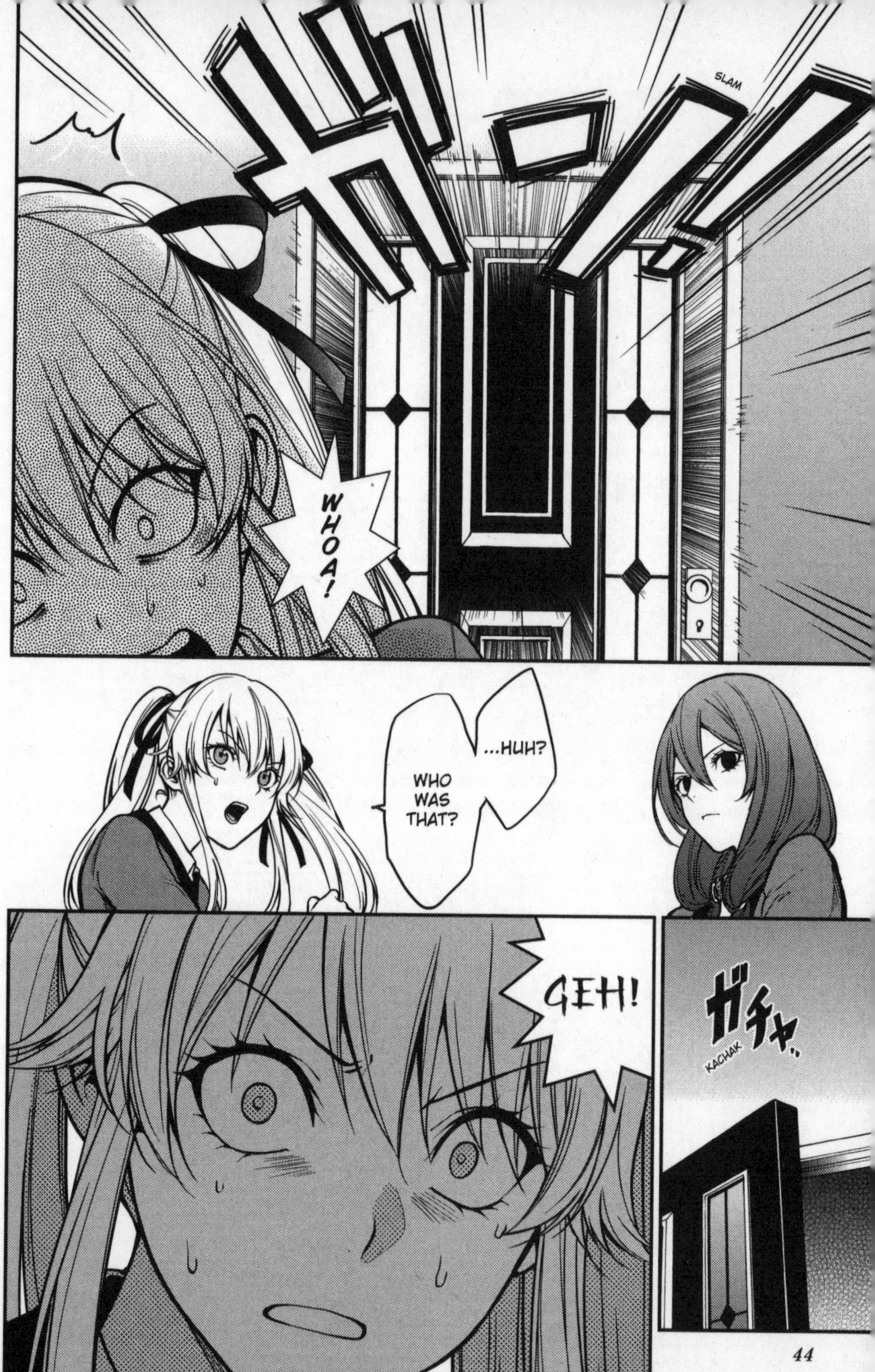
SLAM
WHOA!
...HUH?
WHO WAS THAT?
ガチャ
KACHAK
GEH!

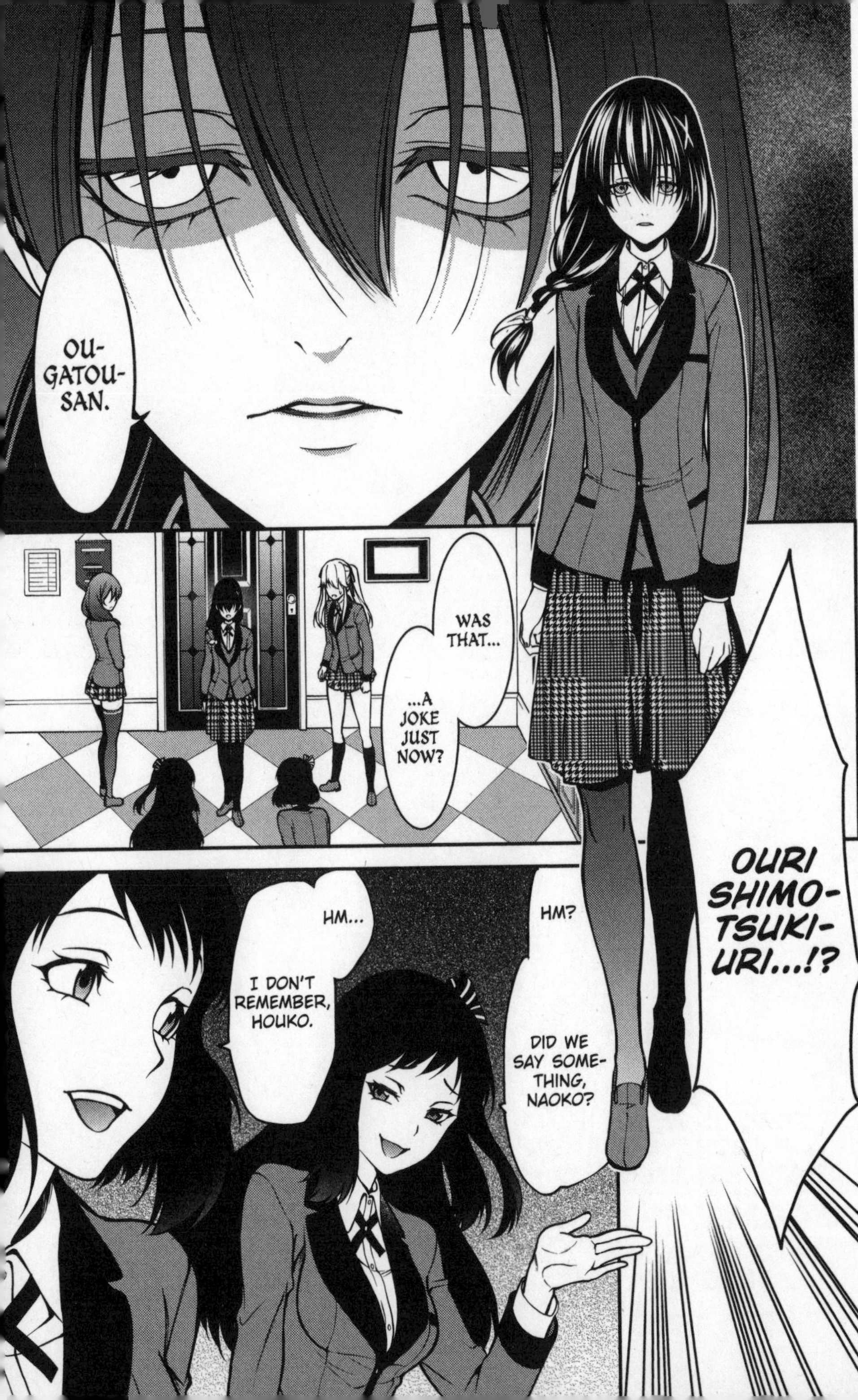
OU-
GATOU-
SAN.
OURI
SHIMO-
TSUKI-
URI...!?
WAS
THAT...
...A
JOKE
JUST
NOW?
HM?
DID WE
SAY SOME-
THING,
NAOKO?
HM...
I DON'T
REMEMBER,
HOUKO.

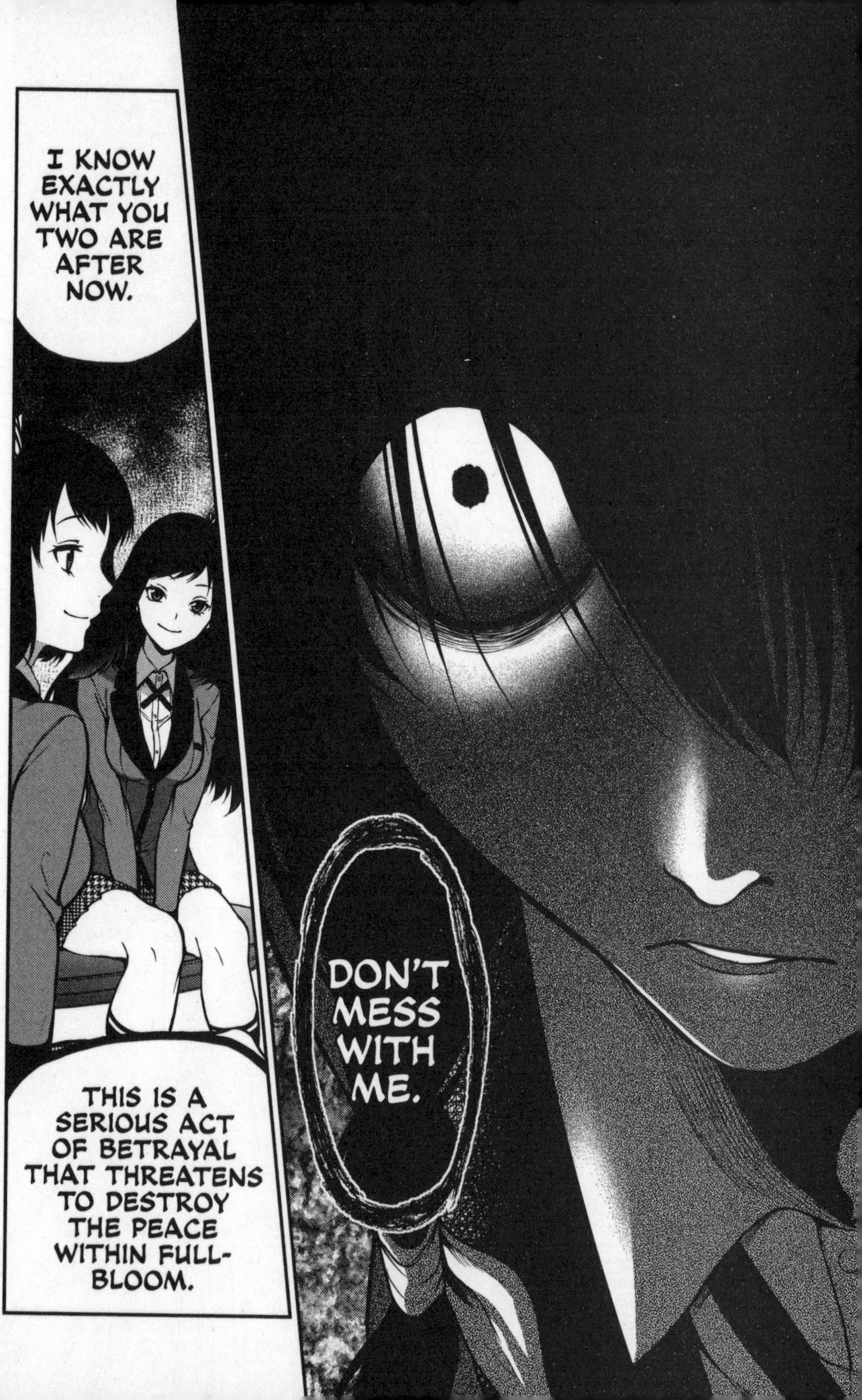
DON'T MESS WITH ME.
I KNOW EXACTLY WHAT YOU TWO ARE AFTER NOW.
THIS IS A SERIOUS ACT OF BETRAYAL THAT THREATENS TO DESTROY THE PEACE WITHIN FULL-BLOOM.

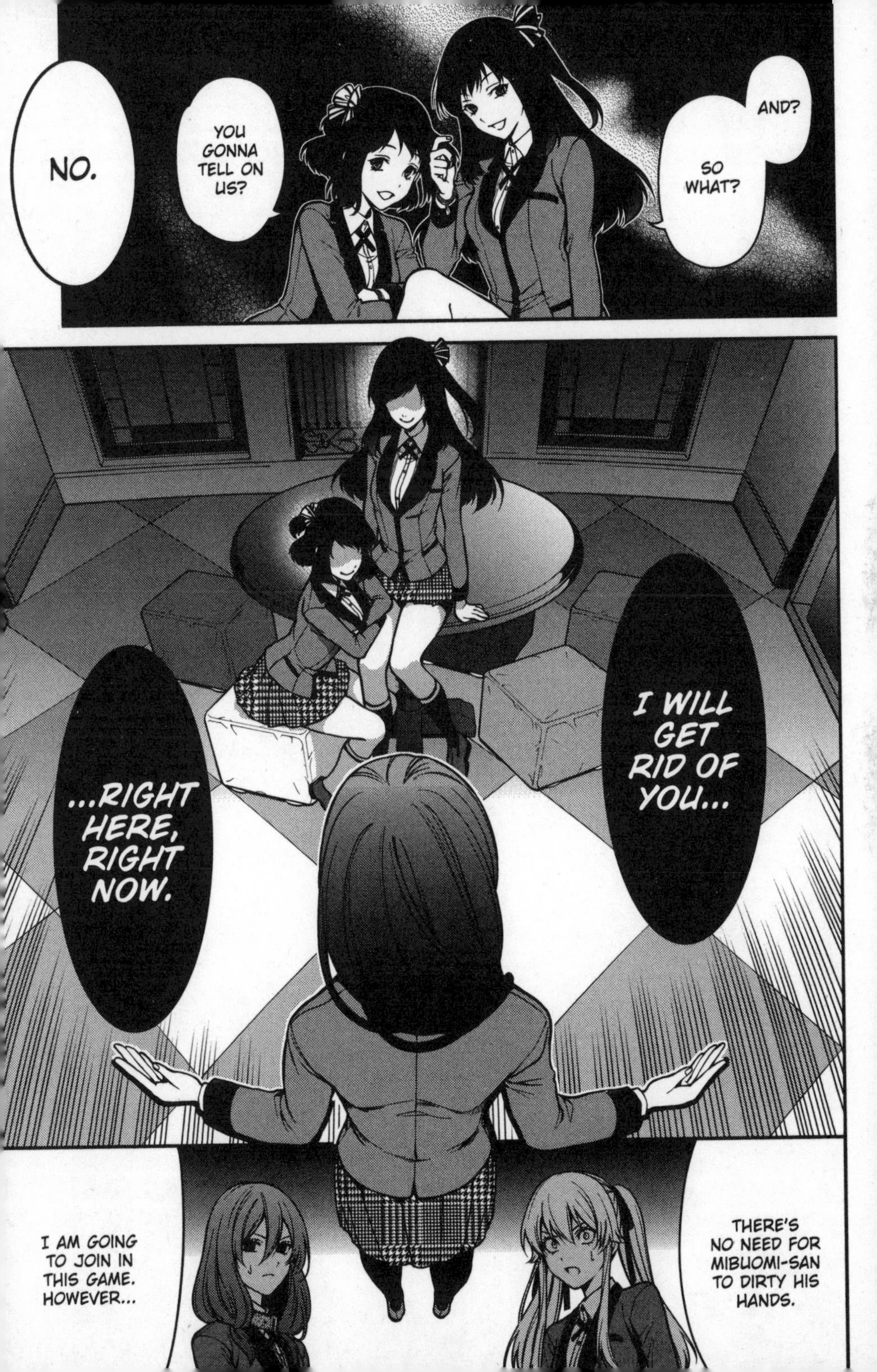
AND? SO WHAT?
YOU GONNA TELL ON US?
NO.
I WILL GET RID OF YOU...
...RIGHT HERE, RIGHT NOW.
THERE'S NO NEED FOR MIBUOMI-SAN TO DIRTY HIS HANDS.
I AM GOING TO JOIN IN THIS GAME. HOWEVER...

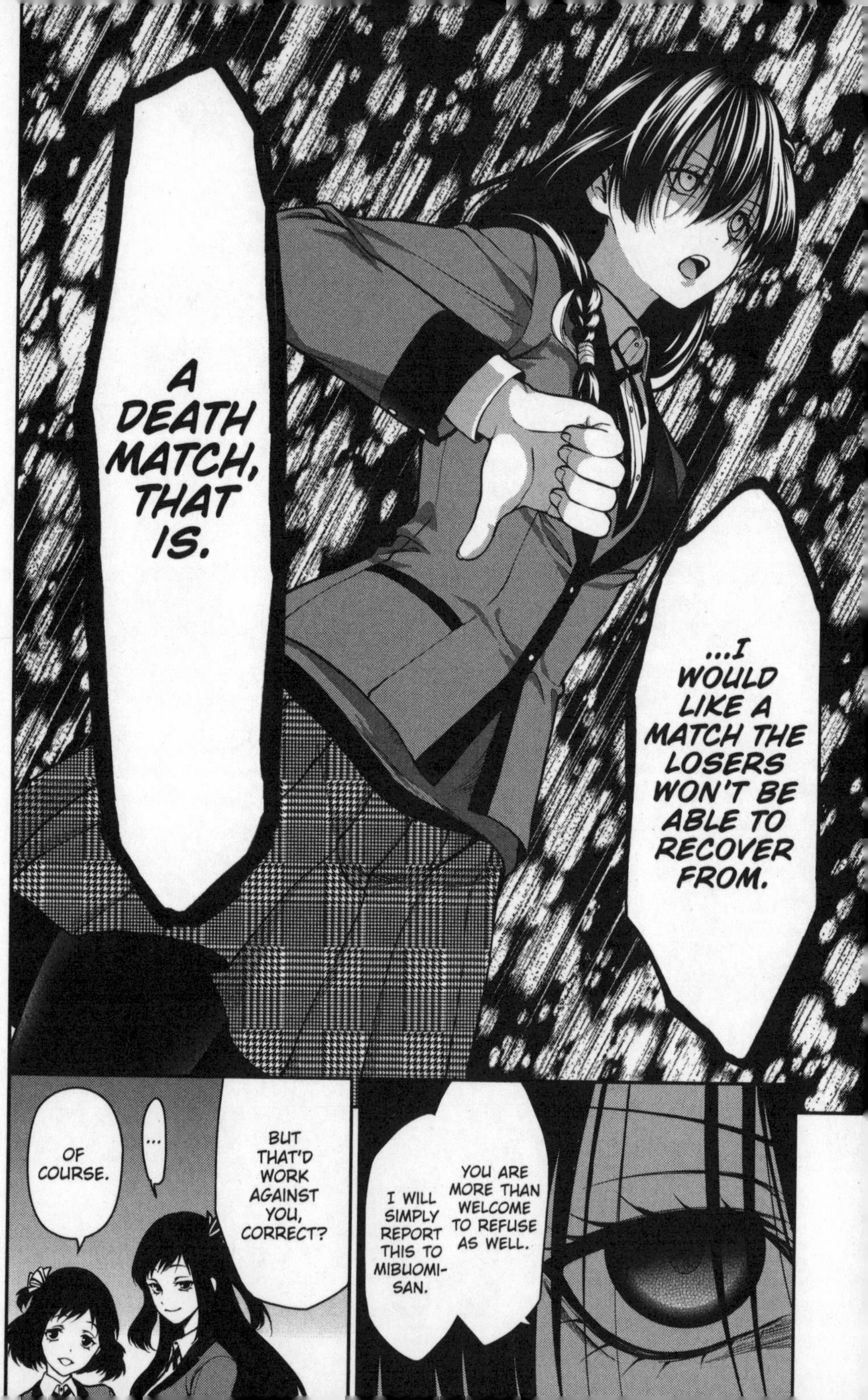
...I WOULD LIKE A MATCH THE LOSERS WON'T BE ABLE TO RECOVER FROM.
A DEATH MATCH, THAT IS.
YOU ARE MORE THAN WELCOME TO REFUSE AS WELL.
I WILL SIMPLY REPORT THIS TO MIBUOMI-SAN.
BUT THAT'D WORK AGAINST YOU, CORRECT?
...
OF COURSE.

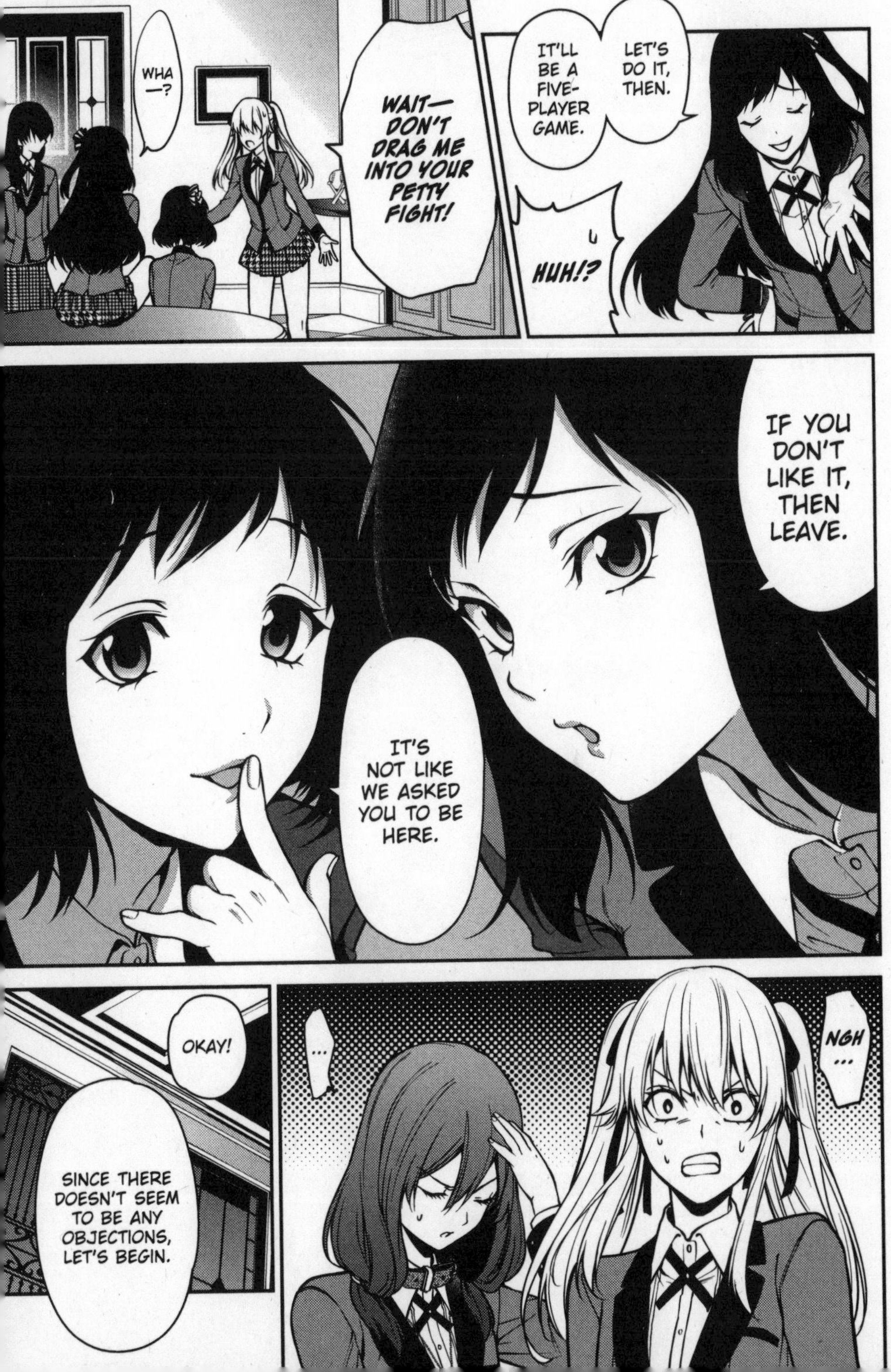
LET'S DO IT, THEN.
IT'LL BE A FIVE-PLAYER GAME.
HUH!?
WAIT—DON'T DRAG ME INTO YOUR PETTY FIGHT!
WHA—?
IF YOU DON'T LIKE IT, THEN LEAVE.
IT'S NOT LIKE WE ASKED YOU TO BE HERE.
NGH...
...
OKAY!
SINCE THERE DOESN'T SEEM TO BE ANY OBJECTIONS, LET'S BEGIN.

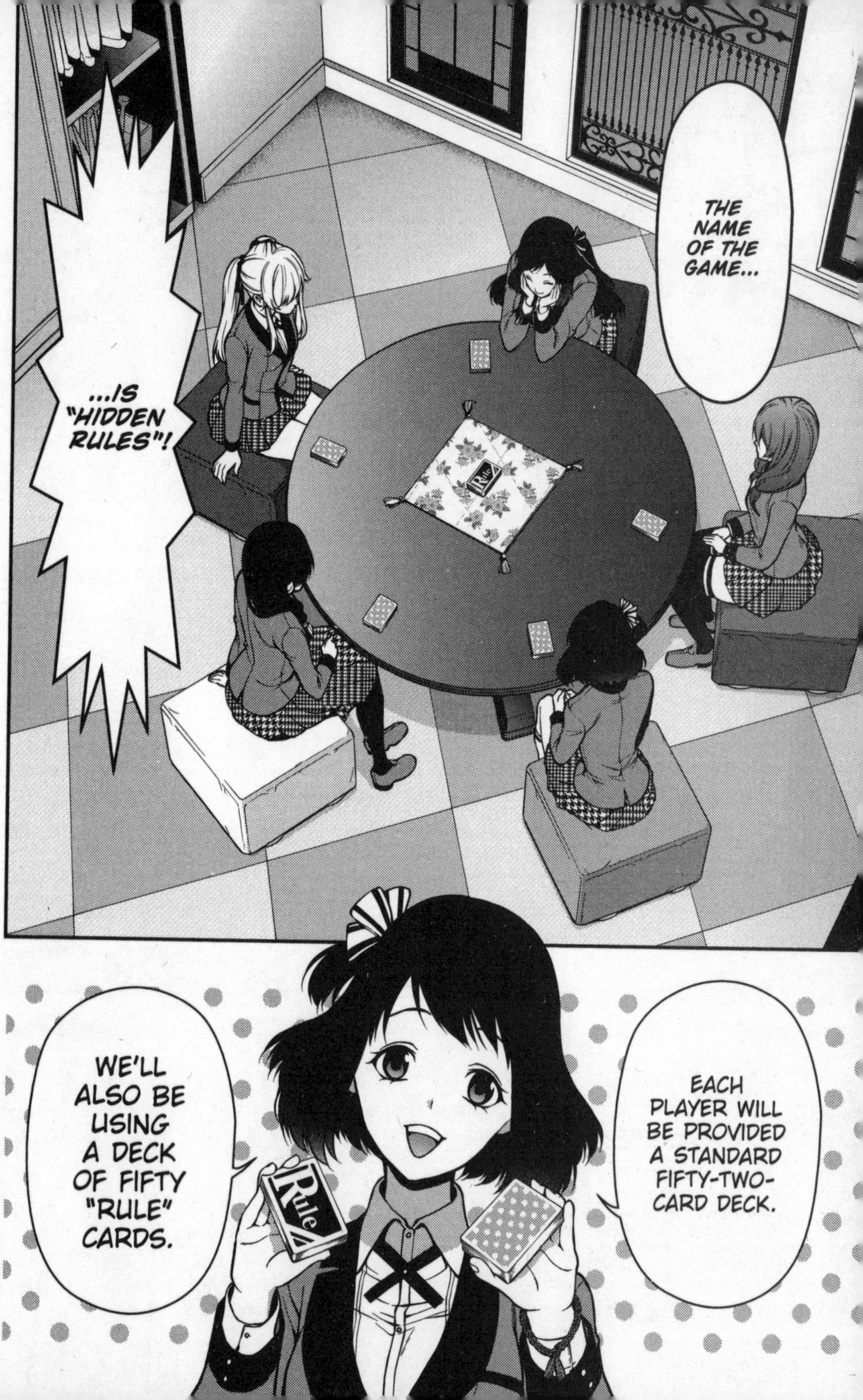
THE NAME OF THE GAME...
...IS "HIDDEN RULES"!
EACH PLAYER WILL BE PROVIDED A STANDARD FIFTY-TWO-CARD DECK.
WE'LL ALSO BE USING A DECK OF FIFTY "RULE" CARDS.

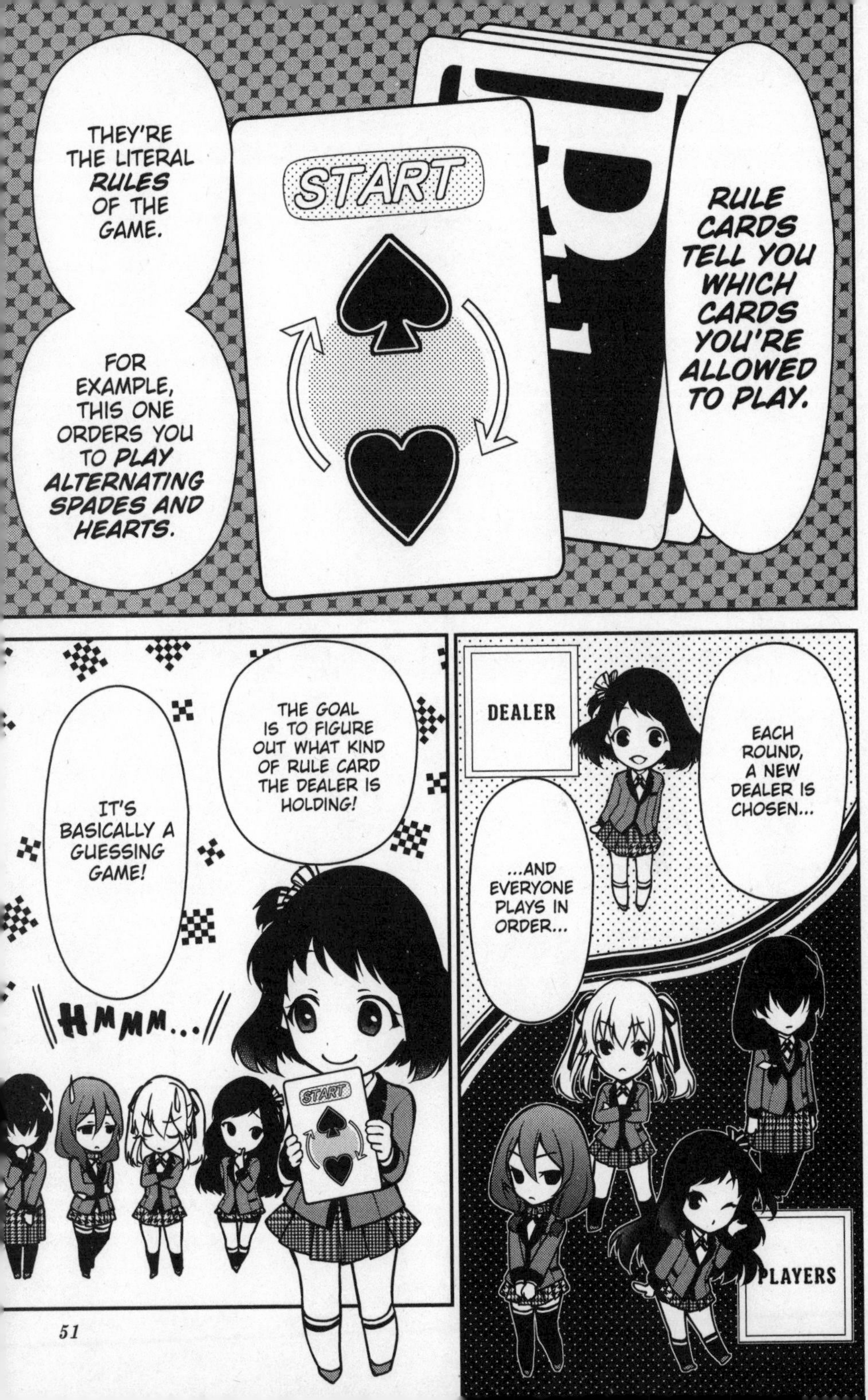
RULE CARDS TELL YOU WHICH CARDS YOU'RE ALLOWED TO PLAY.
START
THEY'RE THE LITERAL RULES OF THE GAME.
FOR EXAMPLE, THIS ONE ORDERS YOU TO PLAY ALTERNATING SPADES AND HEARTS.
EACH ROUND, A NEW DEALER IS CHOSEN...
DEALER
...AND EVERYONE PLAYS IN ORDER...
PLAYERS
THE GOAL IS TO FIGURE OUT WHAT KIND OF RULE CARD THE DEALER IS HOLDING!
IT'S BASICALLY A GUESSING GAME!
HMMM...
START

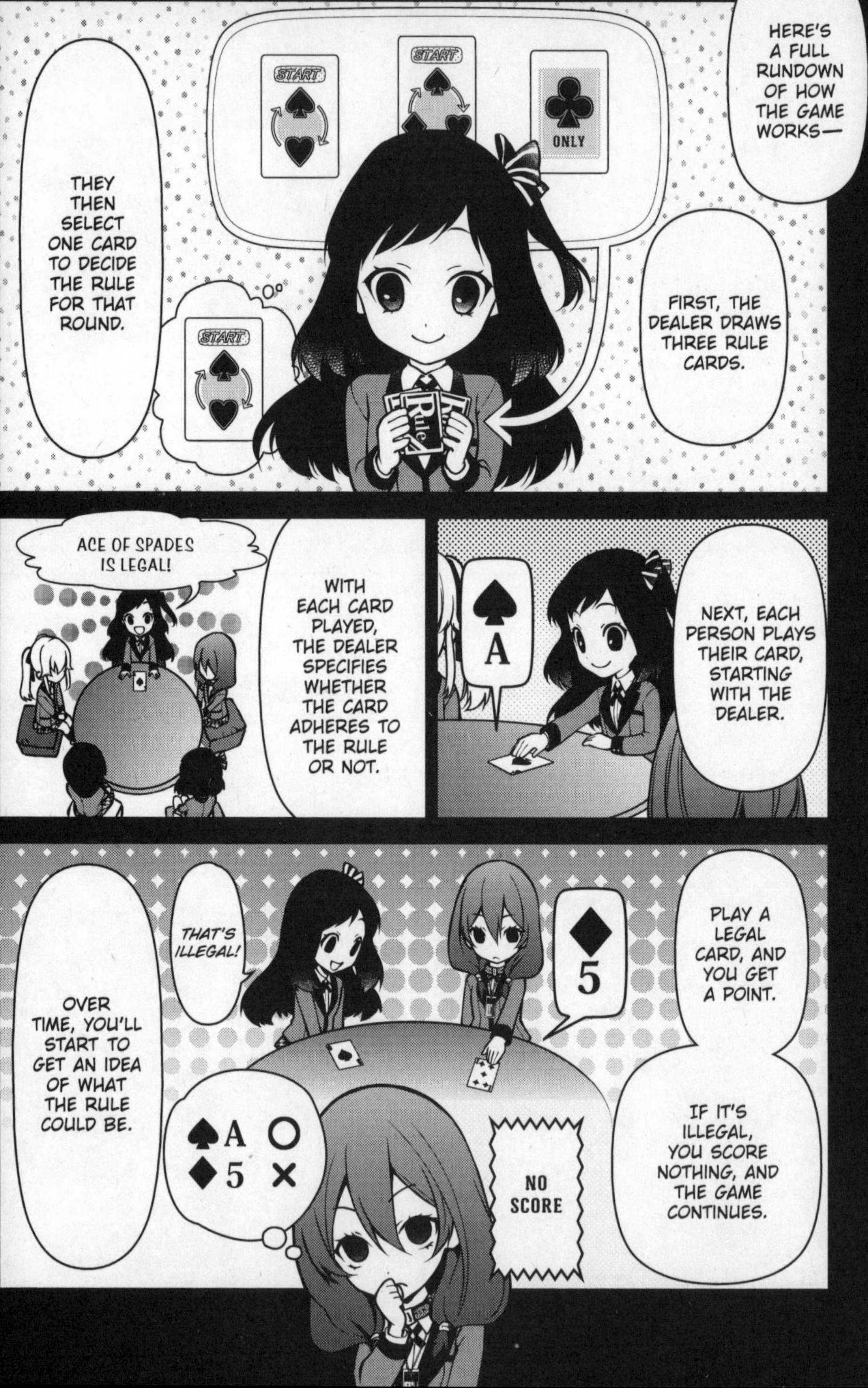
HERE'S A FULL RUNDOWN OF HOW THE GAME WORKS—
FIRST, THE DEALER DRAWS THREE RULE CARDS.
START
START
ONLY
Rule
START
THEY THEN SELECT ONE CARD TO DECIDE THE RULE FOR THAT ROUND.
NEXT, EACH PERSON PLAYS THEIR CARD, STARTING WITH THE DEALER.
A
WITH EACH CARD PLAYED, THE DEALER SPECIFIES WHETHER THE CARD ADHERES TO THE RULE OR NOT.
ACE OF SPADES IS LEGAL!
PLAY A LEGAL CARD, AND YOU GET A POINT.
5
THAT'S ILLEGAL!
IF IT'S ILLEGAL, YOU SCORE NOTHING, AND THE GAME CONTINUES.
NO SCORE
♠A ○
♦5 ×
OVER TIME, YOU'LL START TO GET AN IDEA OF WHAT THE RULE COULD BE.

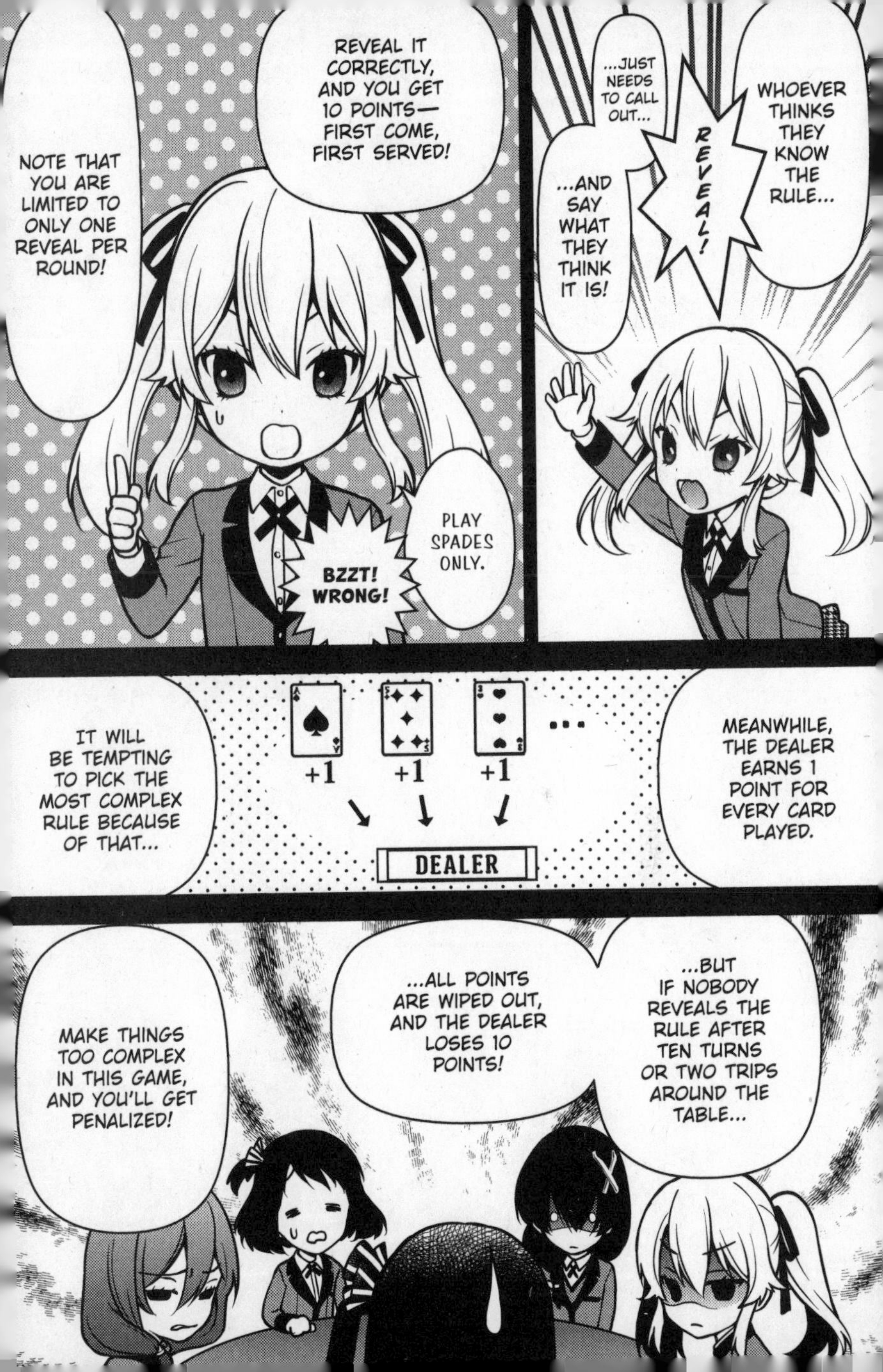
WHOEVER THINKS THEY KNOW THE RULE...
...JUST NEEDS TO CALL OUT...
REVEAL!
...AND SAY WHAT THEY THINK IT IS!
REVEAL IT CORRECTLY, AND YOU GET 10 POINTS— FIRST COME, FIRST SERVED!
NOTE THAT YOU ARE LIMITED TO ONLY ONE REVEAL PER ROUND!
PLAY SPADES ONLY.
BZZT! WRONG!
MEANWHILE, THE DEALER EARNS 1 POINT FOR EVERY CARD PLAYED.
+1
+1
+1
DEALER
IT WILL BE TEMPTING TO PICK THE MOST COMPLEX RULE BECAUSE OF THAT...
...BUT IF NOBODY REVEALS THE RULE AFTER TEN TURNS OR TWO TRIPS AROUND THE TABLE...
...ALL POINTS ARE WIPED OUT, AND THE DEALER LOSES 10 POINTS!
MAKE THINGS TOO COMPLEX IN THIS GAME, AND YOU'LL GET PENALIZED!

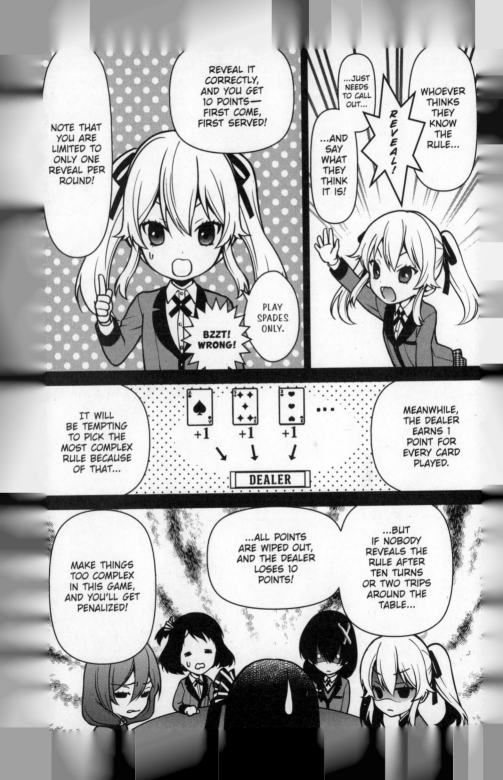

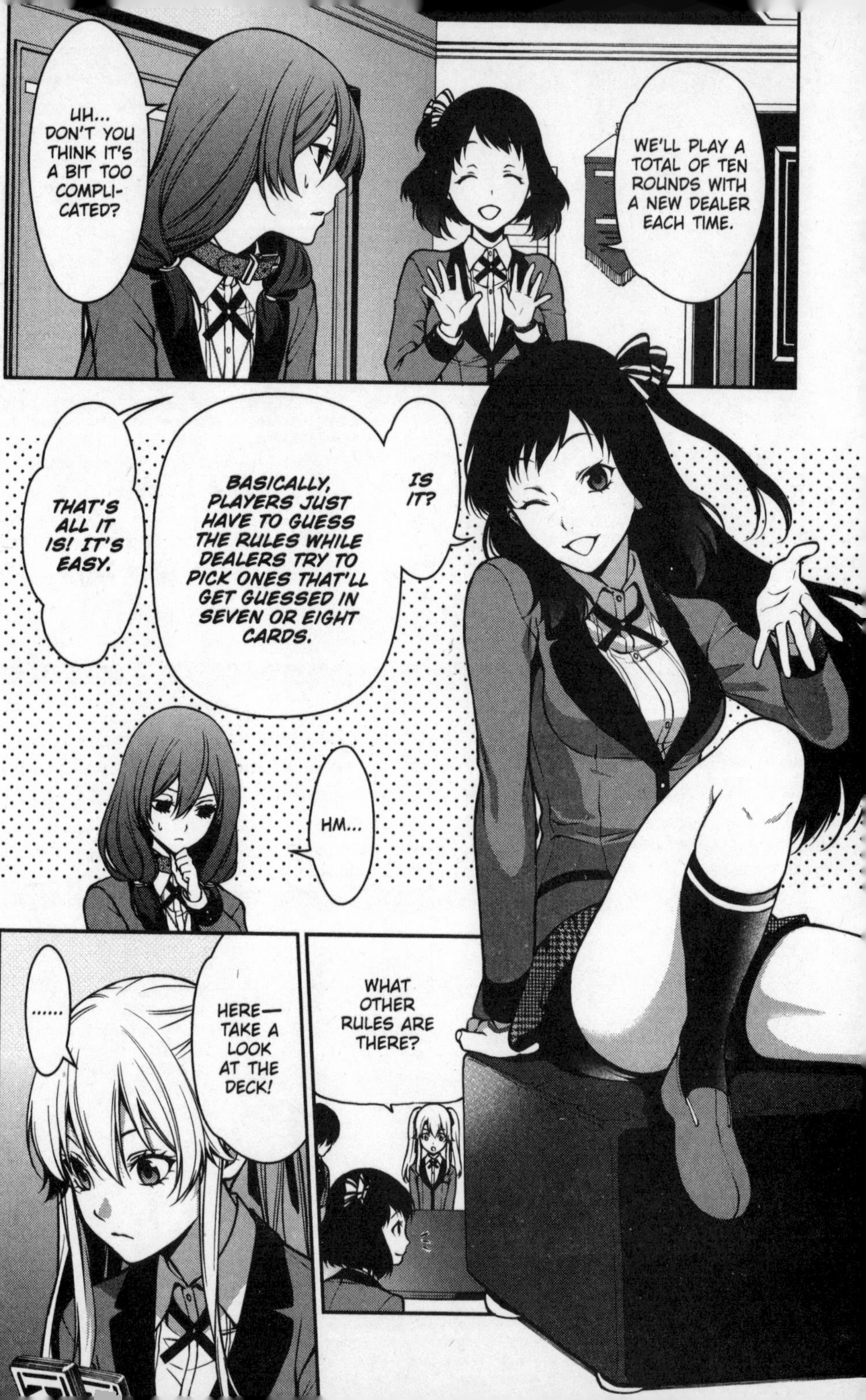
WE'LL PLAY A TOTAL OF TEN ROUNDS WITH A NEW DEALER EACH TIME.
UH... DON'T YOU THINK IT'S A BIT TOO COMPLI-CATED?
IS IT?
BASICALLY, PLAYERS JUST HAVE TO GUESS THE RULES WHILE DEALERS TRY TO PICK ONES THAT'LL GET GUESSED IN SEVEN OR EIGHT CARDS.
THAT'S ALL IT IS! IT'S EASY.
HM...
WHAT OTHER RULES ARE THERE?
HERE— TAKE A LOOK AT THE DECK!
......

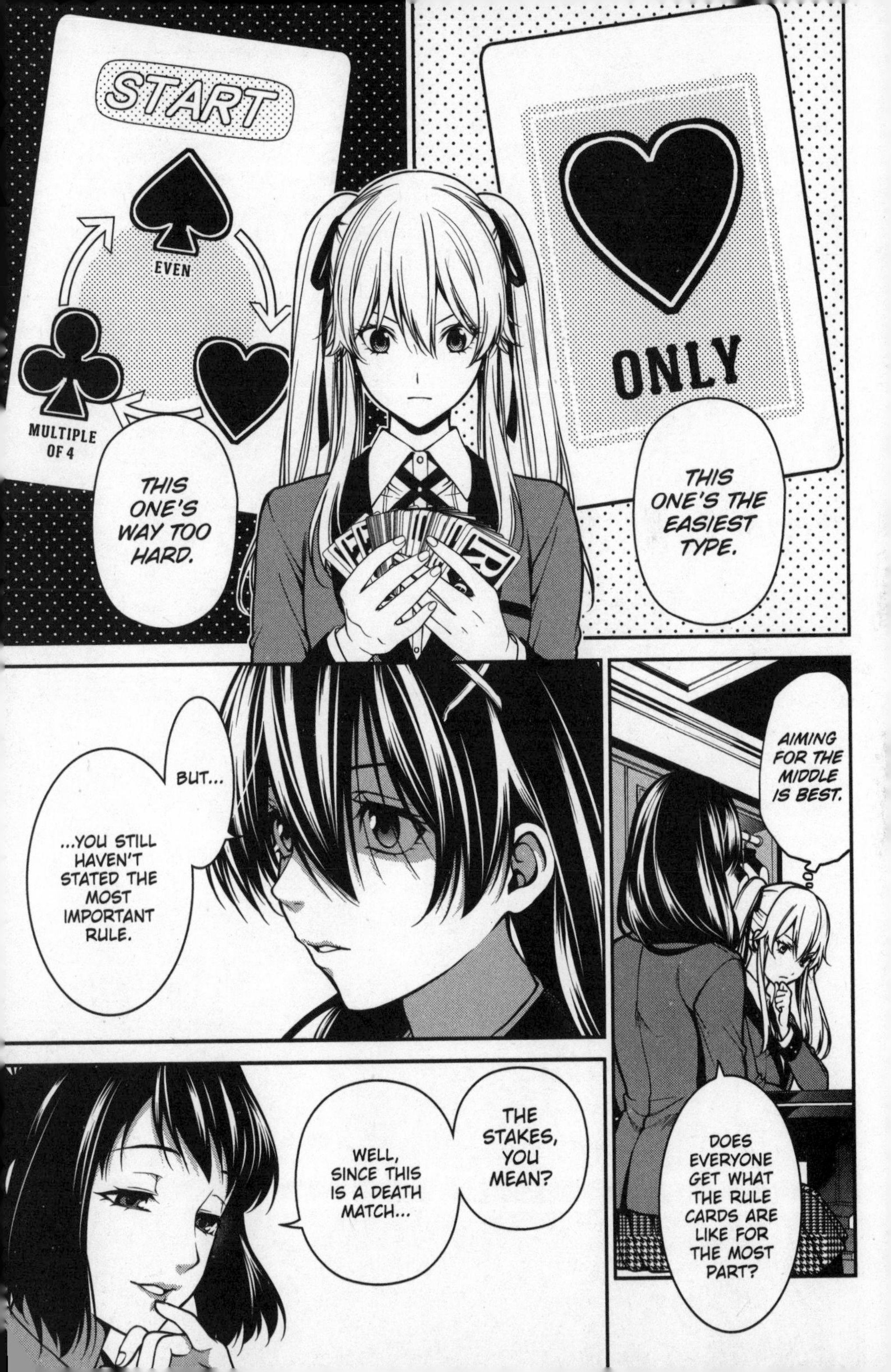
ONLY
THIS ONE'S THE EASIEST TYPE.
START
EVEN
MULTIPLE OF 4
THIS ONE'S WAY TOO HARD.
AIMING FOR THE MIDDLE IS BEST.
DOES EVERYONE GET WHAT THE RULE CARDS ARE LIKE FOR THE MOST PART?
BUT...
...YOU STILL HAVEN'T STATED THE MOST IMPORTANT RULE.
THE STAKES, YOU MEAN?
WELL, SINCE THIS IS A DEATH MATCH...

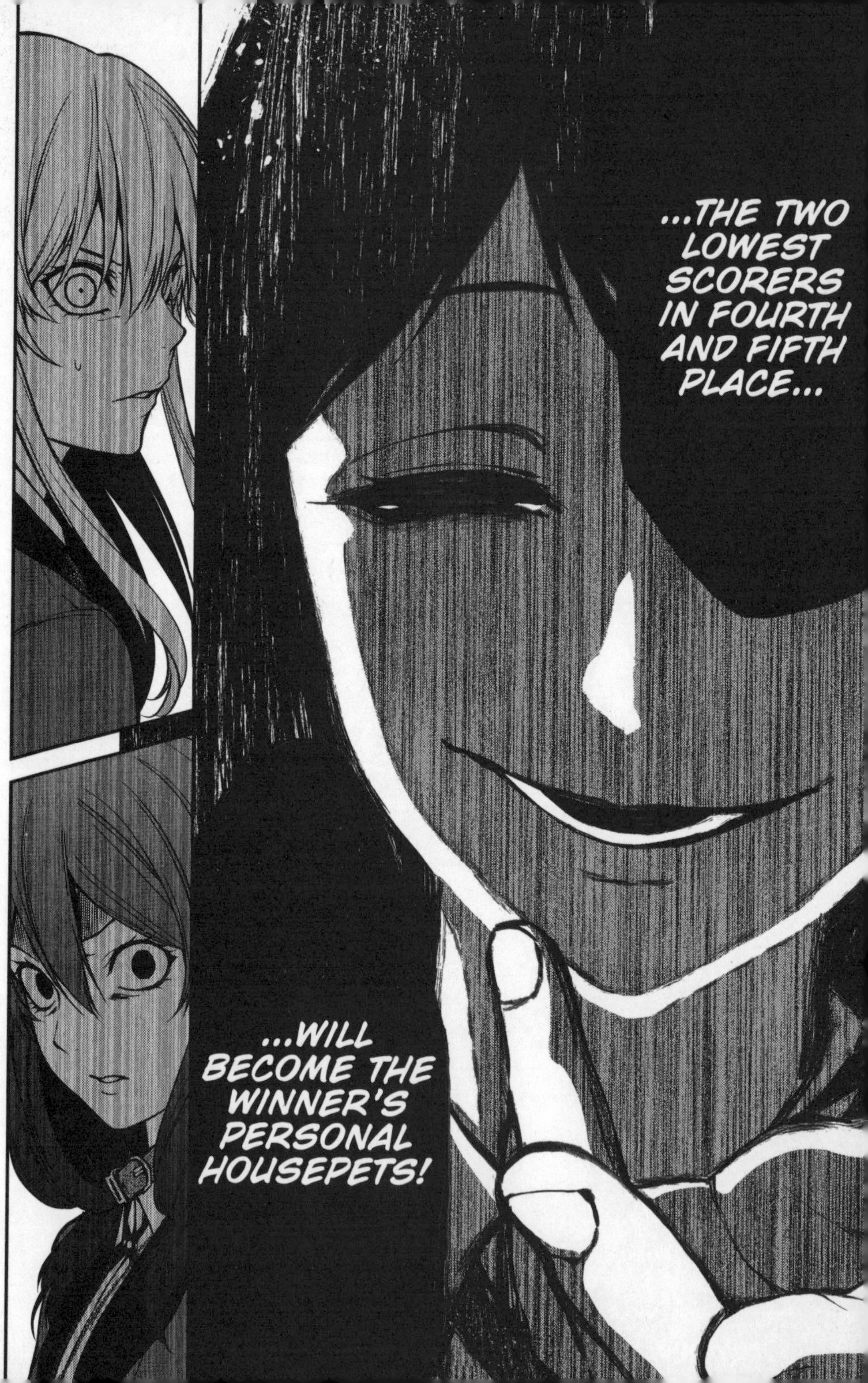
...THE TWO LOWEST SCORERS IN FOURTH AND FIFTH PLACE...
...WILL BECOME THE WINNER'S PERSONAL HOUSEPETS!

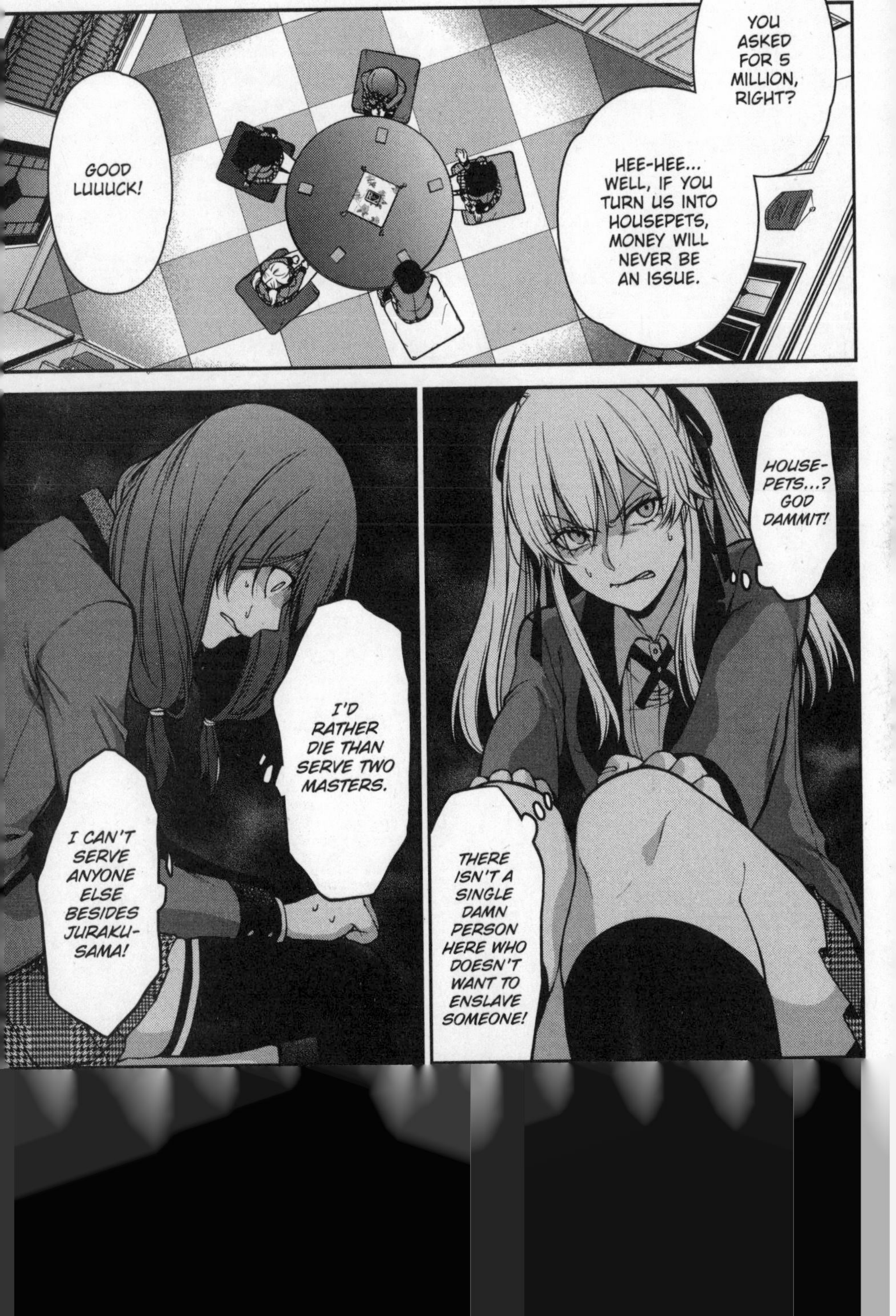
YOU ASKED FOR 5 MILLION, RIGHT?
HEE-HEE... WELL, IF YOU TURN US INTO HOUSEPETS, MONEY WILL NEVER BE AN ISSUE.
GOOD LUUUCK!
HOUSE-PETS...? GOD DAMMIT!
THERE ISN'T A SINGLE DAMN PERSON HERE WHO DOESN'T WANT TO ENSLAVE SOMEONE!
I'D RATHER DIE THAN SERVE TWO MASTERS.
I CAN'T SERVE ANYONE ELSE BESIDES JURAKU-SAMA!

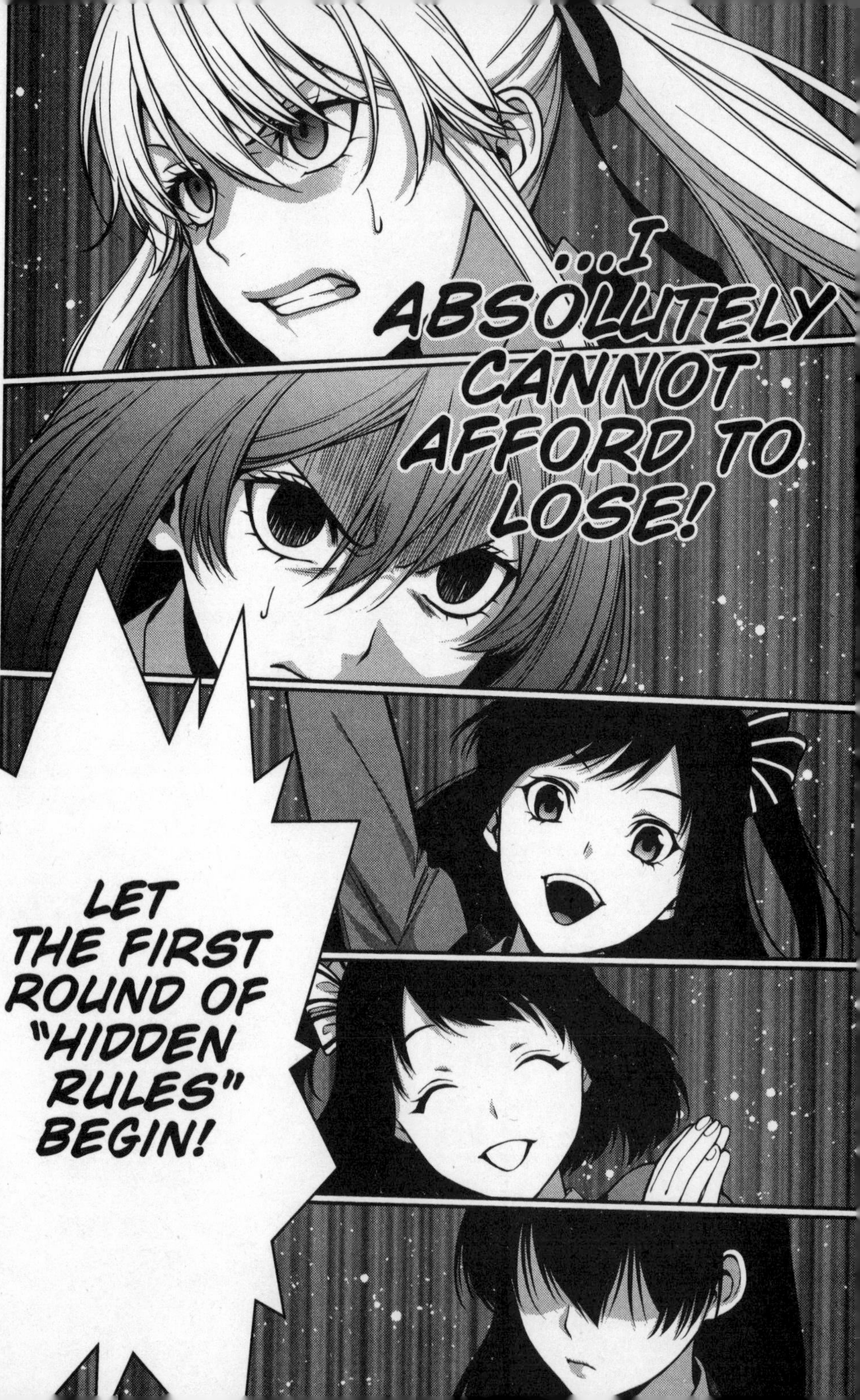
...I ABSOLUTELY CANNOT AFFORD TO LOSE!
LET THE FIRST ROUND OF "HIDDEN RULES" BEGIN!

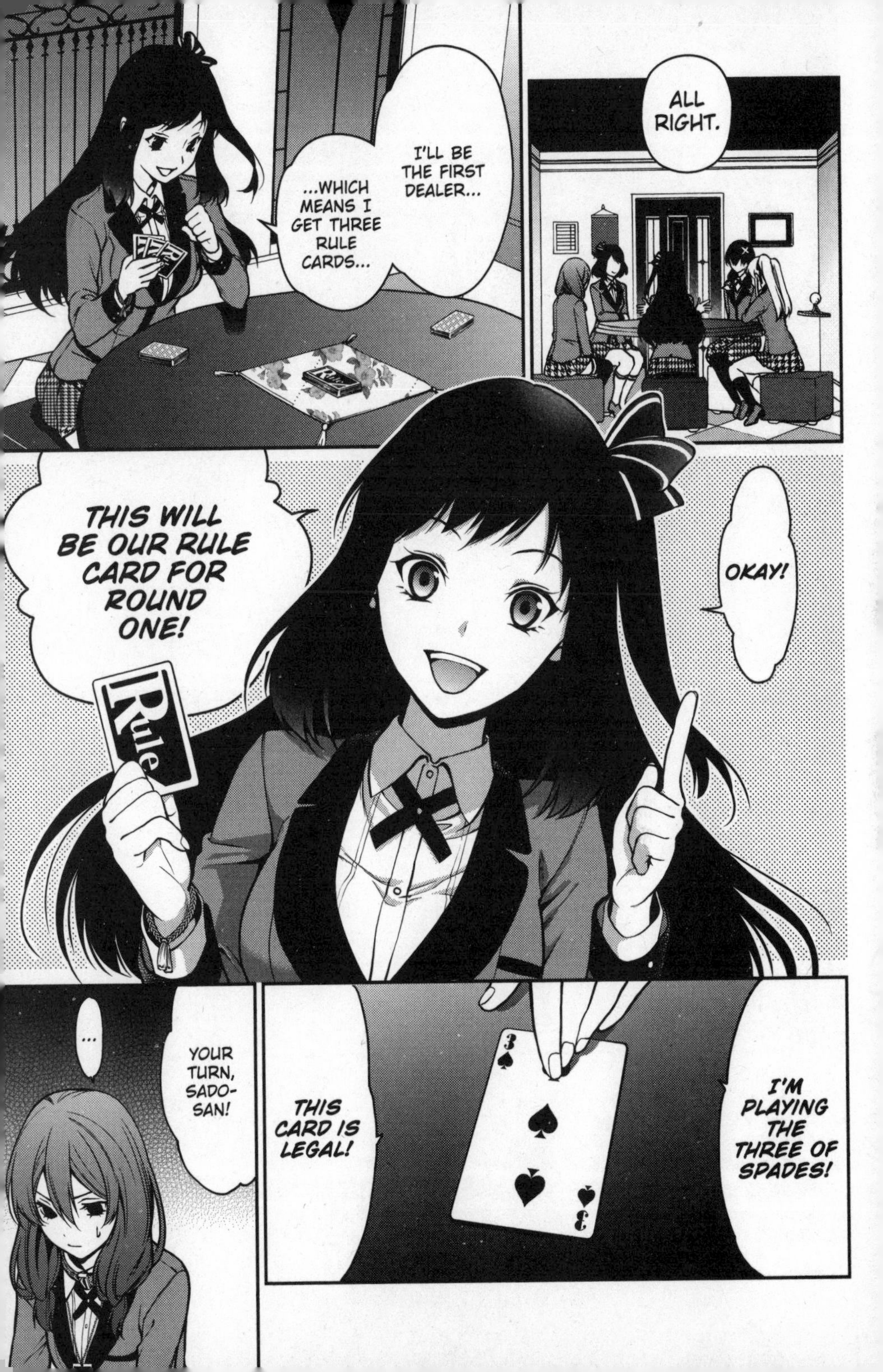
ALL RIGHT.
I'LL BE THE FIRST DEALER...
...WHICH MEANS I GET THREE RULE CARDS...
THIS WILL BE OUR RULE CARD FOR ROUND ONE!
OKAY!
I'M PLAYING THE THREE OF SPADES!
THIS CARD IS LEGAL!
YOUR TURN, SADO-SAN!
...

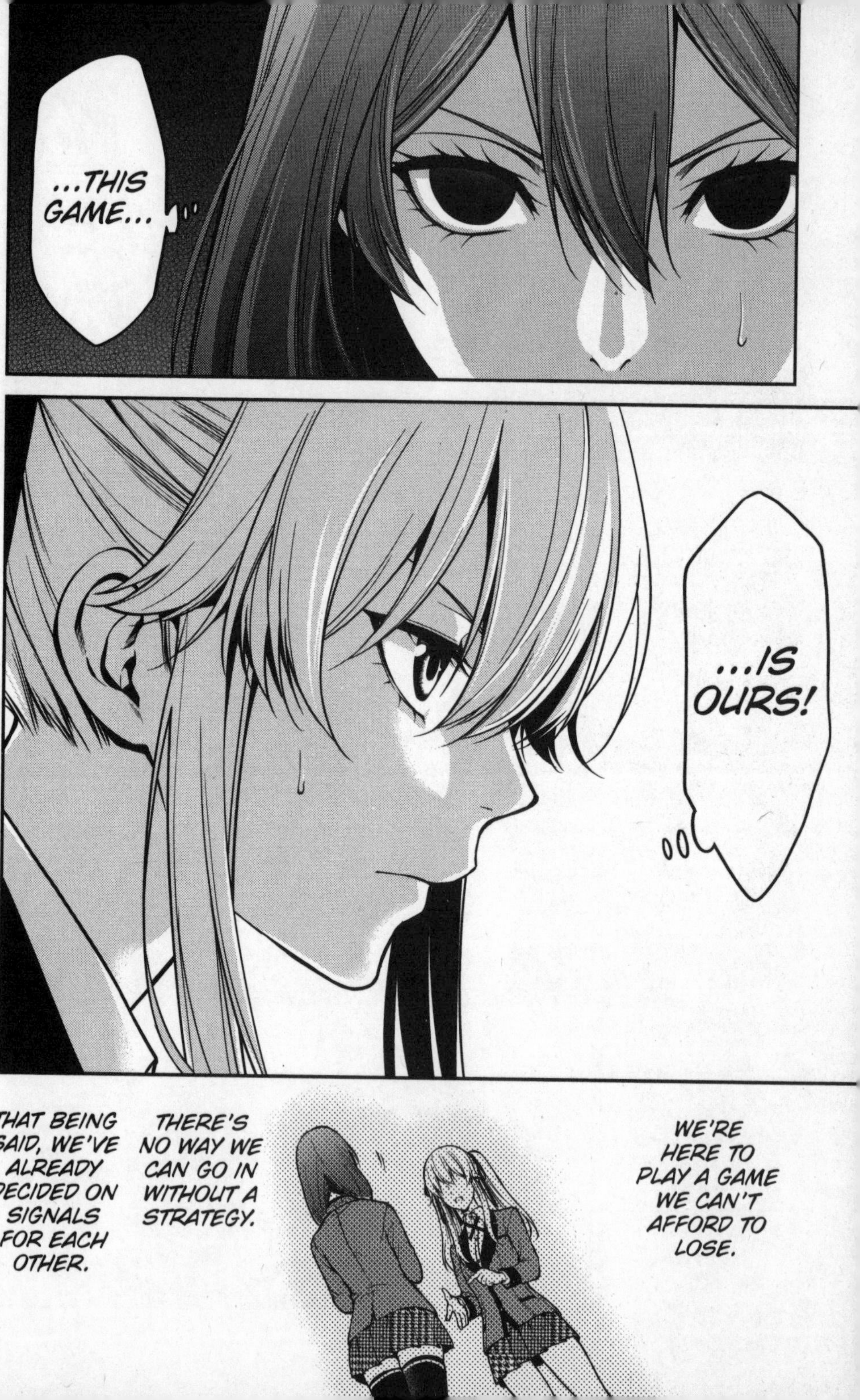
...THIS GAME...
...IS OURS!
WE'RE HERE TO PLAY A GAME WE CAN'T AFFORD TO LOSE.
THERE'S NO WAY WE CAN GO IN WITHOUT A STRATEGY.
THAT BEING SAID, WE'VE ALREADY DECIDED ON SIGNALS FOR EACH OTHER.

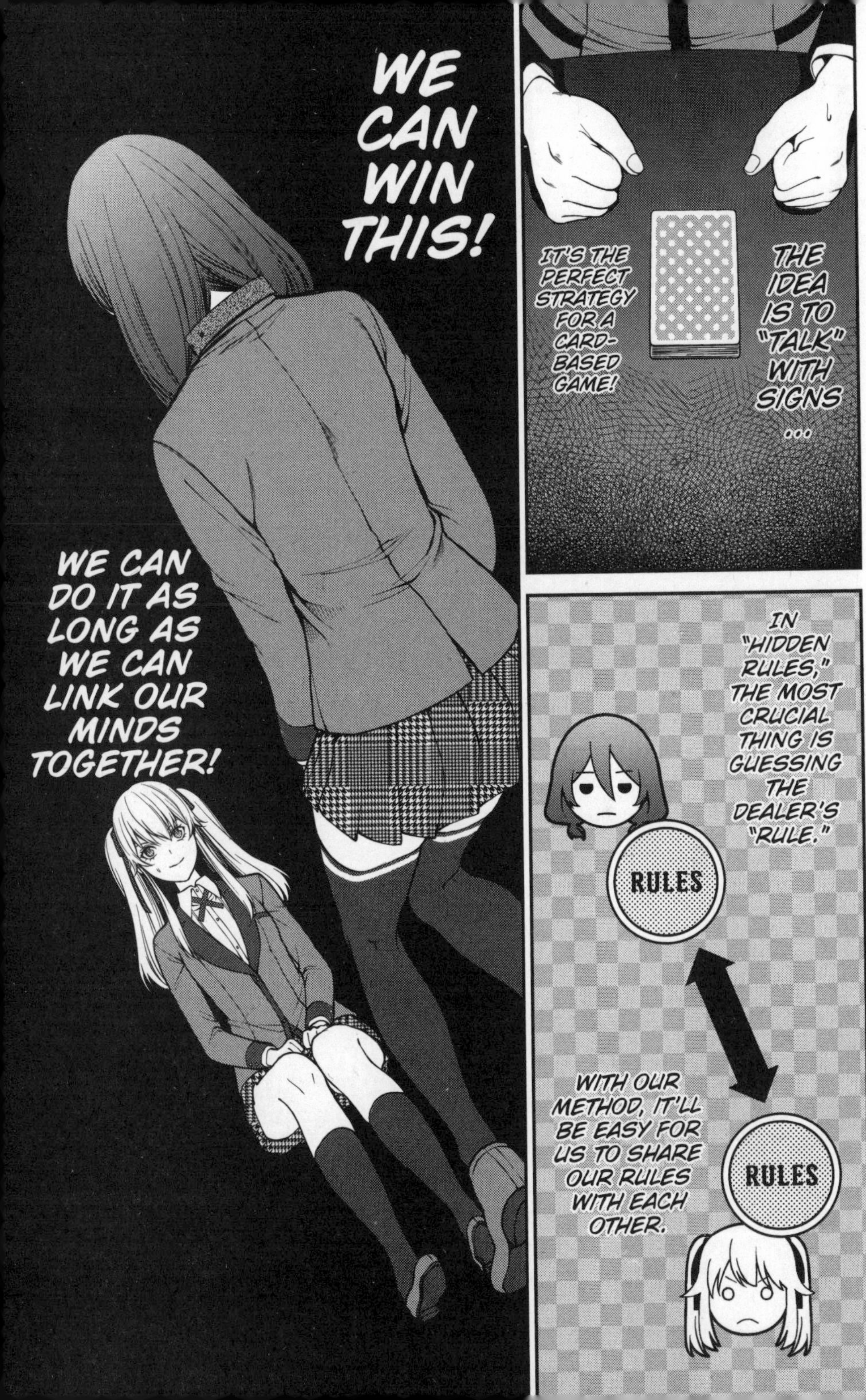
THE IDEA IS TO "TALK" WITH SIGNS...
IT'S THE PERFECT STRATEGY FOR A CARD-BASED GAME!
IN "HIDDEN RULES," THE MOST CRUCIAL THING IS GUESSING THE DEALER'S "RULE."
RULES
WITH OUR METHOD, IT'LL BE EASY FOR US TO SHARE OUR RULES WITH EACH OTHER.
RULES
WE CAN WIN THIS!
WE CAN DO IT AS LONG AS WE CAN LINK OUR MINDS TOGETHER!

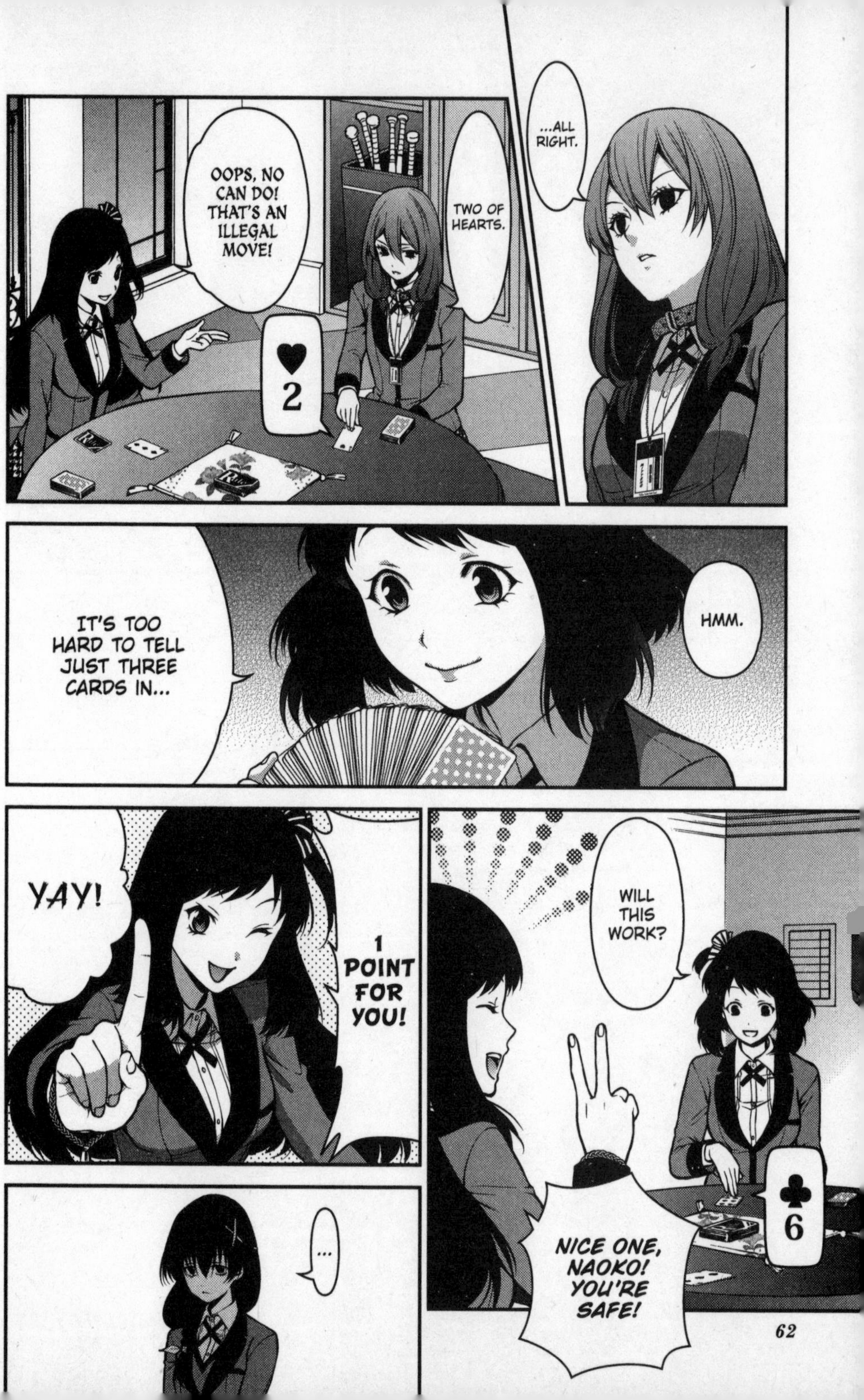
...ALL RIGHT.
TWO OF HEARTS.
OOPS, NO CAN DO! THAT'S AN ILLEGAL MOVE!
♥ 2
HMM.
IT'S TOO HARD TO TELL JUST THREE CARDS IN...
WILL THIS WORK?
♣ 6
NICE ONE, NAOKO! YOU'RE SAFE!
1 POINT FOR YOU!
YAY!
...

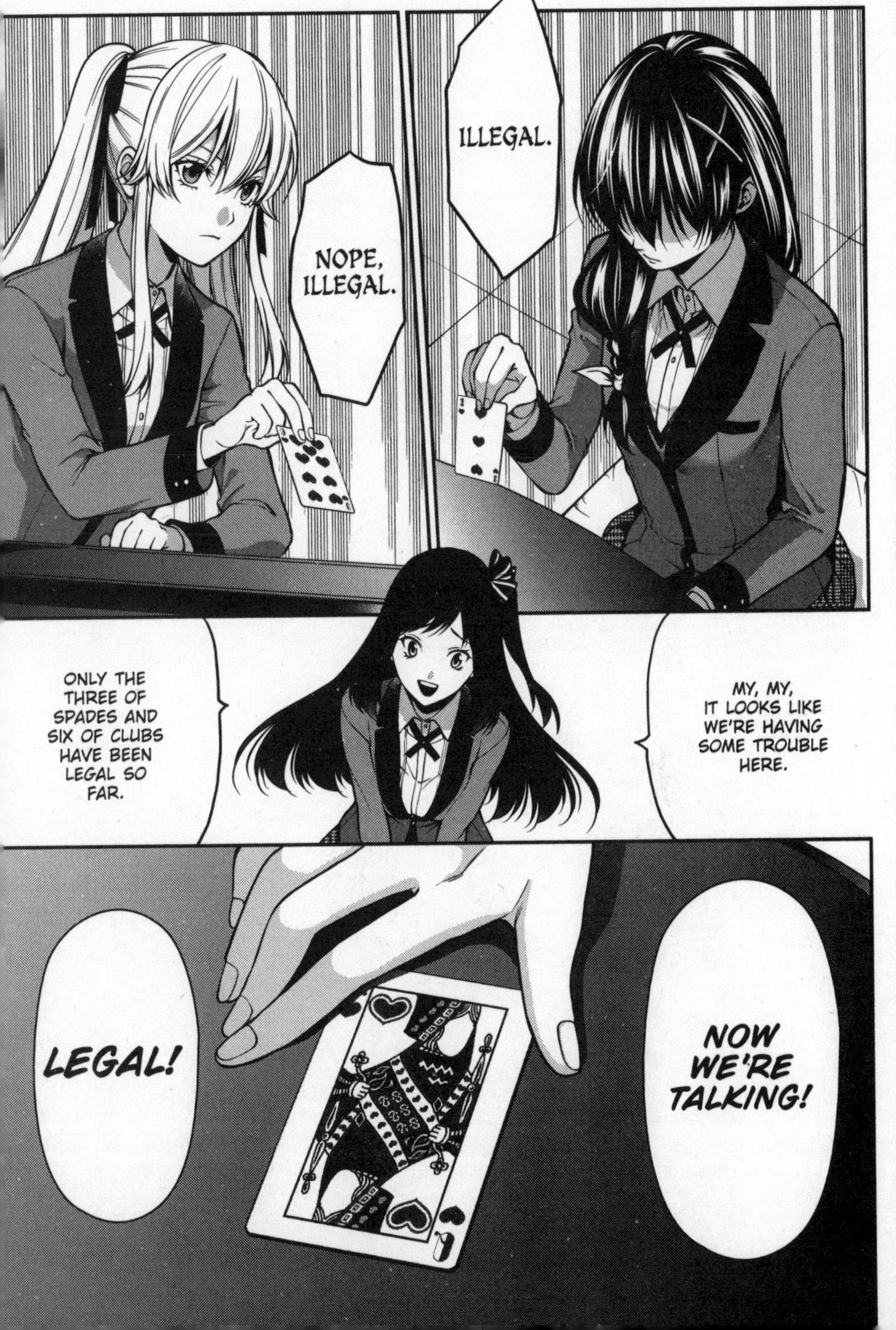
ILLEGAL.
NOPE, ILLEGAL.
MY, MY, IT LOOKS LIKE WE'RE HAVING SOME TROUBLE HERE.
ONLY THE THREE OF SPADES AND SIX OF CLUBS HAVE BEEN LEGAL SO FAR.
NOW WE'RE TALKING!
LEGAL!

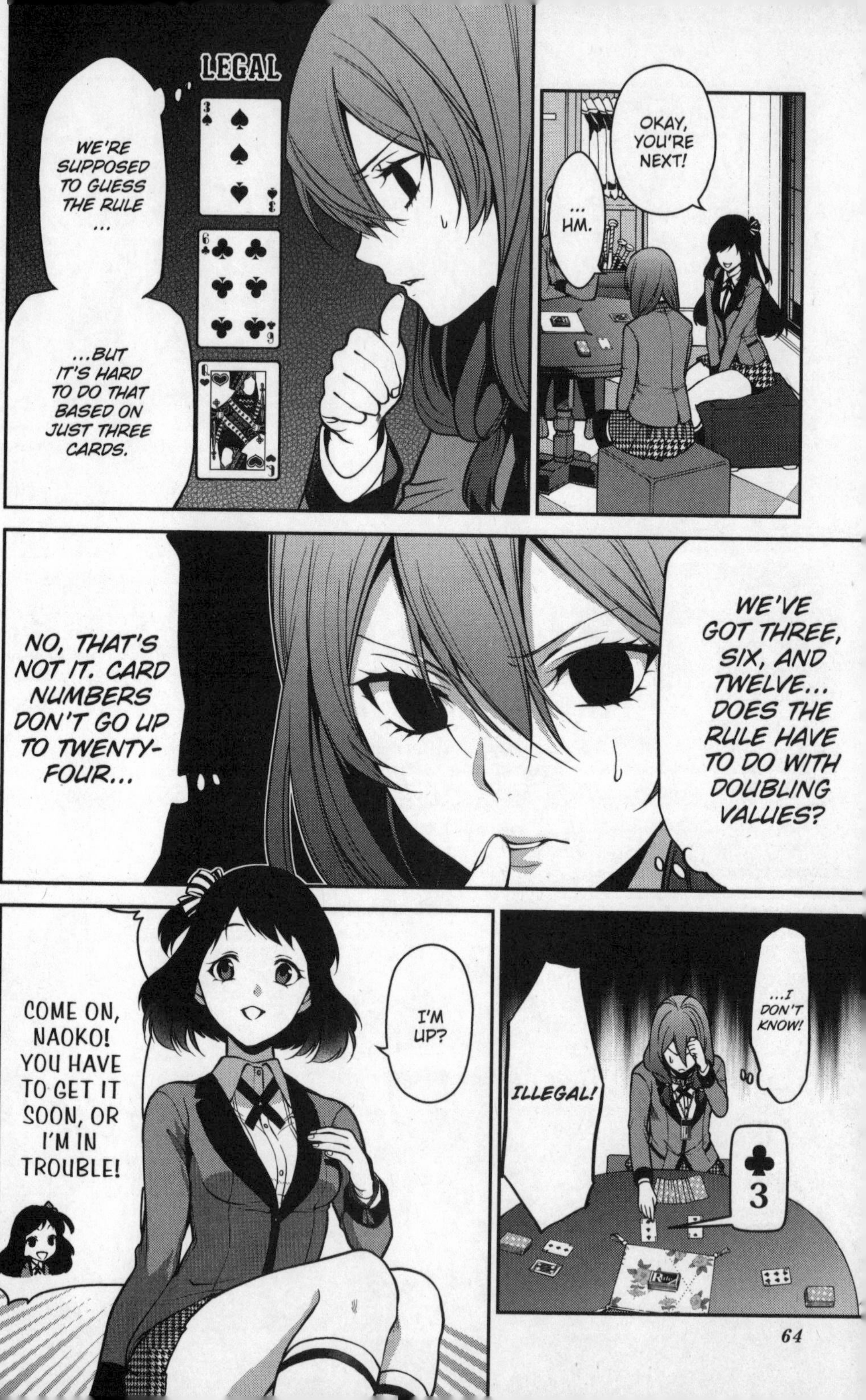
OKAY, YOU'RE NEXT!
... HM.
LEGAL
WE'RE SUPPOSED TO GUESS THE RULE ...
...BUT IT'S HARD TO DO THAT BASED ON JUST THREE CARDS.
WE'VE GOT THREE, SIX, AND TWELVE... DOES THE RULE HAVE TO DO WITH DOUBLING VALUES?
NO, THAT'S NOT IT. CARD NUMBERS DON'T GO UP TO TWENTY-FOUR...
...I DON'T KNOW!
ILLEGAL!
3
I'M UP?
COME ON, NAOKO! YOU HAVE TO GET IT SOON, OR I'M IN TROUBLE!

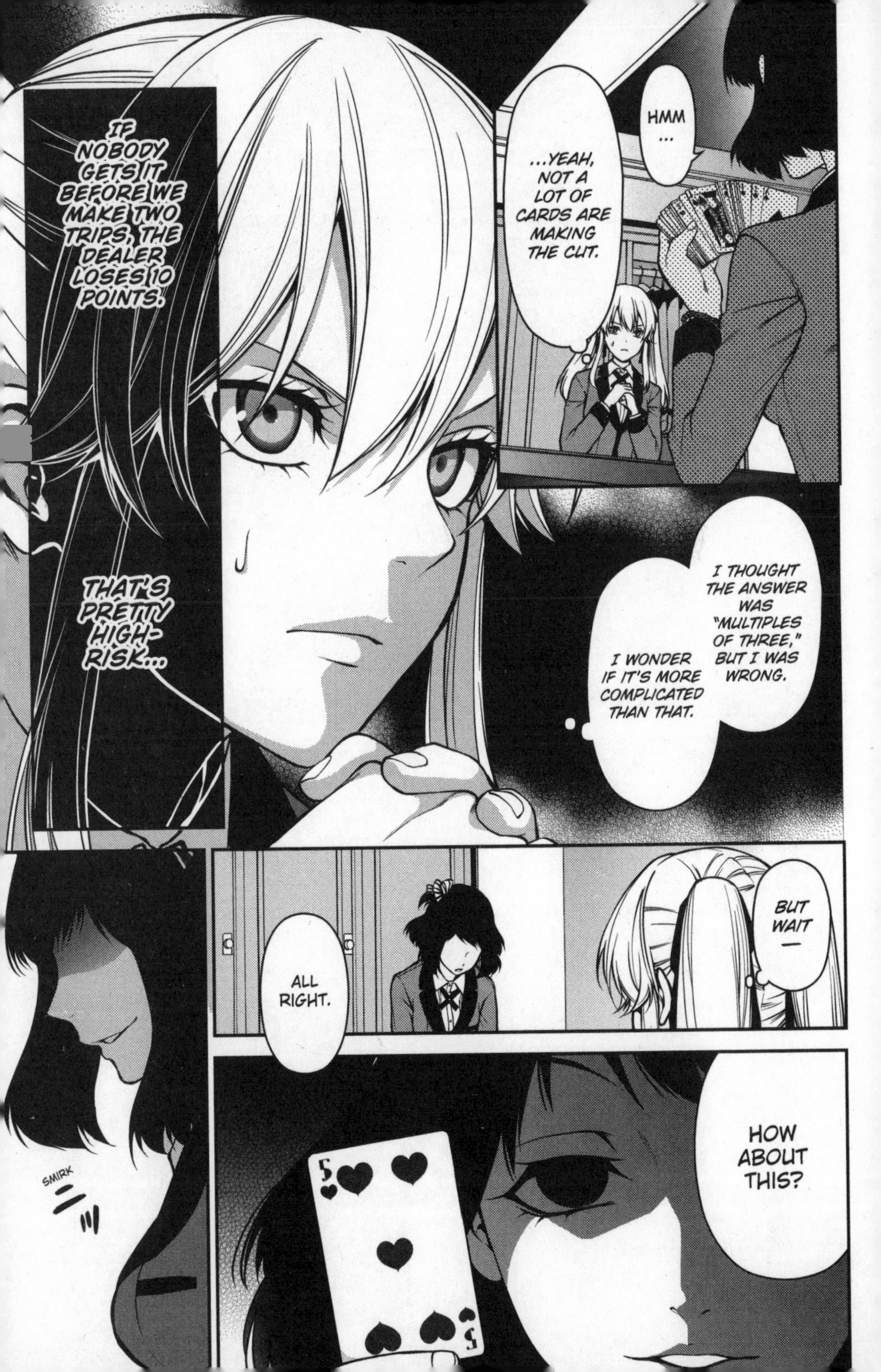
HMM ...
...YEAH, NOT A LOT OF CARDS ARE MAKING THE CUT.
IF NOBODY GETS IT BEFORE WE MAKE TWO TRIPS, THE DEALER LOSES 10 POINTS.
I THOUGHT THE ANSWER WAS "MULTIPLES OF THREE," BUT I WAS WRONG.
I WONDER IF IT'S MORE COMPLICATED THAN THAT.
THAT'S PRETTY HIGH-RISK...
BUT WAIT —
ALL RIGHT.
HOW ABOUT THIS?
SMIRK

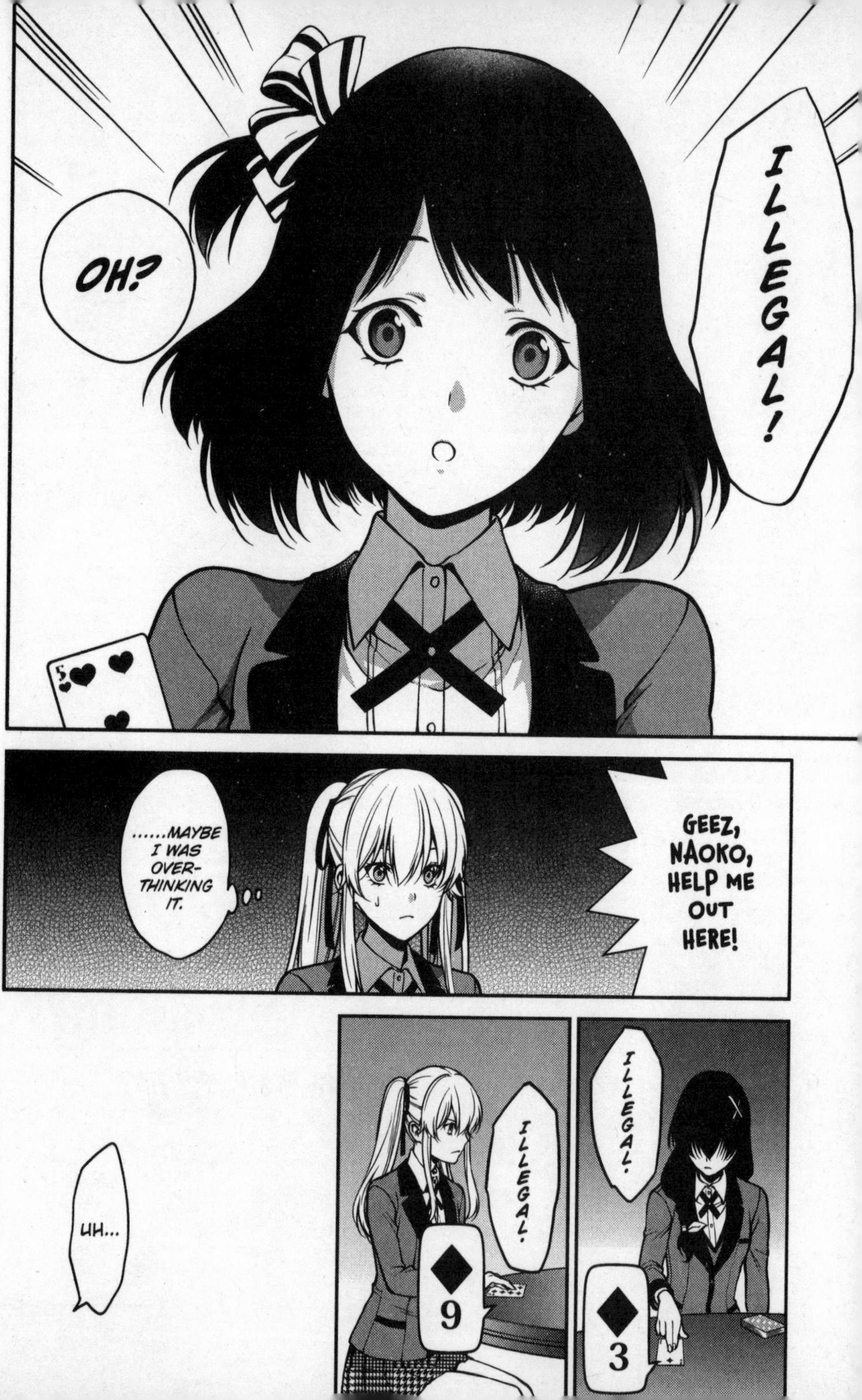
ILLEGAL!
OH?
GEEZ, NAOKO, HELP ME OUT HERE!
......MAYBE I WAS OVER-THINKING IT.
ILLEGAL.
ILLEGAL.
UH...

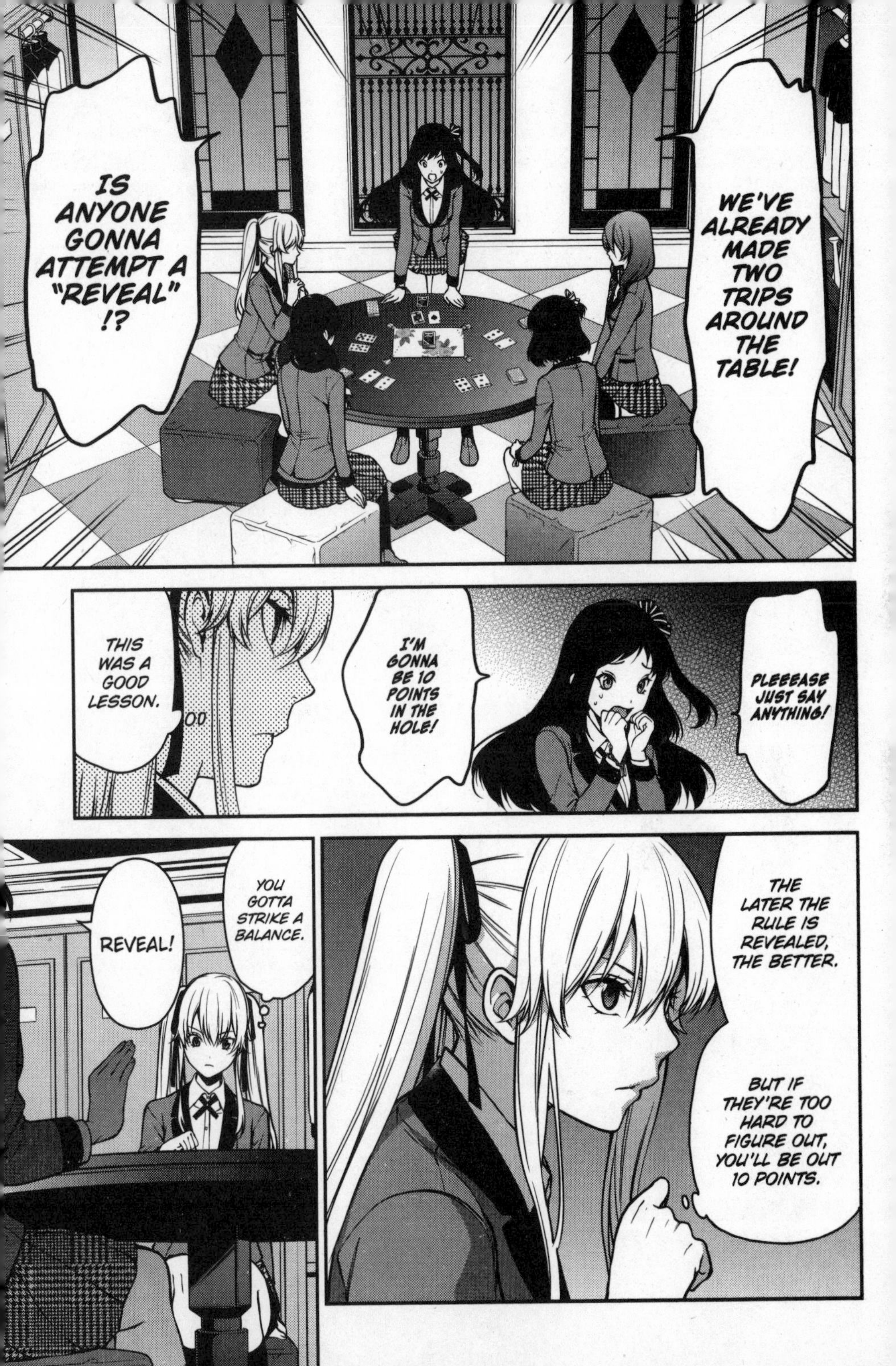
WE'VE ALREADY MADE TWO TRIPS AROUND THE TABLE!
IS ANYONE GONNA ATTEMPT A "REVEAL" !?
PLEEEASE JUST SAY ANYTHING!
I'M GONNA BE 10 POINTS IN THE HOLE!
THIS WAS A GOOD LESSON.
THE LATER THE RULE IS REVEALED, THE BETTER.
BUT IF THEY'RE TOO HARD TO FIGURE OUT, YOU'LL BE OUT 10 POINTS.
YOU GOTTA STRIKE A BALANCE.
REVEAL!

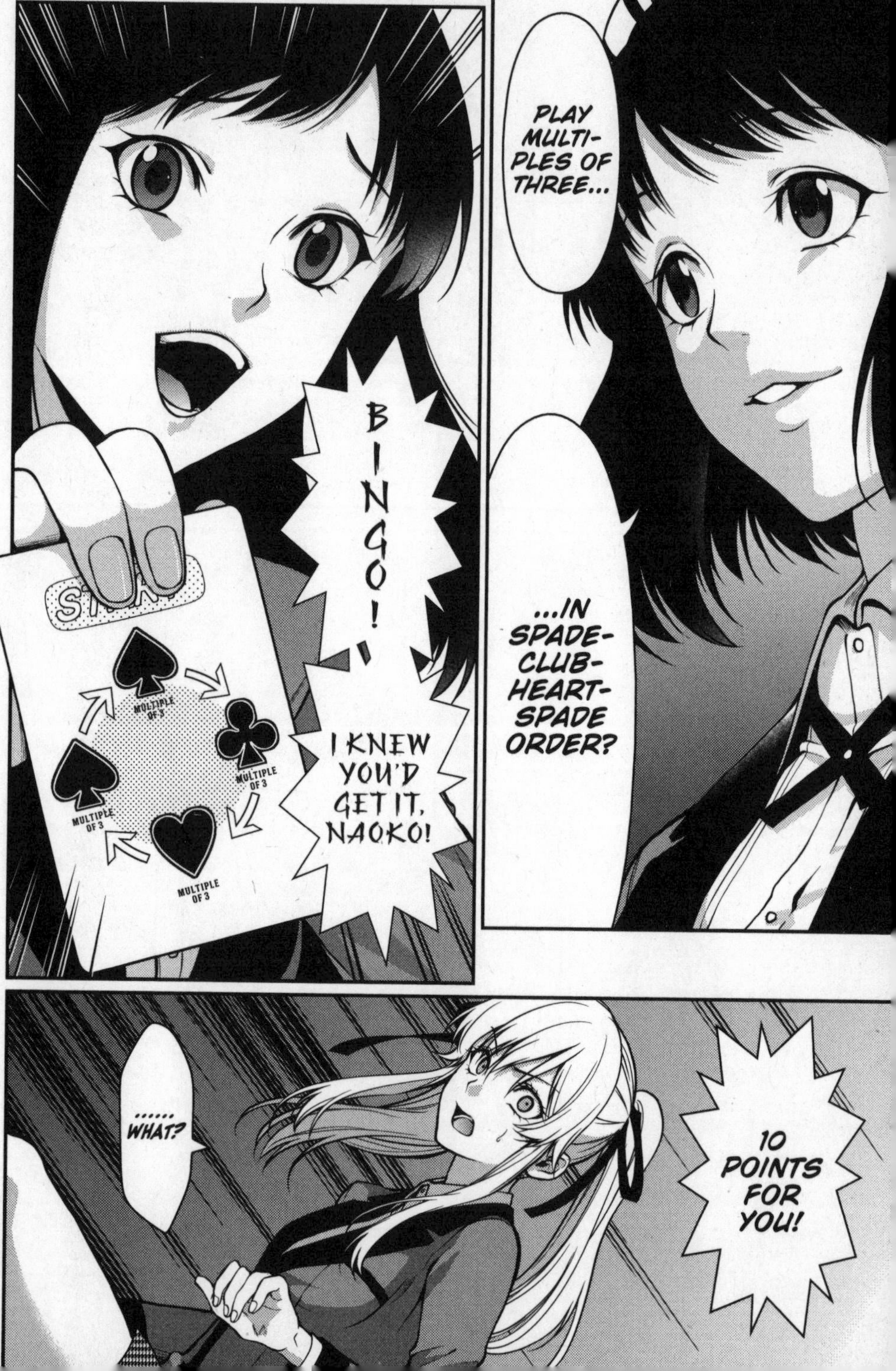
PLAY MULTI-PLES OF THREE...
...IN SPADE-CLUB-HEART-SPADE ORDER?
BINGO!
I KNEW YOU'D GET IT, NAOKO!
MULTIPLE OF 3
MULTIPLE OF 3
MULTIPLE OF 3
MULTIPLE OF 3
10 POINTS FOR YOU!
......WHAT?

Kakegurui Twin

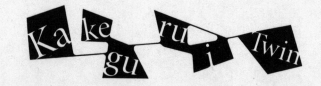

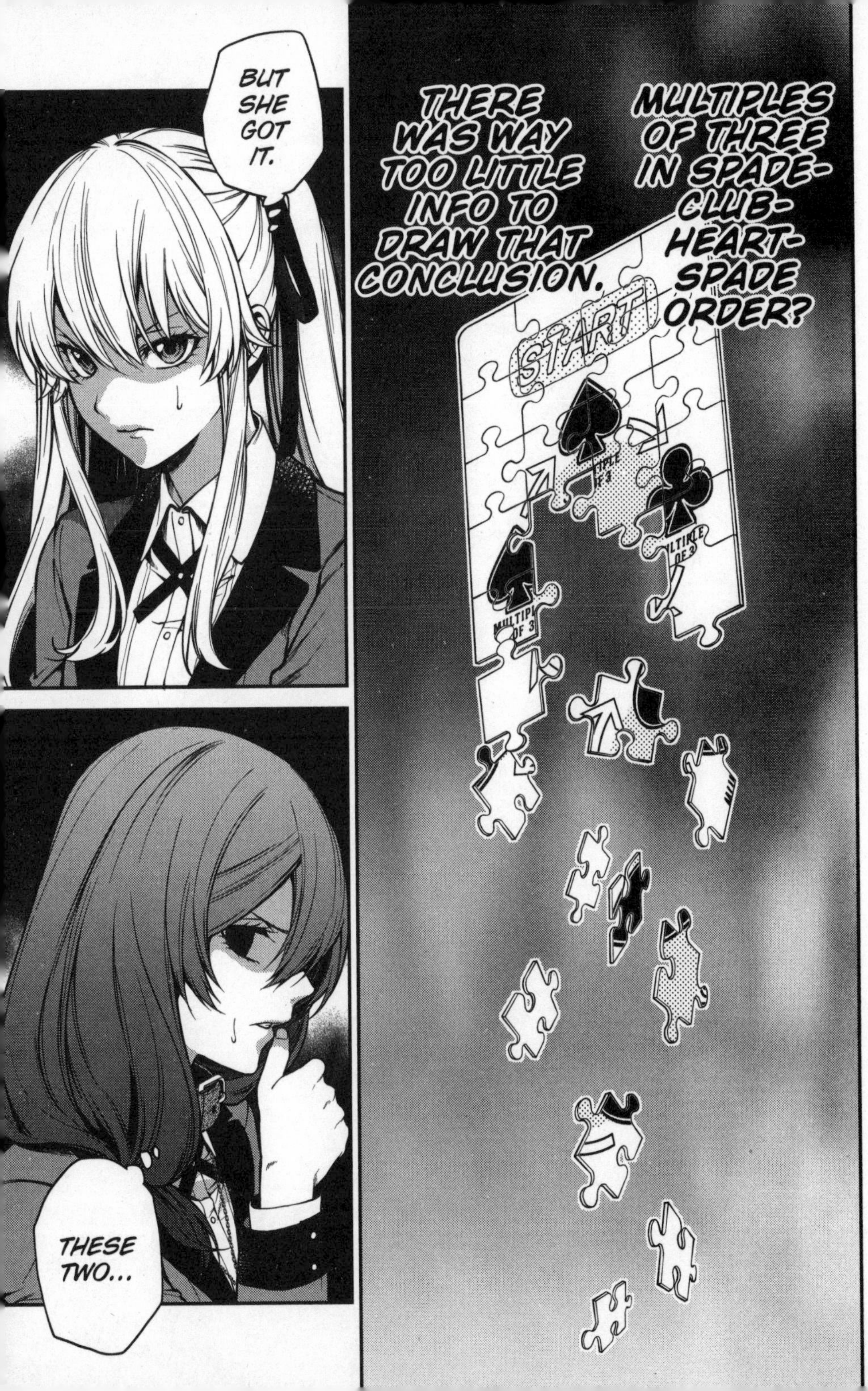
MULTIPLES OF THREE IN SPADE-CLUB-HEART-SPADE ORDER?
THERE WAS WAY TOO LITTLE INFO TO DRAW THAT CONCLUSION.
START
BUT SHE GOT IT.
THESE TWO...

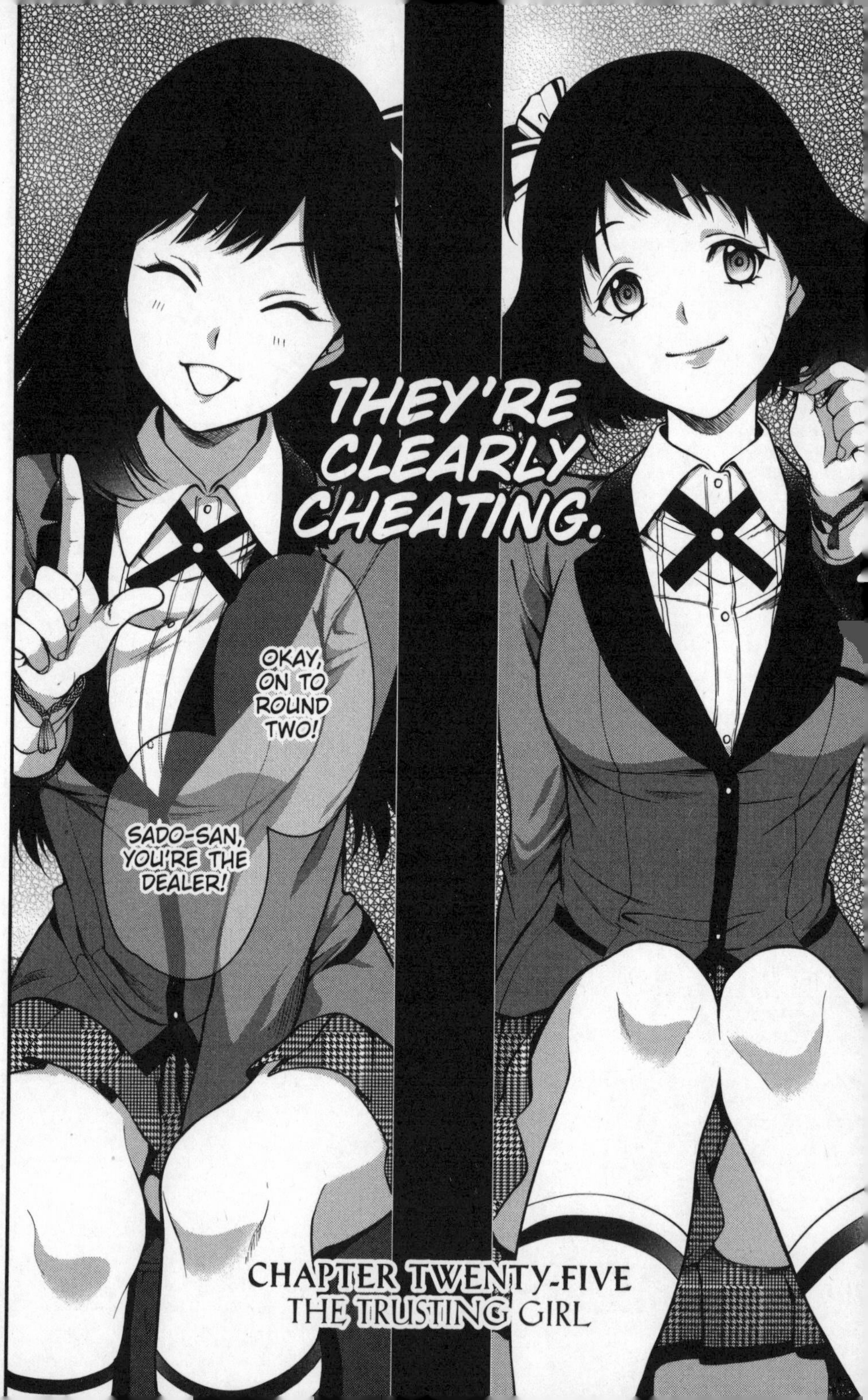
THEY'RE CLEARLY CHEATING.
OKAY, ON TO ROUND TWO!
SADO-SAN, YOU'RE THE DEALER!
CHAPTER TWENTY-FIVE
THE TRUSTING GIRL

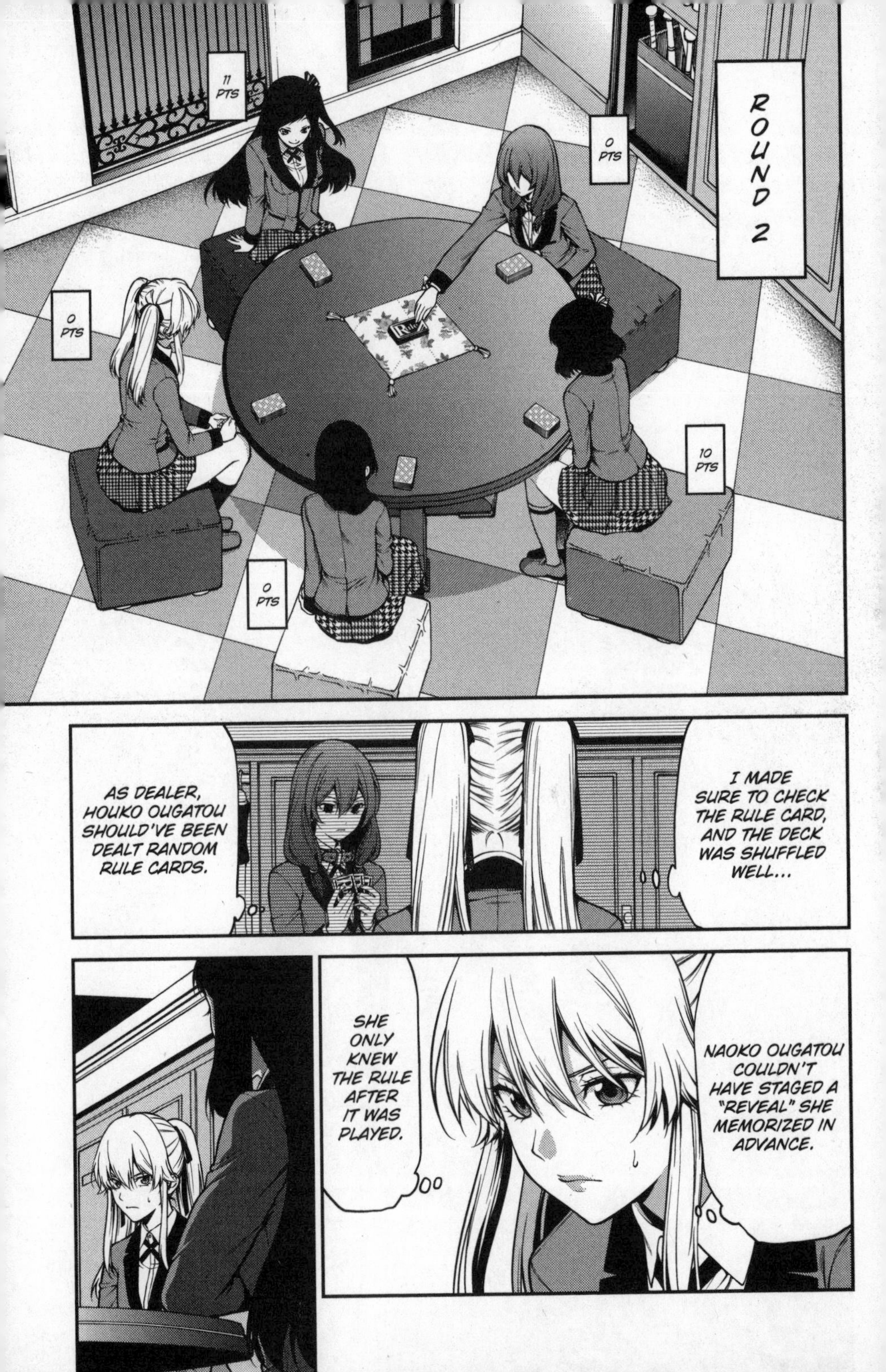
ROUND 2
0 PTS
11 PTS
10 PTS
0 PTS
0 PTS
I MADE SURE TO CHECK THE RULE CARD, AND THE DECK WAS SHUFFLED WELL...
AS DEALER, HOUKO OUGATOU SHOULD'VE BEEN DEALT RANDOM RULE CARDS.
NAOKO OUGATOU COULDN'T HAVE STAGED A "REVEAL" SHE MEMORIZED IN ADVANCE.
SHE ONLY KNEW THE RULE AFTER IT WAS PLAYED.

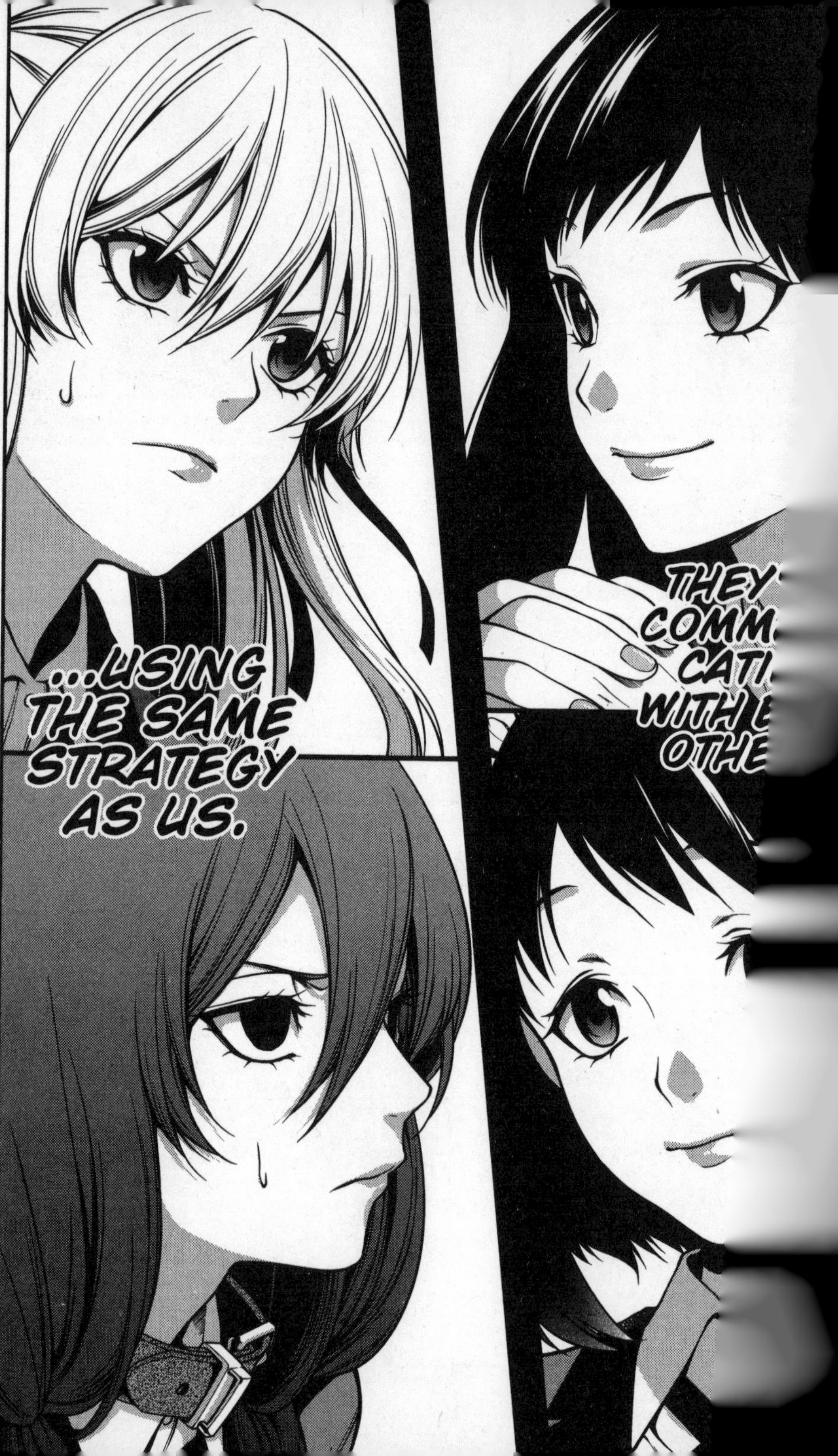
THEY
COMM
CATI
WITH
OTHE
...USING THE SAME STRATEGY AS US.

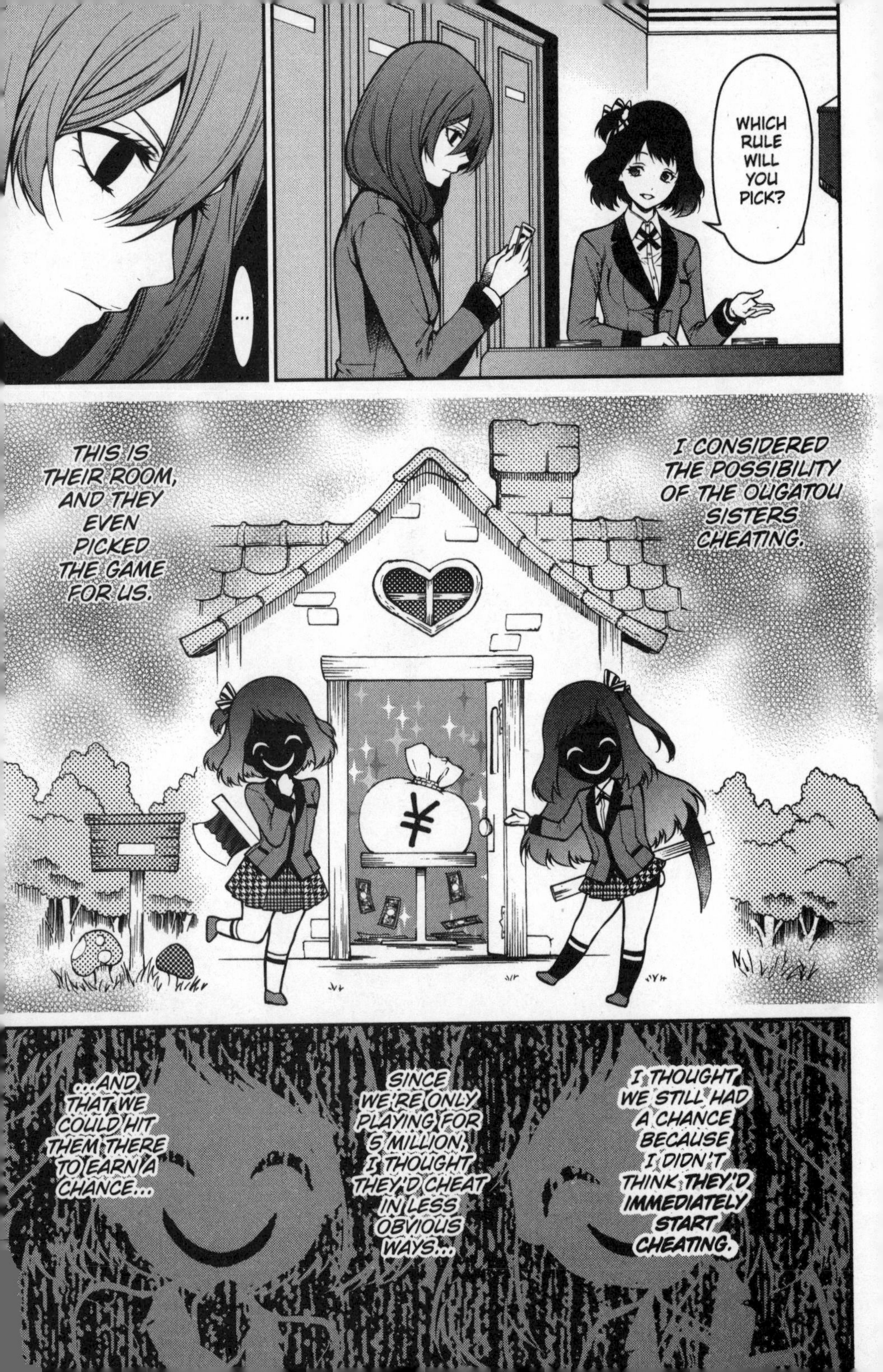
WHICH RULE WILL YOU PICK?
...
I CONSIDERED THE POSSIBILITY OF THE OUGATOU SISTERS CHEATING.
THIS IS THEIR ROOM, AND THEY EVEN PICKED THE GAME FOR US.
I THOUGHT WE STILL HAD A CHANCE BECAUSE I DIDN'T THINK THEY'D IMMEDIATELY START CHEATING.
SINCE WE'RE ONLY PLAYING FOR 5 MILLION, I THOUGHT THEY'D CHEAT IN LESS OBVIOUS WAYS...
...AND THAT WE COULD HIT THEM THERE TO EARN A CHANCE...

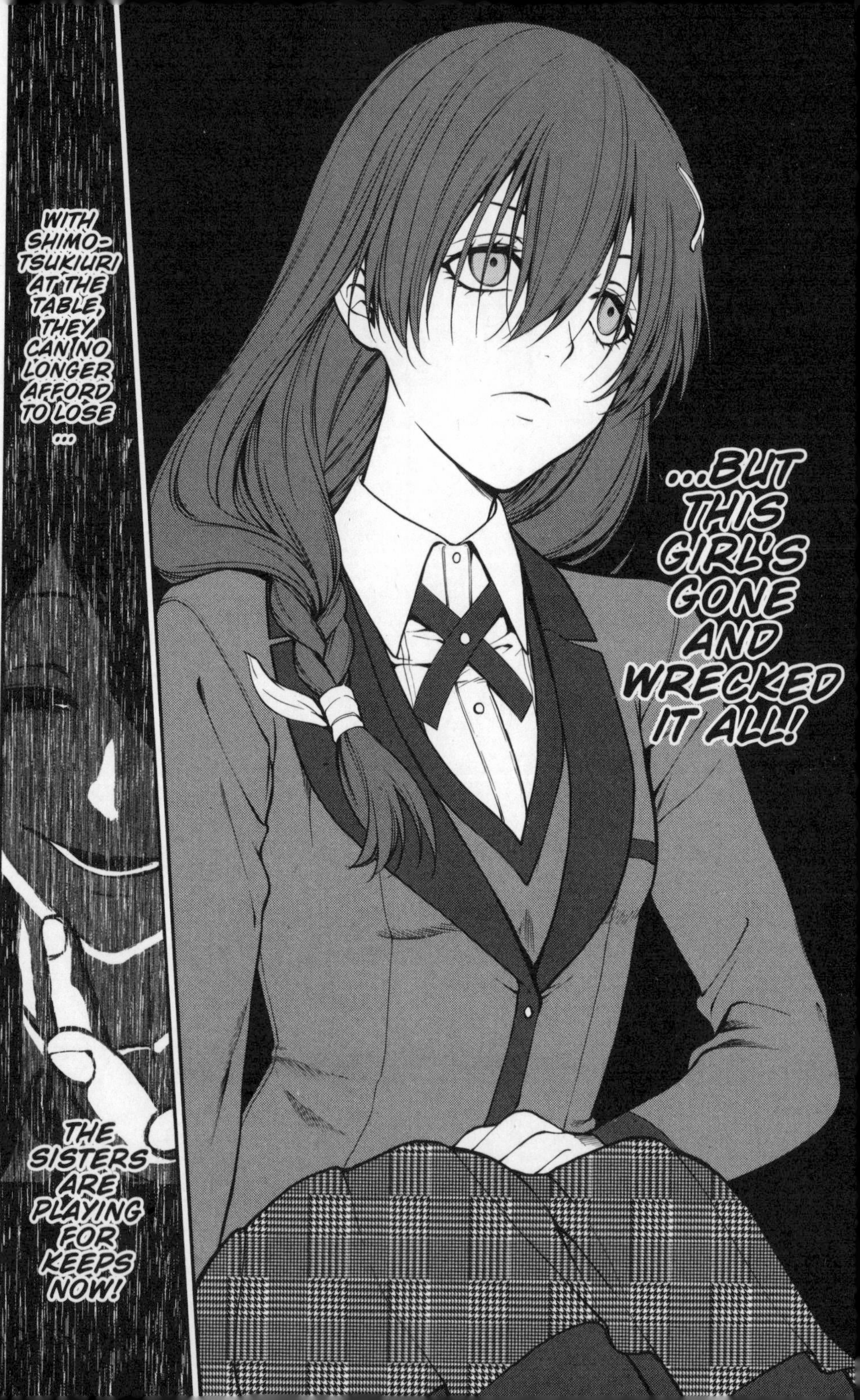
WITH SHIMO-TSUKIURI AT THE TABLE, THEY CAN NO LONGER AFFORD TO LOSE ...
...BUT THIS GIRL'S GONE AND WRECKED IT ALL!
THE SISTERS ARE PLAYING FOR KEEPS NOW!

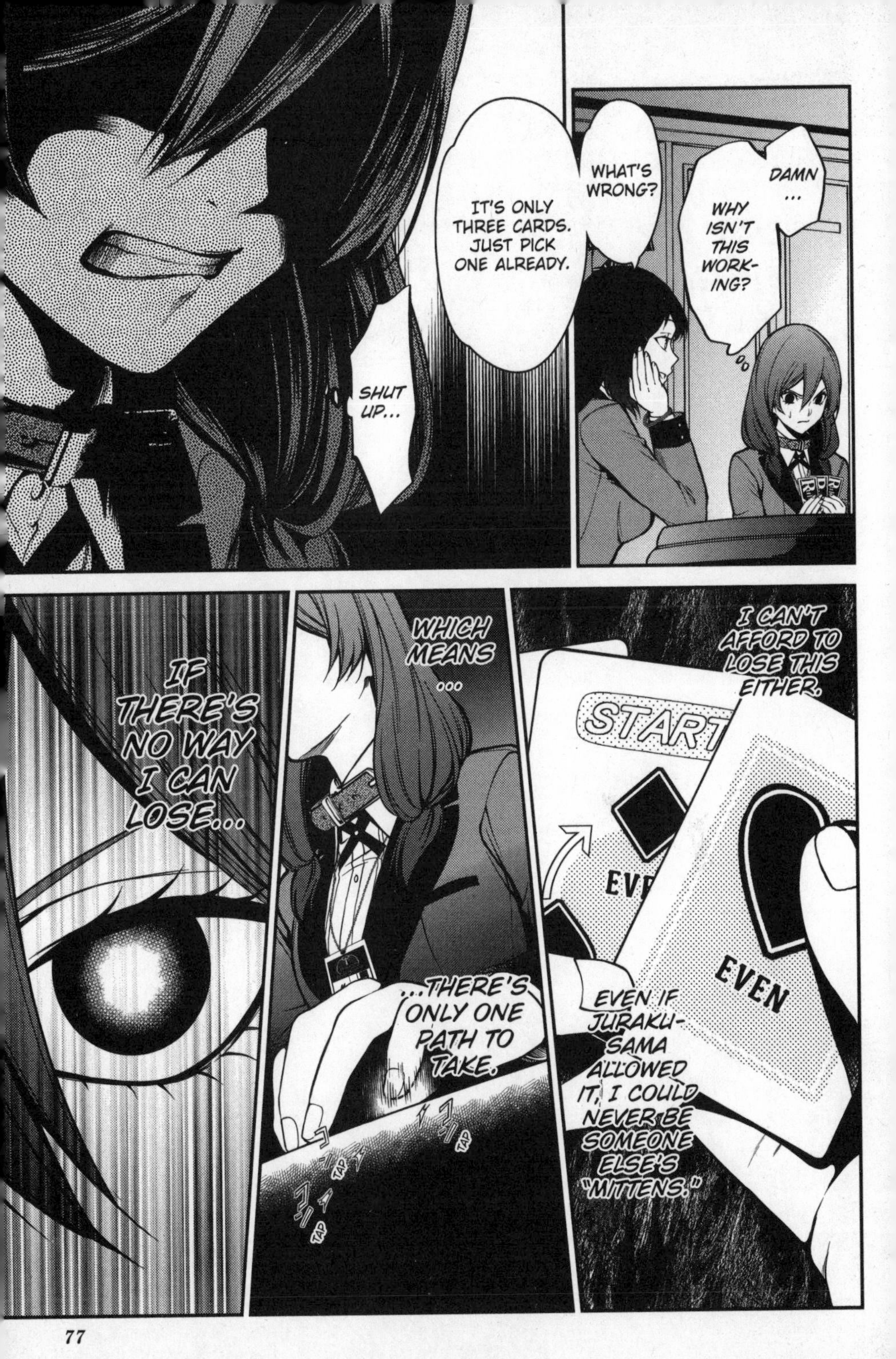
DAMN...
WHY ISN'T THIS WORKING?
WHAT'S WRONG?
IT'S ONLY THREE CARDS. JUST PICK ONE ALREADY.
SHUT UP...
I CAN'T AFFORD TO LOSE THIS EITHER.
START
EVEN
EVEN
EVEN IF JURAKU-SAMA ALLOWED IT, I COULD NEVER BE SOMEONE ELSE'S "MITTENS."
WHICH MEANS...
...THERE'S ONLY ONE PATH TO TAKE.
TAP
TAP
TAP
IF THERE'S NO WAY I CAN LOSE...

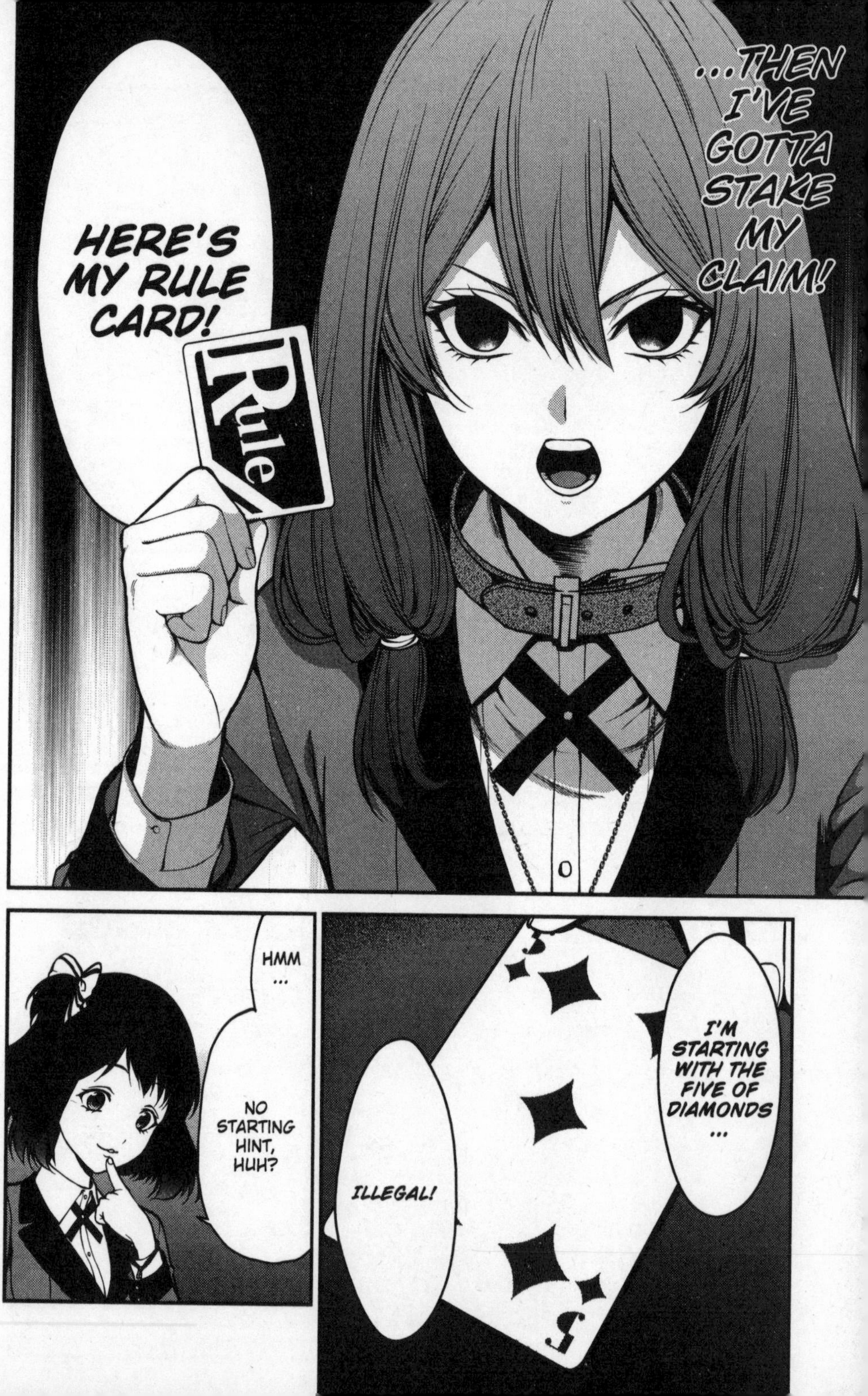
...THEN I'VE GOTTA STAKE MY CLAIM!
HERE'S MY RULE CARD!
Rule
I'M STARTING WITH THE FIVE OF DIAMONDS ...
ILLEGAL!
HMM ...
NO STARTING HINT, HUH?

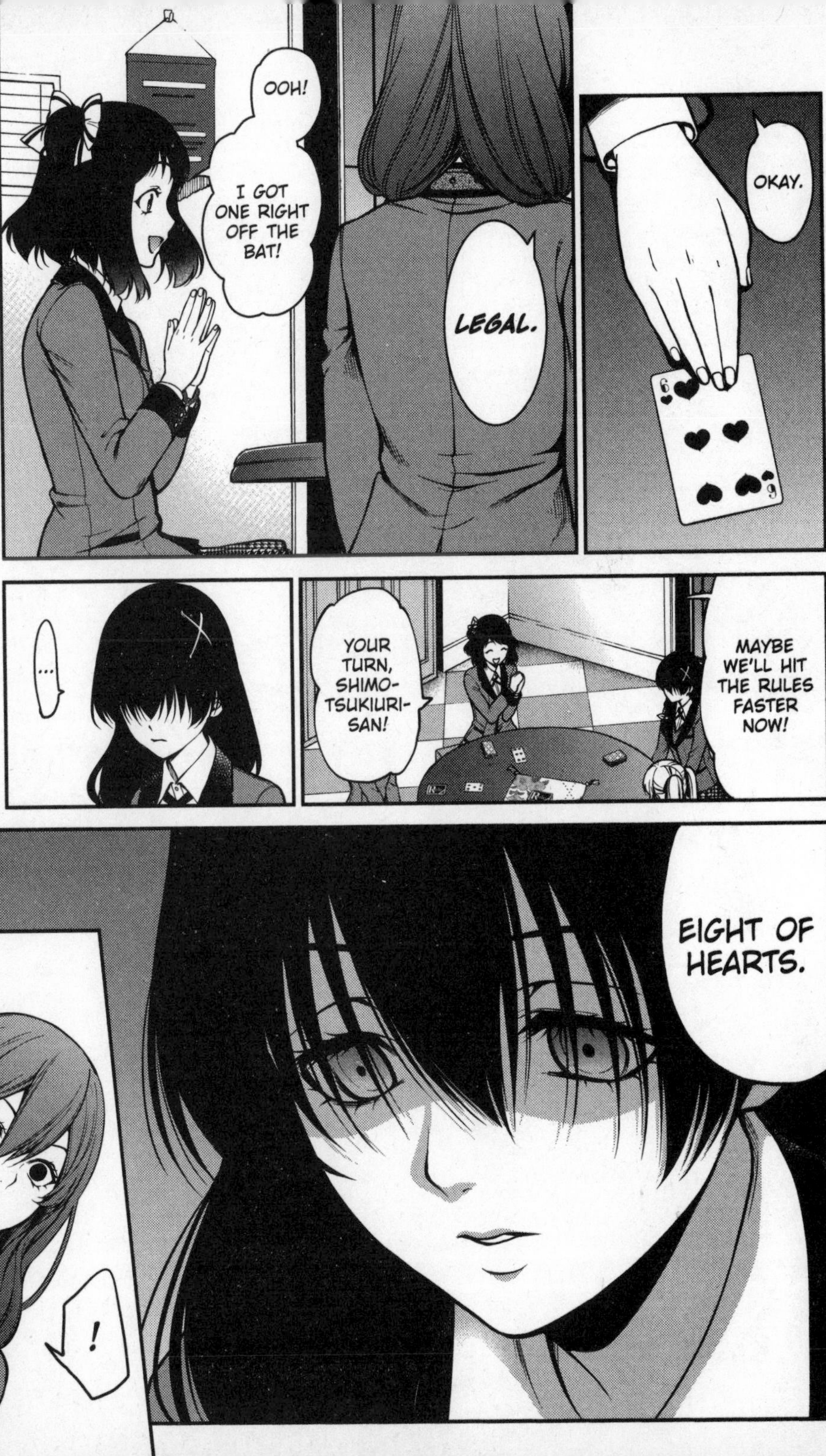
OKAY.
LEGAL.
OOH!
I GOT ONE RIGHT OFF THE BAT!
MAYBE WE'LL HIT THE RULES FASTER NOW!
YOUR TURN, SHIMO-TSUKIURI-SAN!
...
EIGHT OF HEARTS.
!

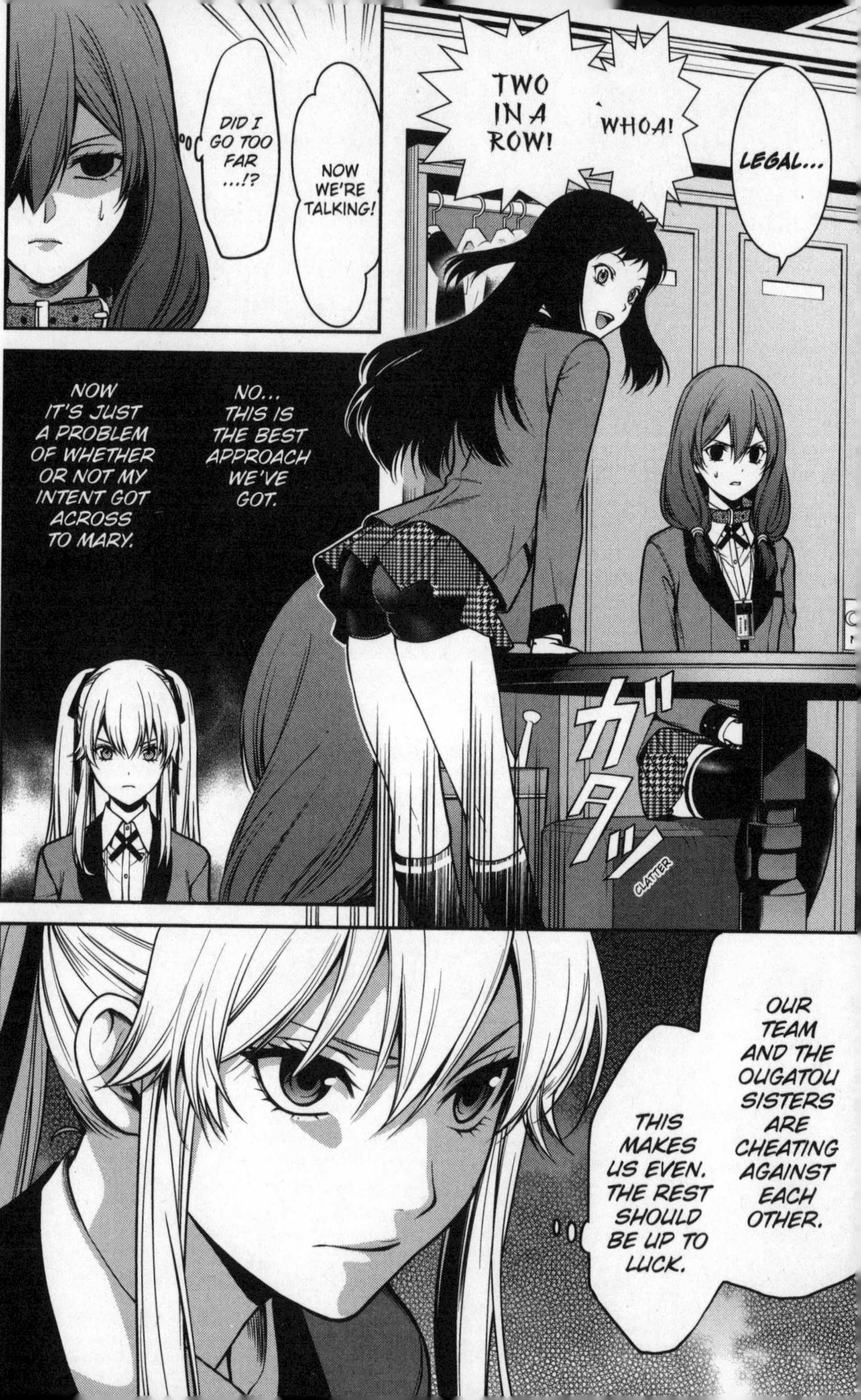
LEGAL...
WHOA!
TWO IN A ROW!
ガタッ
CLATTER
NOW WE'RE TALKING!
DID I GO TOO FAR ...!?
NO... THIS IS THE BEST APPROACH WE'VE GOT.
NOW IT'S JUST A PROBLEM OF WHETHER OR NOT MY INTENT GOT ACROSS TO MARY.
OUR TEAM AND THE OUGATOU SISTERS ARE CHEATING AGAINST EACH OTHER.
THIS MAKES US EVEN. THE REST SHOULD BE UP TO LUCK.

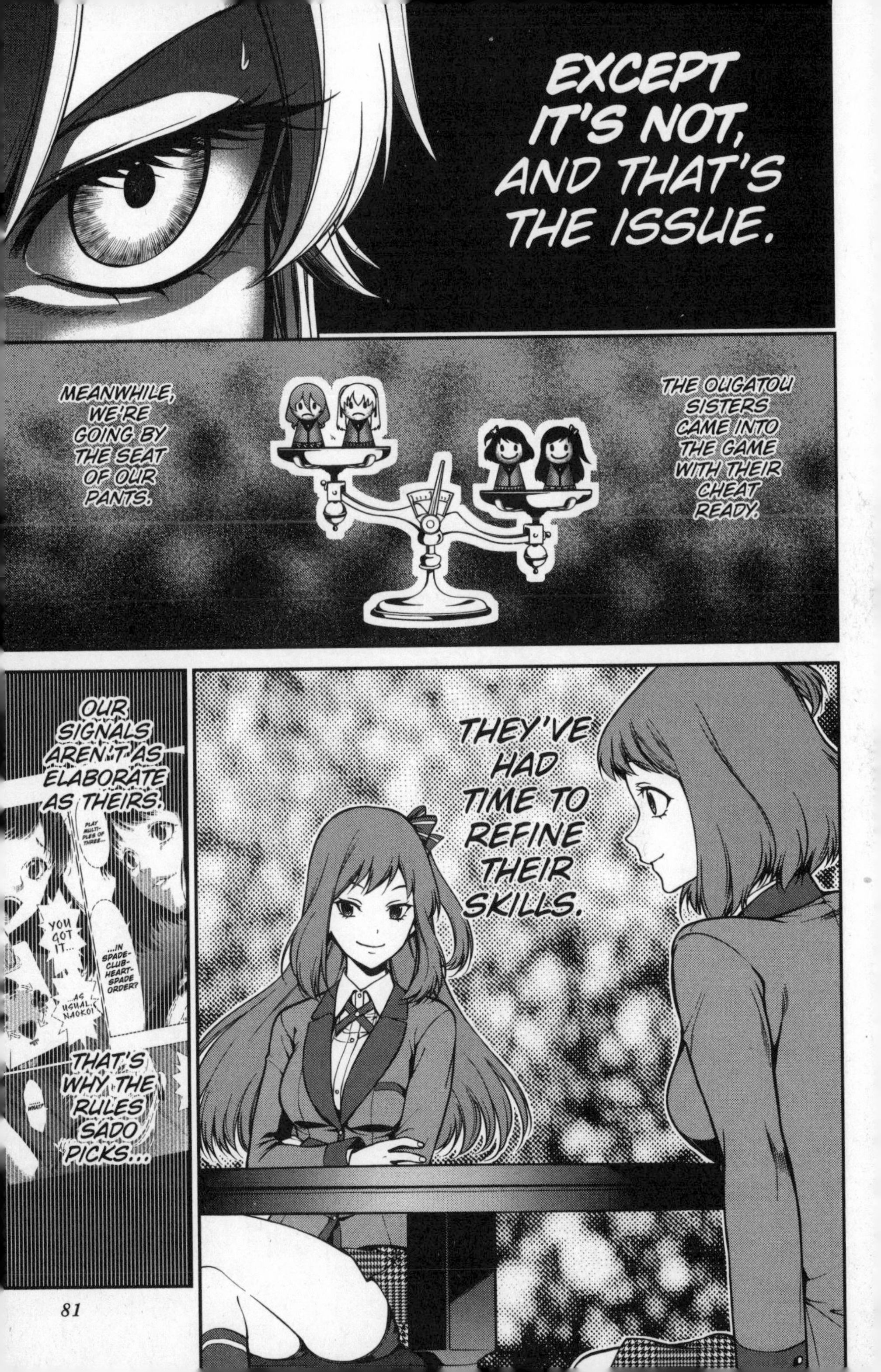
EXCEPT IT'S NOT, AND THAT'S THE ISSUE.
THE OUGATOU SISTERS CAME INTO THE GAME WITH THEIR CHEAT READY.
MEANWHILE, WE'RE GOING BY THE SEAT OF OUR PANTS.
THEY'VE HAD TIME TO REFINE THEIR SKILLS.
OUR SIGNALS AREN'T AS ELABORATE AS THEIRS.
PLAY MULTI-PLES OF THREE...
...IN SPADE-CLUB-HEART-SPADE ORDER?
YOU GOT IT...
...AS USUAL, NAOKO!
THAT'S WHY THE RULES SADO PICKS...
......WHAT?

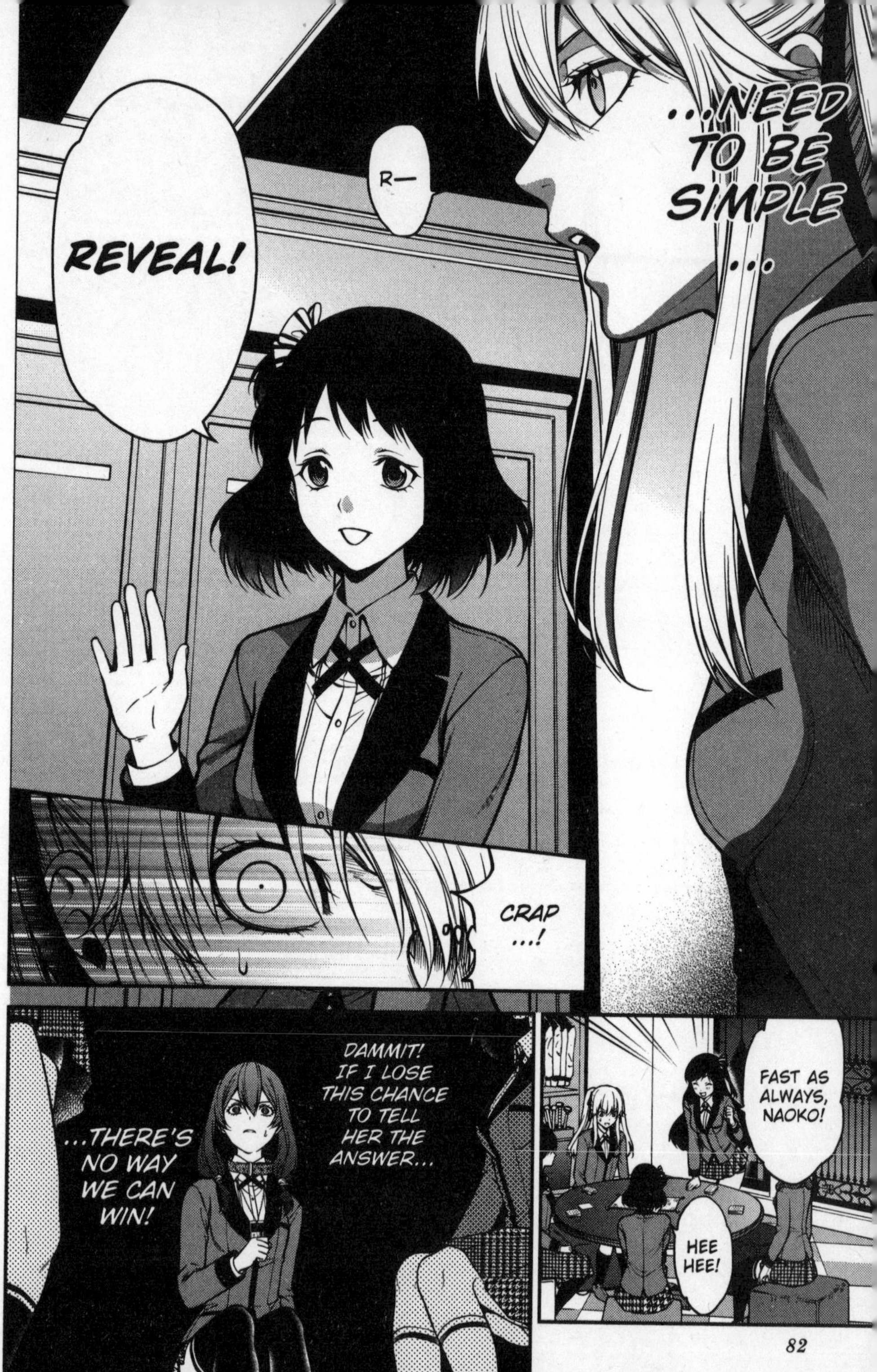
...NEED TO BE SIMPLE ...
R—
REVEAL!
CRAP ...!
FAST AS ALWAYS, NAOKO!
HEE HEE!
DAMMIT! IF I LOSE THIS CHANCE TO TELL HER THE ANSWER...
...THERE'S NO WAY WE CAN WIN!

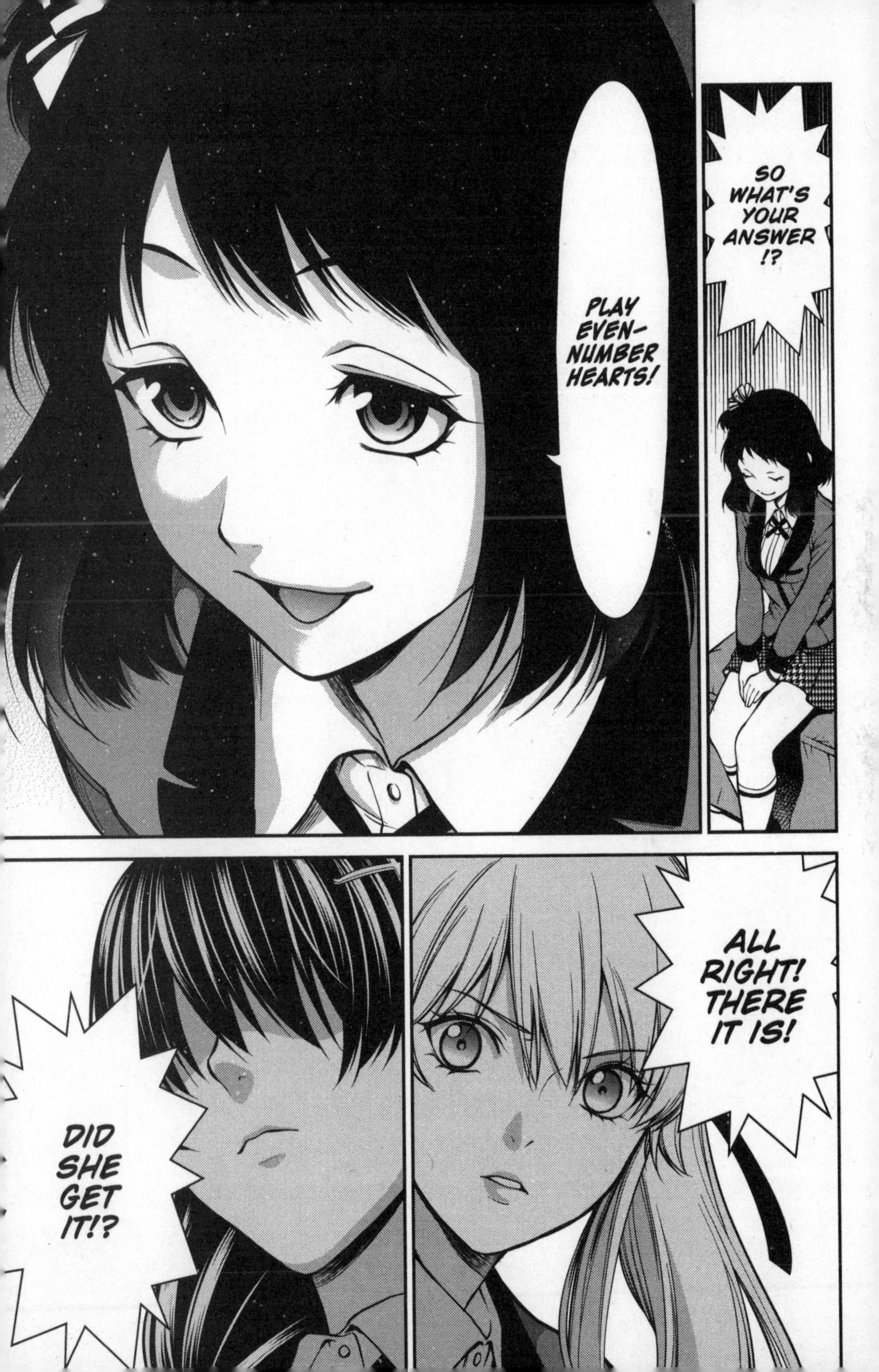
SO WHAT'S YOUR ANSWER !?
PLAY EVEN-NUMBER HEARTS!
ALL RIGHT! THERE IT IS!
DID SHE GET IT!?

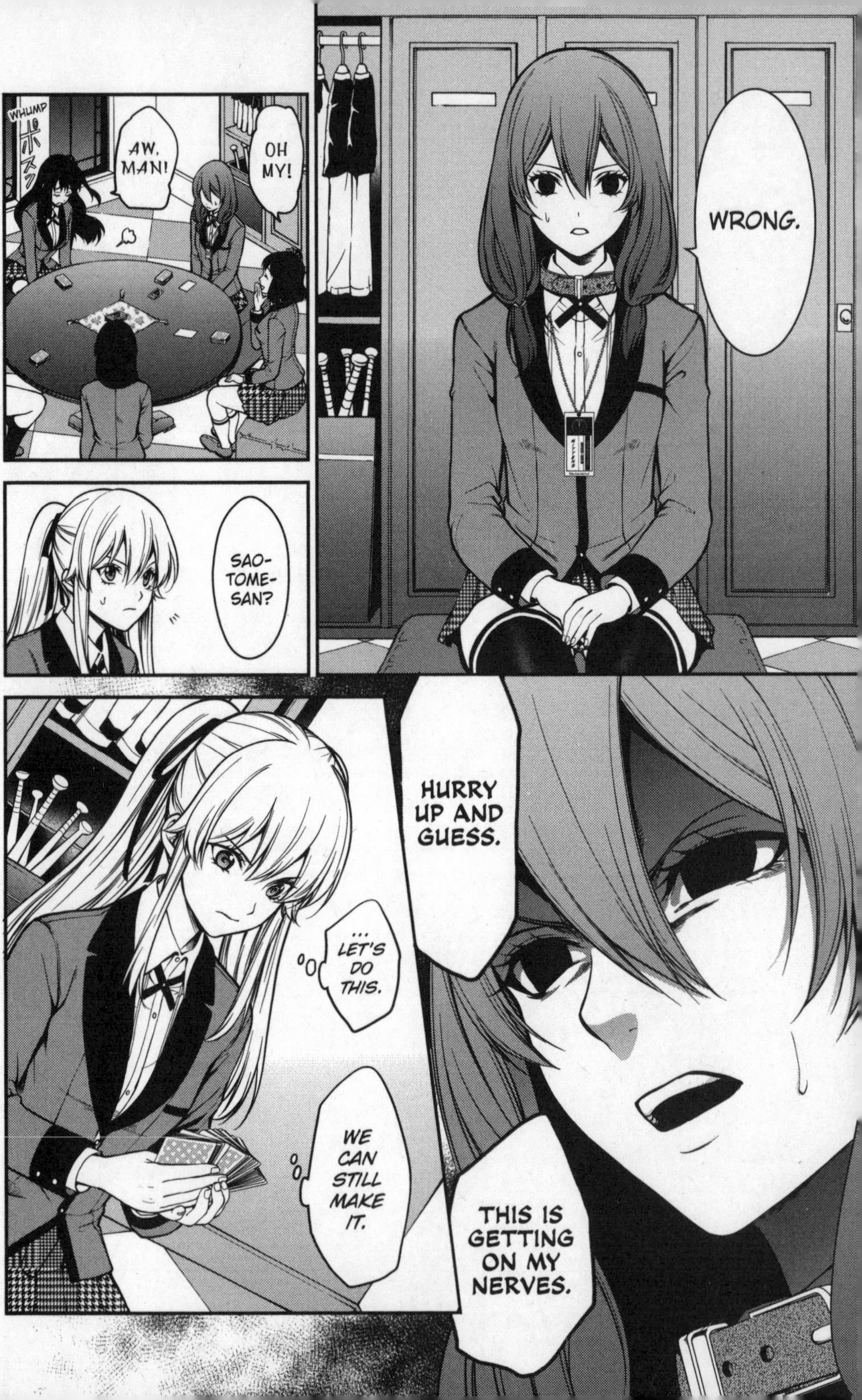
WRONG.
OH MY!
AW, MAN!
WHUMP
ボスッ
SAO-TOME-SAN?
HURRY UP AND GUESS.
THIS IS GETTING ON MY NERVES.
...LET'S DO THIS.
WE CAN STILL MAKE IT.

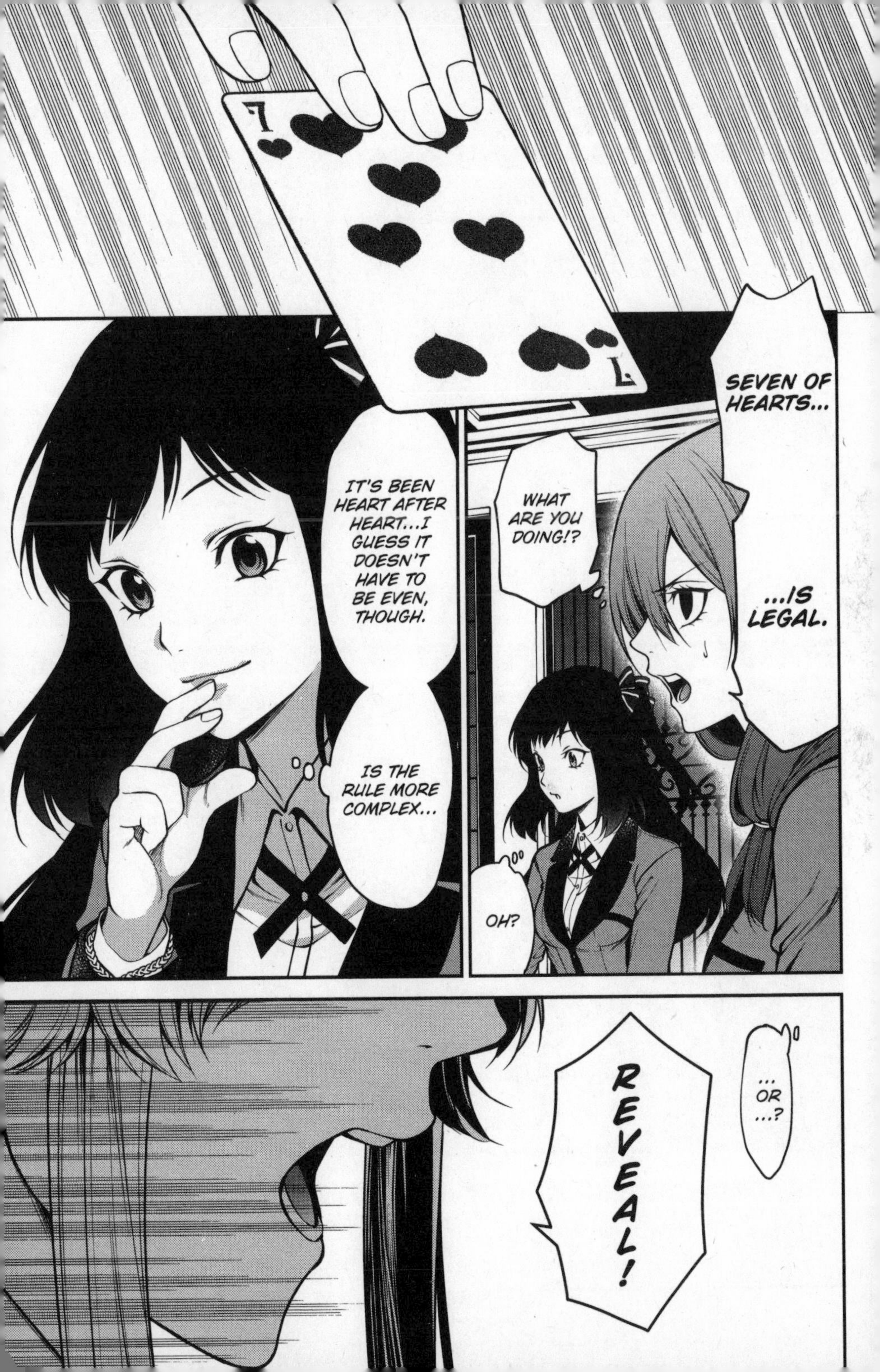
SEVEN OF HEARTS...
...IS LEGAL.
WHAT ARE YOU DOING!?
OH?
IT'S BEEN HEART AFTER HEART...I GUESS IT DOESN'T HAVE TO BE EVEN, THOUGH.
IS THE RULE MORE COMPLEX...
...OR ...?
REVEAL!

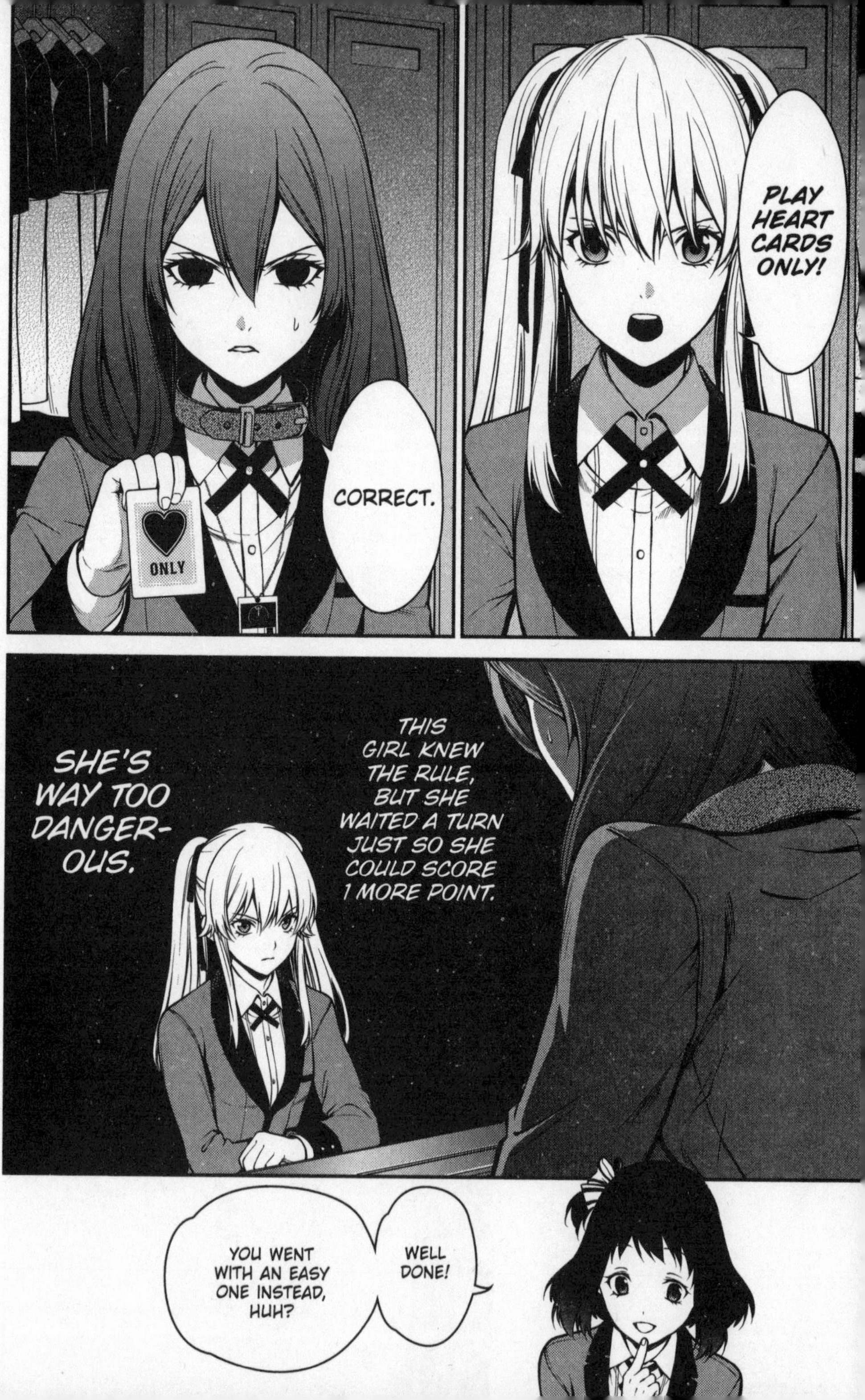
PLAY HEART CARDS ONLY!
ONLY
CORRECT.
THIS GIRL KNEW THE RULE, BUT SHE WAITED A TURN JUST SO SHE COULD SCORE 1 MORE POINT.
SHE'S WAY TOO DANGER-OUS.
WELL DONE!
YOU WENT WITH AN EASY ONE INSTEAD, HUH?

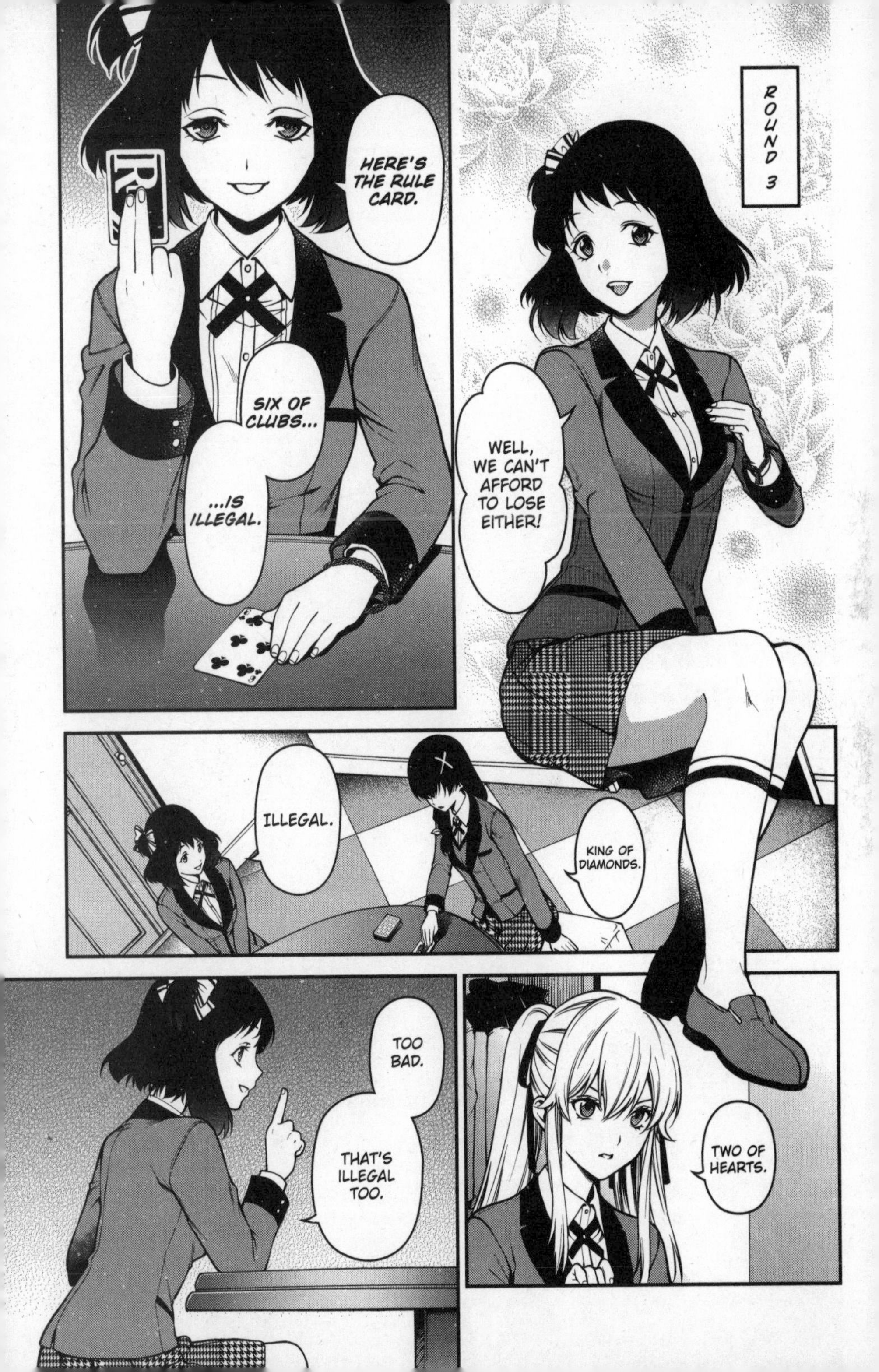
ROUND 3
WELL, WE CAN'T AFFORD TO LOSE EITHER!
HERE'S THE RULE CARD.
SIX OF CLUBS...
...IS ILLEGAL.
KING OF DIAMONDS.
ILLEGAL.
TWO OF HEARTS.
TOO BAD.
THAT'S ILLEGAL TOO.

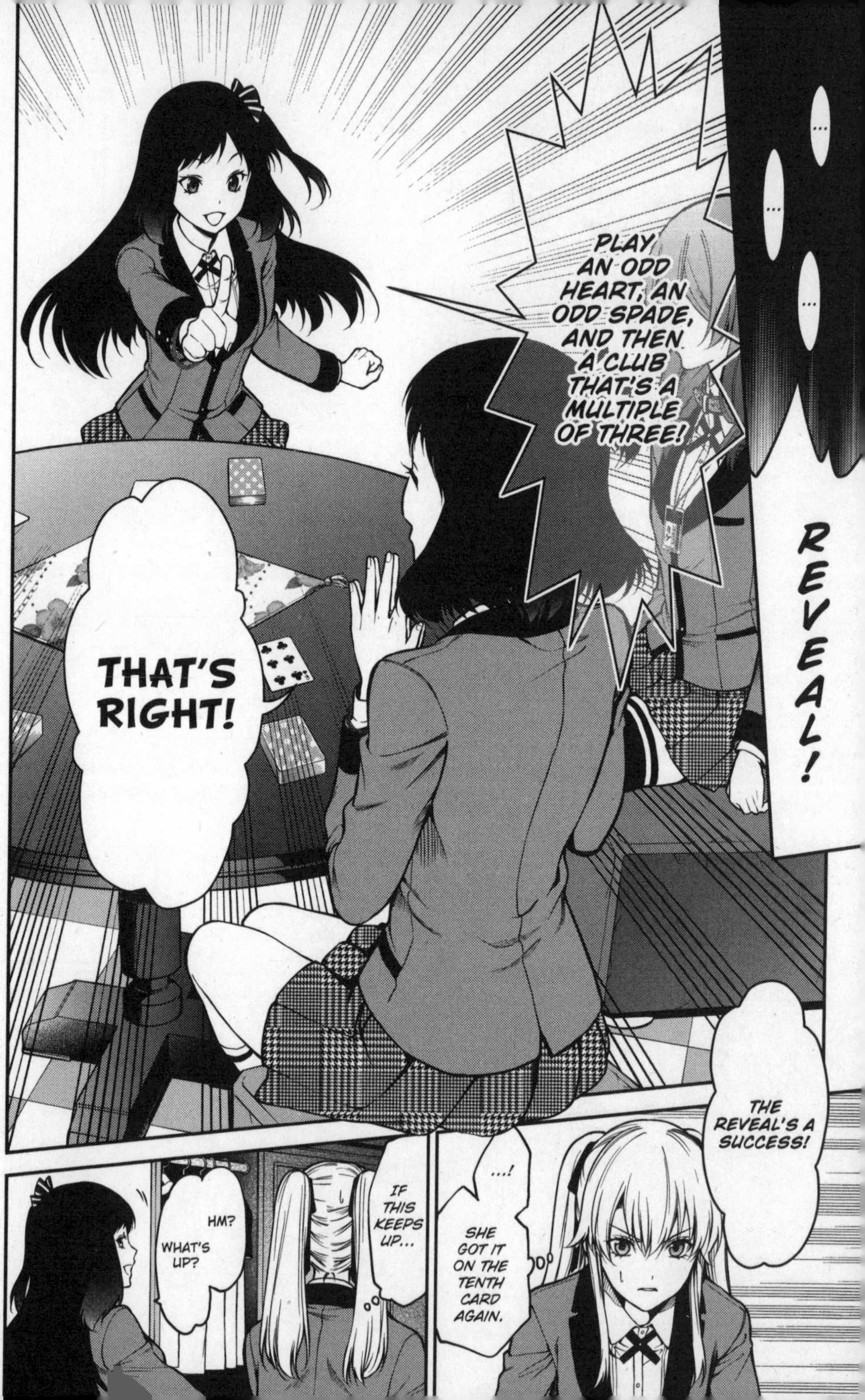
...
...
...
REVEAL!
PLAY AN ODD HEART, AN ODD SPADE, AND THEN A CLUB THAT'S A MULTIPLE OF THREE!
THAT'S RIGHT!
THE REVEAL'S A SUCCESS!
...!
SHE GOT IT ON THE TENTH CARD AGAIN.
IF THIS KEEPS UP...
HM?
WHAT'S UP?

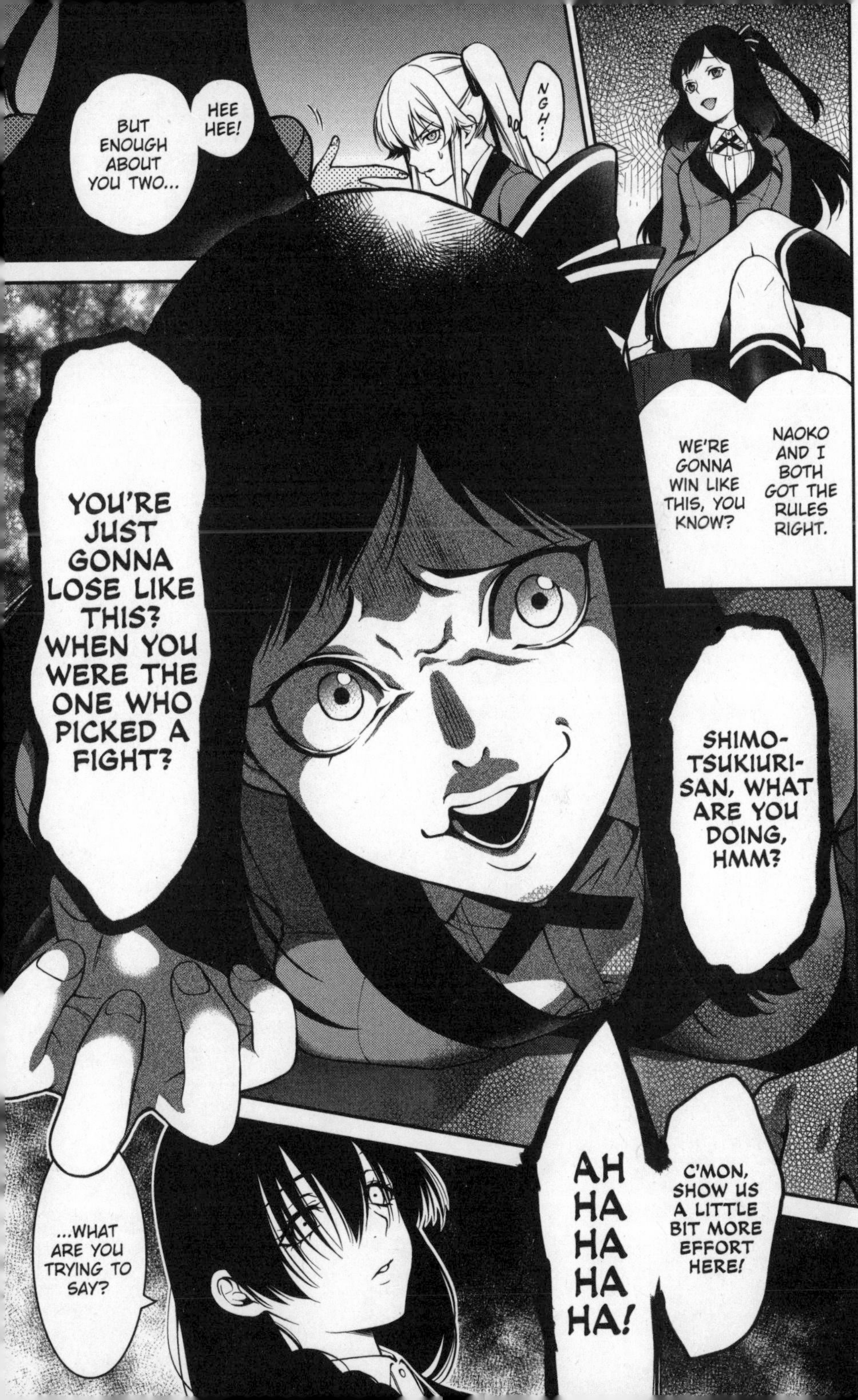
NGH...
HEE HEE!
BUT ENOUGH ABOUT YOU TWO...
NAOKO AND I BOTH GOT THE RULES RIGHT.
WE'RE GONNA WIN LIKE THIS, YOU KNOW?
SHIMO-TSUKIURI-SAN, WHAT ARE YOU DOING, HMM?
YOU'RE JUST GONNA LOSE LIKE THIS? WHEN YOU WERE THE ONE WHO PICKED A FIGHT?
C'MON, SHOW US A LITTLE BIT MORE EFFORT HERE!
AH HA HA HA HA!
...WHAT ARE YOU TRYING TO SAY?

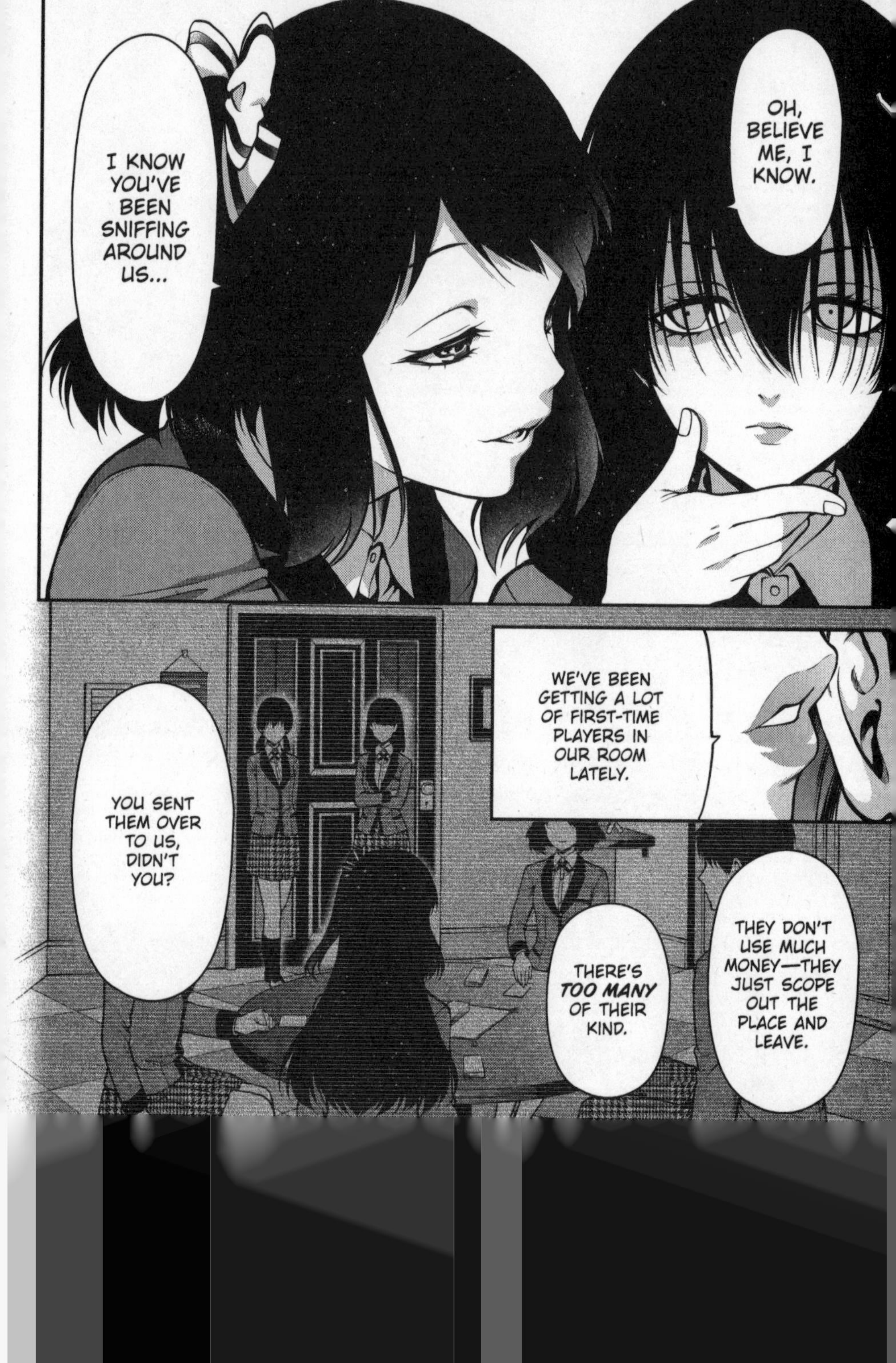
OH, BELIEVE ME, I KNOW.
I KNOW YOU'VE BEEN SNIFFING AROUND US...
WE'VE BEEN GETTING A LOT OF FIRST-TIME PLAYERS IN OUR ROOM LATELY.
THEY DON'T USE MUCH MONEY—THEY JUST SCOPE OUT THE PLACE AND LEAVE.
THERE'S *TOO MANY* OF THEIR KIND.
YOU SENT THEM OVER TO US, DIDN'T YOU?

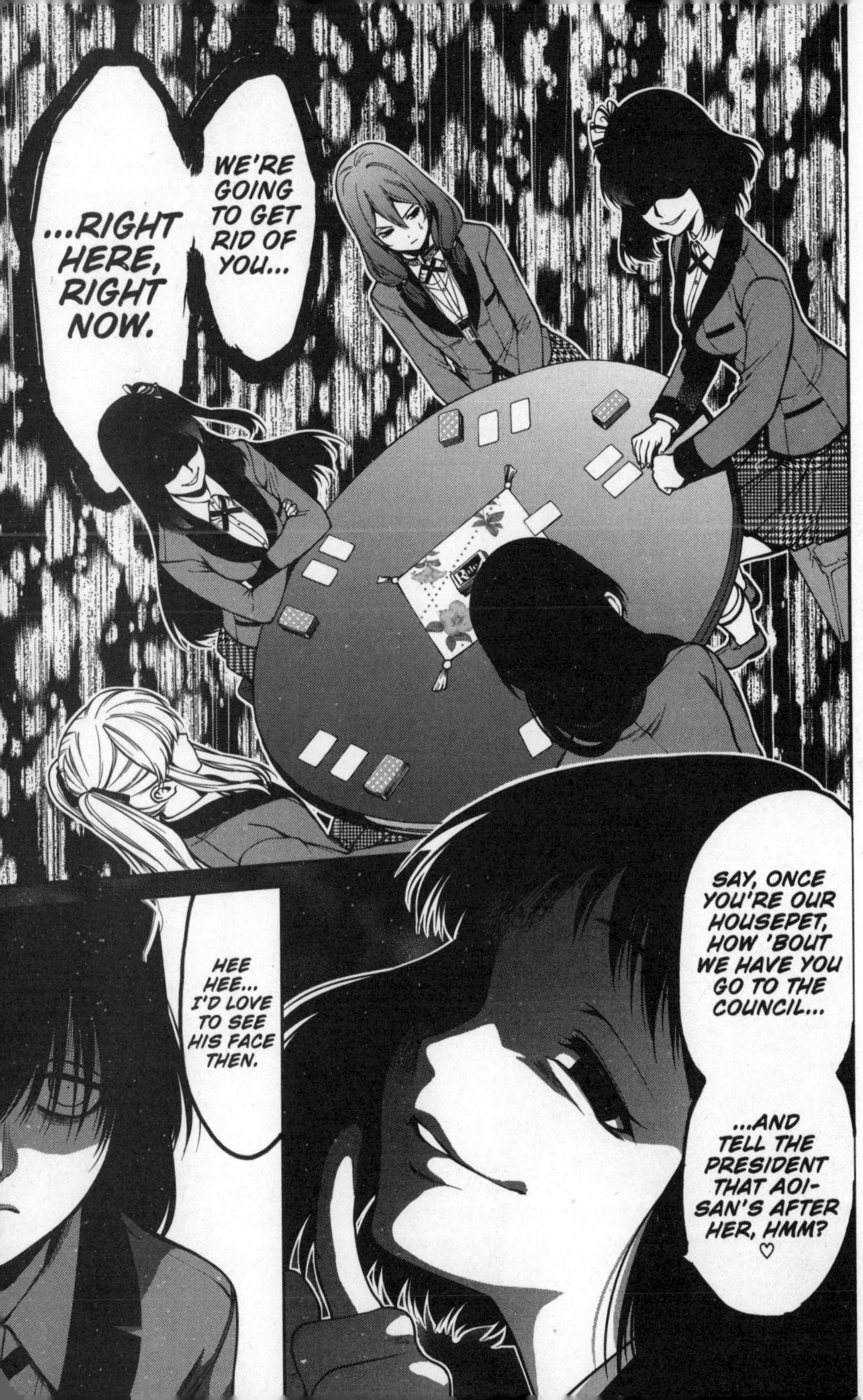
WE'RE GOING TO GET RID OF YOU...
...RIGHT HERE, RIGHT NOW.
SAY, ONCE YOU'RE OUR HOUSEPET, HOW 'BOUT WE HAVE YOU GO TO THE COUNCIL...
...AND TELL THE PRESIDENT THAT AOI-SAN'S AFTER HER, HMM? ♡
HEE HEE... I'D LOVE TO SEE HIS FACE THEN.

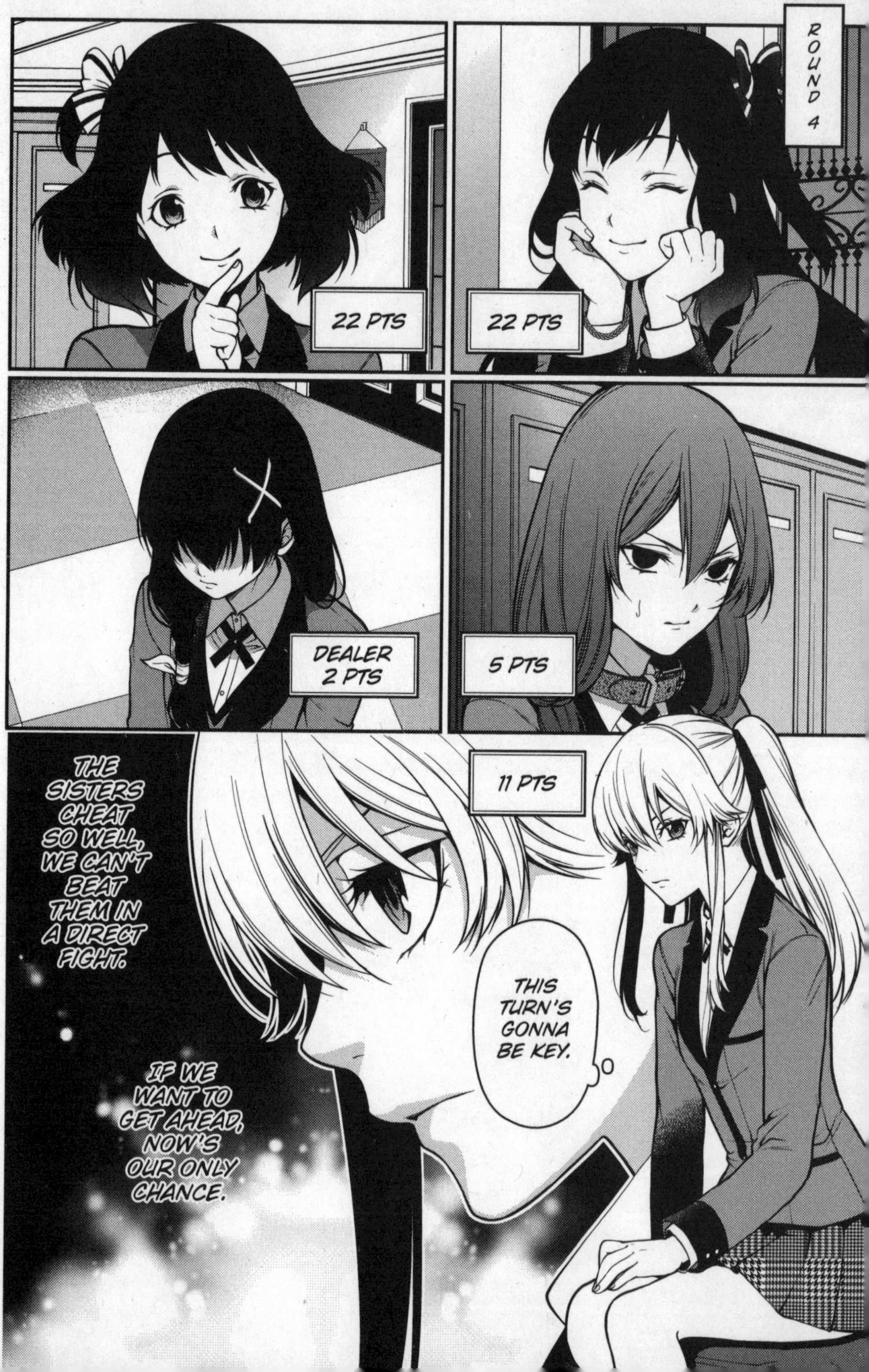
ROUND 4
22 PTS
22 PTS
5 PTS
DEALER 2 PTS
11 PTS
THIS TURN'S GONNA BE KEY.
THE SISTERS CHEAT SO WELL, WE CAN'T BEAT THEM IN A DIRECT FIGHT.
IF WE WANT TO GET AHEAD, NOW'S OUR ONLY CHANCE.

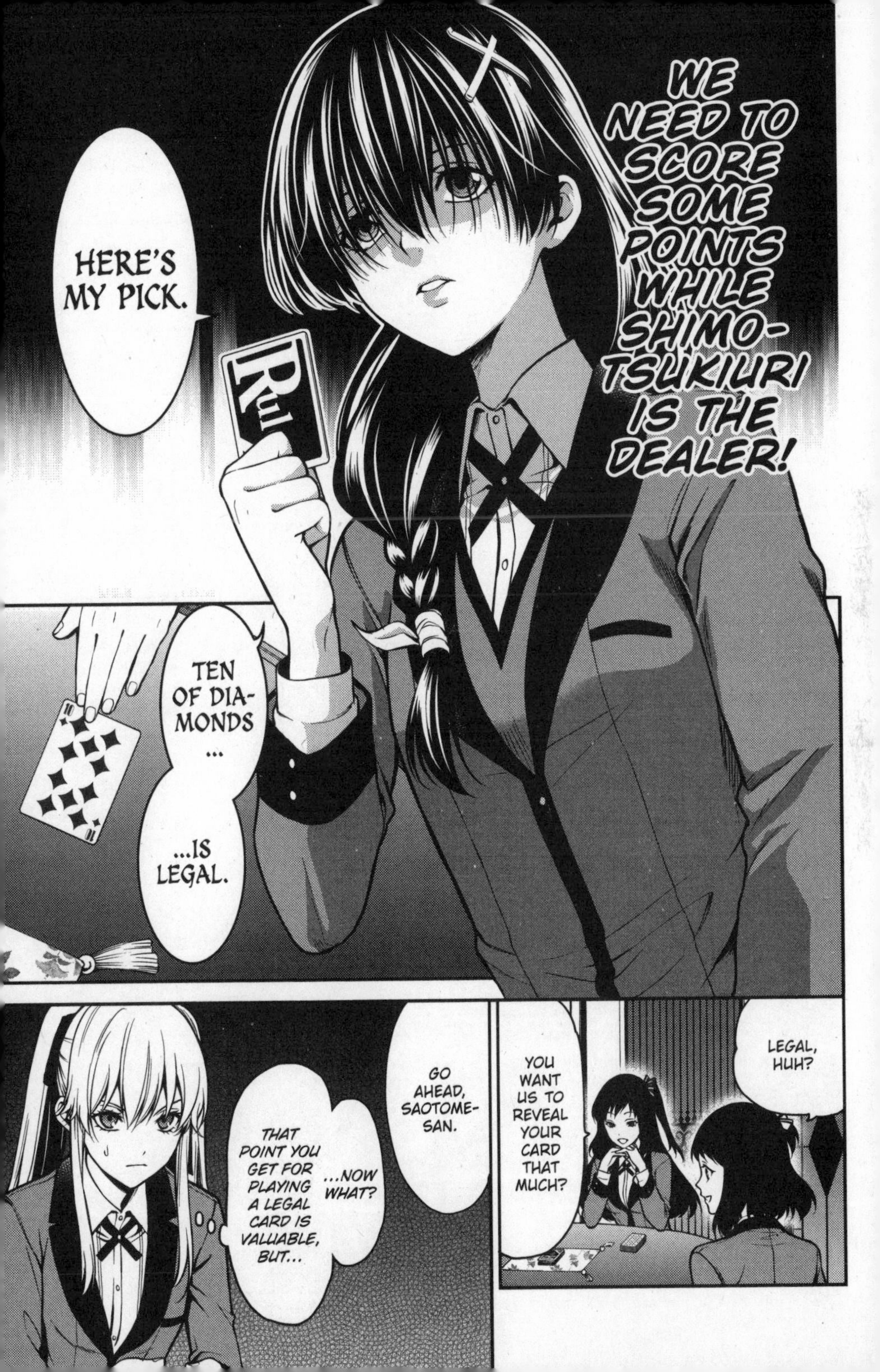
WE NEED TO SCORE SOME POINTS WHILE SHIMO-TSUKIURI IS THE DEALER!
HERE'S MY PICK.
TEN OF DIA-MONDS ...
...IS LEGAL.
LEGAL, HUH?
YOU WANT US TO REVEAL YOUR CARD THAT MUCH?
GO AHEAD, SAOTOME-SAN.
THAT POINT YOU GET FOR PLAYING A LEGAL CARD IS VALUABLE, BUT...
...NOW WHAT?

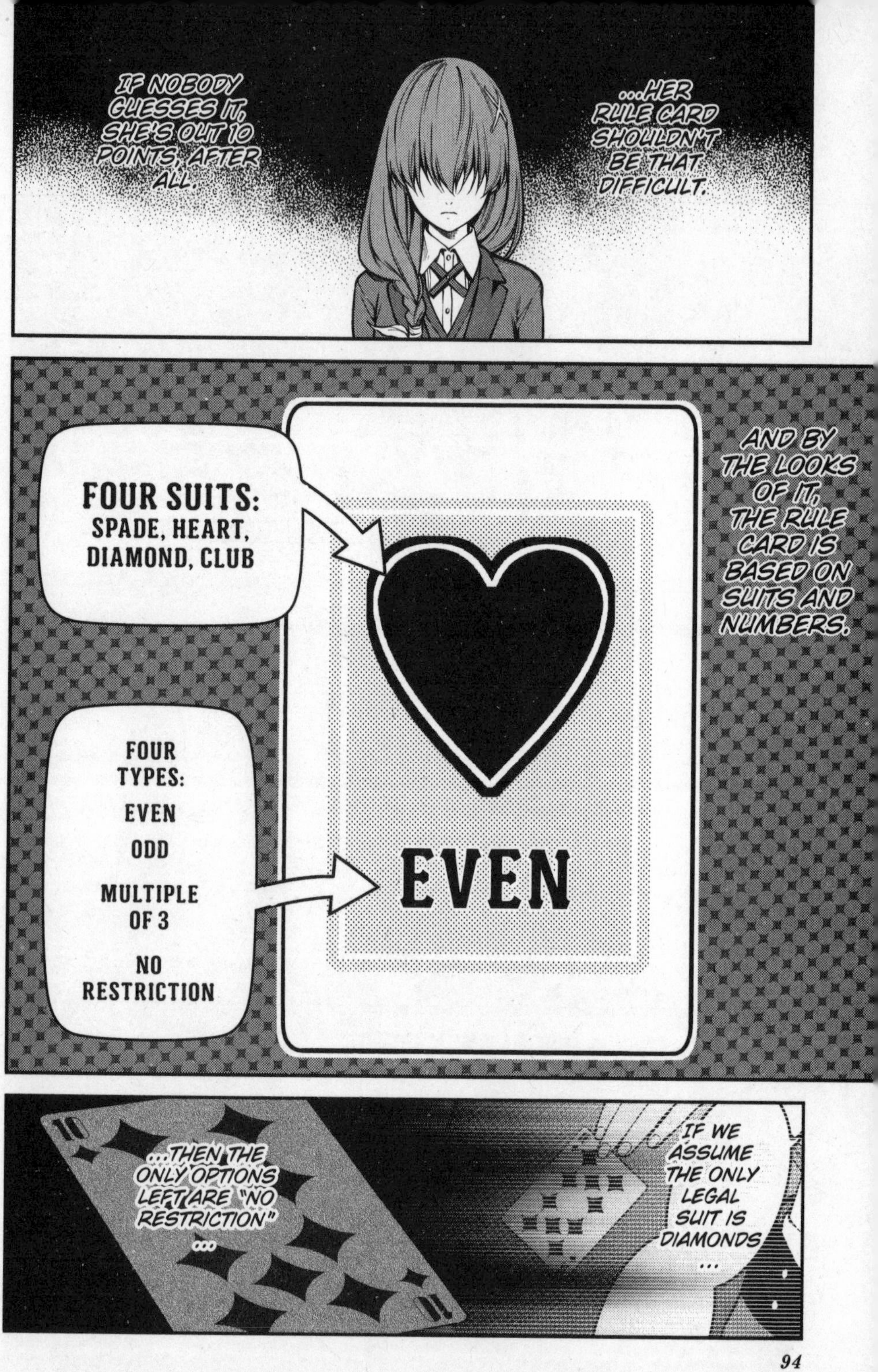
...HER RULE CARD SHOULDN'T BE THAT DIFFICULT.
IF NOBODY GUESSES IT, SHE'S OUT 10 POINTS, AFTER ALL.
AND BY THE LOOKS OF IT, THE RULE CARD IS BASED ON SUITS AND NUMBERS.
FOUR SUITS: SPADE, HEART, DIAMOND, CLUB
EVEN
FOUR TYPES: EVEN ODD MULTIPLE OF 3 NO RESTRICTION
IF WE ASSUME THE ONLY LEGAL SUIT IS DIAMONDS...
...THEN THE ONLY OPTIONS LEFT ARE "NO RESTRICTION"...

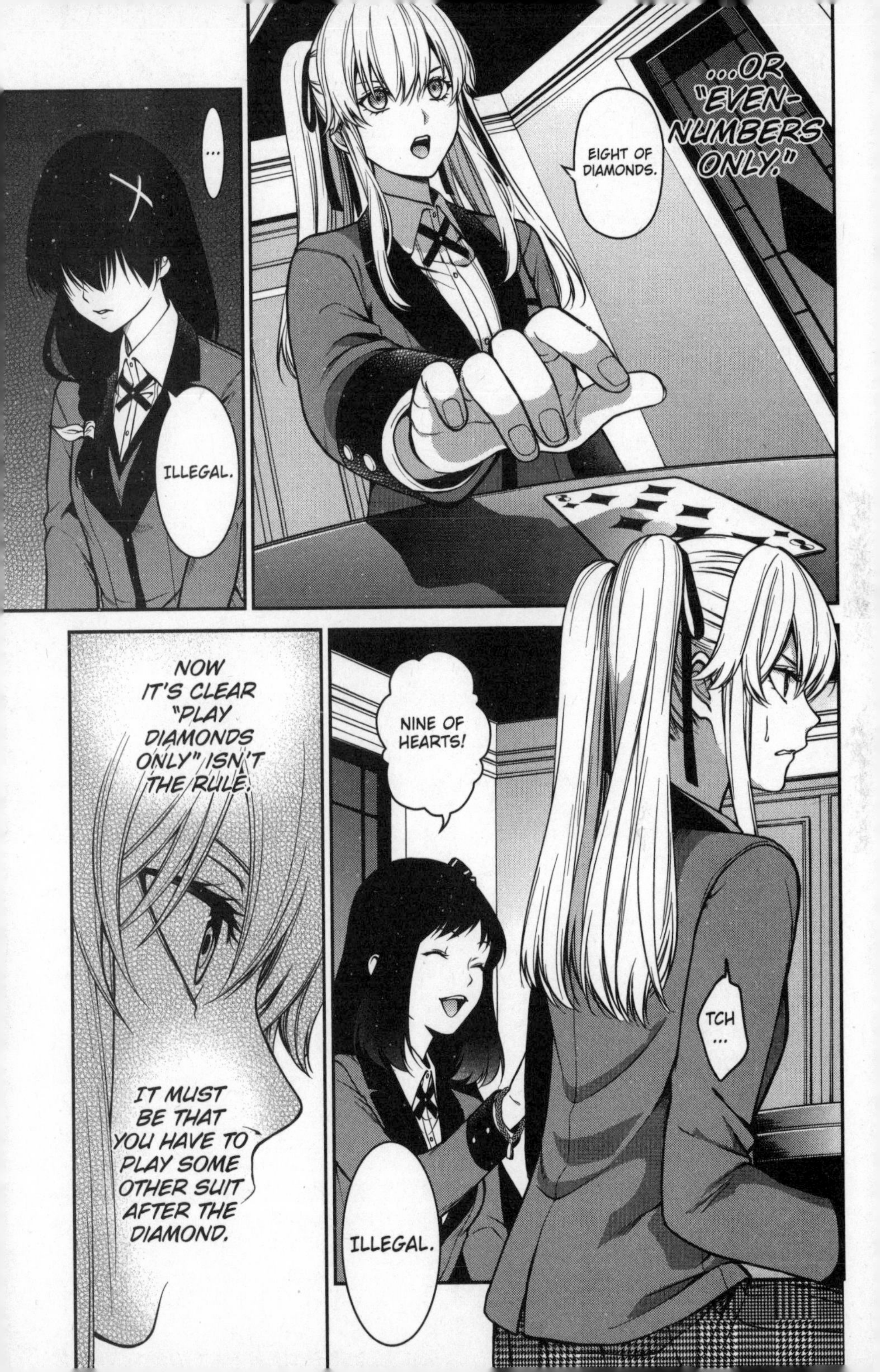
...OR "EVEN-NUMBERS ONLY."
EIGHT OF DIAMONDS.
...
ILLEGAL.
NINE OF HEARTS!
TCH...
ILLEGAL.
NOW IT'S CLEAR "PLAY DIAMONDS ONLY" ISN'T THE RULE.
IT MUST BE THAT YOU HAVE TO PLAY SOME OTHER SUIT AFTER THE DIAMOND.

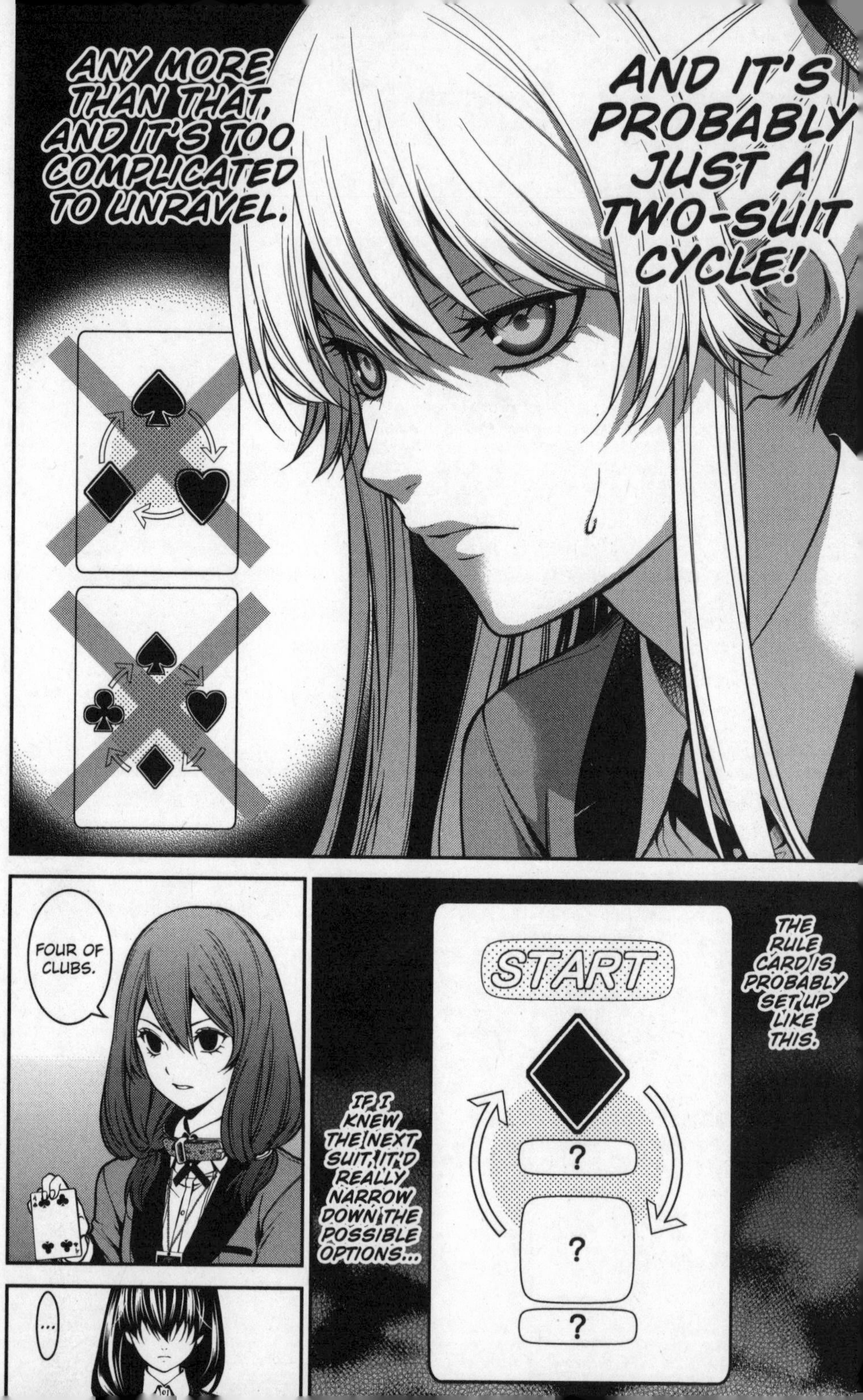
AND IT'S PROBABLY JUST A TWO-SUIT CYCLE!
ANY MORE THAN THAT, AND IT'S TOO COMPLICATED TO UNRAVEL.
THE RULE CARD IS PROBABLY SET UP LIKE THIS.
START
?
?
?
IF I KNEW THE NEXT SUIT, IT'D REALLY NARROW DOWN THE POSSIBLE OPTIONS...
FOUR OF CLUBS.
...

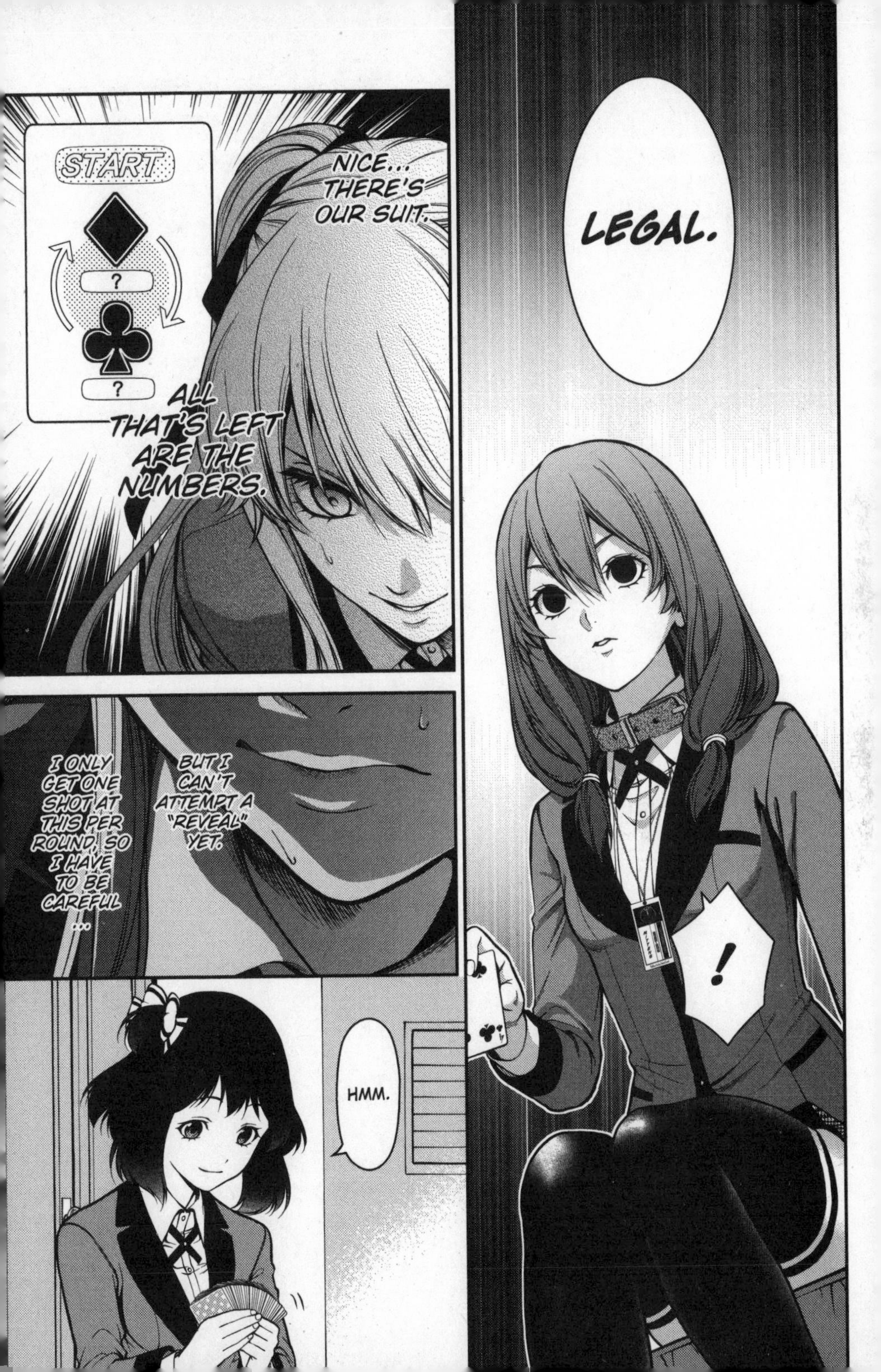
LEGAL.
!
START
?
?
NICE... THERE'S OUR SUIT.
ALL THAT'S LEFT ARE THE NUMBERS.
BUT I CAN'T ATTEMPT A "REVEAL" YET.
I ONLY GET ONE SHOT AT THIS PER ROUND, SO I HAVE TO BE CAREFUL...
HMM.

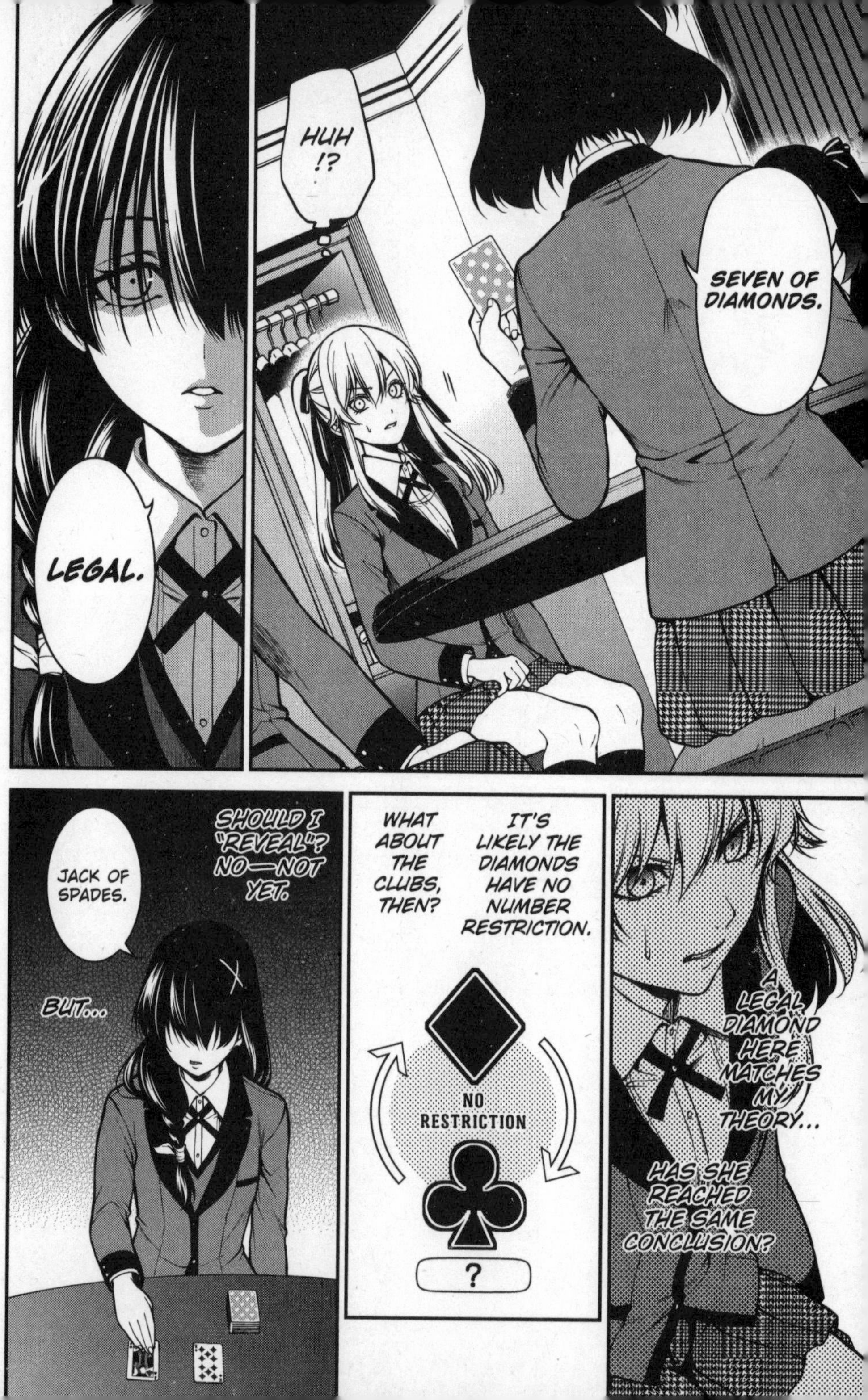
SEVEN OF DIAMONDS.
HUH !?
LEGAL.
A LEGAL DIAMOND HERE MATCHES MY THEORY...
HAS SHE REACHED THE SAME CONCLUSION?
IT'S LIKELY THE DIAMONDS HAVE NO NUMBER RESTRICTION.
WHAT ABOUT THE CLUBS, THEN?
NO RESTRICTION
?
SHOULD I "REVEAL"? NO—NOT YET.
JACK OF SPADES.
BUT...

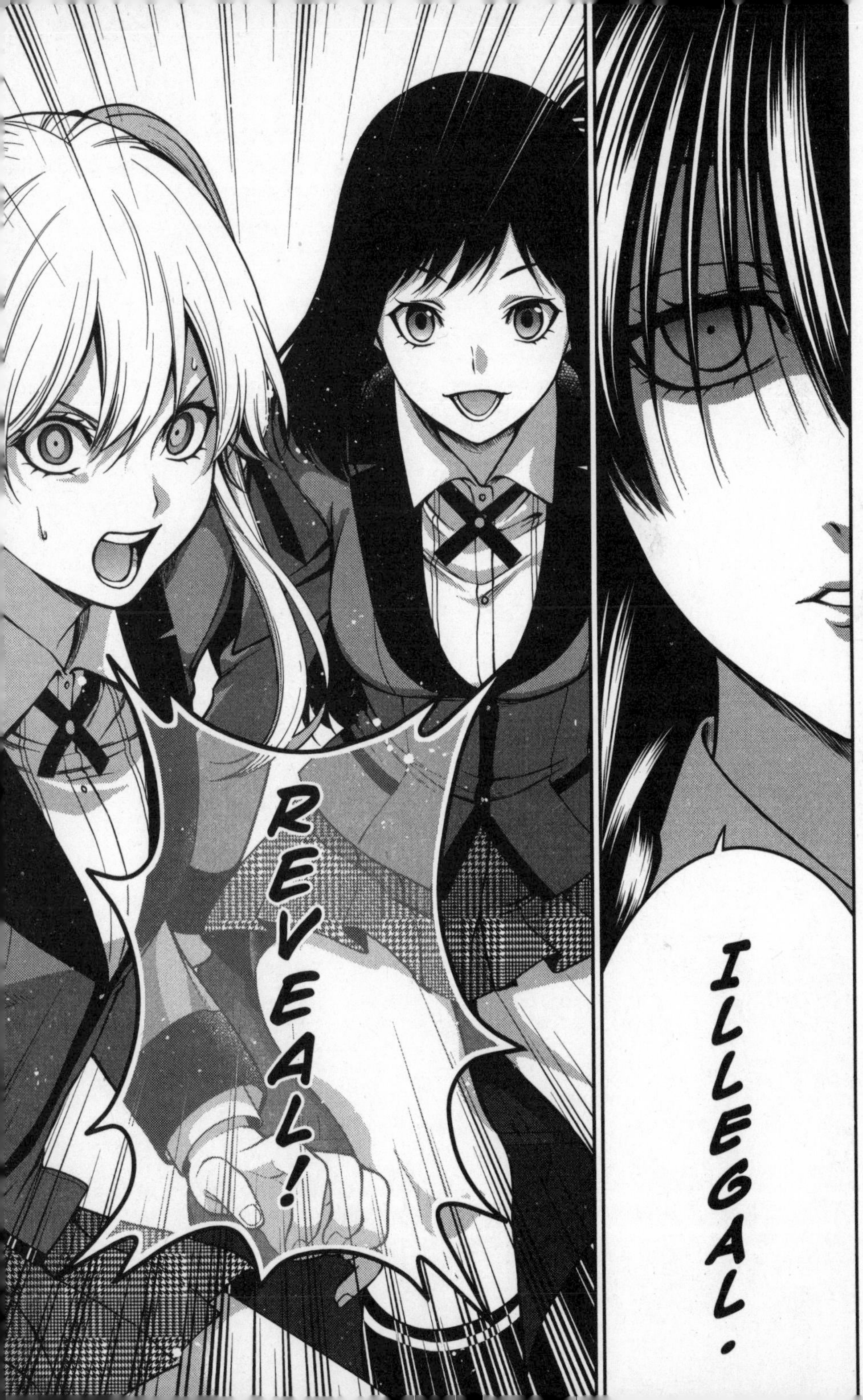
ILLEGAL.
REVEAL!

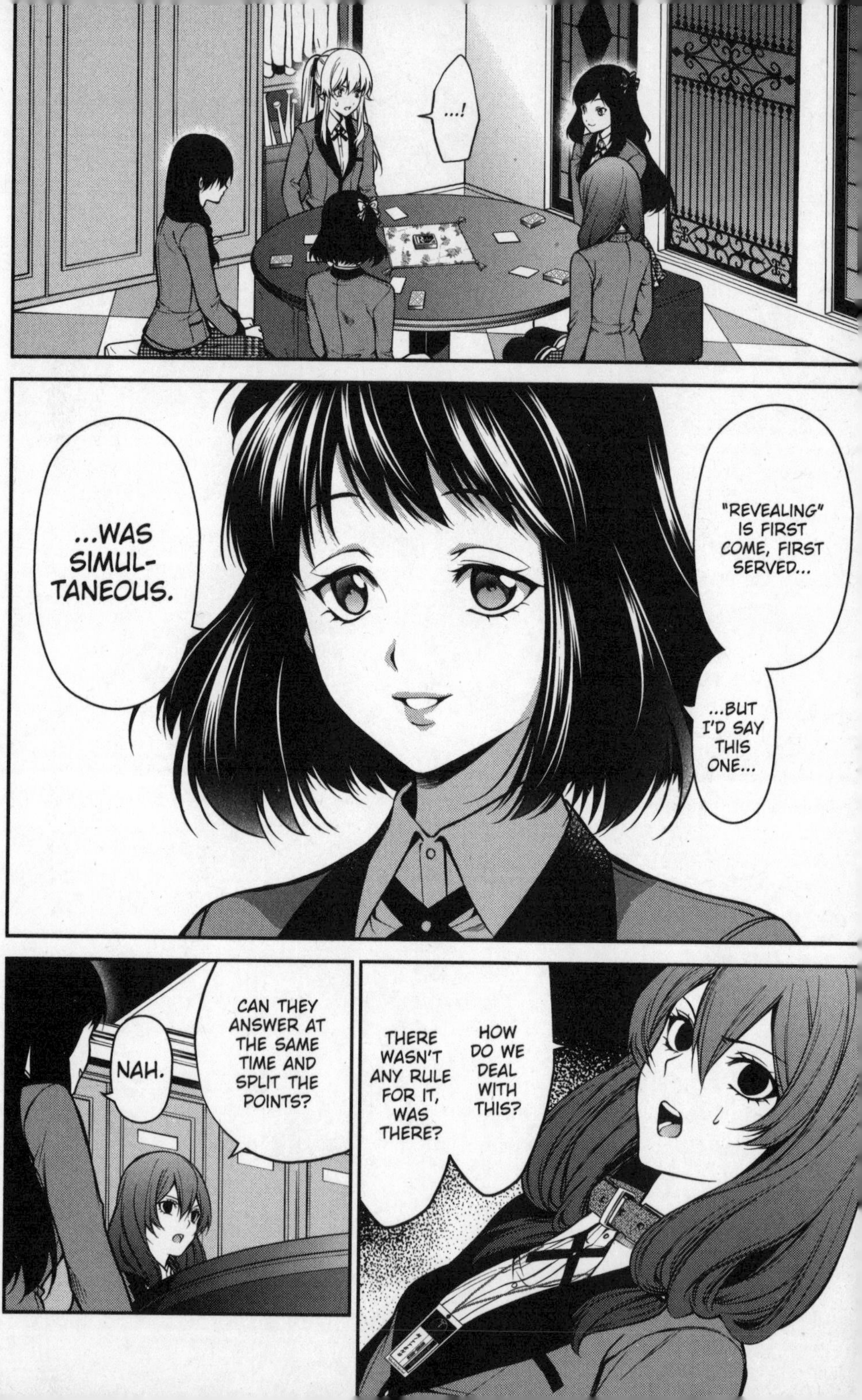
...!
"REVEALING" IS FIRST COME, FIRST SERVED...
...BUT I'D SAY THIS ONE...
...WAS SIMUL-TANEOUS.
HOW DO WE DEAL WITH THIS?
THERE WASN'T ANY RULE FOR IT, WAS THERE?
CAN THEY ANSWER AT THE SAME TIME AND SPLIT THE POINTS?
NAH.

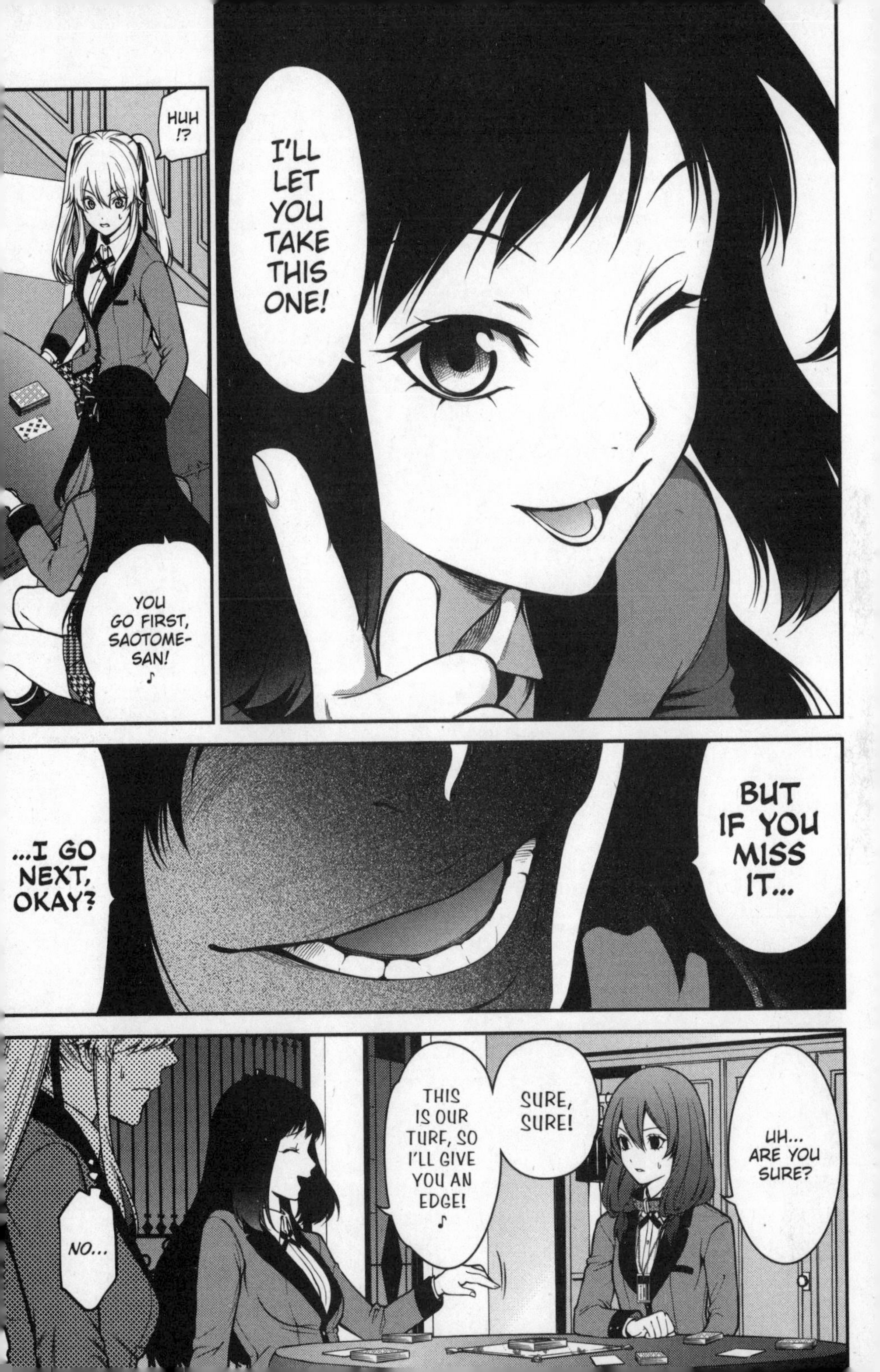
I'LL LET YOU TAKE THIS ONE!
HUH !?
YOU GO FIRST, SAOTOME-SAN! ♪
BUT IF YOU MISS IT...
...I GO NEXT, OKAY?
UH... ARE YOU SURE?
SURE, SURE!
THIS IS OUR TURF, SO I'LL GIVE YOU AN EDGE! ♪
NO...

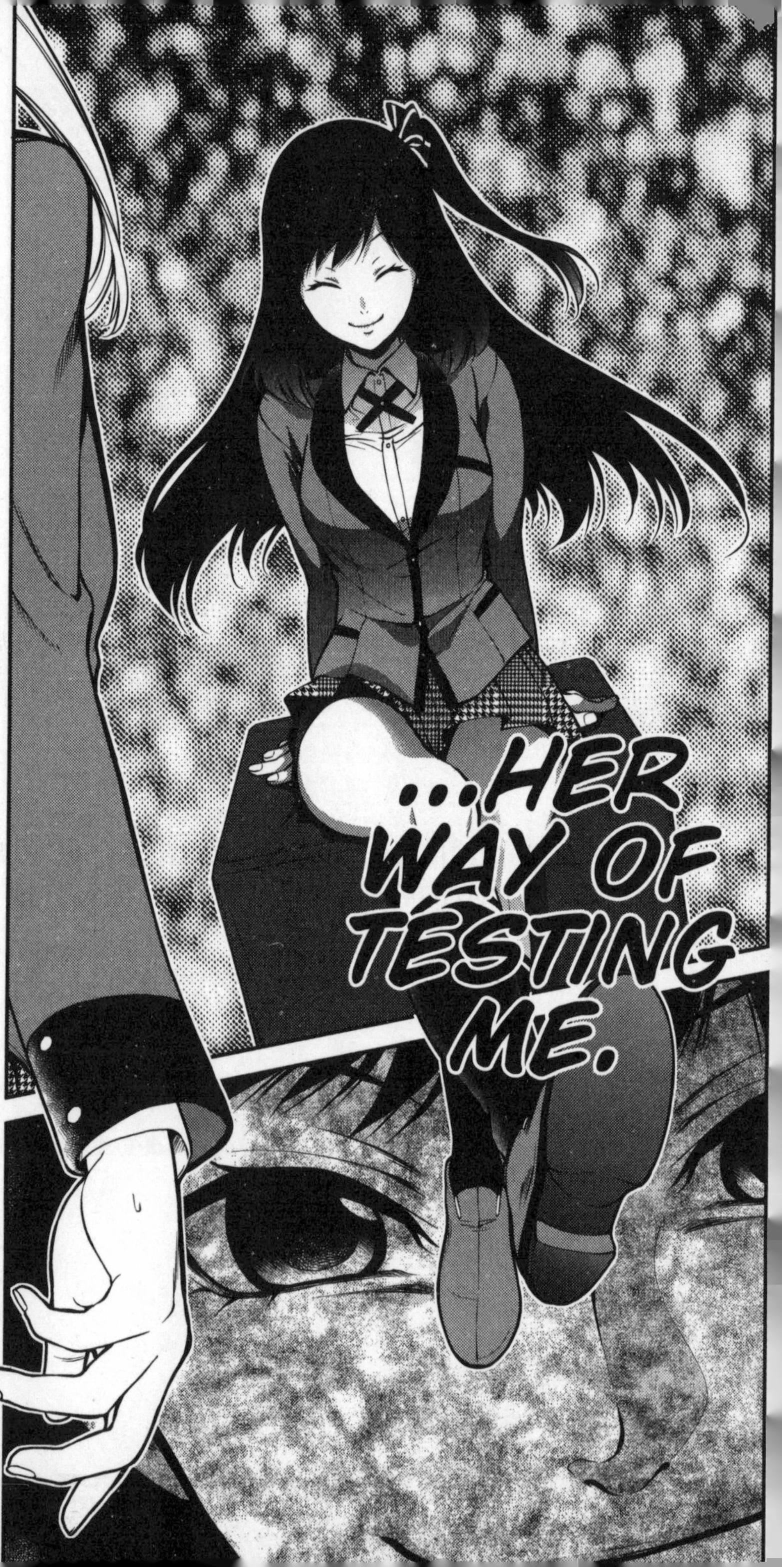
...HER WAY OF TESTING ME.

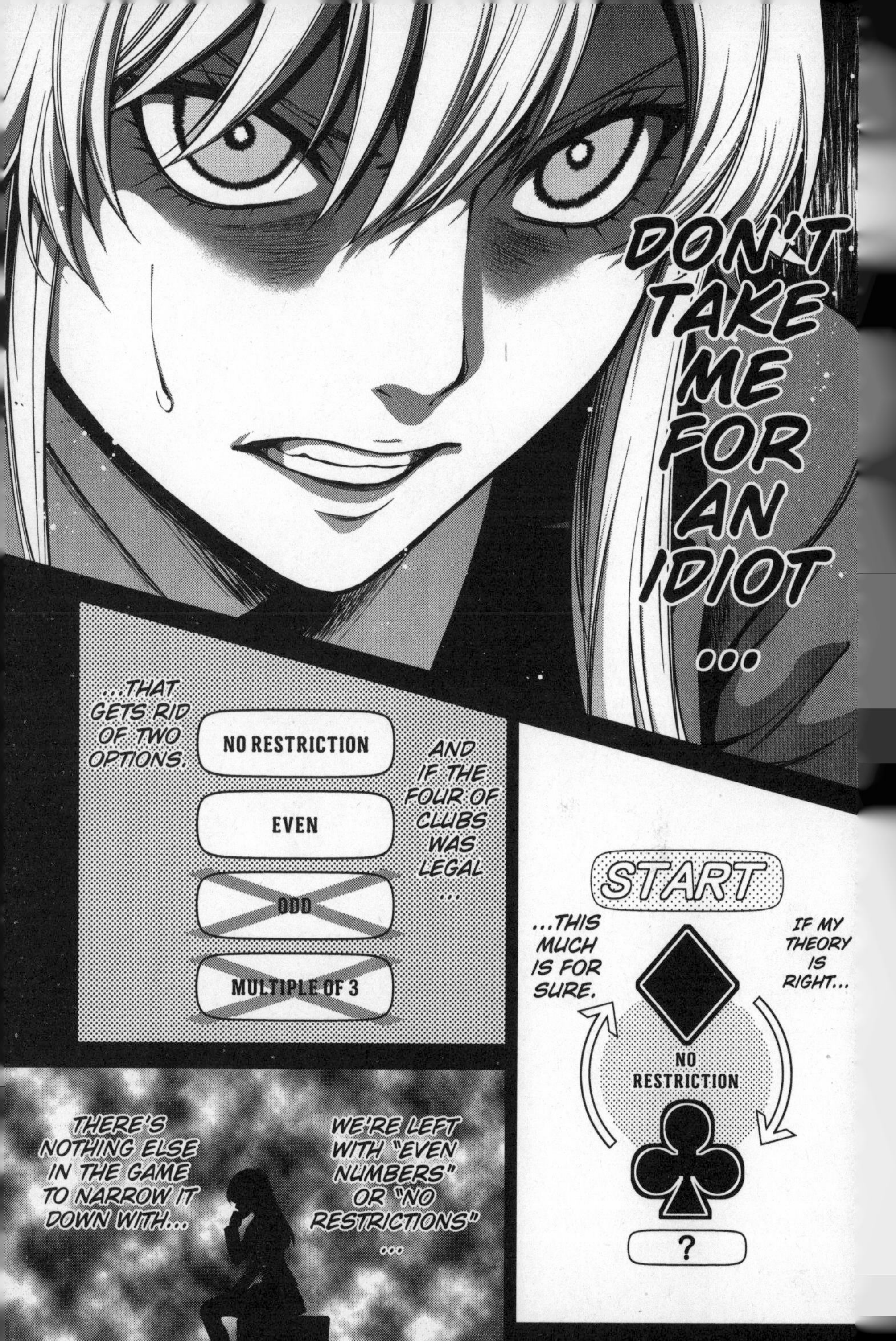
DON'T TAKE ME FOR AN IDIOT...
IF MY THEORY IS RIGHT...
START
...THIS MUCH IS FOR SURE.
NO RESTRICTION
?
AND IF THE FOUR OF CLUBS WAS LEGAL...
...THAT GETS RID OF TWO OPTIONS.
NO RESTRICTION
EVEN
ODD
MULTIPLE OF 3
WE'RE LEFT WITH "EVEN NUMBERS" OR "NO RESTRICTIONS"...
THERE'S NOTHING ELSE IN THE GAME TO NARROW IT DOWN WITH...

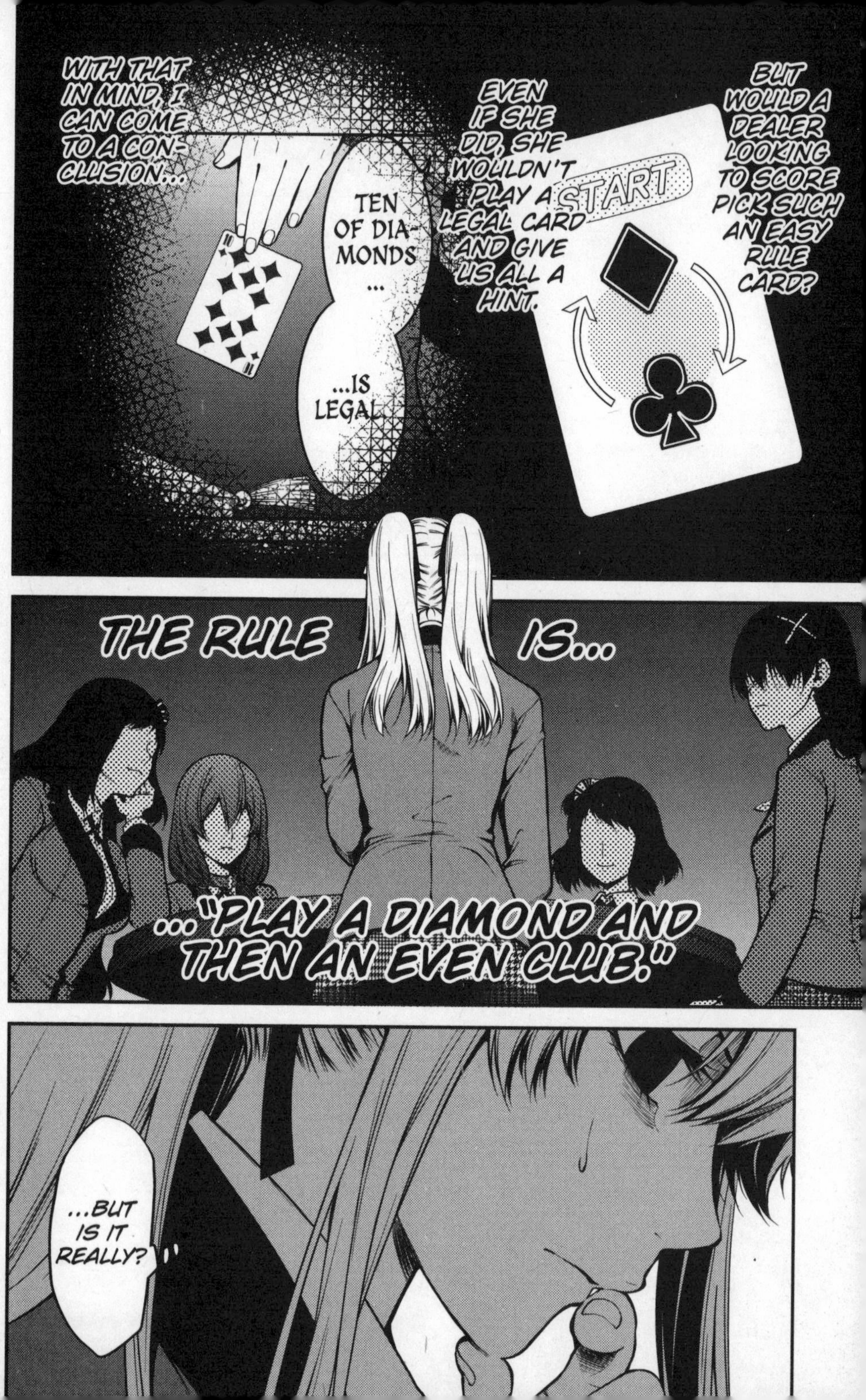
BUT WOULD A DEALER LOOKING TO SCORE PICK SUCH AN EASY RULE CARD?
START
EVEN IF SHE DID, SHE WOULDN'T PLAY A LEGAL CARD AND GIVE US ALL A HINT.
TEN OF DIAMONDS ...
...IS LEGAL
WITH THAT IN MIND, I CAN COME TO A CONCLUSION...
THE RULE IS...
..."PLAY A DIAMOND AND THEN AN EVEN CLUB."
...BUT IS IT REALLY?

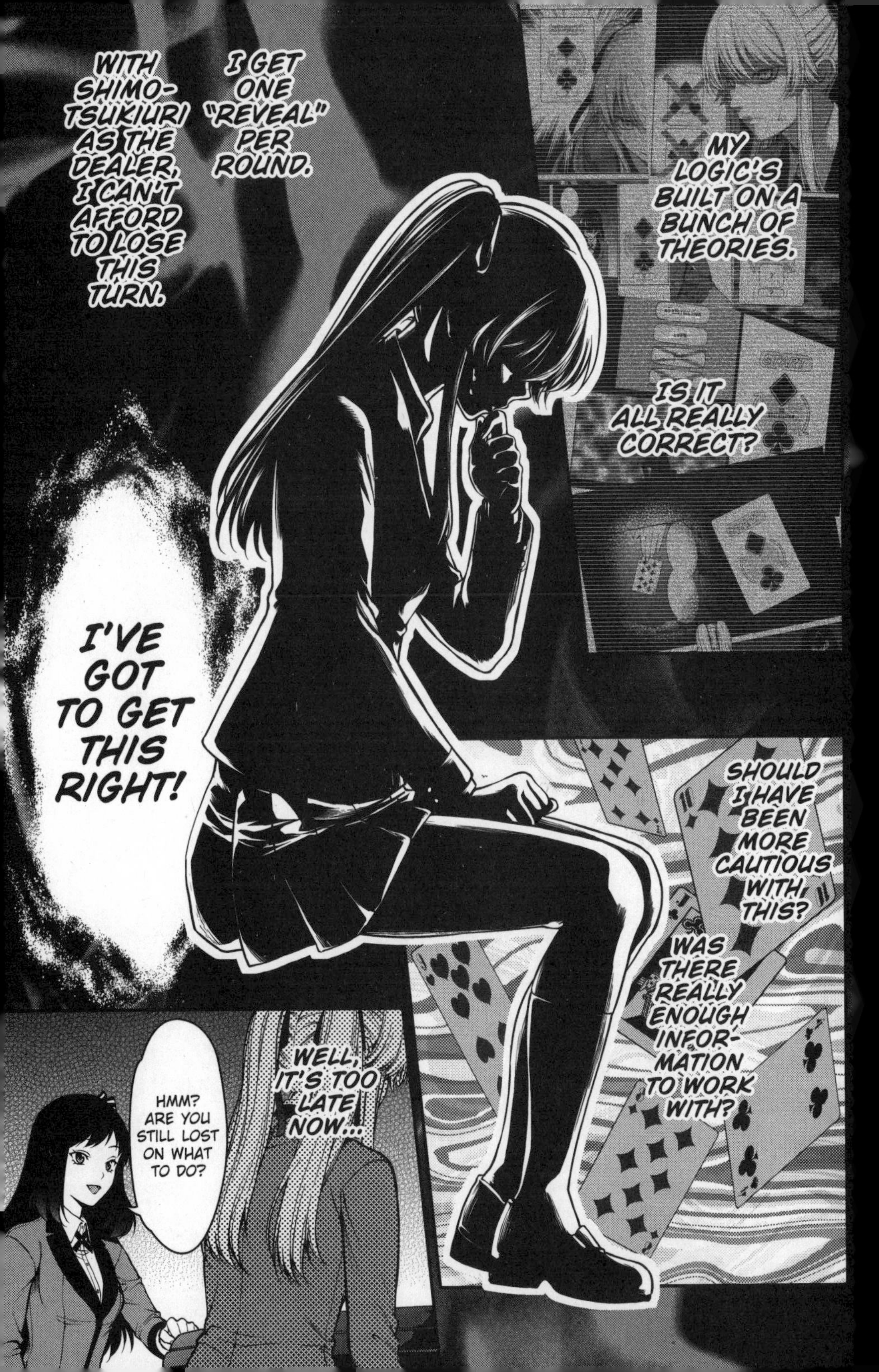
I GET ONE "REVEAL" PER ROUND.
WITH SHIMOTSUKIURI AS THE DEALER, I CAN'T AFFORD TO LOSE THIS TURN.
MY LOGIC'S BUILT ON A BUNCH OF THEORIES.
IS IT ALL REALLY CORRECT?
SHOULD I HAVE BEEN MORE CAUTIOUS WITH THIS?
WAS THERE REALLY ENOUGH INFORMATION TO WORK WITH?
I'VE GOT TO GET THIS RIGHT!
WELL, IT'S TOO LATE NOW...
HMM? ARE YOU STILL LOST ON WHAT TO DO?

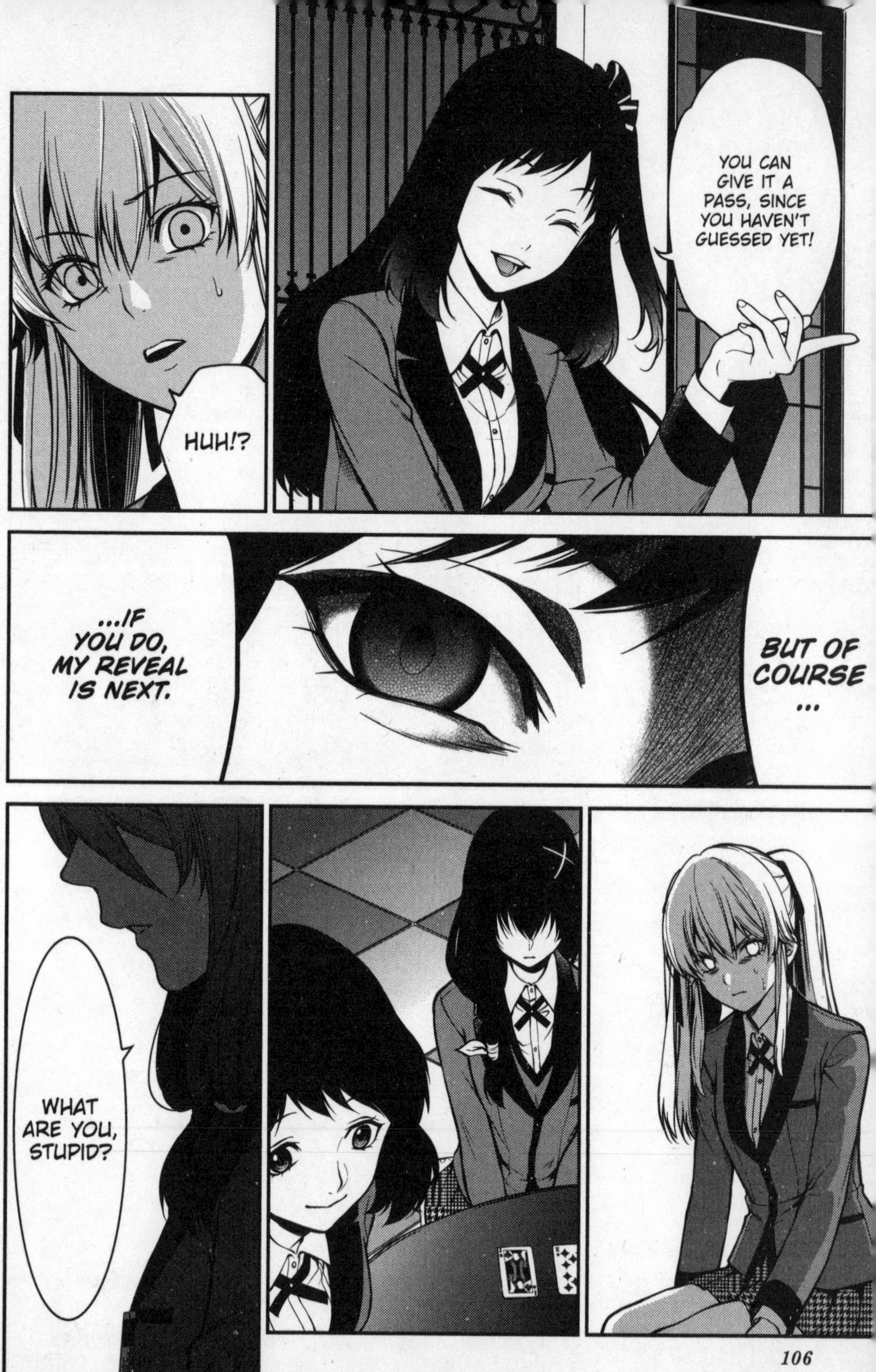
YOU CAN GIVE IT A PASS, SINCE YOU HAVEN'T GUESSED YET!
HUH!?
BUT OF COURSE ...
...IF YOU DO, MY REVEAL IS NEXT.
WHAT ARE YOU, STUPID?

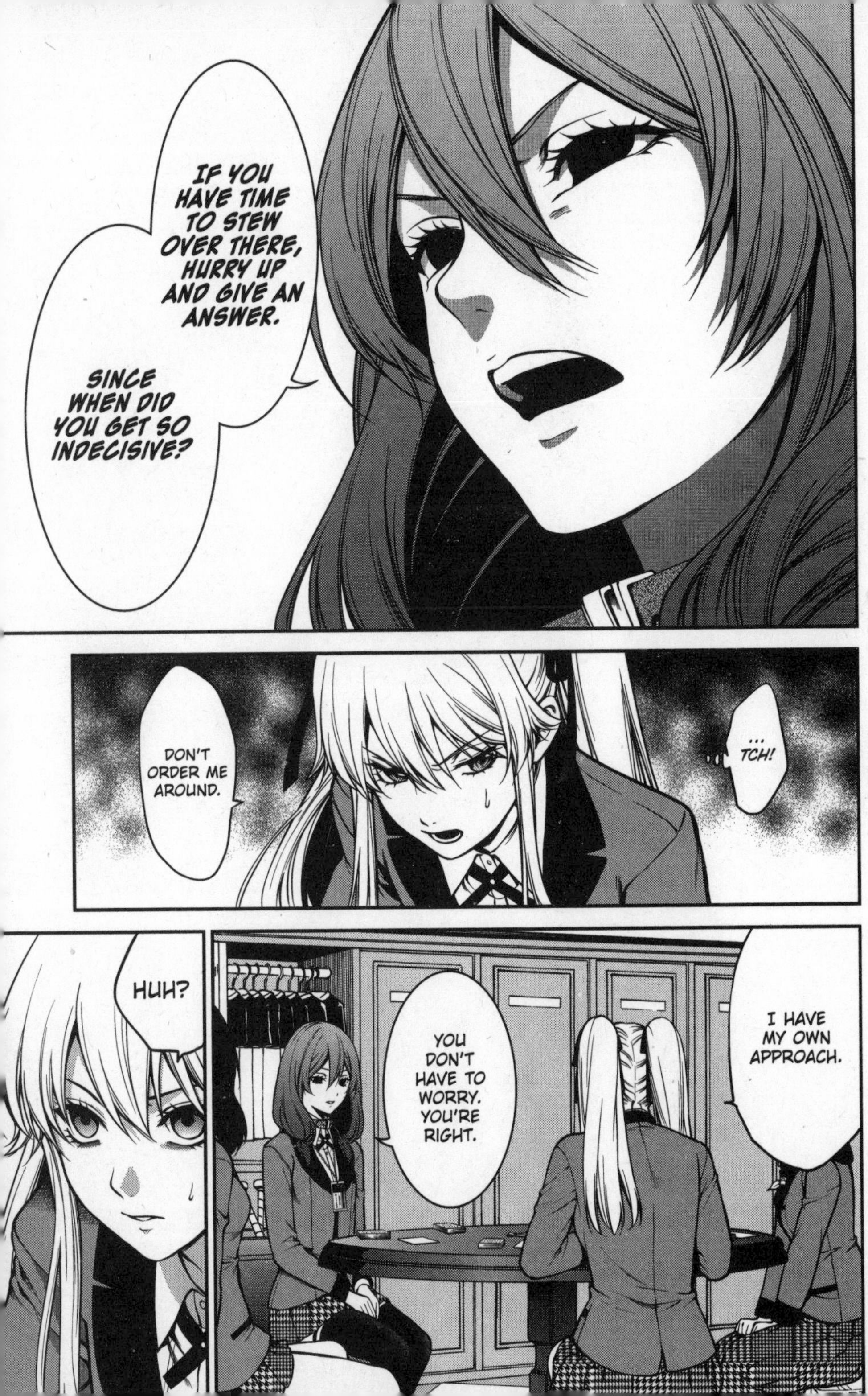
IF YOU HAVE TIME TO STEW OVER THERE, HURRY UP AND GIVE AN ANSWER.
SINCE WHEN DID YOU GET SO INDECISIVE?
...TCH!
DON'T ORDER ME AROUND.
I HAVE MY OWN APPROACH.
YOU DON'T HAVE TO WORRY. YOU'RE RIGHT.
HUH?

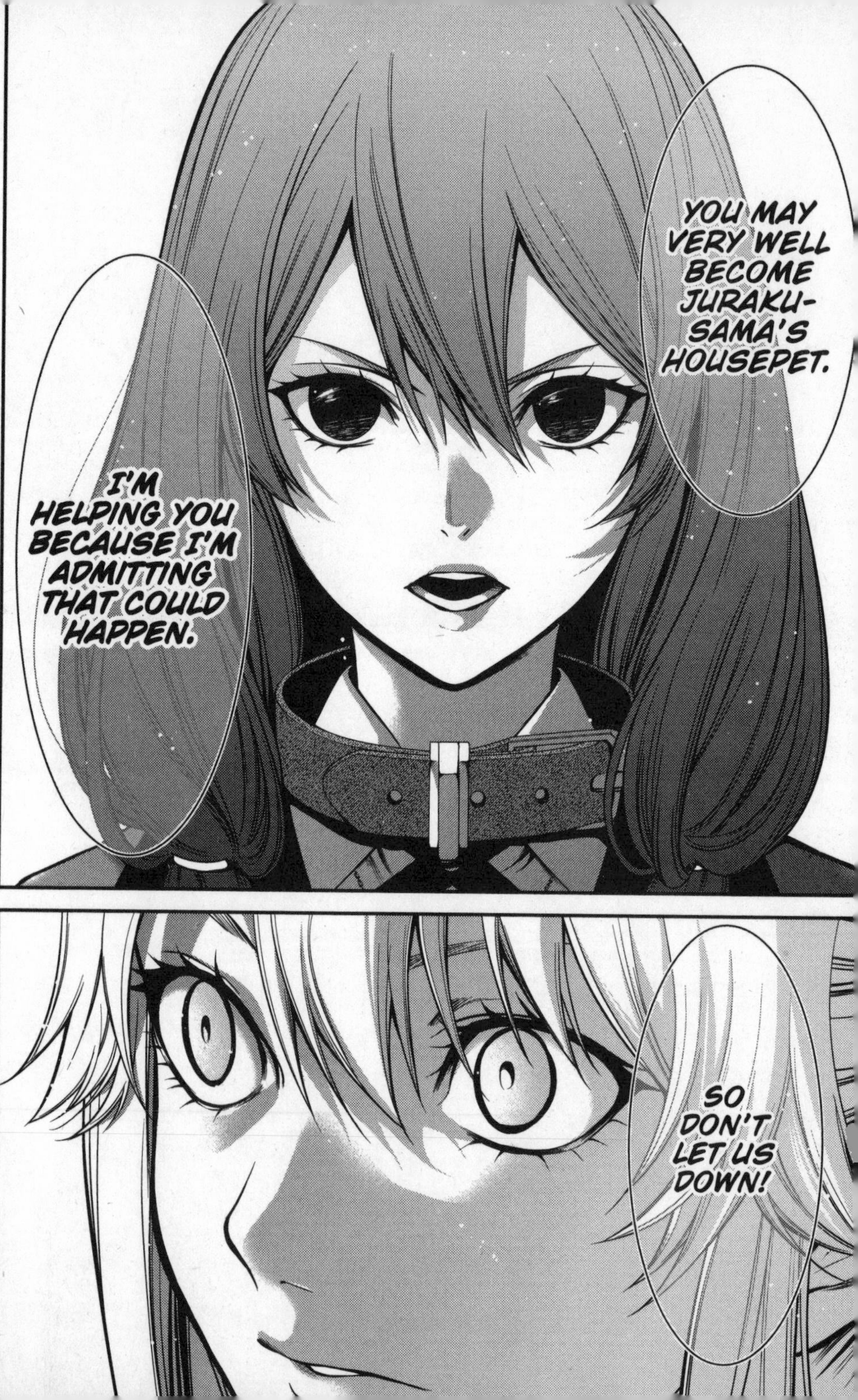
YOU MAY VERY WELL BECOME JURAKU-SAMA'S HOUSEPET.
I'M HELPING YOU BECAUSE I'M ADMITTING THAT COULD HAPPEN.
SO DON'T LET US DOWN!

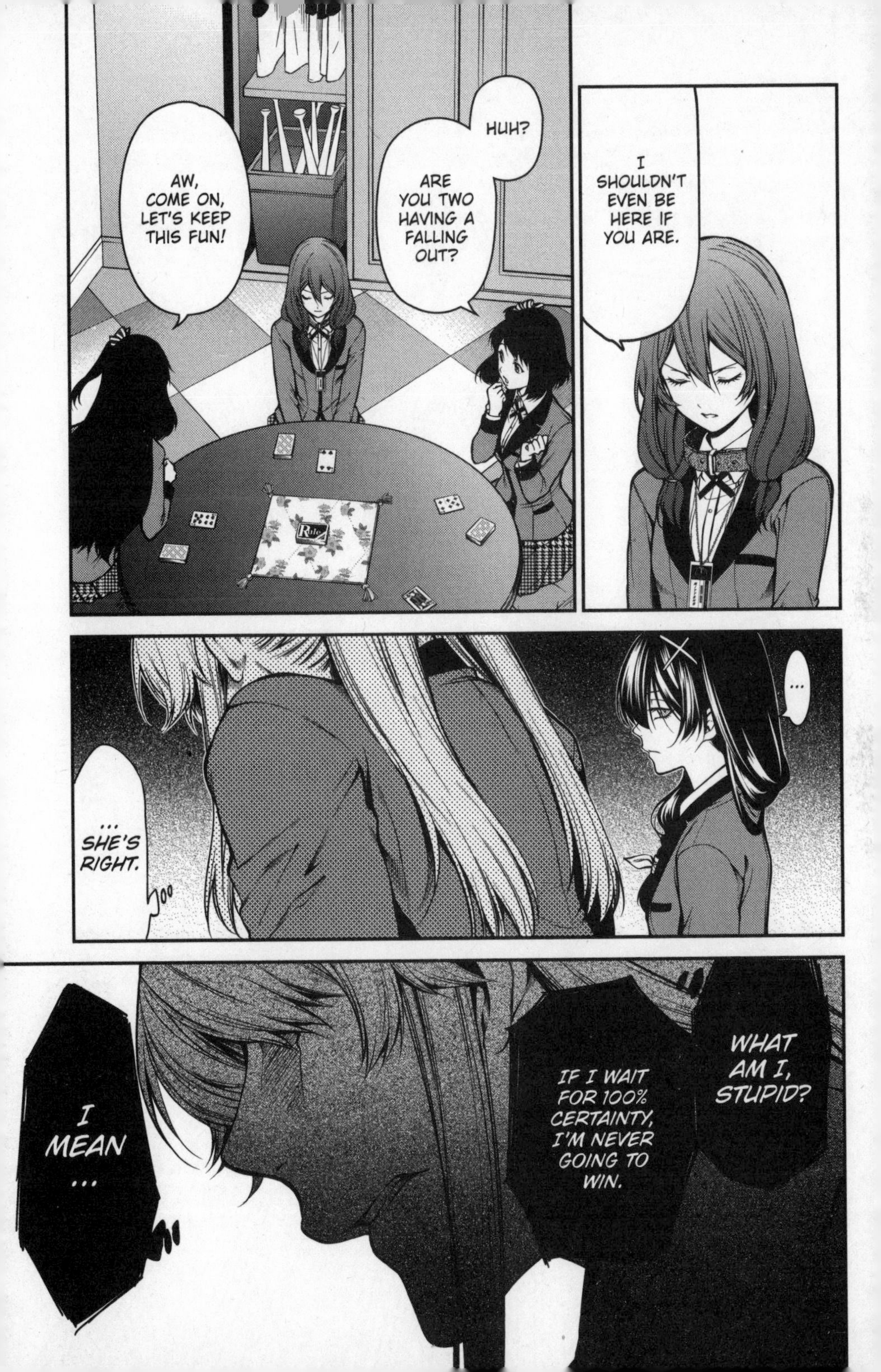
I SHOULDN'T EVEN BE HERE IF YOU ARE.
HUH?
ARE YOU TWO HAVING A FALLING OUT?
AW, COME ON, LET'S KEEP THIS FUN!
...
... SHE'S RIGHT.
WHAT AM I, STUPID?
IF I WAIT FOR 100% CERTAINTY, I'M NEVER GOING TO WIN.
I MEAN ...

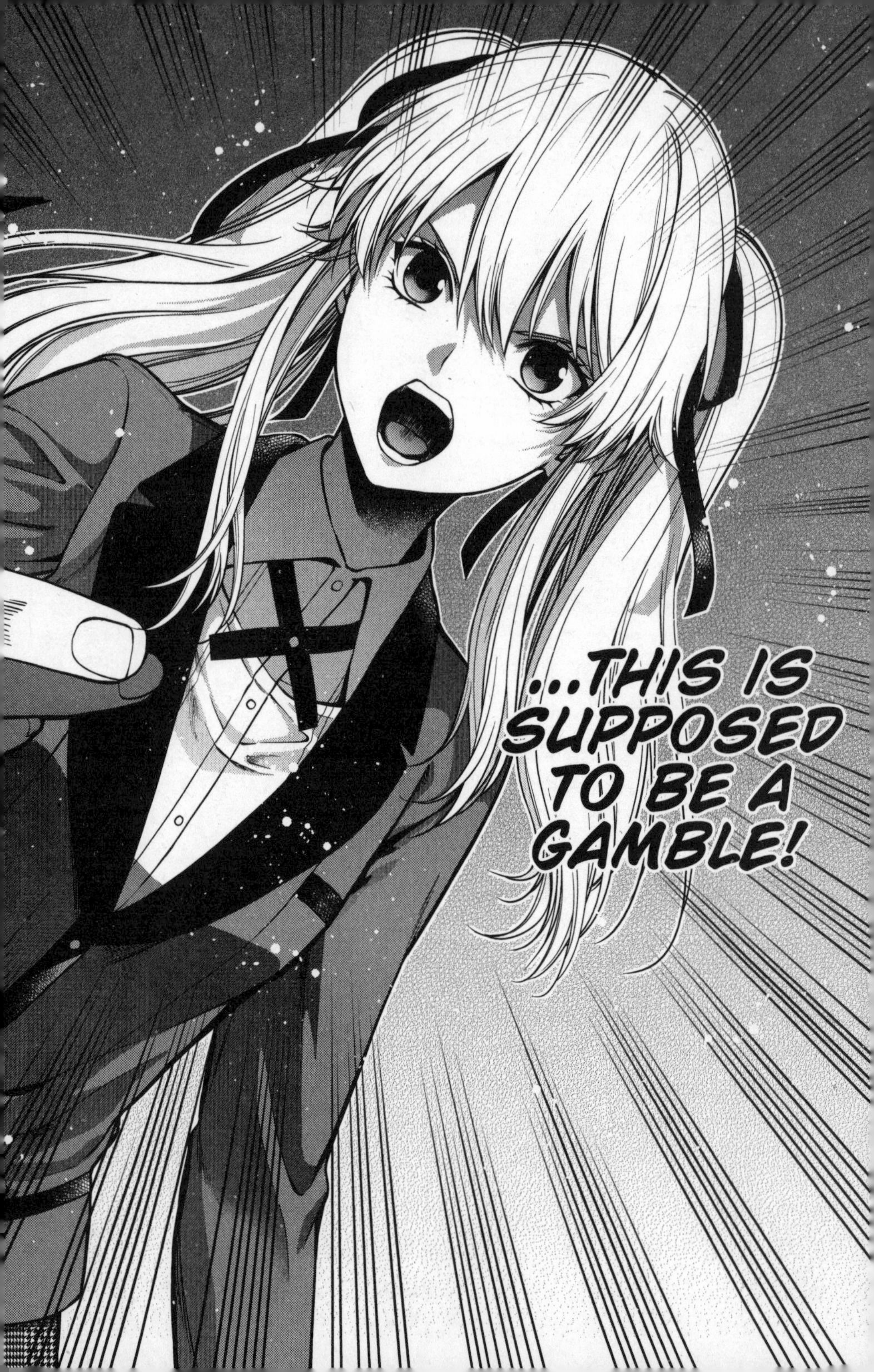
...THIS IS SUPPOSED TO BE A GAMBLE!

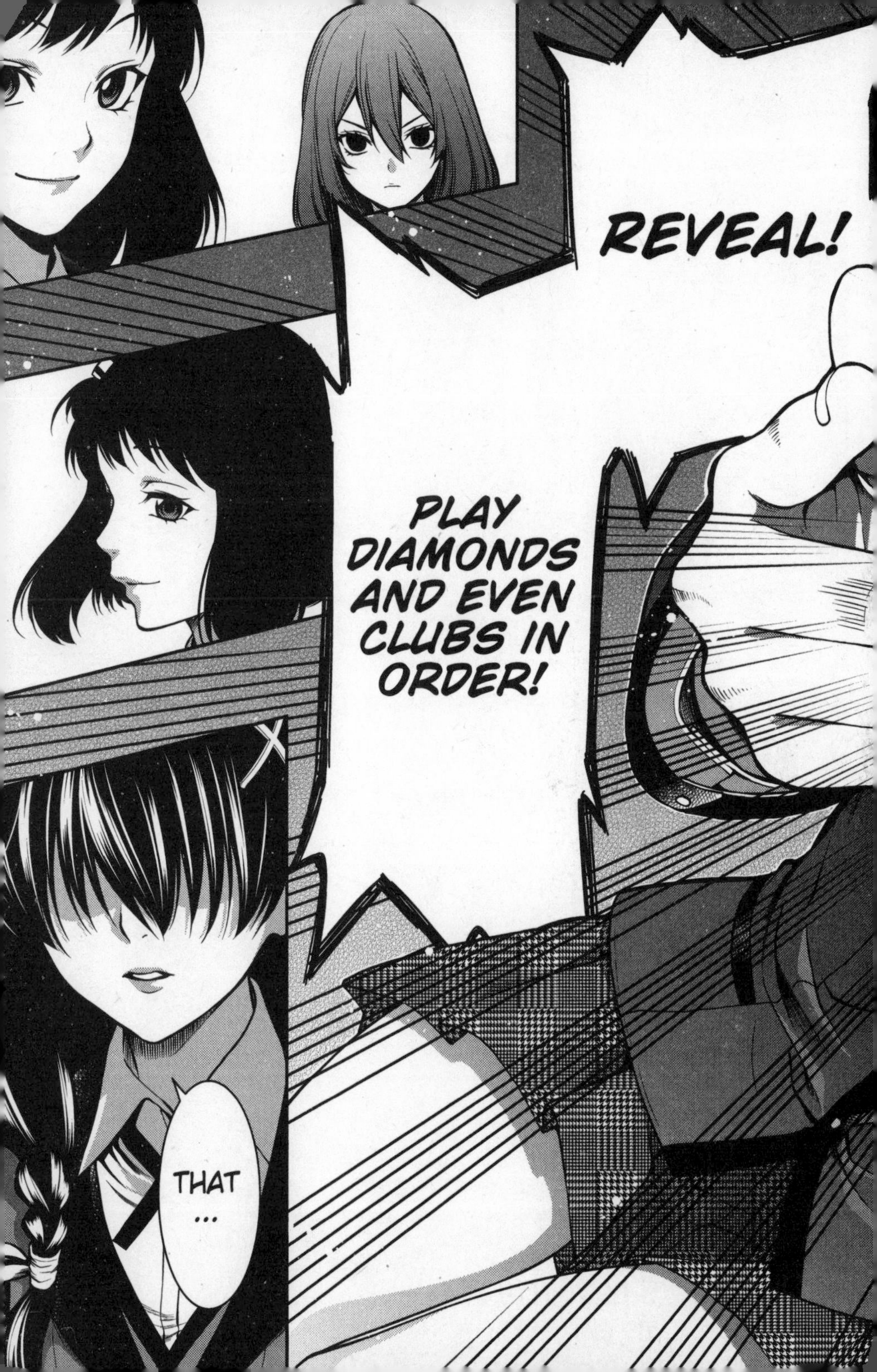
REVEAL!
PLAY DIAMONDS AND EVEN CLUBS IN ORDER!
THAT ...

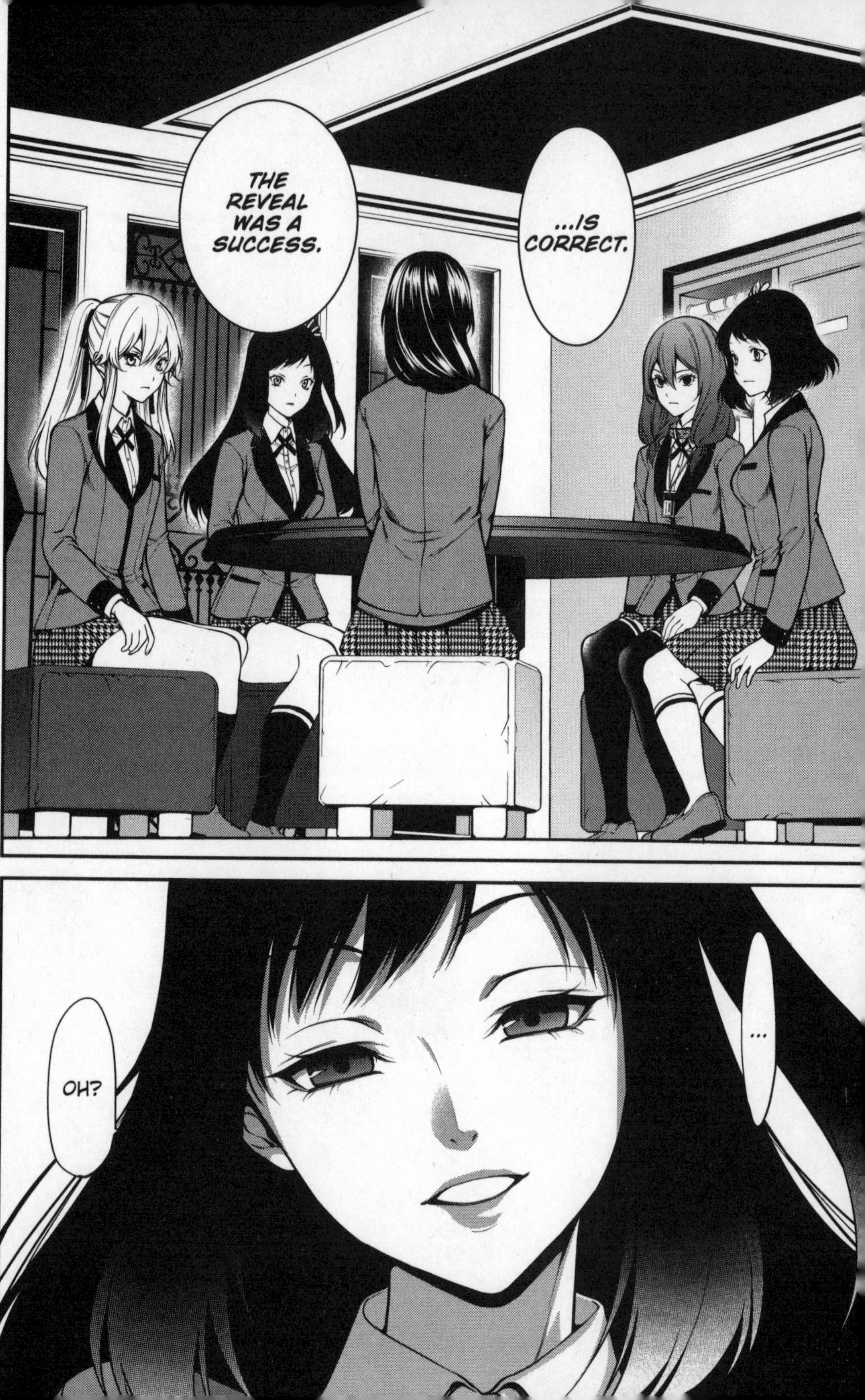
THE REVEAL WAS A SUCCESS.
...IS CORRECT.
...
OH?

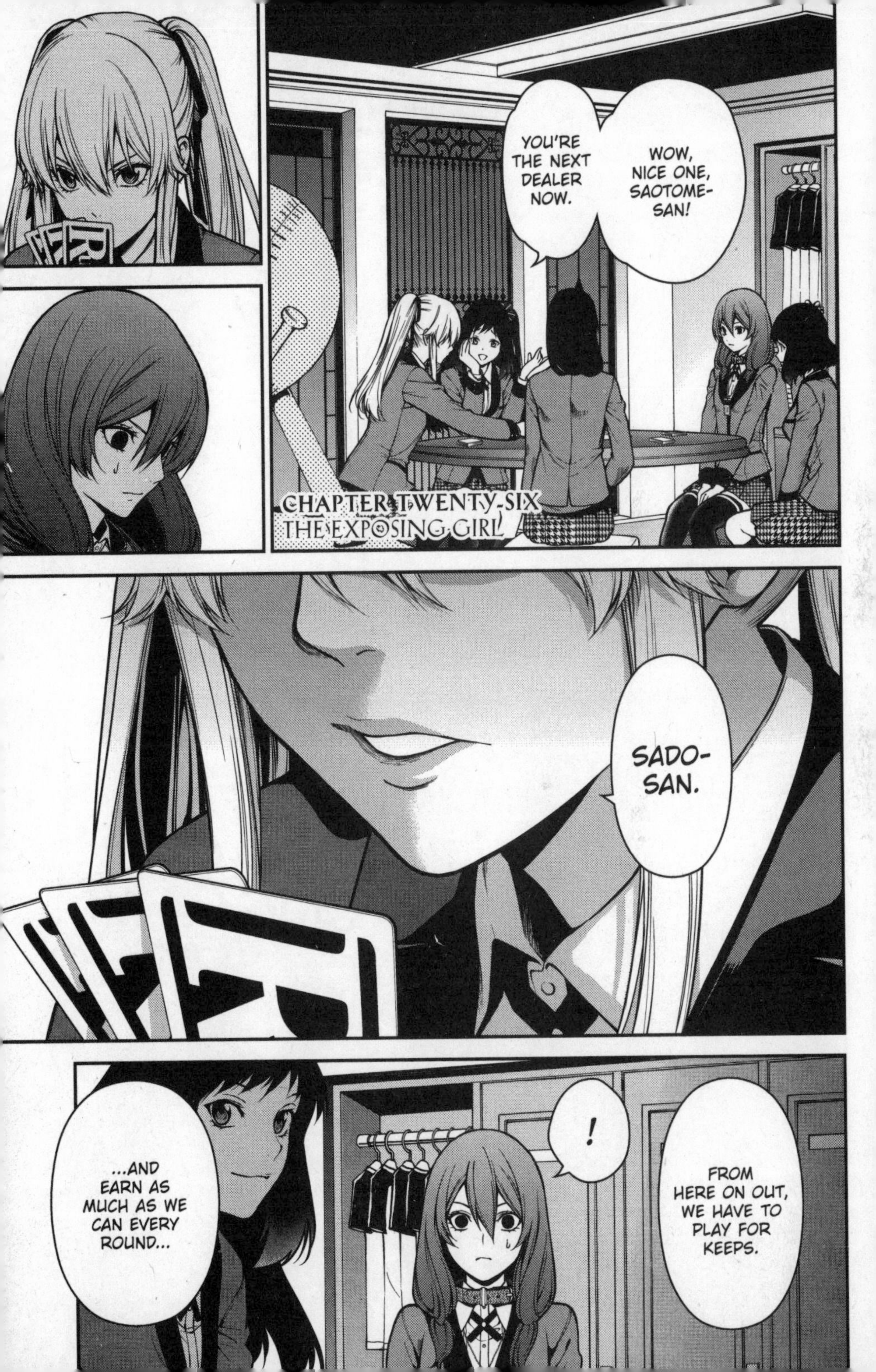
WOW, NICE ONE, SAOTOME-SAN!
YOU'RE THE NEXT DEALER NOW.
CHAPTER TWENTY-SIX THE EXPOSING GIRL
SADO-SAN.
FROM HERE ON OUT, WE HAVE TO PLAY FOR KEEPS.
!
...AND EARN AS MUCH AS WE CAN EVERY ROUND...

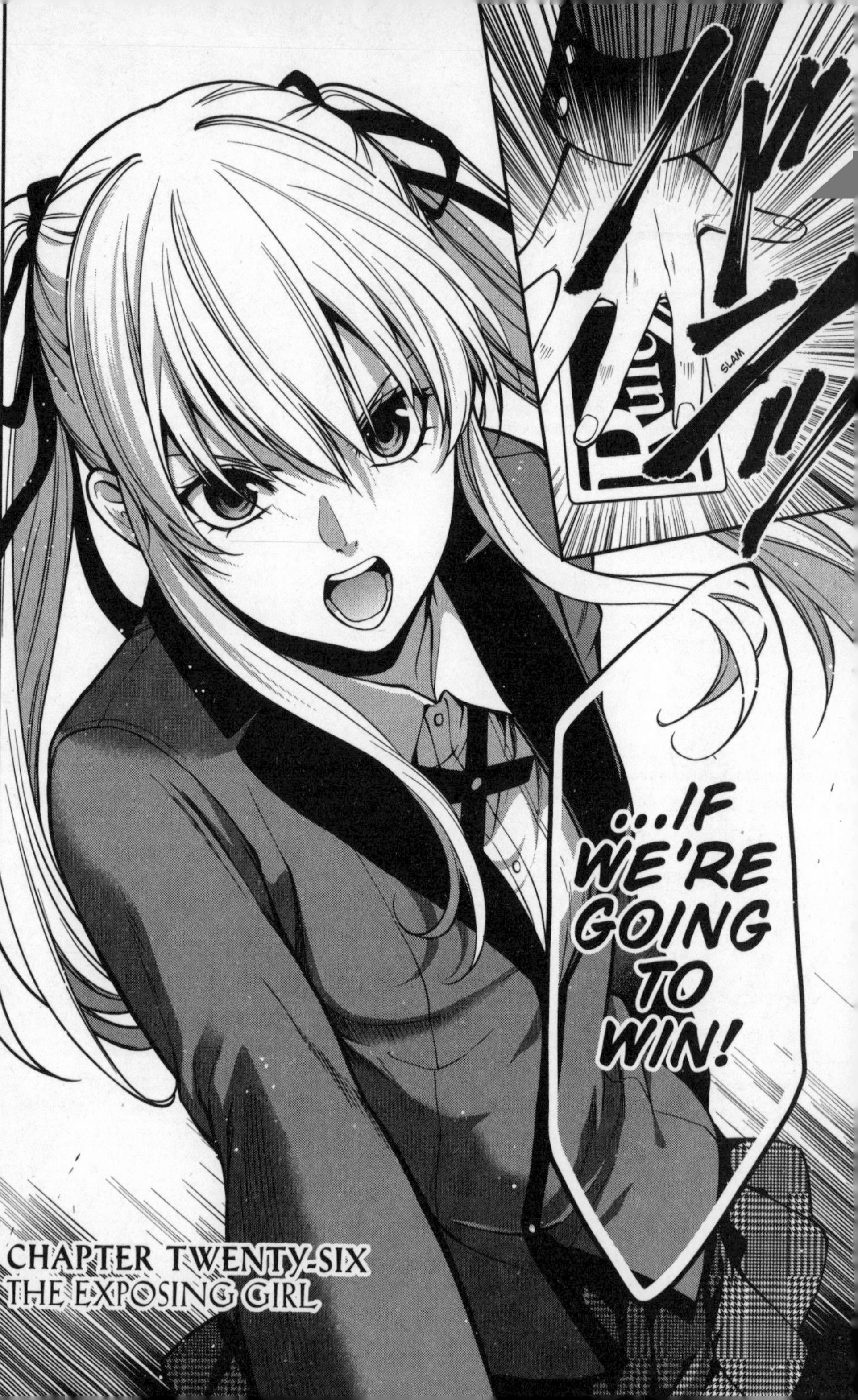
SLAM
...IF WE'RE GOING TO WIN!

CHAPTER TWENTY-SIX
THE EXPOSING GIRL

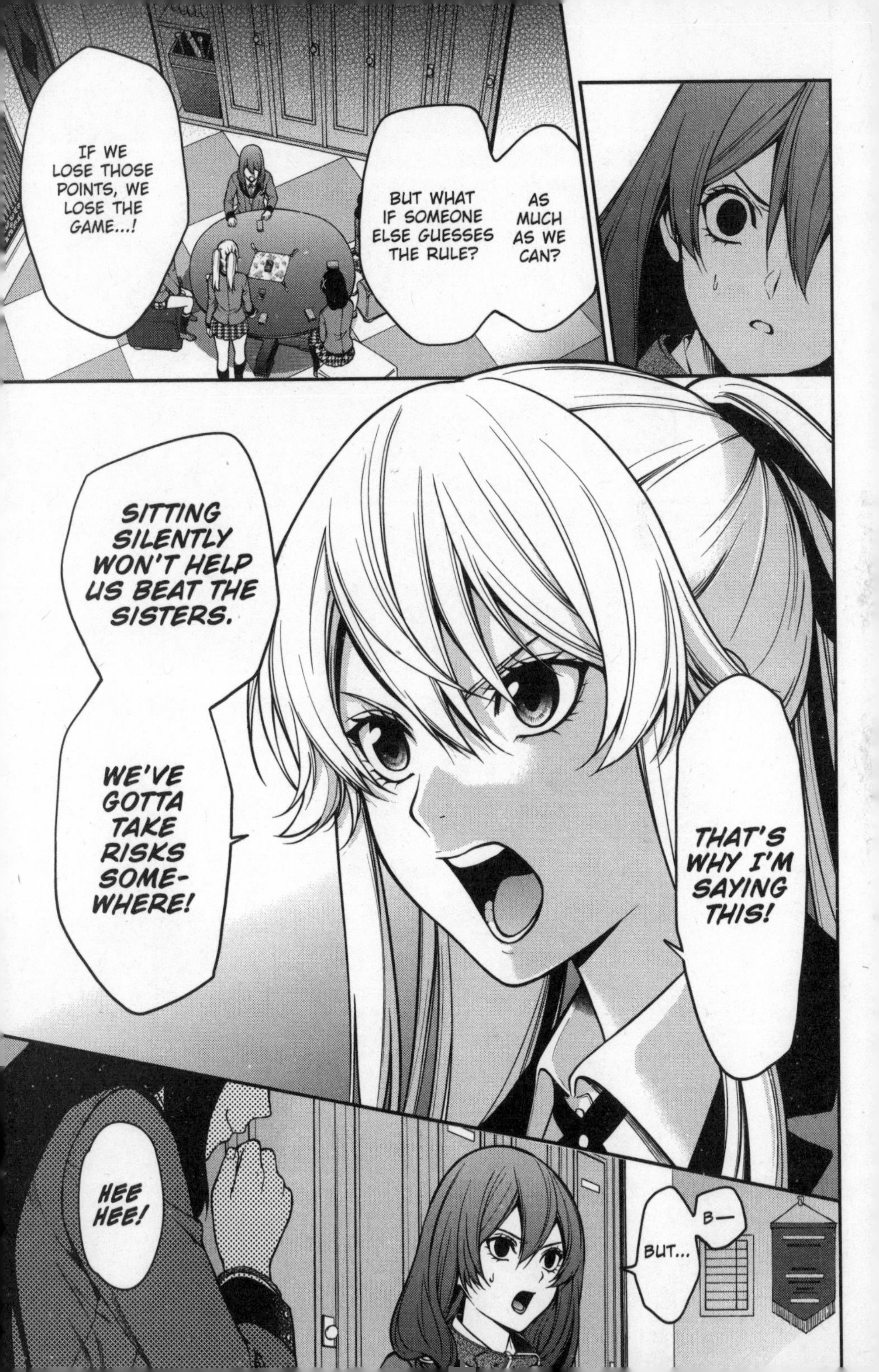
AS MUCH AS WE CAN?
BUT WHAT IF SOMEONE ELSE GUESSES THE RULE?
IF WE LOSE THOSE POINTS, WE LOSE THE GAME...!
SITTING SILENTLY WON'T HELP US BEAT THE SISTERS.
WE'VE GOTTA TAKE RISKS SOME-WHERE!
THAT'S WHY I'M SAYING THIS!
B—
BUT...
HEE HEE!

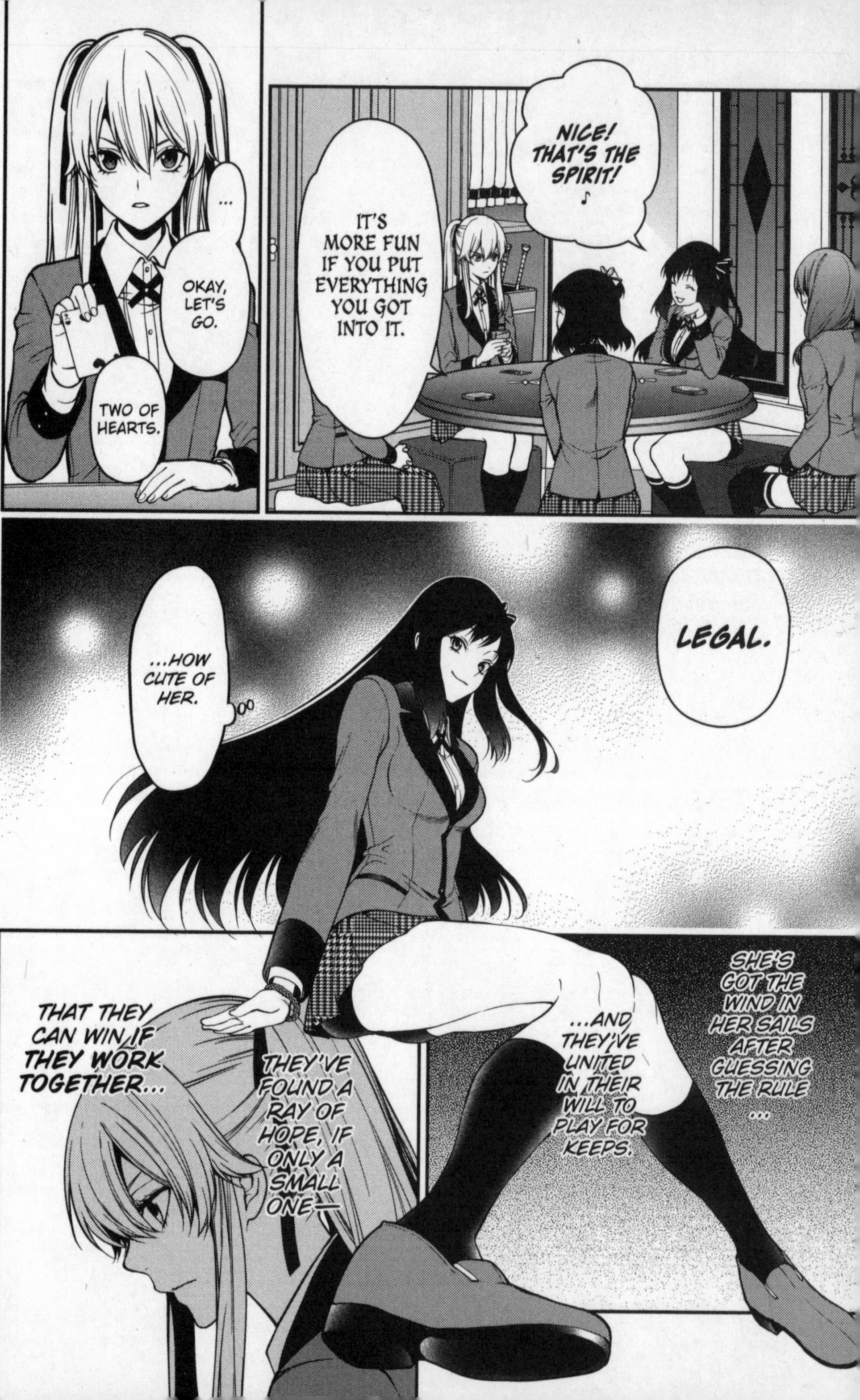
NICE! THAT'S THE SPIRIT! ♪
IT'S MORE FUN IF YOU PUT EVERYTHING YOU GOT INTO IT.
...
OKAY, LET'S GO.
TWO OF HEARTS.
LEGAL.
...HOW CUTE OF HER.
SHE'S GOT THE WIND IN HER SAILS AFTER GUESSING THE RULE...
...AND THEY'VE UNITED IN THEIR WILL TO PLAY FOR KEEPS.
THEY'VE FOUND A RAY OF HOPE, IF ONLY A SMALL ONE—
THAT THEY CAN WIN IF THEY WORK TOGETHER...

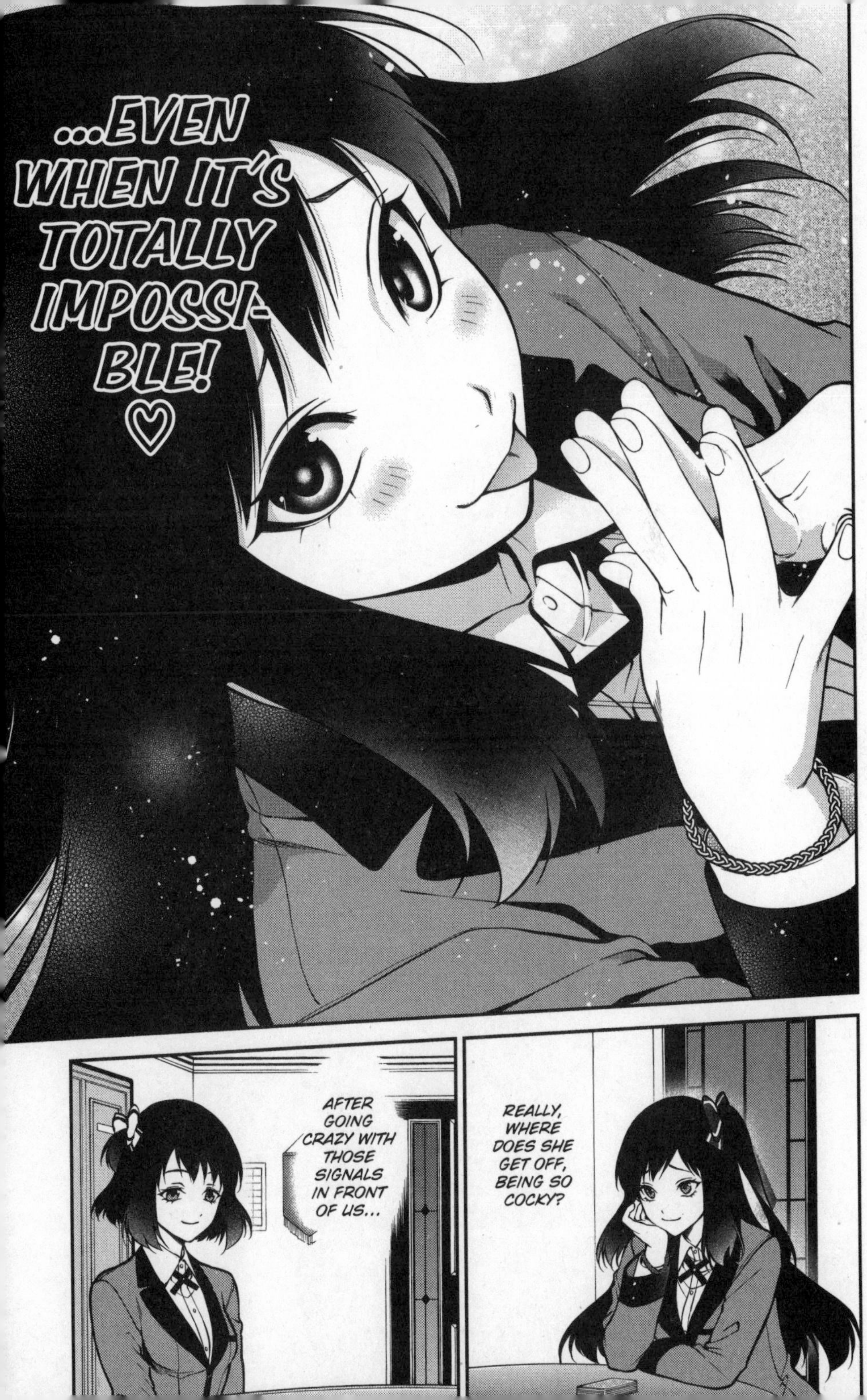
...EVEN WHEN IT'S TOTALLY IMPOSSIBLE! ♡
REALLY, WHERE DOES SHE GET OFF, BEING SO COCKY?
AFTER GOING CRAZY WITH THOSE SIGNALS IN FRONT OF US...

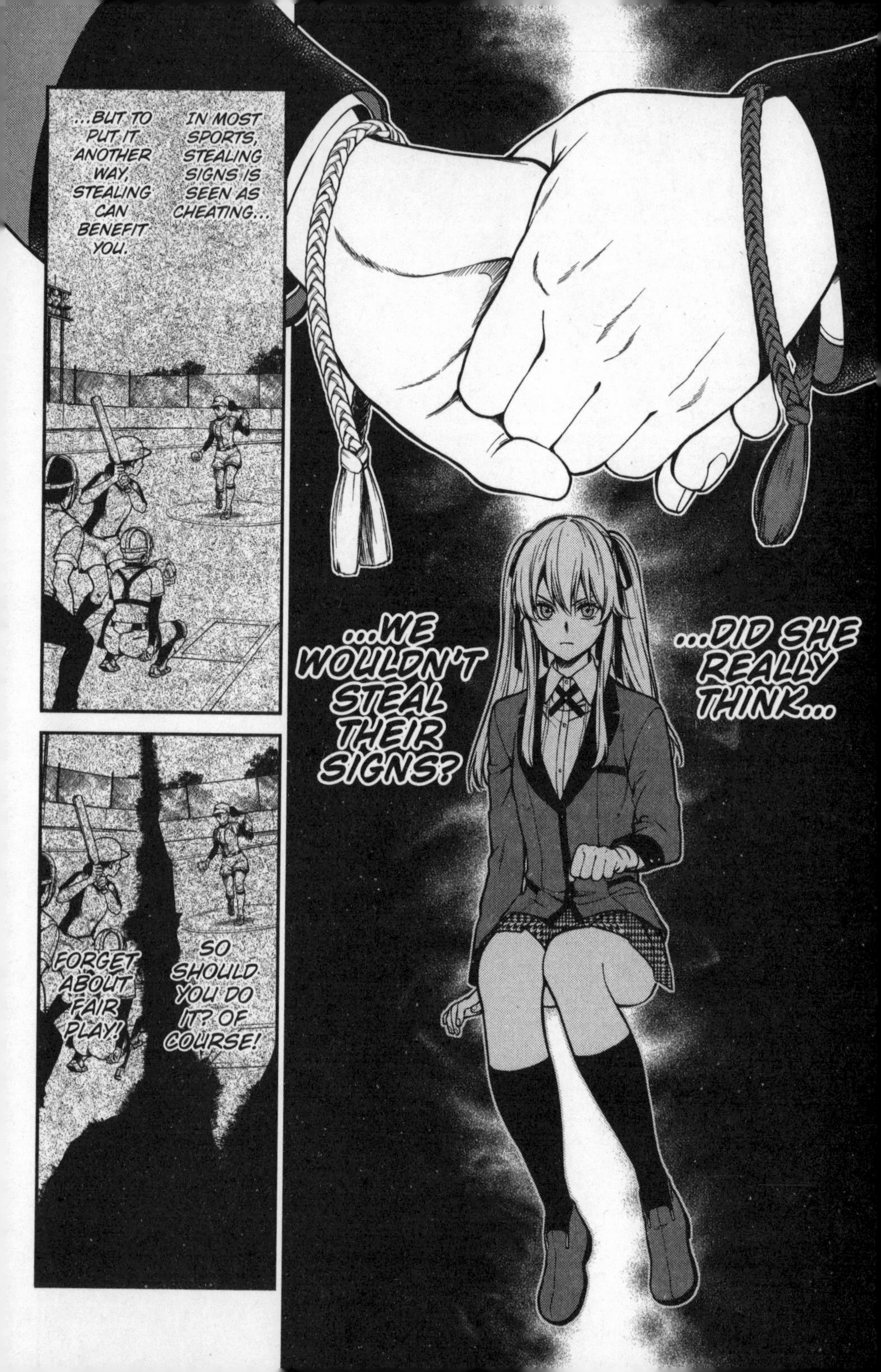
...DID SHE REALLY THINK...
...WE WOULDN'T STEAL THEIR SIGNS?
IN MOST SPORTS, STEALING SIGNS IS SEEN AS CHEATING...
...BUT TO PUT IT ANOTHER WAY, STEALING CAN BENEFIT YOU.
SO SHOULD YOU DO IT? OF COURSE!
FORGET ABOUT FAIR PLAY!

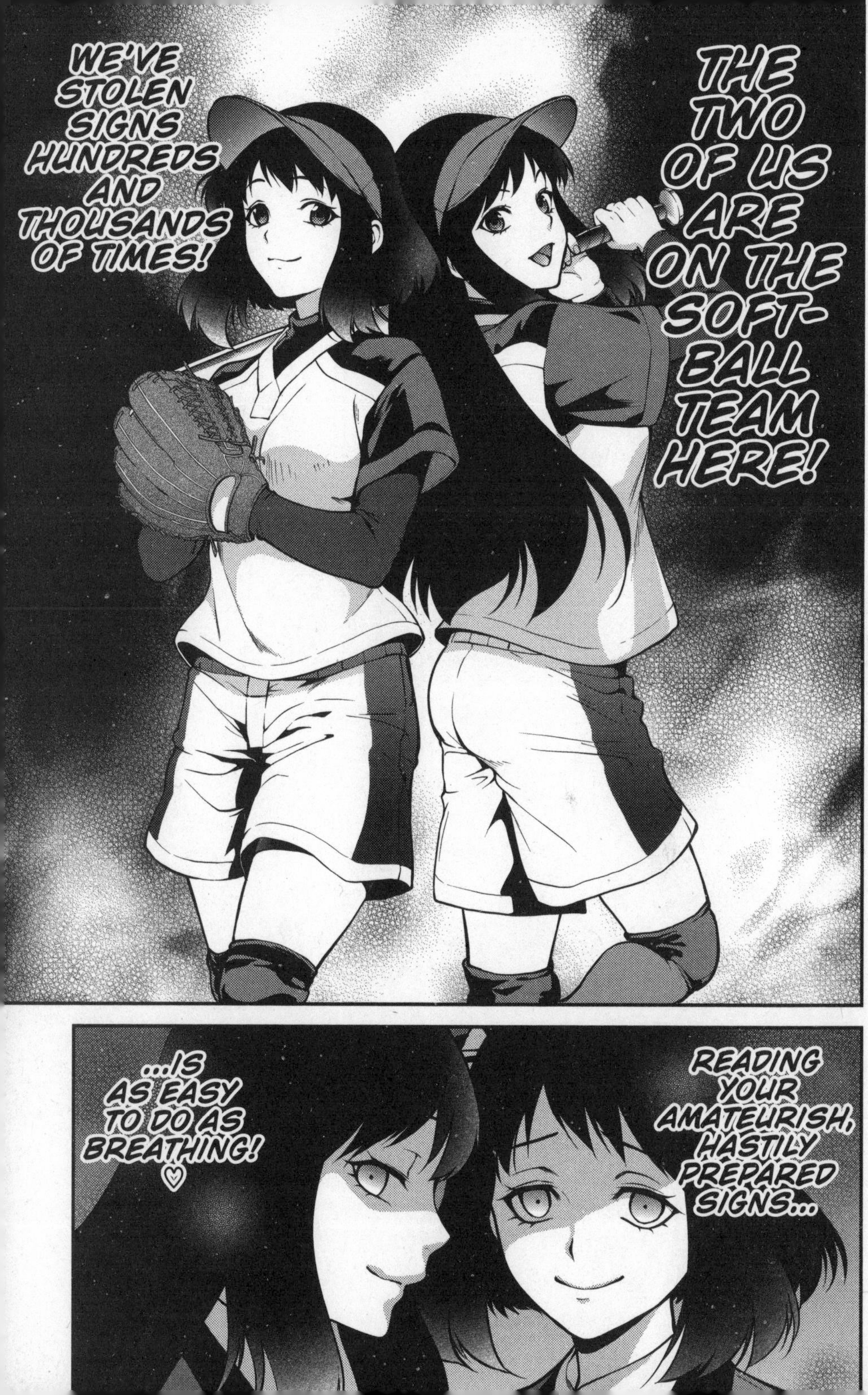
THE TWO OF US ARE ON THE SOFT-BALL TEAM HERE!
WE'VE STOLEN SIGNS HUNDREDS AND THOUSANDS OF TIMES!
READING YOUR AMATEURISH, HASTILY PREPARED SIGNS...
...IS AS EASY TO DO AS BREATHING! ♡

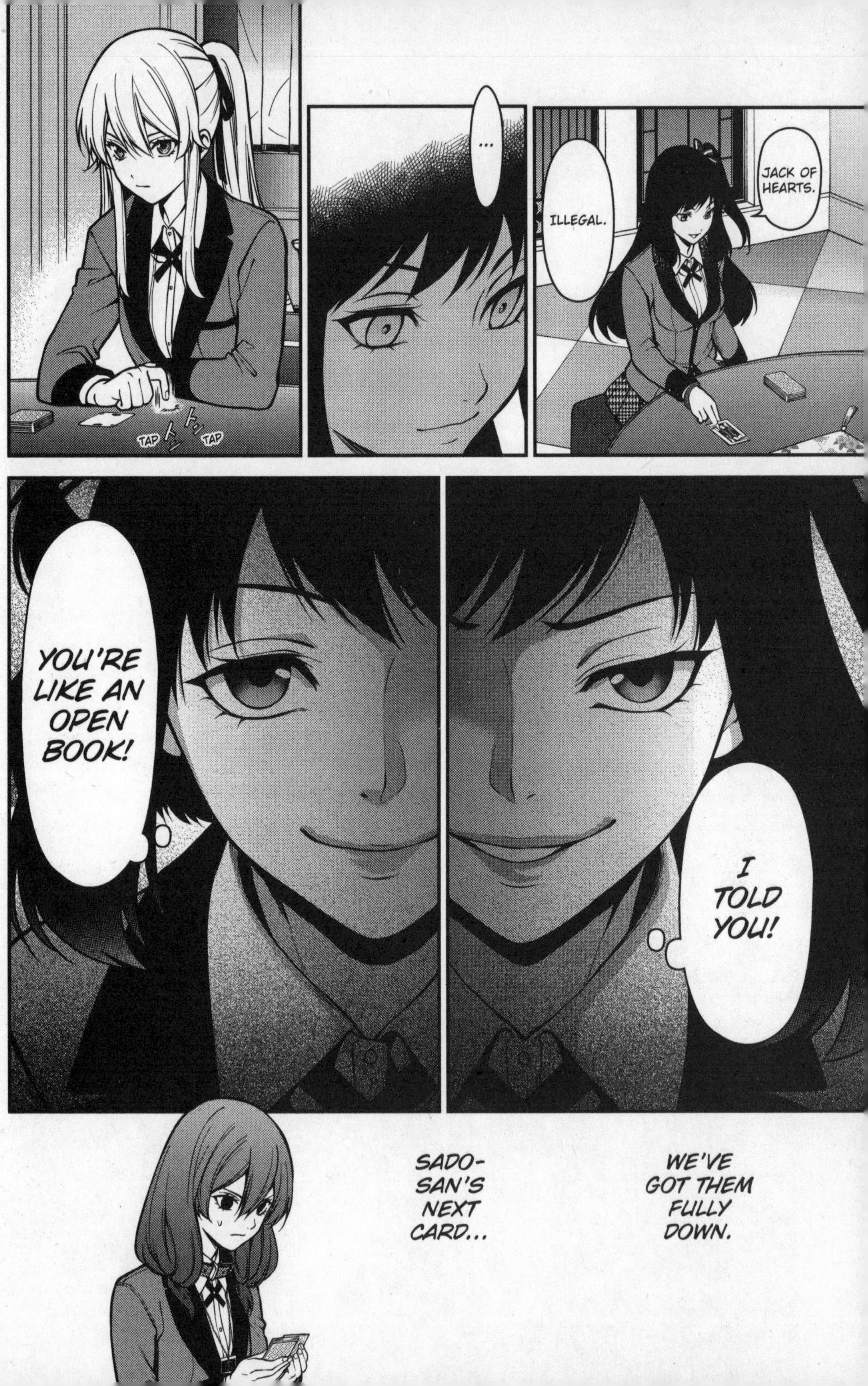
JACK OF HEARTS.
ILLEGAL.
...
TAP
TAP
I TOLD YOU!
YOU'RE LIKE AN OPEN BOOK!
WE'VE GOT THEM FULLY DOWN.
SADO-SAN'S NEXT CARD...

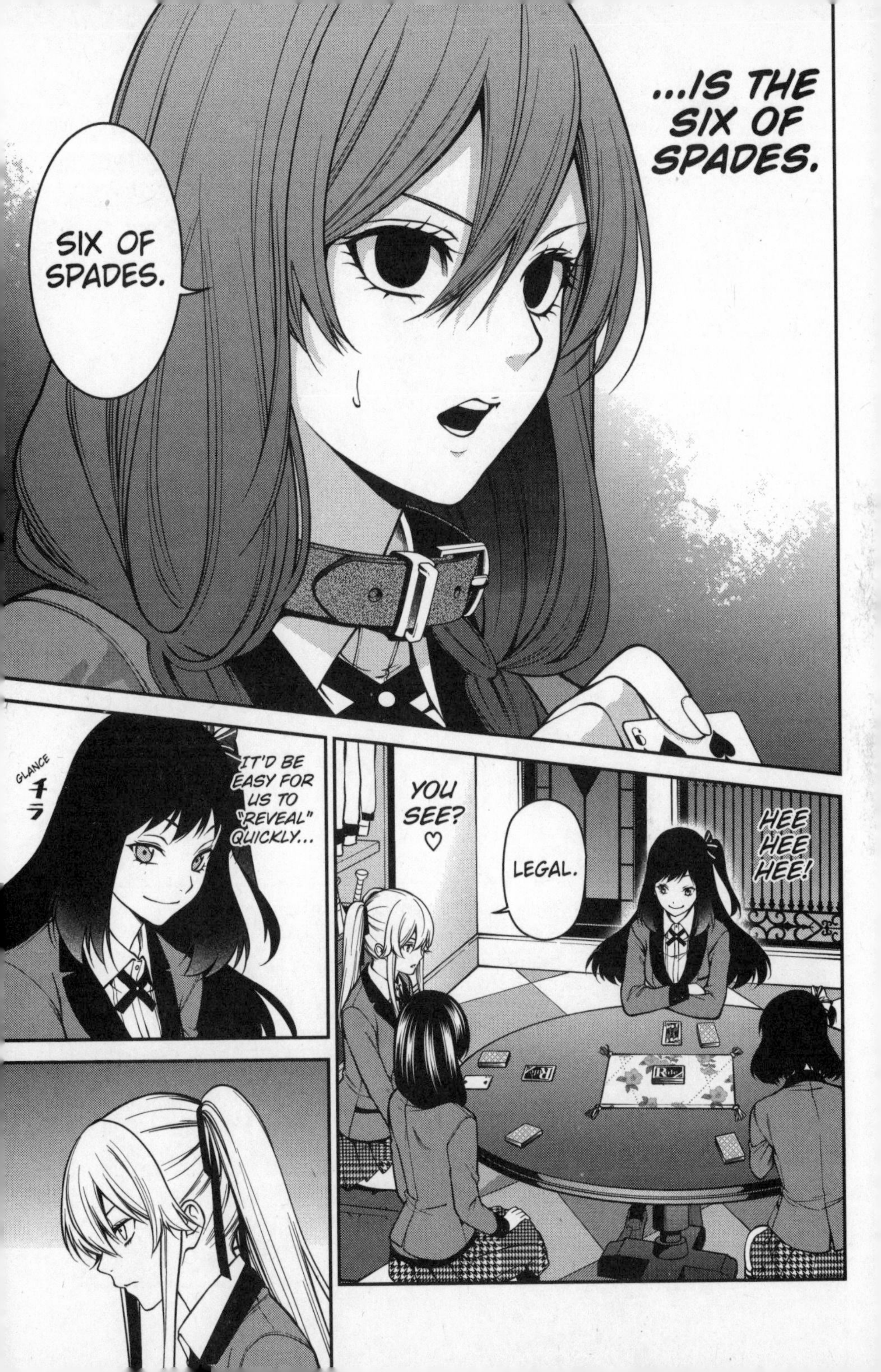
...IS THE SIX OF SPADES.
SIX OF SPADES.
HEE HEE HEE!
LEGAL.
YOU SEE? ♡
IT'D BE EASY FOR US TO "REVEAL" QUICKLY...
GLANCE
チラ

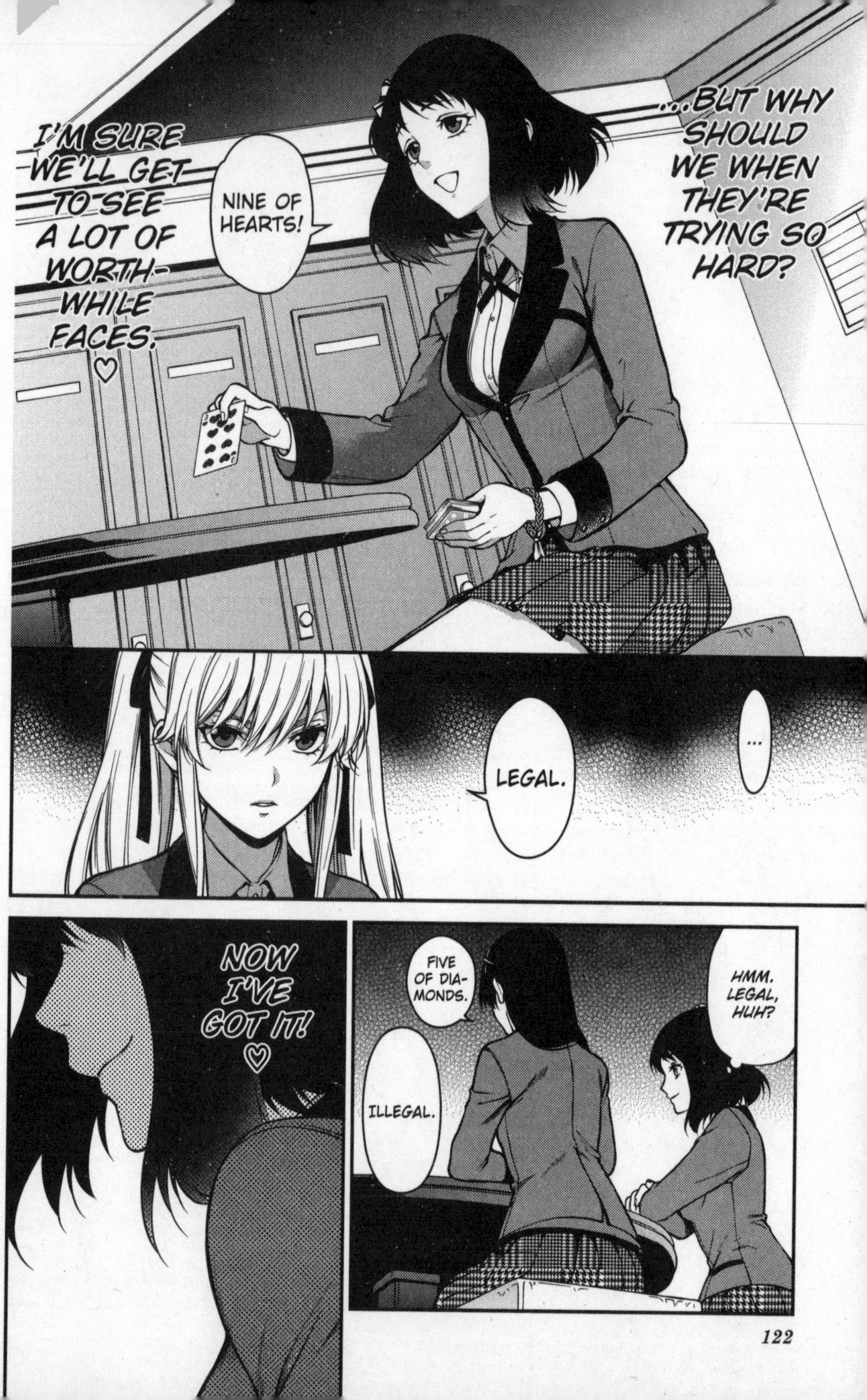
...BUT WHY SHOULD WE WHEN THEY'RE TRYING SO HARD?
NINE OF HEARTS!
I'M SURE WE'LL GET TO SEE A LOT OF WORTH-WHILE FACES. ♡
...
LEGAL.
HMM. LEGAL, HUH?
FIVE OF DIA-MONDS.
ILLEGAL.
NOW I'VE GOT IT! ♡

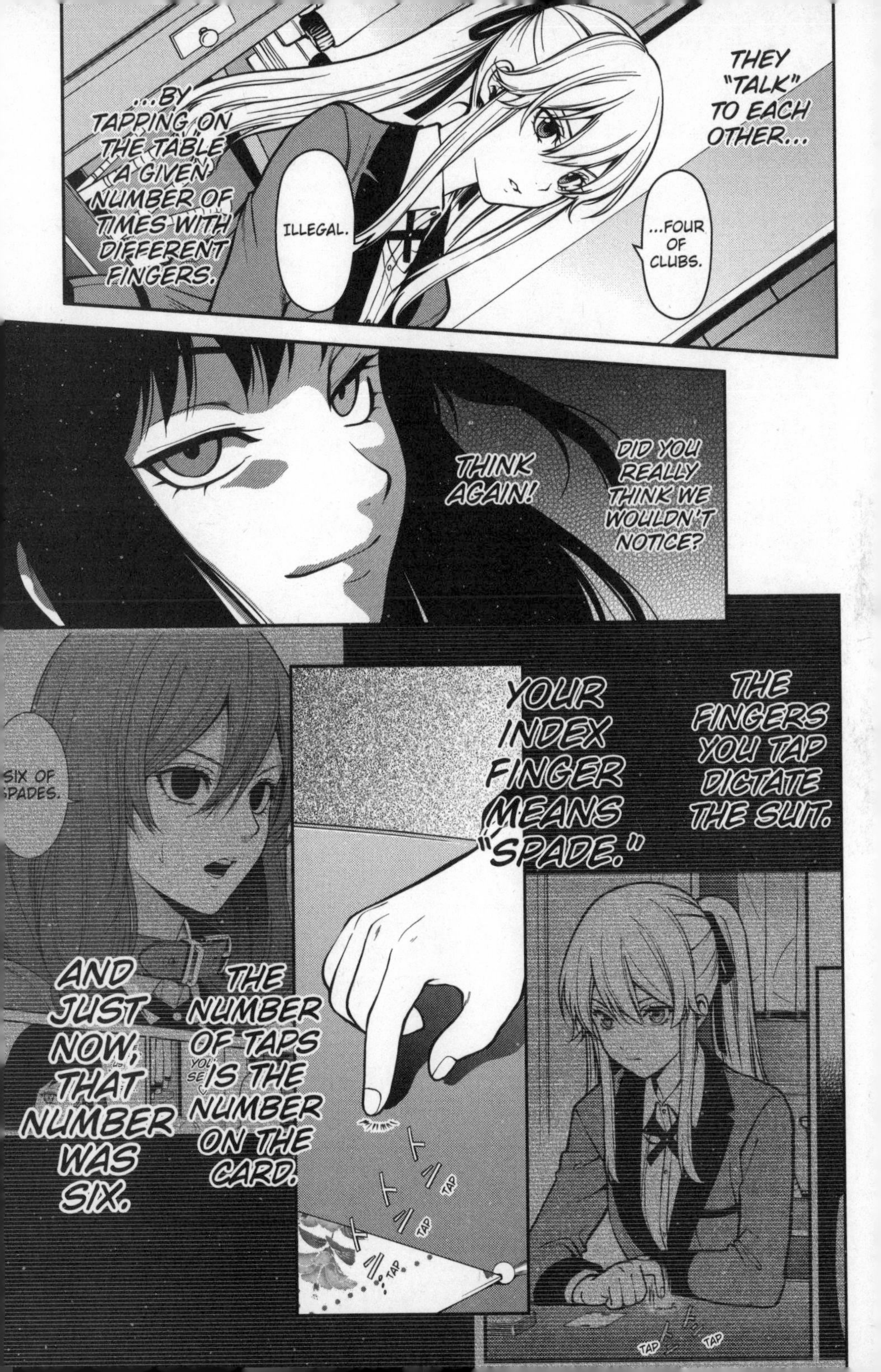
THEY "TALK" TO EACH OTHER...
...FOUR OF CLUBS.
ILLEGAL.
...BY TAPPING ON THE TABLE A GIVEN NUMBER OF TIMES WITH DIFFERENT FINGERS.
DID YOU REALLY THINK WE WOULDN'T NOTICE?
THINK AGAIN!
THE FINGERS YOU TAP DICTATE THE SUIT.
YOUR INDEX FINGER MEANS "SPADE."
TAP TAP
TAP TAP TAP
THE NUMBER OF TAPS IS THE NUMBER ON THE CARD.
AND JUST NOW, THAT NUMBER WAS SIX.
SIX OF SPADES.

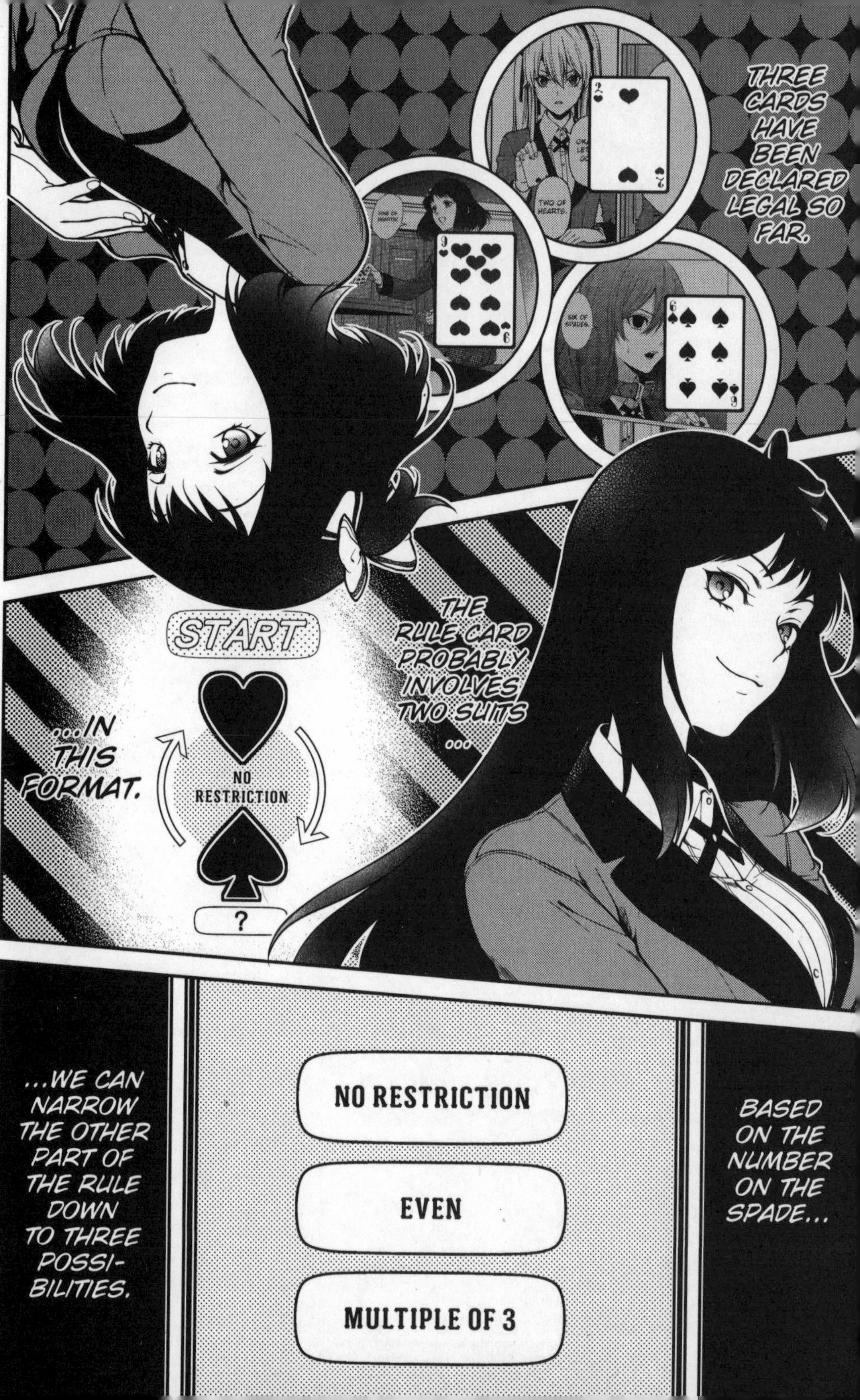
THREE CARDS HAVE BEEN DECLARED LEGAL SO FAR.
TWO OF HEARTS.
SIX OF SPADES.
THE RULE CARD PROBABLY INVOLVES TWO SUITS...
...IN THIS FORMAT.
START
NO RESTRICTION
?
BASED ON THE NUMBER ON THE SPADE...
...WE CAN NARROW THE OTHER PART OF THE RULE DOWN TO THREE POSSI-BILITIES.
NO RESTRICTION
EVEN
MULTIPLE OF 3

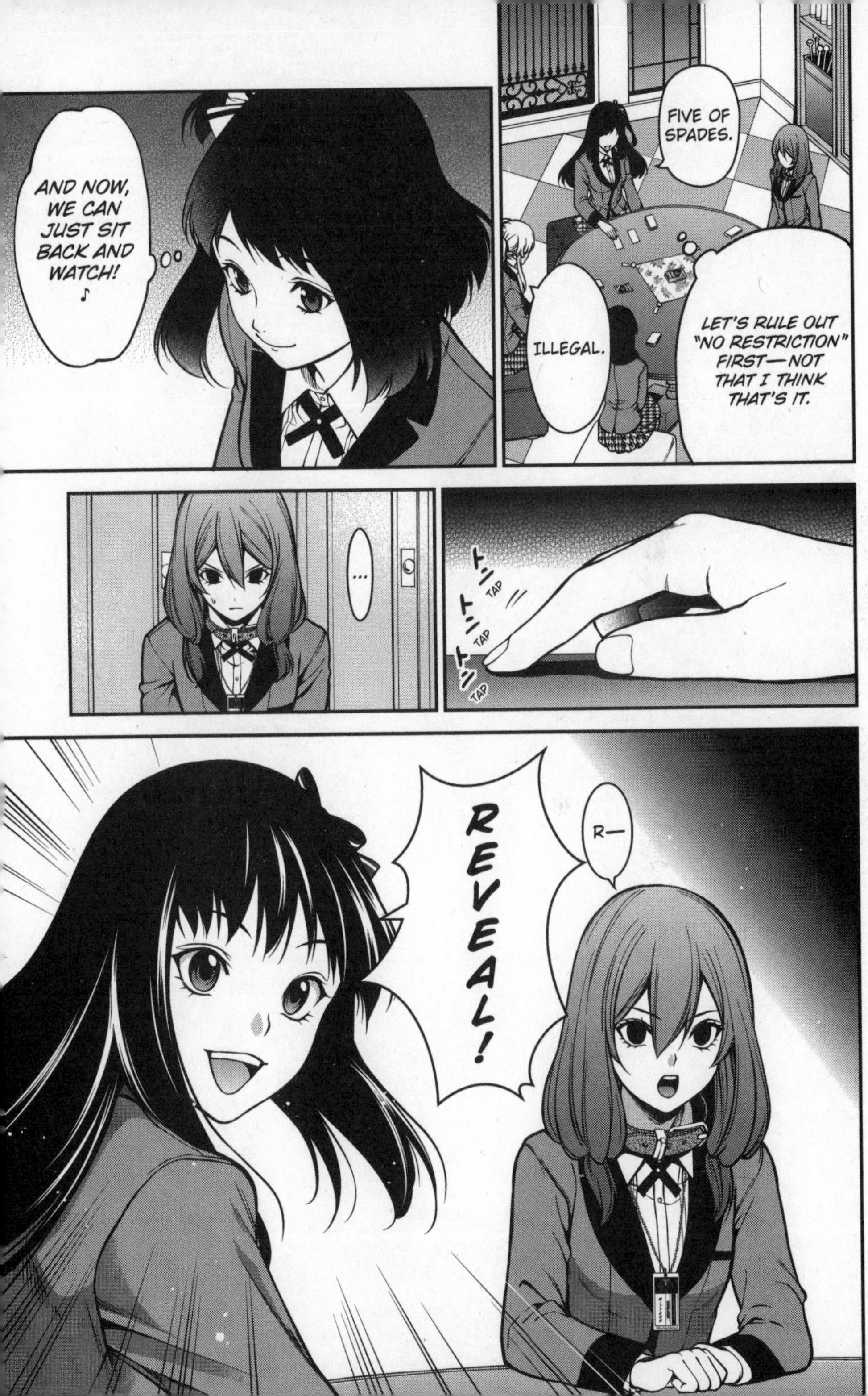
FIVE OF SPADES.
LET'S RULE OUT "NO RESTRICTION" FIRST—NOT THAT I THINK THAT'S IT.
ILLEGAL.
AND NOW, WE CAN JUST SIT BACK AND WATCH! ♪
TAP
TAP
TAP
...
R—
REVEAL!

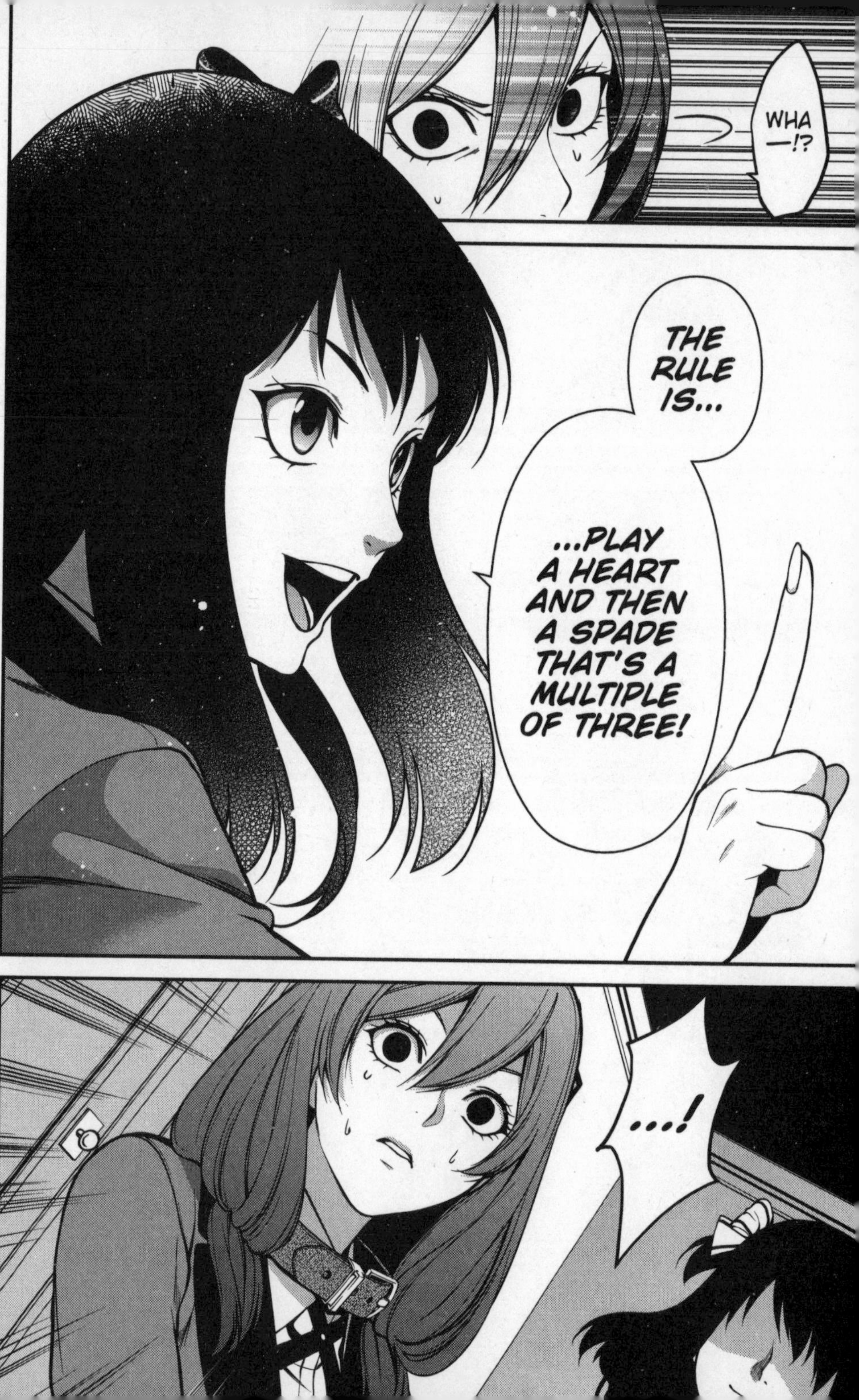
WHA—!?
THE RULE IS...
...PLAY A HEART AND THEN A SPADE THAT'S A MULTIPLE OF THREE!
...!

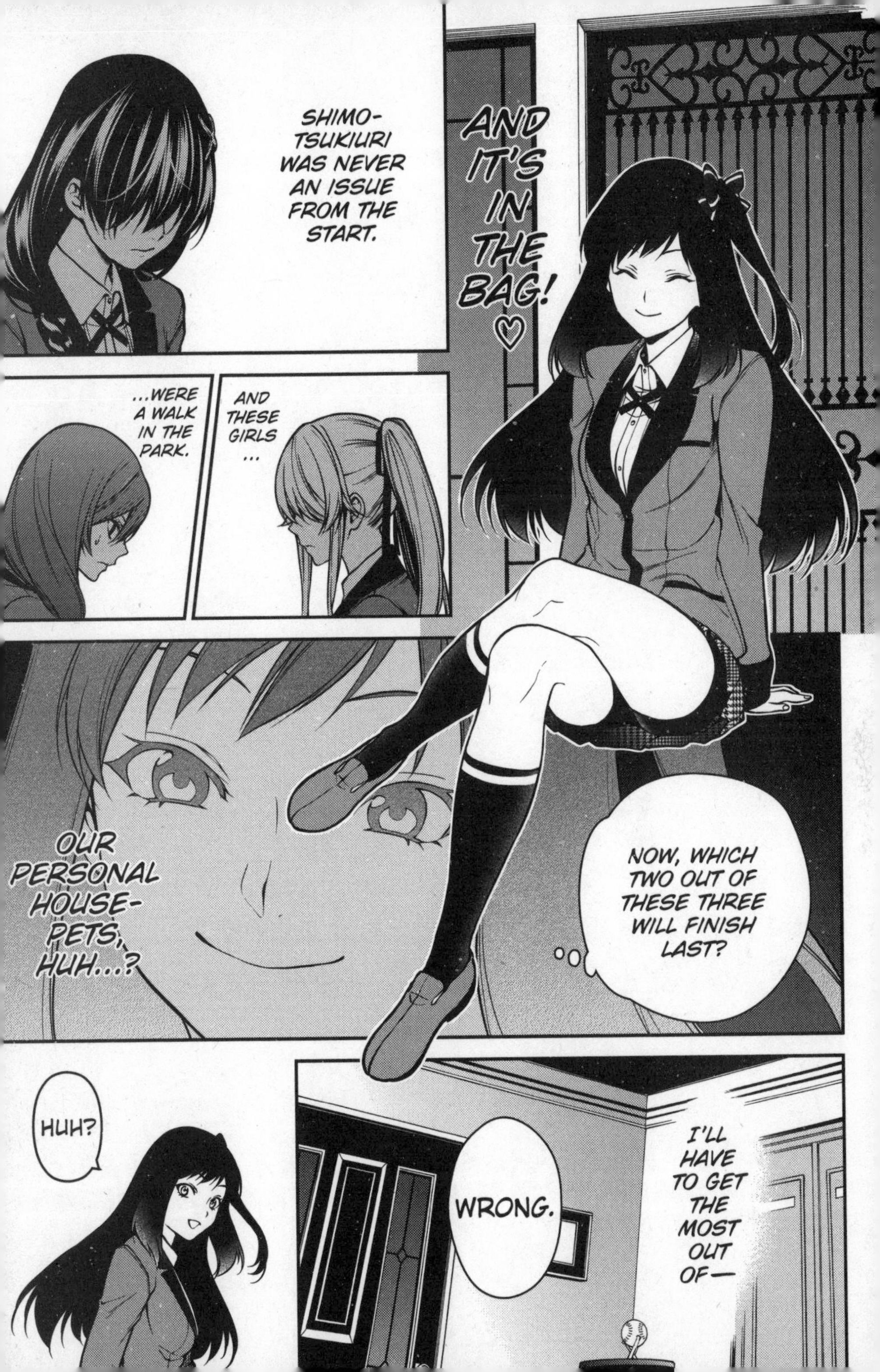
AND IT'S IN THE BAG! ♡
SHIMO-TSUKIURI WAS NEVER AN ISSUE FROM THE START.
AND THESE GIRLS ...
...WERE A WALK IN THE PARK.
NOW, WHICH TWO OUT OF THESE THREE WILL FINISH LAST?
OUR PERSONAL HOUSE-PETS, HUH...?
I'LL HAVE TO GET THE MOST OUT OF—
WRONG.
HUH?

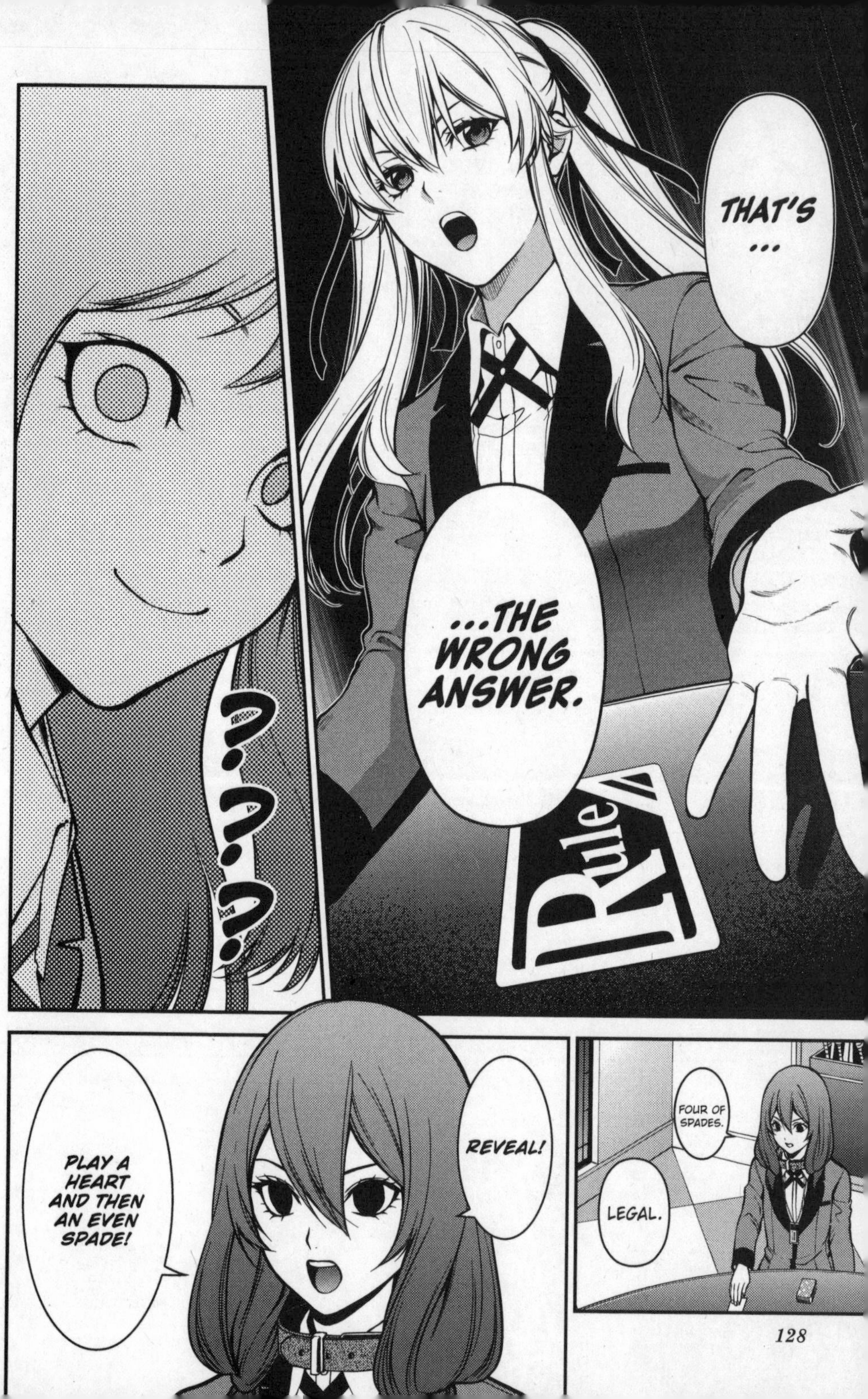
THAT'S ...
...THE WRONG ANSWER.
?!?!?!
FOUR OF SPADES.
LEGAL.
REVEAL!
PLAY A HEART AND THEN AN EVEN SPADE!

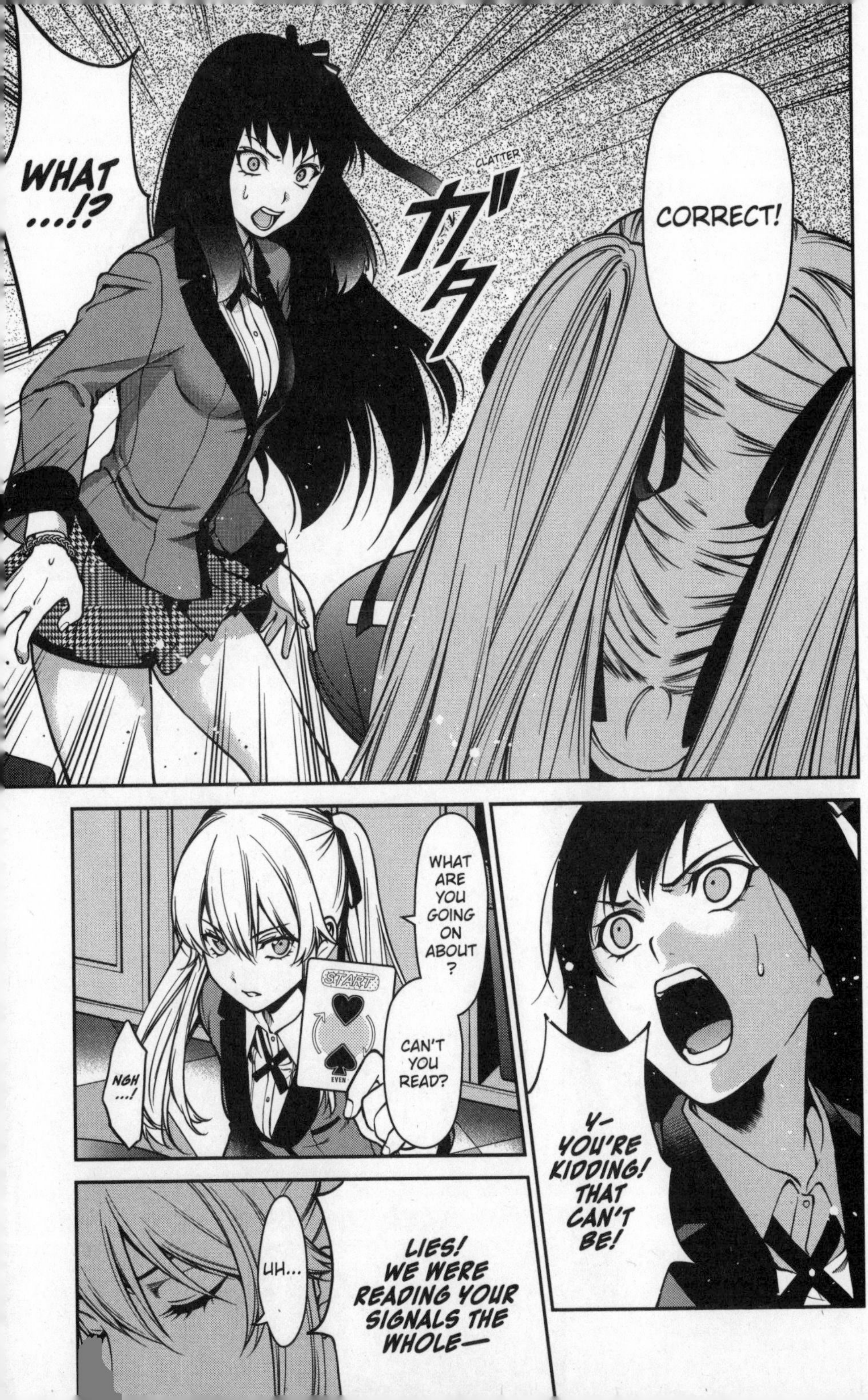
CORRECT!
CLATTER
WHAT ...!?
Y- YOU'RE KIDDING! THAT CAN'T BE!
WHAT ARE YOU GOING ON ABOUT?
CAN'T YOU READ?
START
EVEN
NGH ...!
LIES! WE WERE READING YOUR SIGNALS THE WHOLE—
UH...

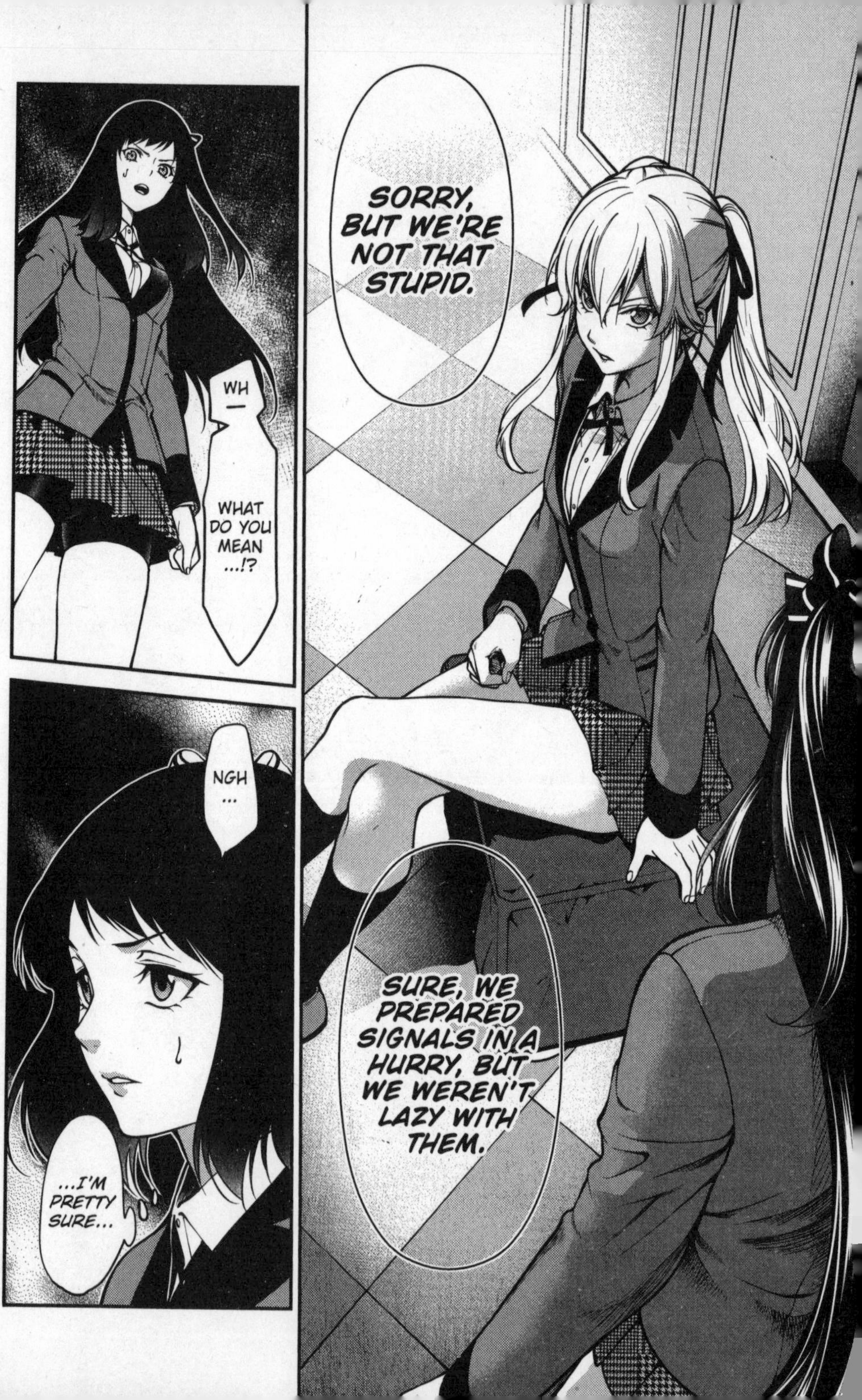
SORRY, BUT WE'RE NOT THAT STUPID.
SURE, WE PREPARED SIGNALS IN A HURRY, BUT WE WEREN'T LAZY WITH THEM.
WH—
WHAT DO YOU MEAN ...!?
NGH ...
...I'M PRETTY SURE...

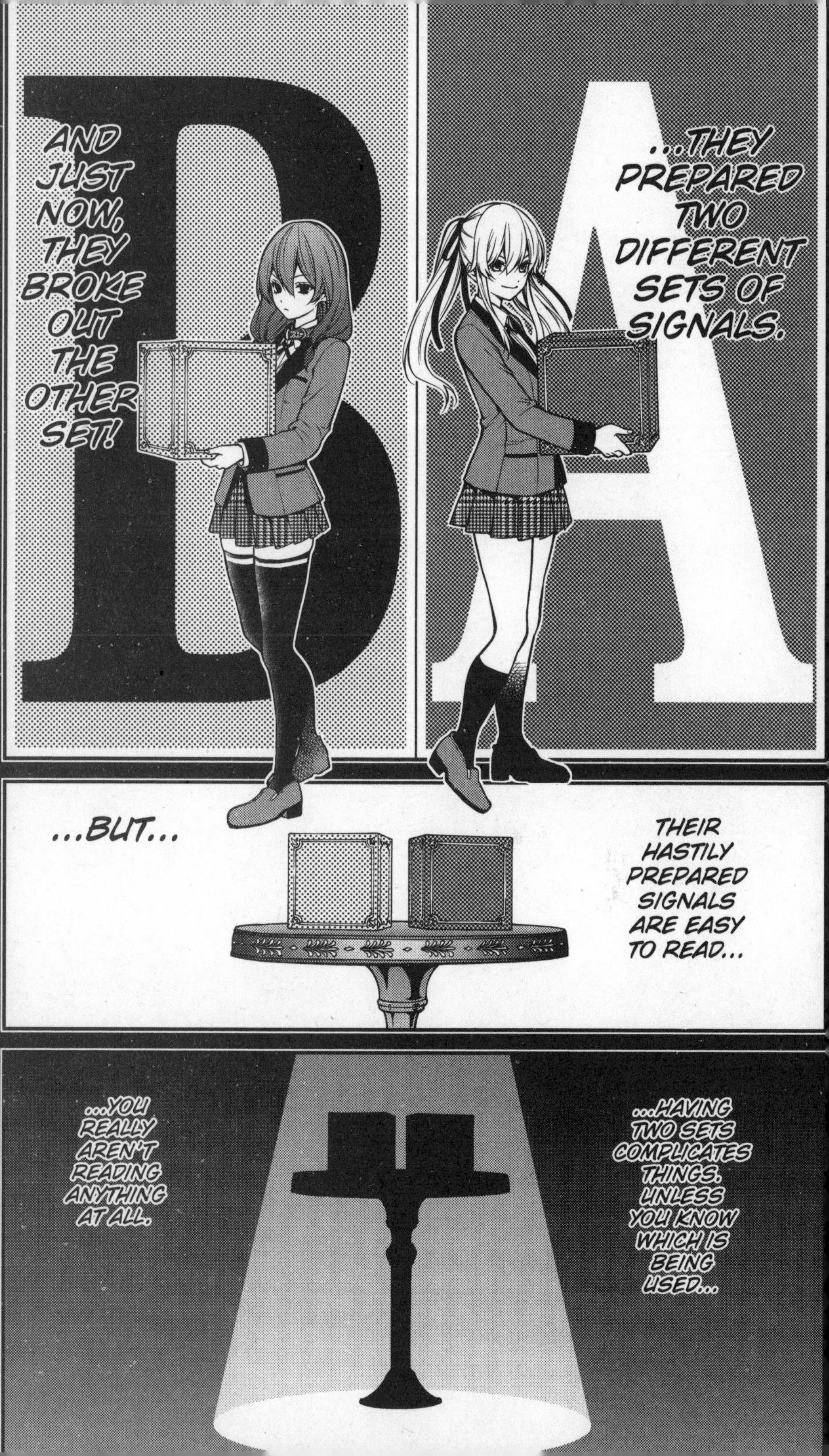
...THEY PREPARED TWO DIFFERENT SETS OF SIGNALS.
AND JUST NOW, THEY BROKE OUT THE OTHER SET!
THEIR HASTILY PREPARED SIGNALS ARE EASY TO READ...
...BUT...
...HAVING TWO SETS COMPLICATES THINGS. UNLESS YOU KNOW WHICH IS BEING USED...
...YOU REALLY AREN'T READING ANYTHING AT ALL.

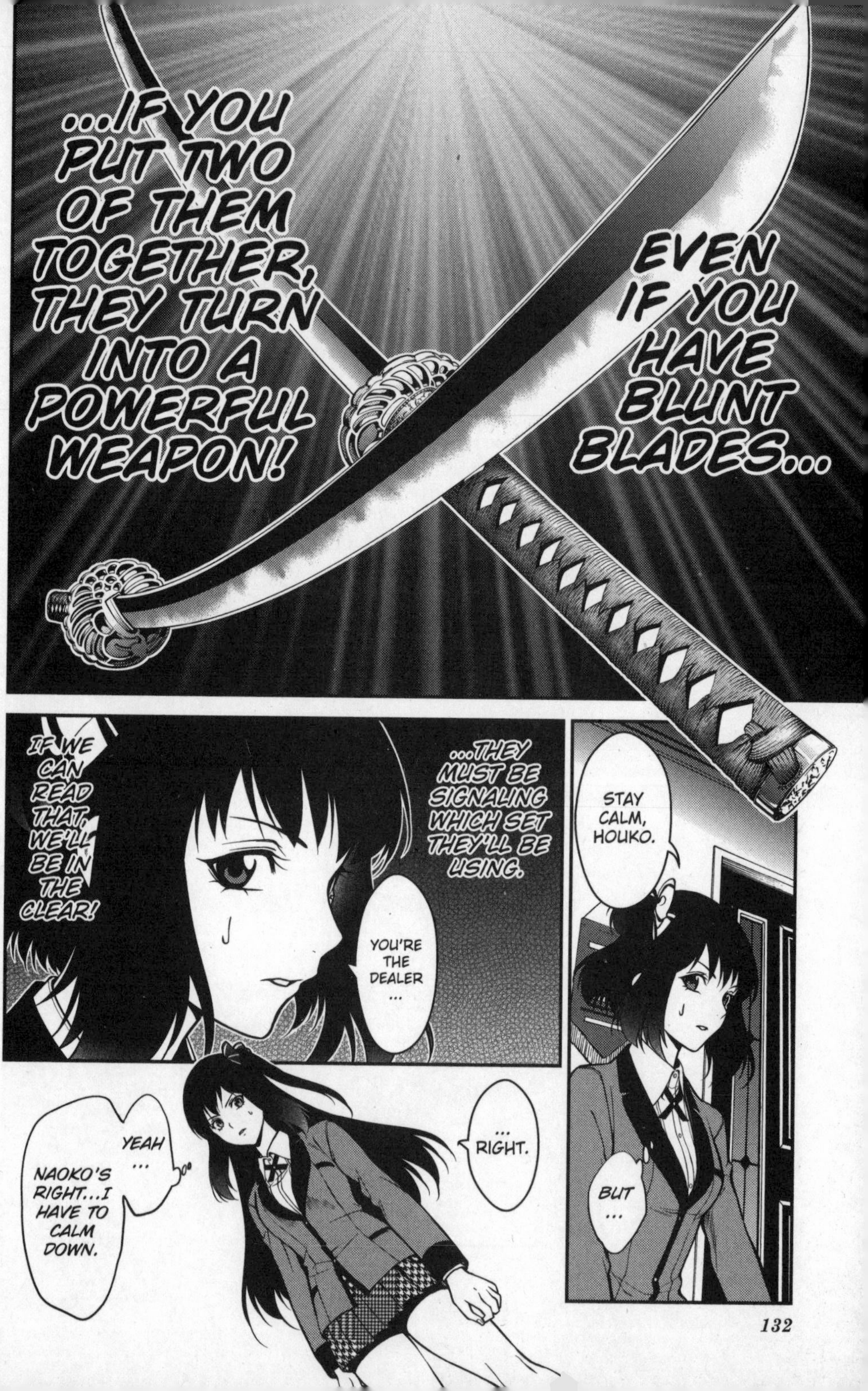
EVEN IF YOU HAVE BLUNT BLADES...
...IF YOU PUT TWO OF THEM TOGETHER, THEY TURN INTO A POWERFUL WEAPON!
STAY CALM, HOUKO.
BUT...
...THEY MUST BE SIGNALING WHICH SET THEY'LL BE USING.
IF WE CAN READ THAT, WE'LL BE IN THE CLEAR!
YOU'RE THE DEALER...
...RIGHT.
YEAH...
NAOKO'S RIGHT...I HAVE TO CALM DOWN.

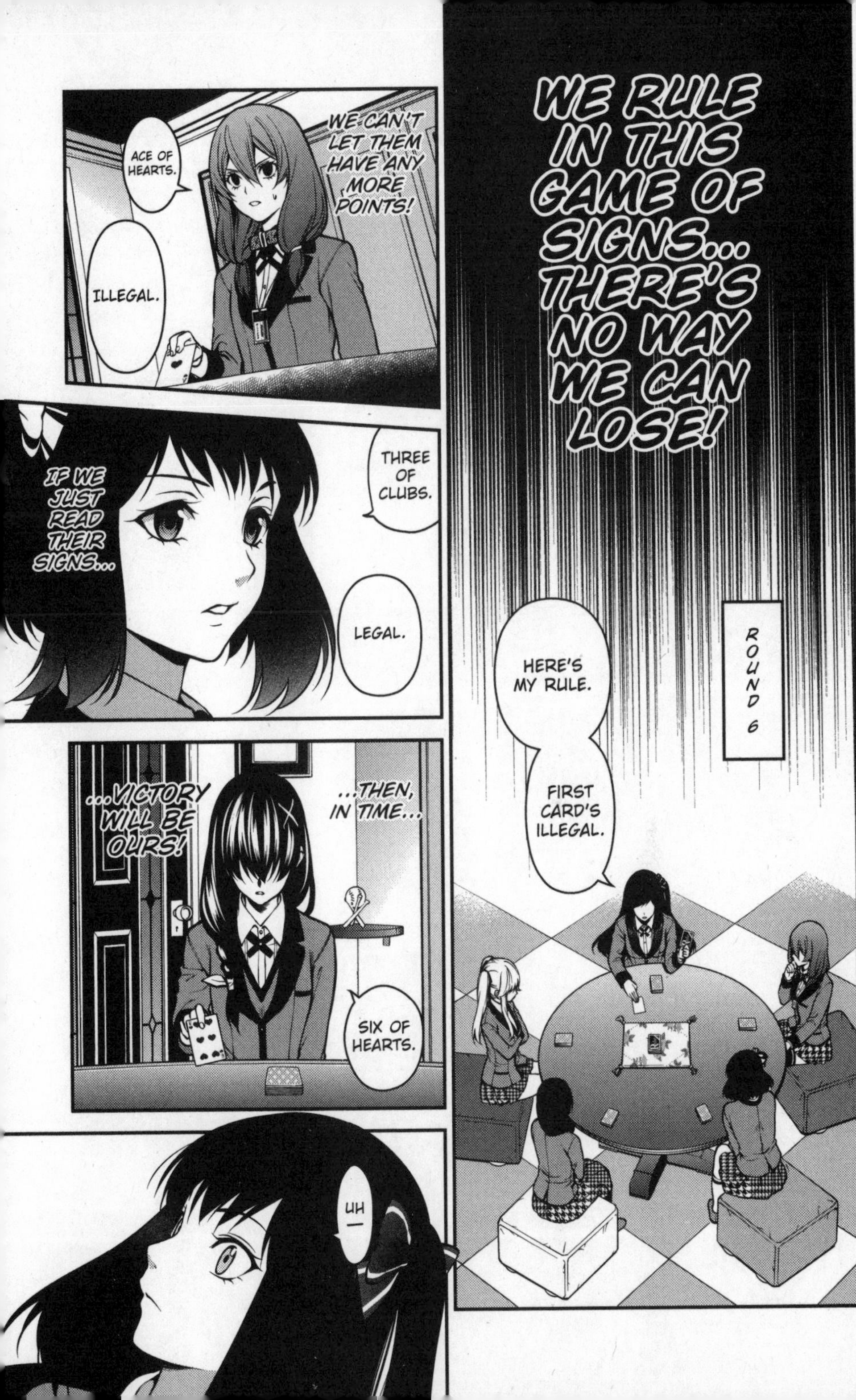
WE RULE IN THIS GAME OF SIGNS... THERE'S NO WAY WE CAN LOSE!
ROUND 6
HERE'S MY RULE.
FIRST CARD'S ILLEGAL.
WE CAN'T LET THEM HAVE ANY MORE POINTS!
ACE OF HEARTS.
ILLEGAL.
THREE OF CLUBS.
IF WE JUST READ THEIR SIGNS...
LEGAL.
...THEN, IN TIME...
...VICTORY WILL BE OURS!
SIX OF HEARTS.
UH—

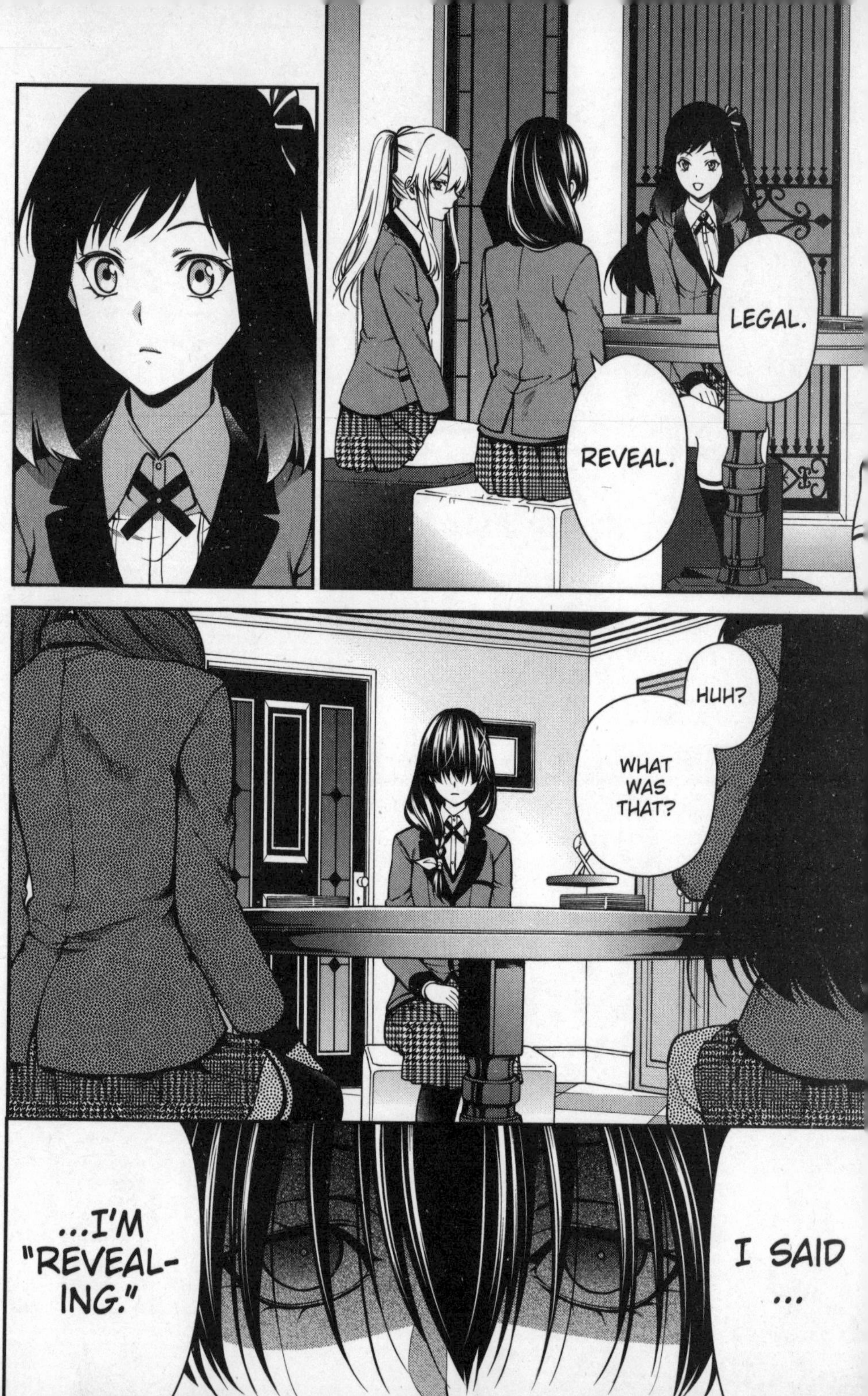
LEGAL.
REVEAL.
HUH?
WHAT WAS THAT?
I SAID ...
...I'M "REVEAL-ING."

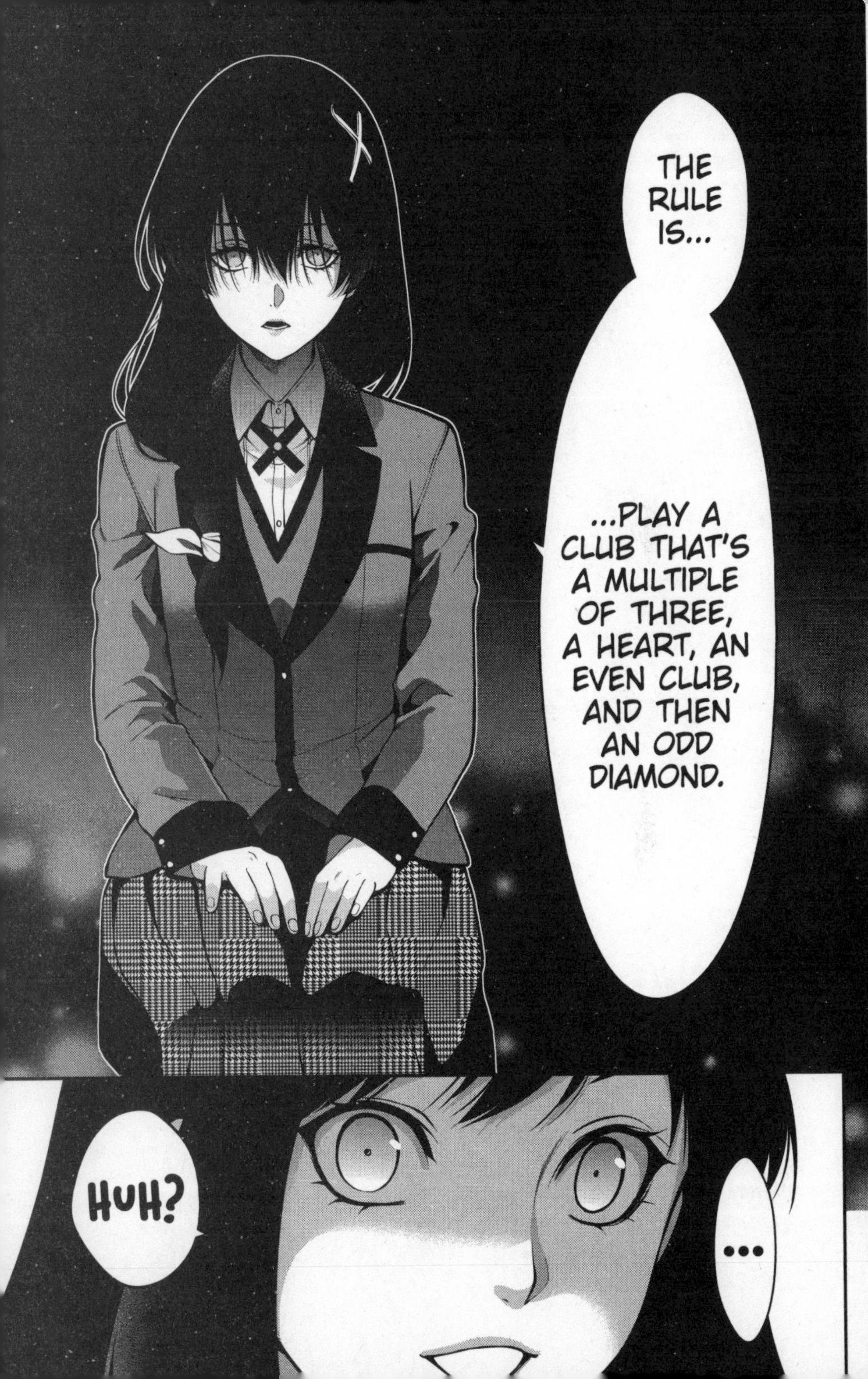
THE RULE IS...
...PLAY A CLUB THAT'S A MULTIPLE OF THREE, A HEART, AN EVEN CLUB, AND THEN AN ODD DIAMOND.
...
HUH?

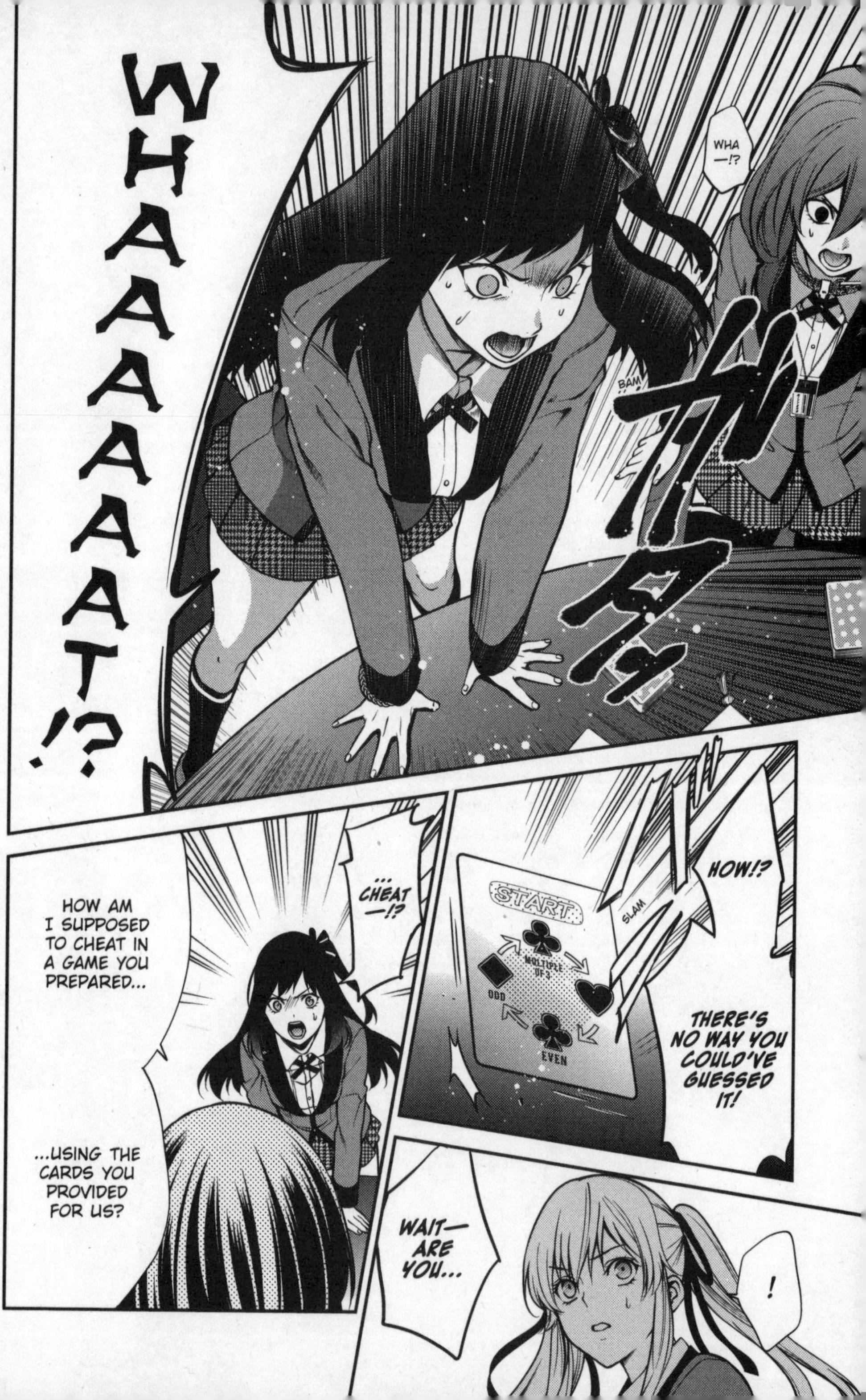
WHA—!?
BAM
WHAAAAAT!?
HOW!?
SLAM
START
MULTIPLE OF 3
ODD
EVEN
THERE'S NO WAY YOU COULD'VE GUESSED IT!
!
WAIT— ARE YOU...
...CHEAT—!?
HOW AM I SUPPOSED TO CHEAT IN A GAME YOU PREPARED...
...USING THE CARDS YOU PROVIDED FOR US?

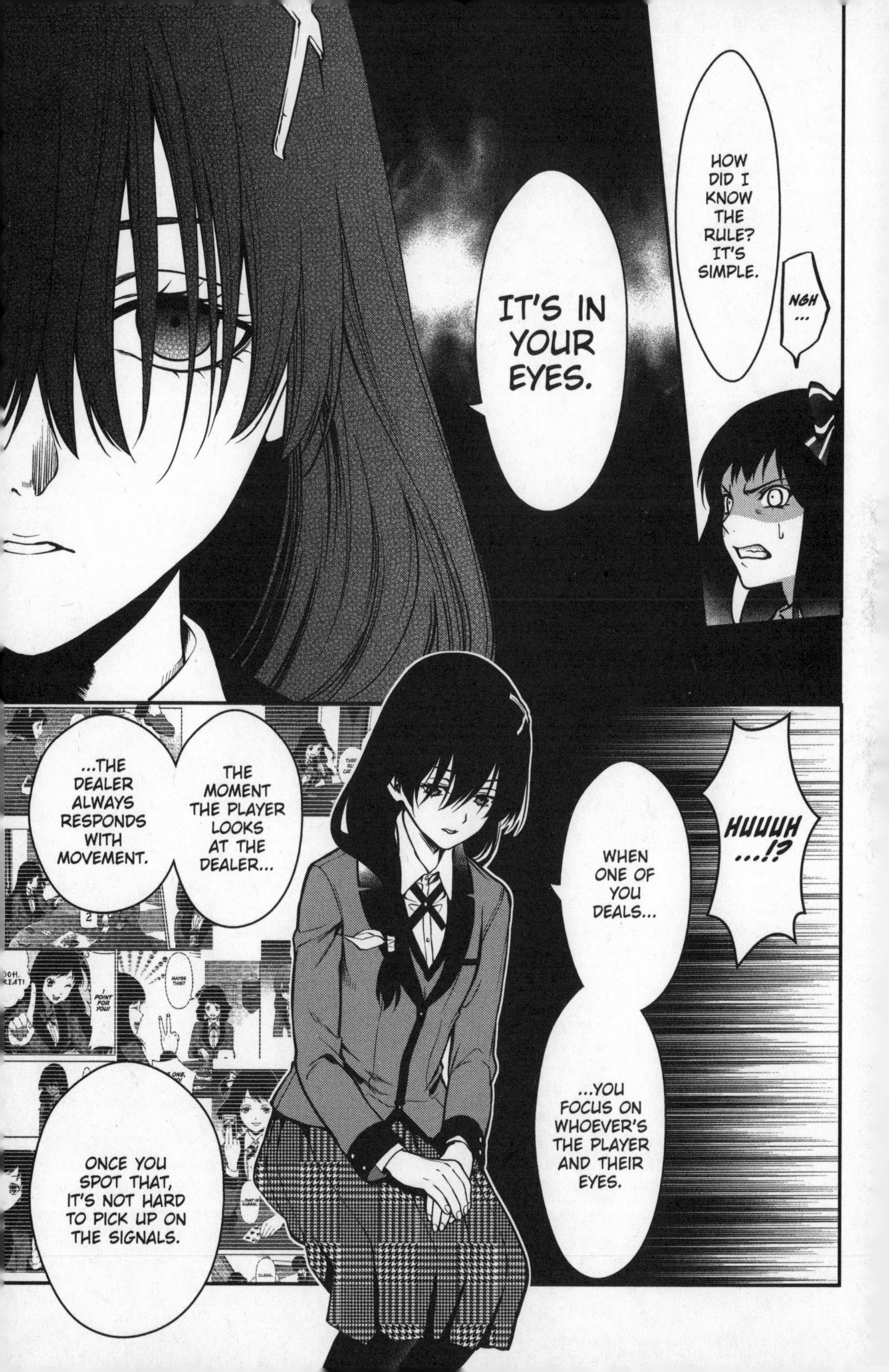
HOW DID I KNOW THE RULE? IT'S SIMPLE.
NGH...
IT'S IN YOUR EYES.
HUUUH...!?
WHEN ONE OF YOU DEALS...
...YOU FOCUS ON WHOEVER'S THE PLAYER AND THEIR EYES.
THE MOMENT THE PLAYER LOOKS AT THE DEALER...
...THE DEALER ALWAYS RESPONDS WITH MOVEMENT.
ONCE YOU SPOT THAT, IT'S NOT HARD TO PICK UP ON THE SIGNALS.

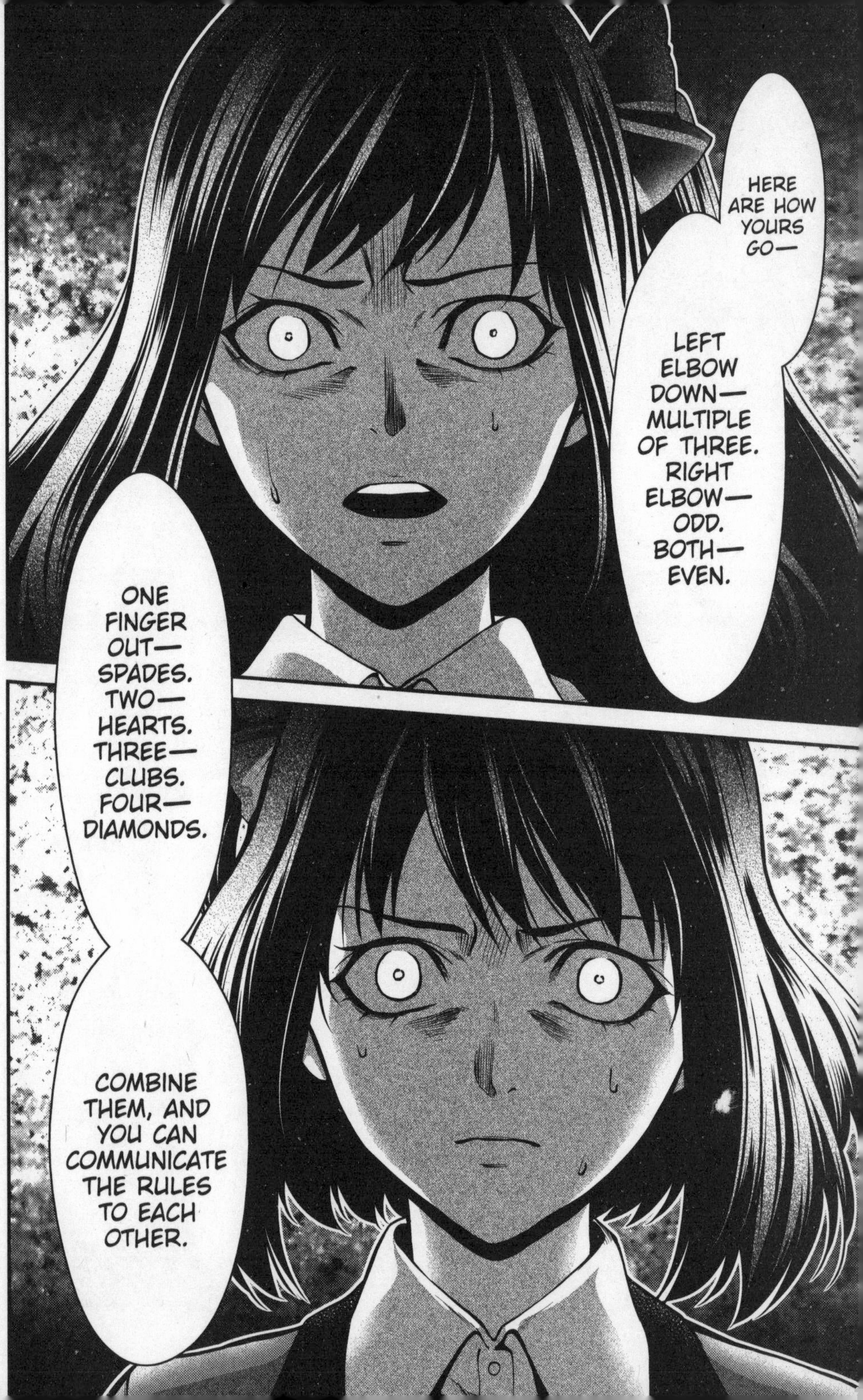
HERE ARE HOW YOURS GO—
LEFT ELBOW DOWN—MULTIPLE OF THREE. RIGHT ELBOW—ODD. BOTH—EVEN.
ONE FINGER OUT—SPADES. TWO—HEARTS. THREE—CLUBS. FOUR—DIAMONDS.
COMBINE THEM, AND YOU CAN COMMUNICATE THE RULES TO EACH OTHER.

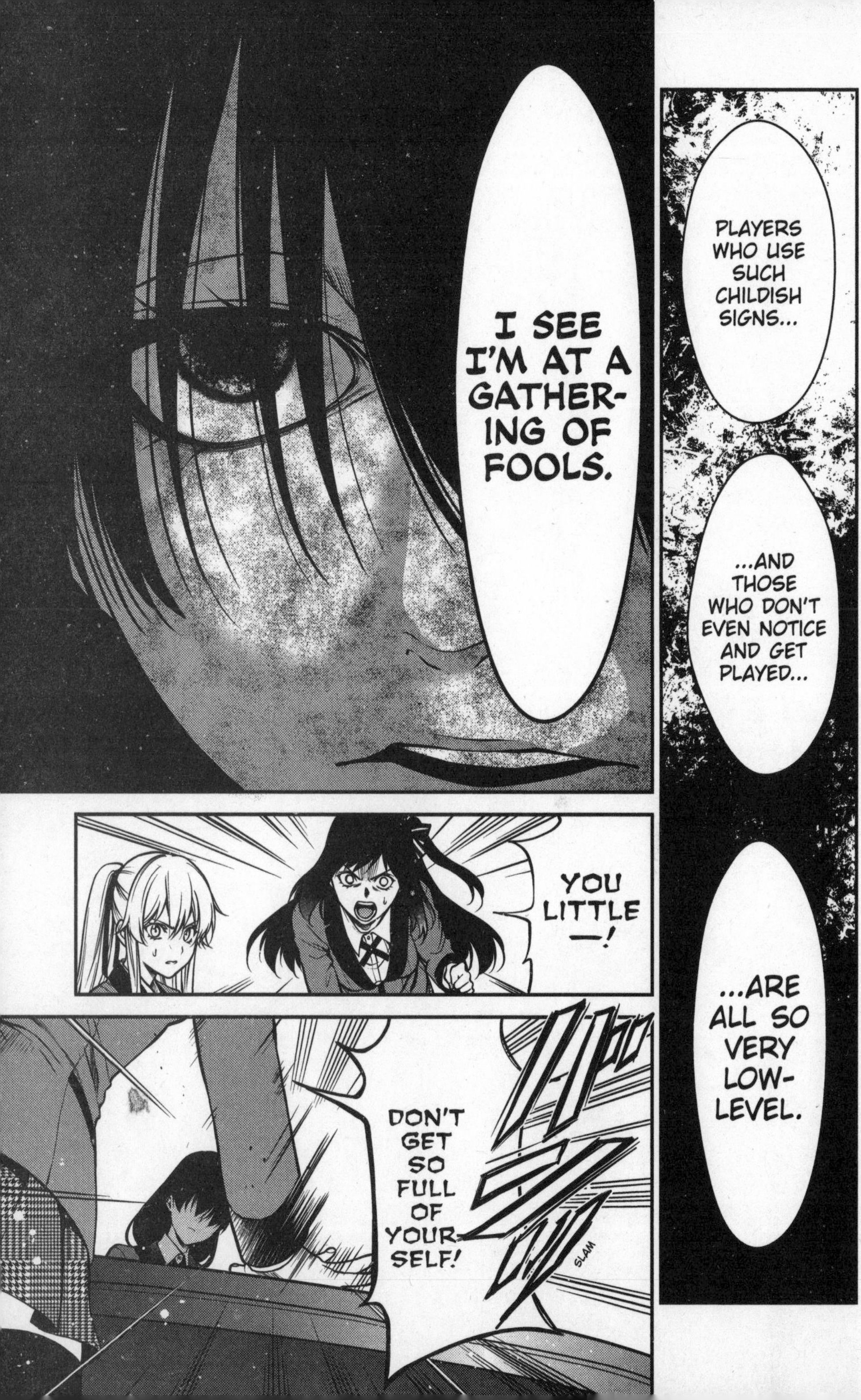
PLAYERS WHO USE SUCH CHILDISH SIGNS...
...AND THOSE WHO DON'T EVEN NOTICE AND GET PLAYED...
...ARE ALL SO VERY LOW-LEVEL.
I SEE I'M AT A GATHER-ING OF FOOLS.
YOU LITTLE —!
DON'T GET SO FULL OF YOUR-SELF!
SLAM

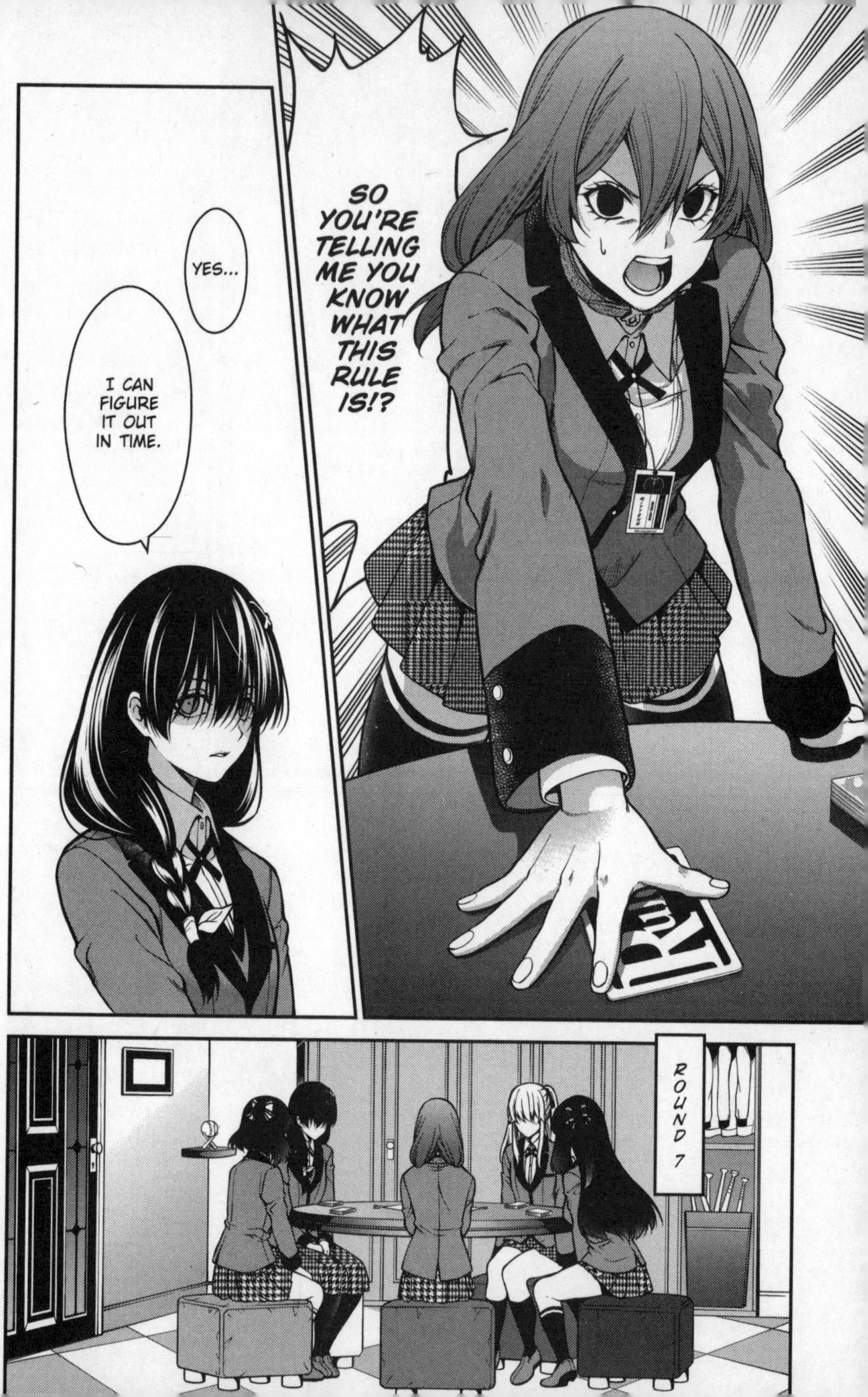
SO YOU'RE TELLING ME YOU KNOW WHAT THIS RULE IS!?
YES...
I CAN FIGURE IT OUT IN TIME.
ROUND 7

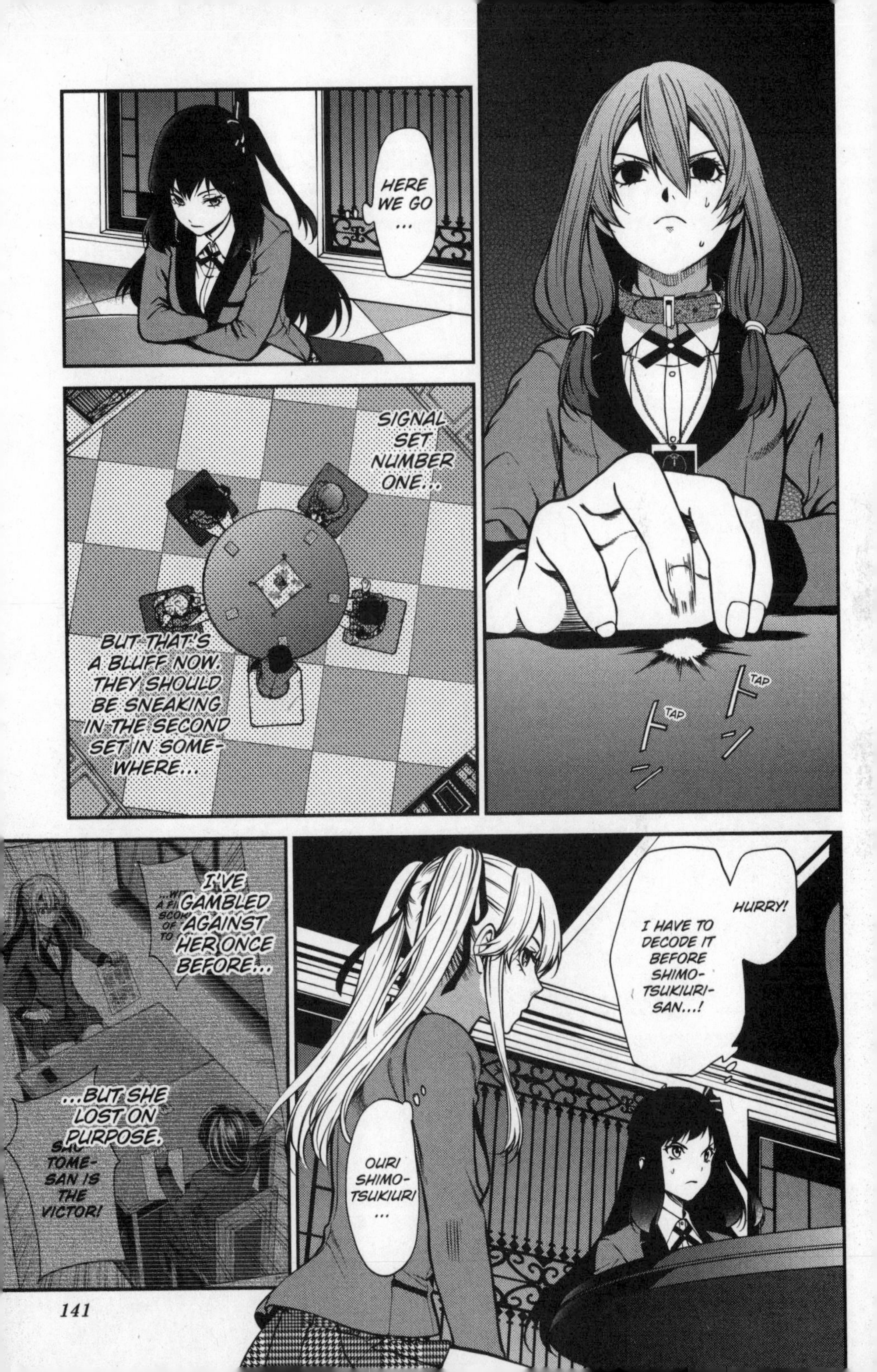
TAP
TAP
HERE WE GO ...
SIGNAL SET NUMBER ONE...
BUT THAT'S A BLUFF NOW. THEY SHOULD BE SNEAKING IN THE SECOND SET IN SOME-WHERE...
HURRY!
I HAVE TO DECODE IT BEFORE SHIMO-TSUKIURI-SAN...!
OURI SHIMO-TSUKIURI ...
I'VE GAMBLED AGAINST HER ONCE BEFORE...
...BUT SHE LOST ON PURPOSE.
TOME-SAN IS THE VICTOR!

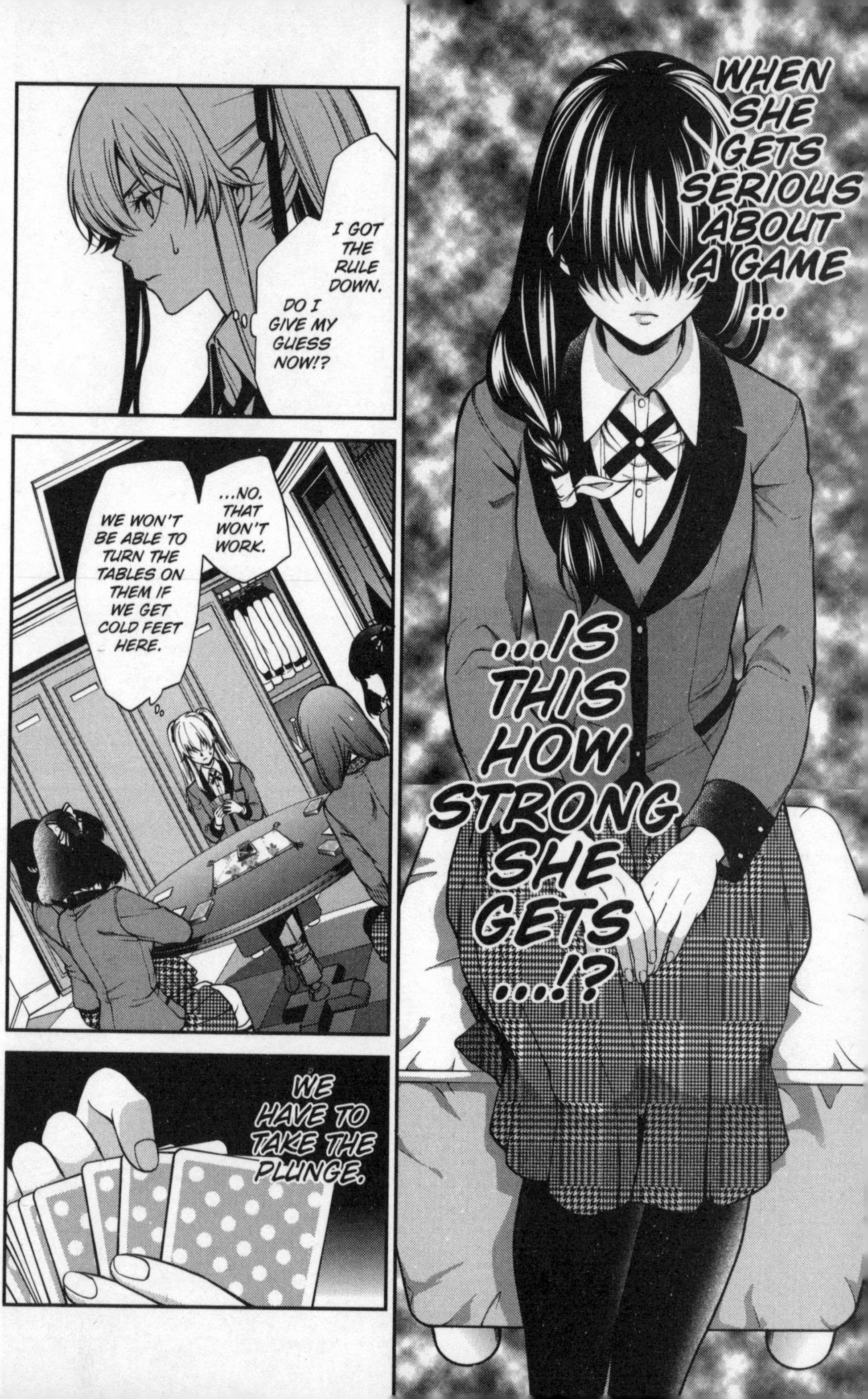
WHEN SHE GETS SERIOUS ABOUT A GAME ...
...IS THIS HOW STRONG SHE GETS ...!?
I GOT THE RULE DOWN.
DO I GIVE MY GUESS NOW!?
...NO. THAT WON'T WORK.
WE WON'T BE ABLE TO TURN THE TABLES ON THEM IF WE GET COLD FEET HERE.
WE HAVE TO TAKE THE PLUNGE.

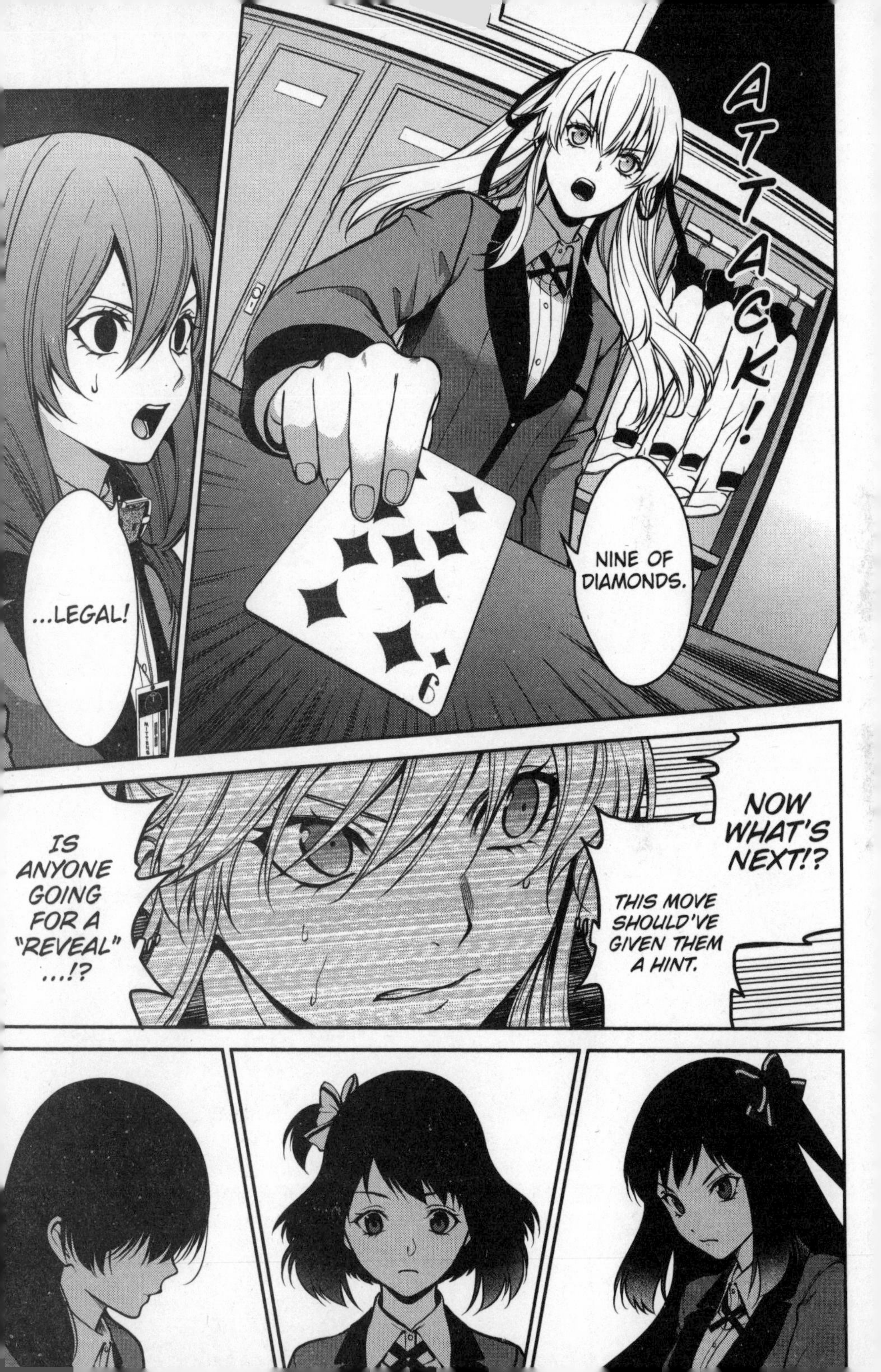
ATTACK!
NINE OF DIAMONDS.
...LEGAL!
NOW WHAT'S NEXT!?
THIS MOVE SHOULD'VE GIVEN THEM A HINT.
IS ANYONE GOING FOR A "REVEAL" ...!?

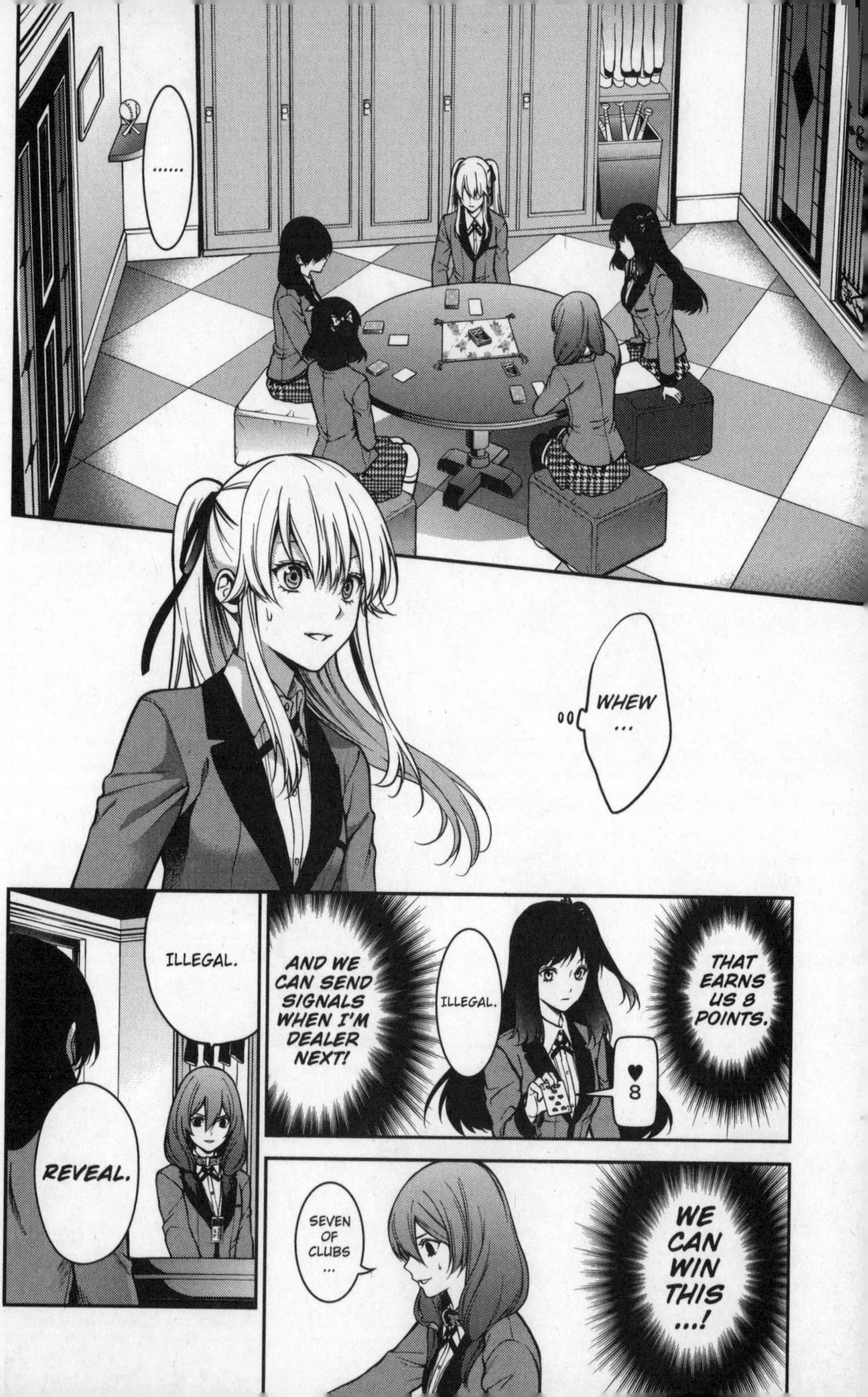
......
...WHEW...
THAT EARNS US 8 POINTS.
ILLEGAL.
♥ 8
AND WE CAN SEND SIGNALS WHEN I'M DEALER NEXT!
WE CAN WIN THIS...!
SEVEN OF CLUBS...
ILLEGAL.
REVEAL.

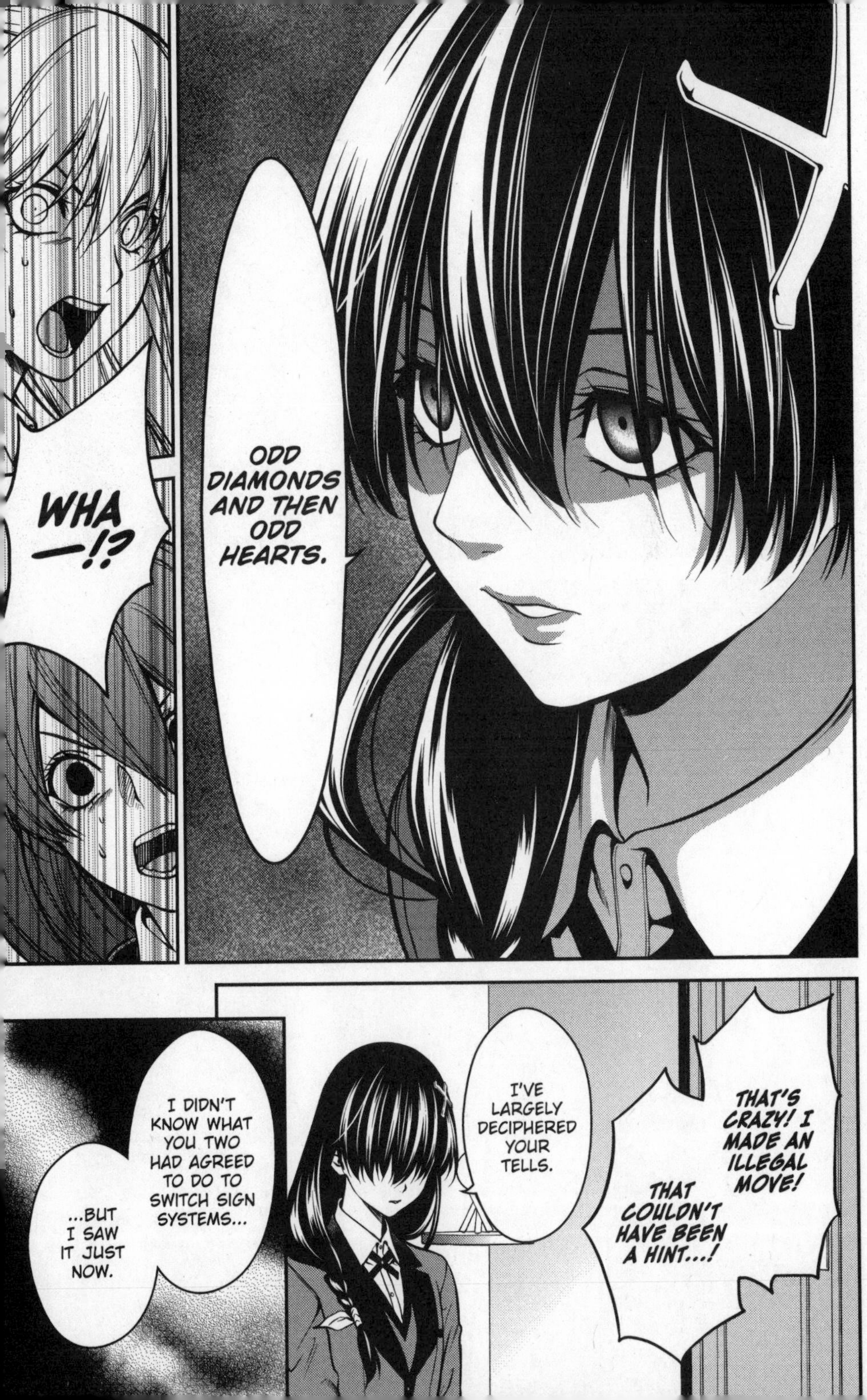
ODD DIAMONDS AND THEN ODD HEARTS.
WHA—!?
THAT'S CRAZY! I MADE AN ILLEGAL MOVE!
THAT COULDN'T HAVE BEEN A HINT...!
I'VE LARGELY DECIPHERED YOUR TELLS.
I DIDN'T KNOW WHAT YOU TWO HAD AGREED TO DO TO SWITCH SIGN SYSTEMS...
...BUT I SAW IT JUST NOW.

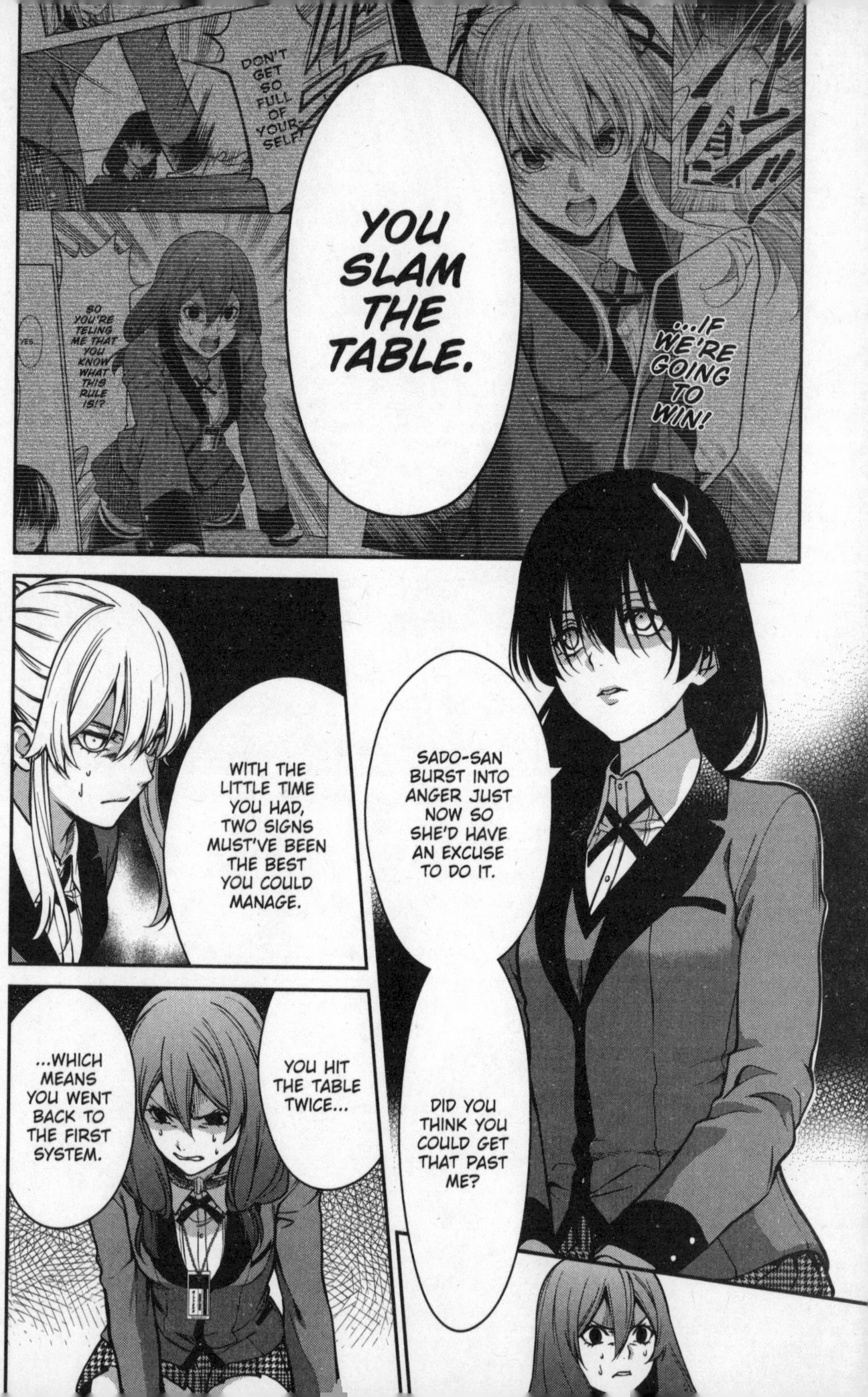
DON'T GET SO FULL OF YOURSELF!
SO YOU'RE TELING ME THAT YOU KNOW WHAT THIS RULE IS!?
YES...
...IF WE'RE GOING TO WIN!
YOU SLAM THE TABLE.
SADO-SAN BURST INTO ANGER JUST NOW SO SHE'D HAVE AN EXCUSE TO DO IT.
DID YOU THINK YOU COULD GET THAT PAST ME?
WITH THE LITTLE TIME YOU HAD, TWO SIGNS MUST'VE BEEN THE BEST YOU COULD MANAGE.
YOU HIT THE TABLE TWICE...
...WHICH MEANS YOU WENT BACK TO THE FIRST SYSTEM.

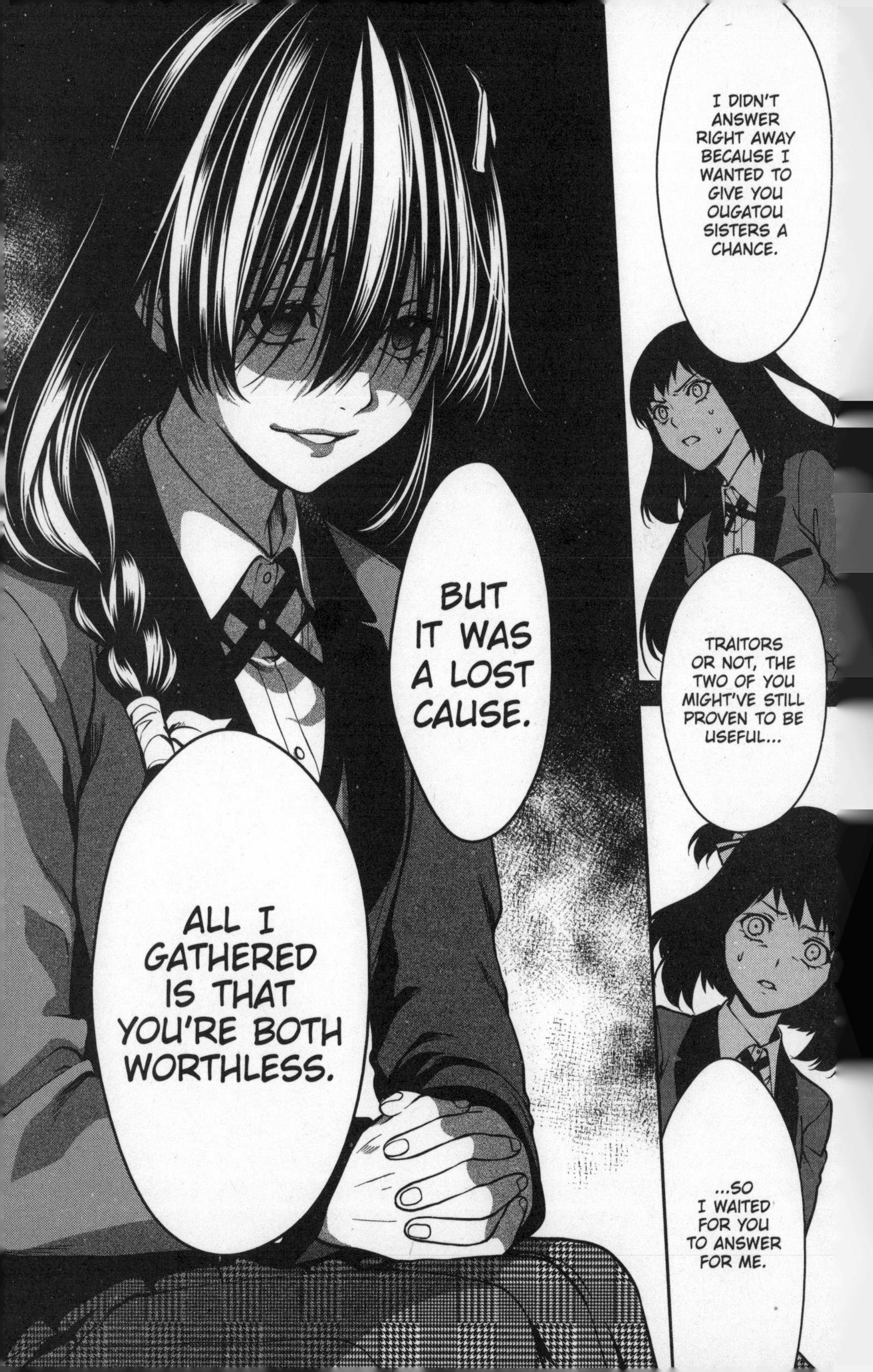
I DIDN'T ANSWER RIGHT AWAY BECAUSE I WANTED TO GIVE YOU OUGATOU SISTERS A CHANCE.
TRAITORS OR NOT, THE TWO OF YOU MIGHT'VE STILL PROVEN TO BE USEFUL...
...SO I WAITED FOR YOU TO ANSWER FOR ME.
BUT IT WAS A LOST CAUSE.
ALL I GATHERED IS THAT YOU'RE BOTH WORTHLESS.

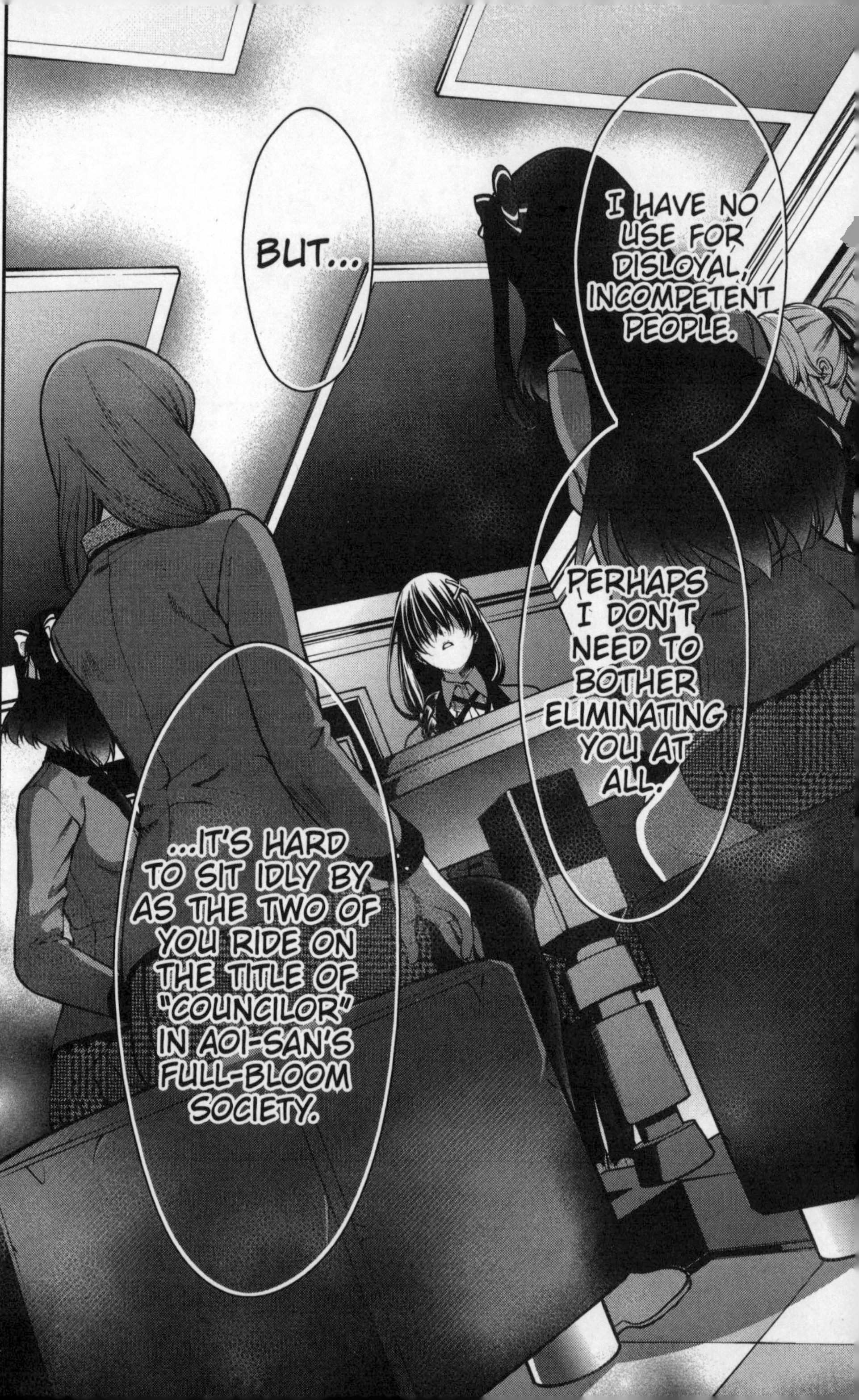
I HAVE NO USE FOR DISLOYAL, INCOMPETENT PEOPLE.
PERHAPS I DON'T NEED TO BOTHER ELIMINATING YOU AT ALL.
BUT...
...IT'S HARD TO SIT IDLY BY AS THE TWO OF YOU RIDE ON THE TITLE OF "COUNCILOR" IN AOI-SAN'S FULL-BLOOM SOCIETY.

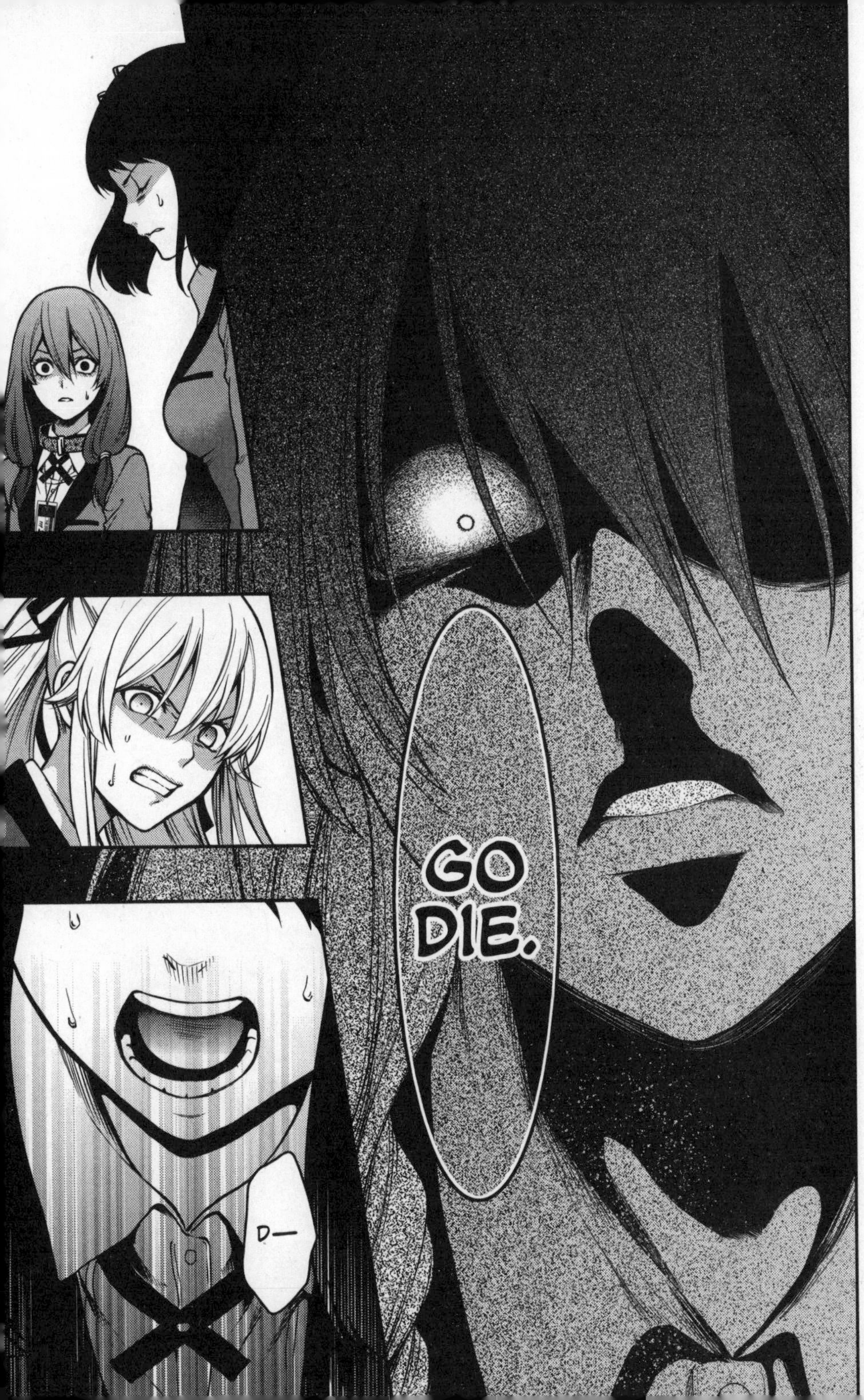
GO DIE.
D—

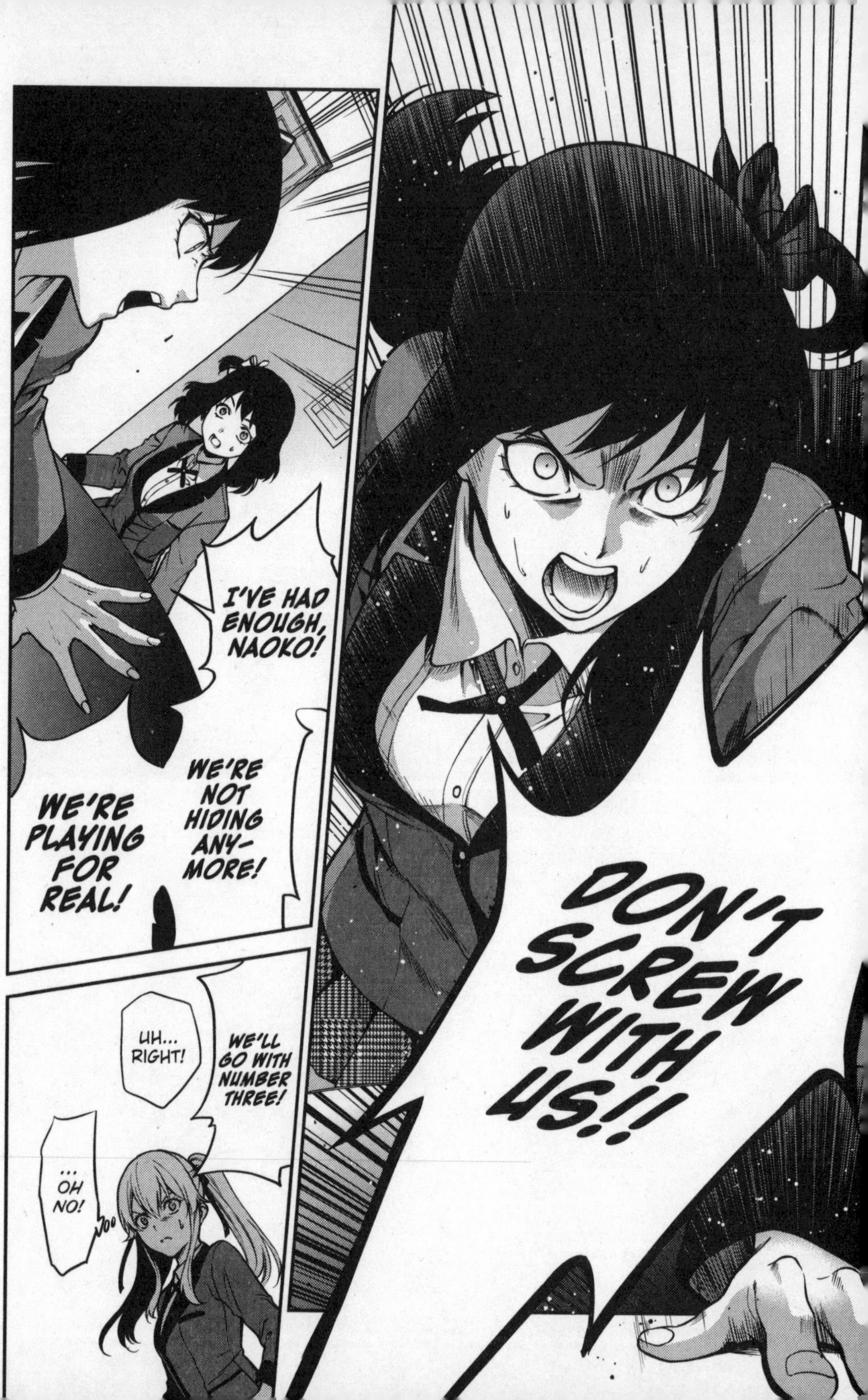
DON'T SCREW WITH US!!
I'VE HAD ENOUGH, NAOKO!
WE'RE NOT HIDING ANY-MORE!
WE'RE PLAYING FOR REAL!
WE'LL GO WITH NUMBER THREE!
UH... RIGHT!
... OH NO!

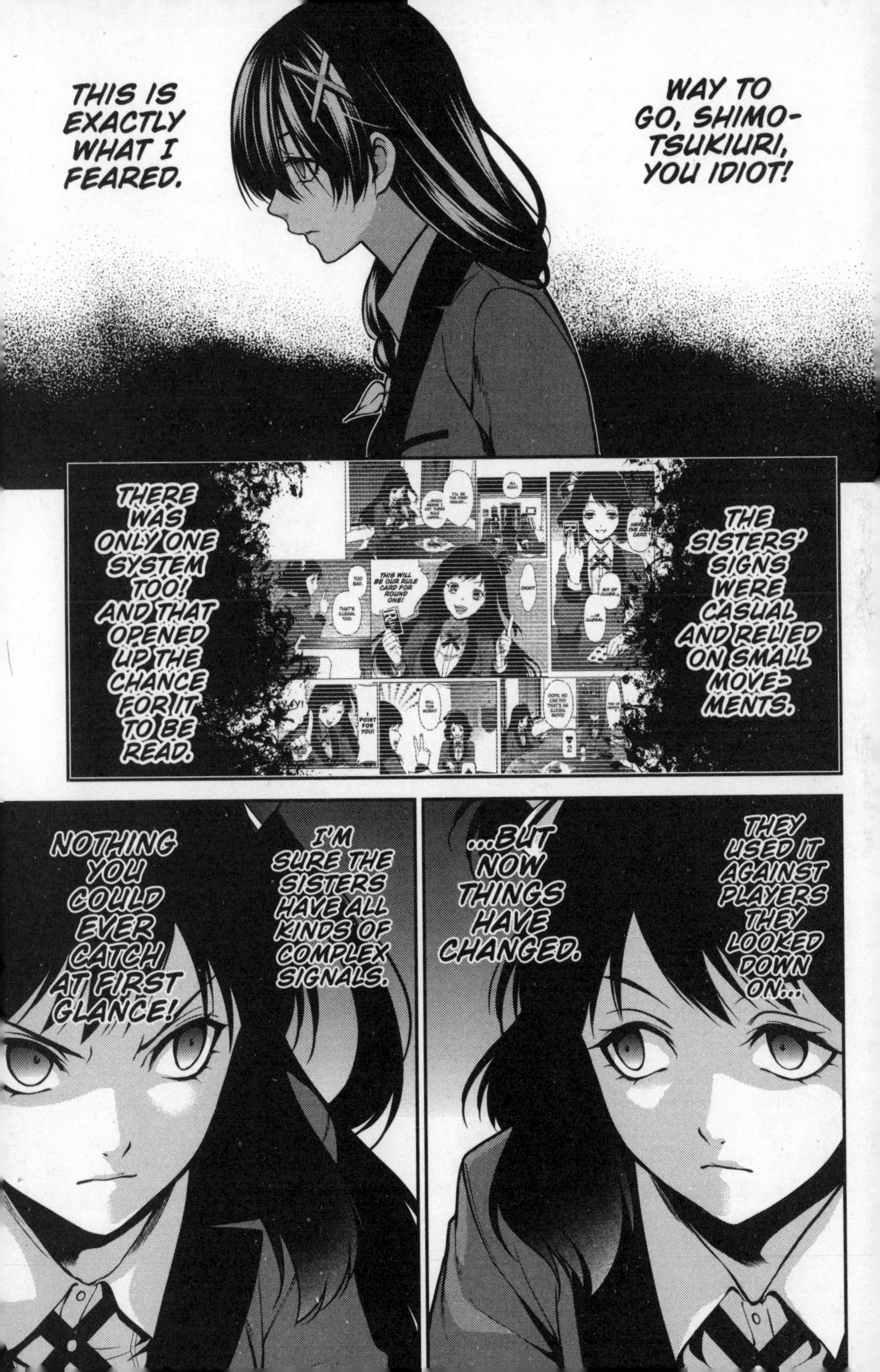
WAY TO GO, SHIMO-TSUKIURI, YOU IDIOT!
THIS IS EXACTLY WHAT I FEARED.
THE SISTERS' SIGNS WERE CASUAL AND RELIED ON SMALL MOVE-MENTS.
THERE WAS ONLY ONE SYSTEM TOO! AND THAT OPENED UP THE CHANCE FOR IT TO BE READ.
THEY USED IT AGAINST PLAYERS THEY LOOKED DOWN ON...
...BUT NOW THINGS HAVE CHANGED.
I'M SURE THE SISTERS HAVE ALL KINDS OF COMPLEX SIGNALS.
NOTHING YOU COULD EVER CATCH AT FIRST GLANCE!

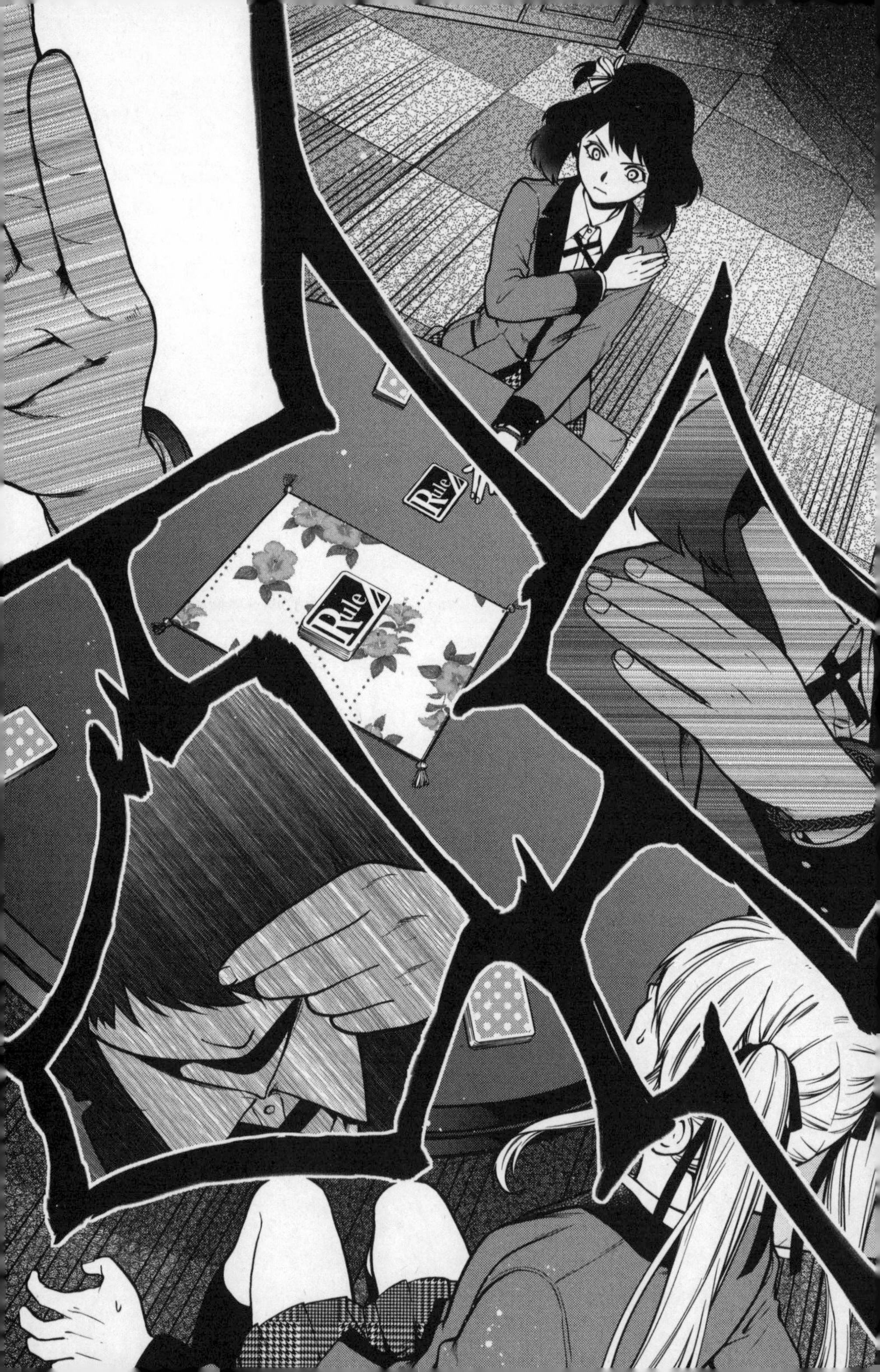
Rule
Rule

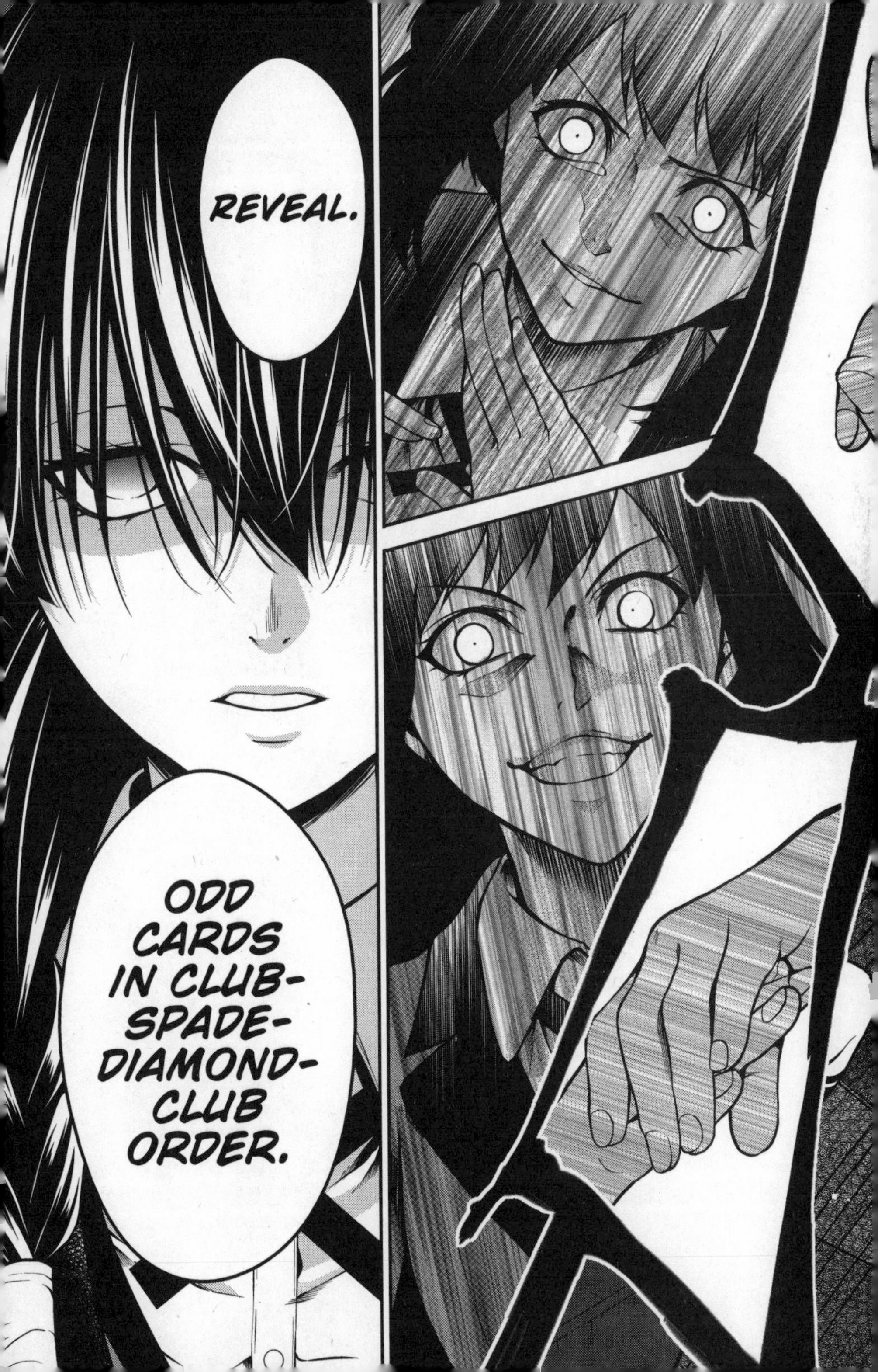
REVEAL.
ODD CARDS IN CLUB-SPADE-DIAMOND-CLUB ORDER.

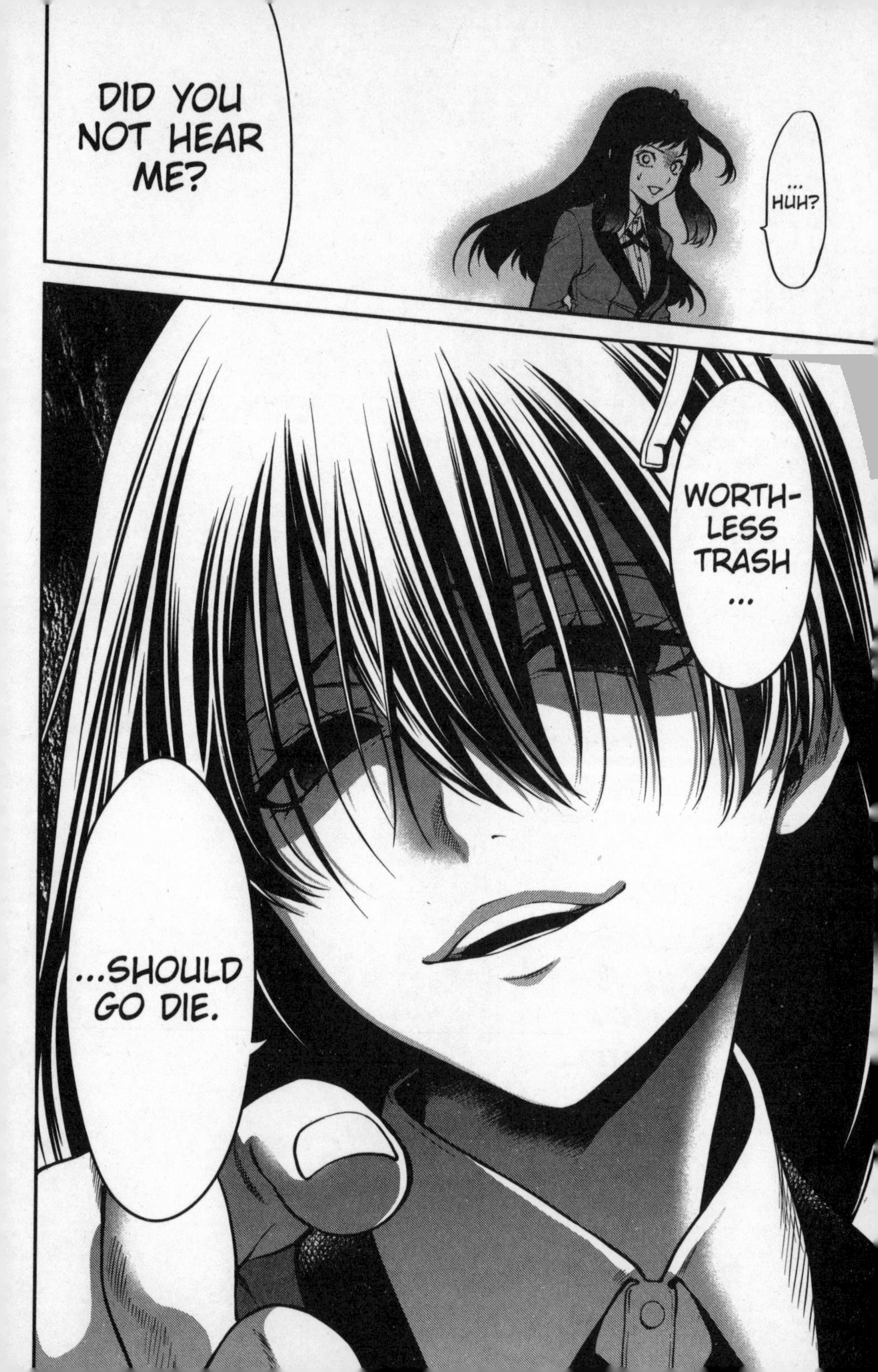

... HUH?
DID YOU NOT HEAR ME?
WORTH-LESS TRASH ...
...SHOULD GO DIE.

CHAPTER TWENTY-SEVEN
THE FOOLISH GIRL

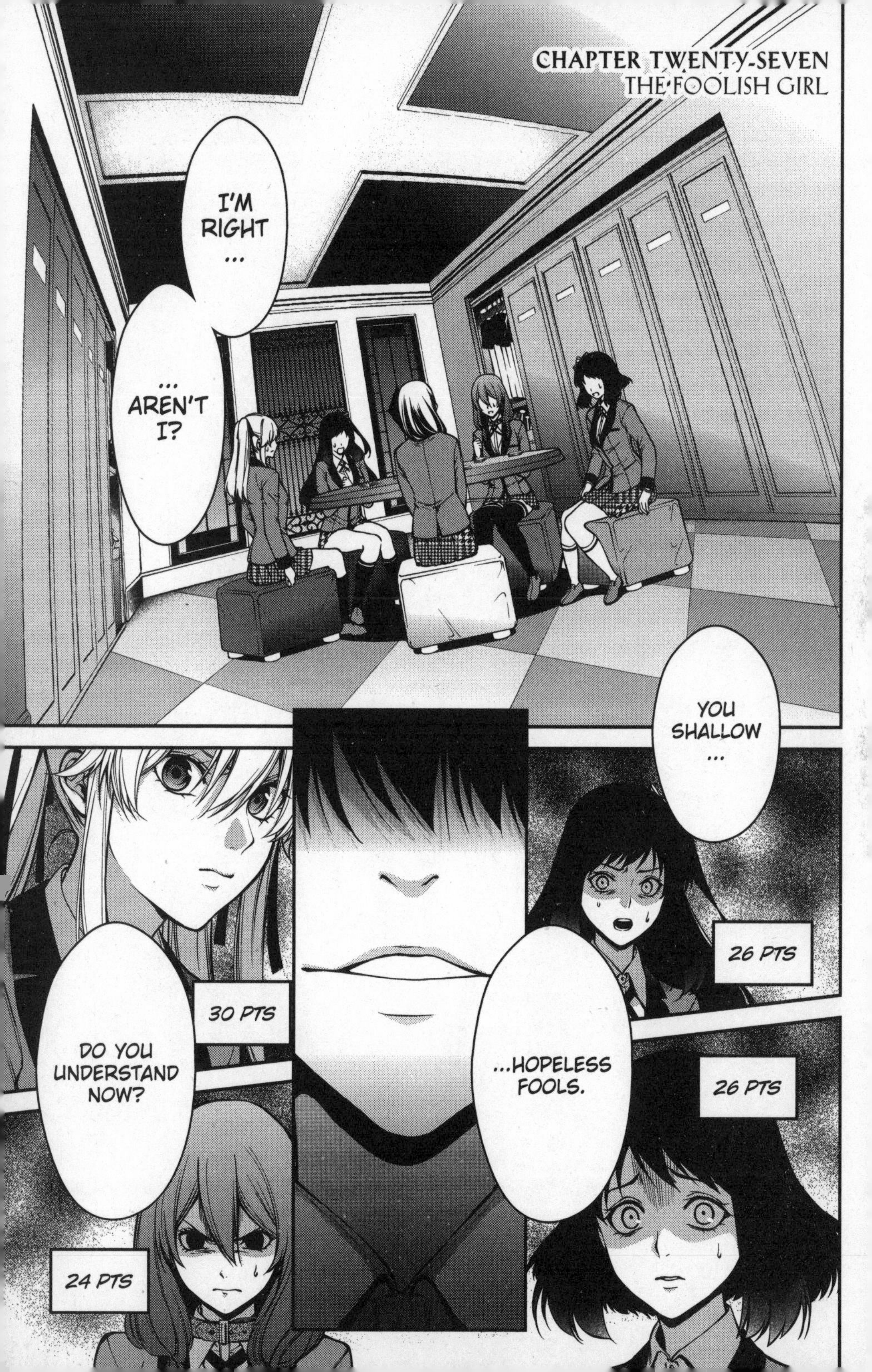
I'M RIGHT ...
... AREN'T I?
YOU SHALLOW ...
26 PTS
26 PTS
...HOPELESS FOOLS.
30 PTS
DO YOU UNDERSTAND NOW?
24 PTS

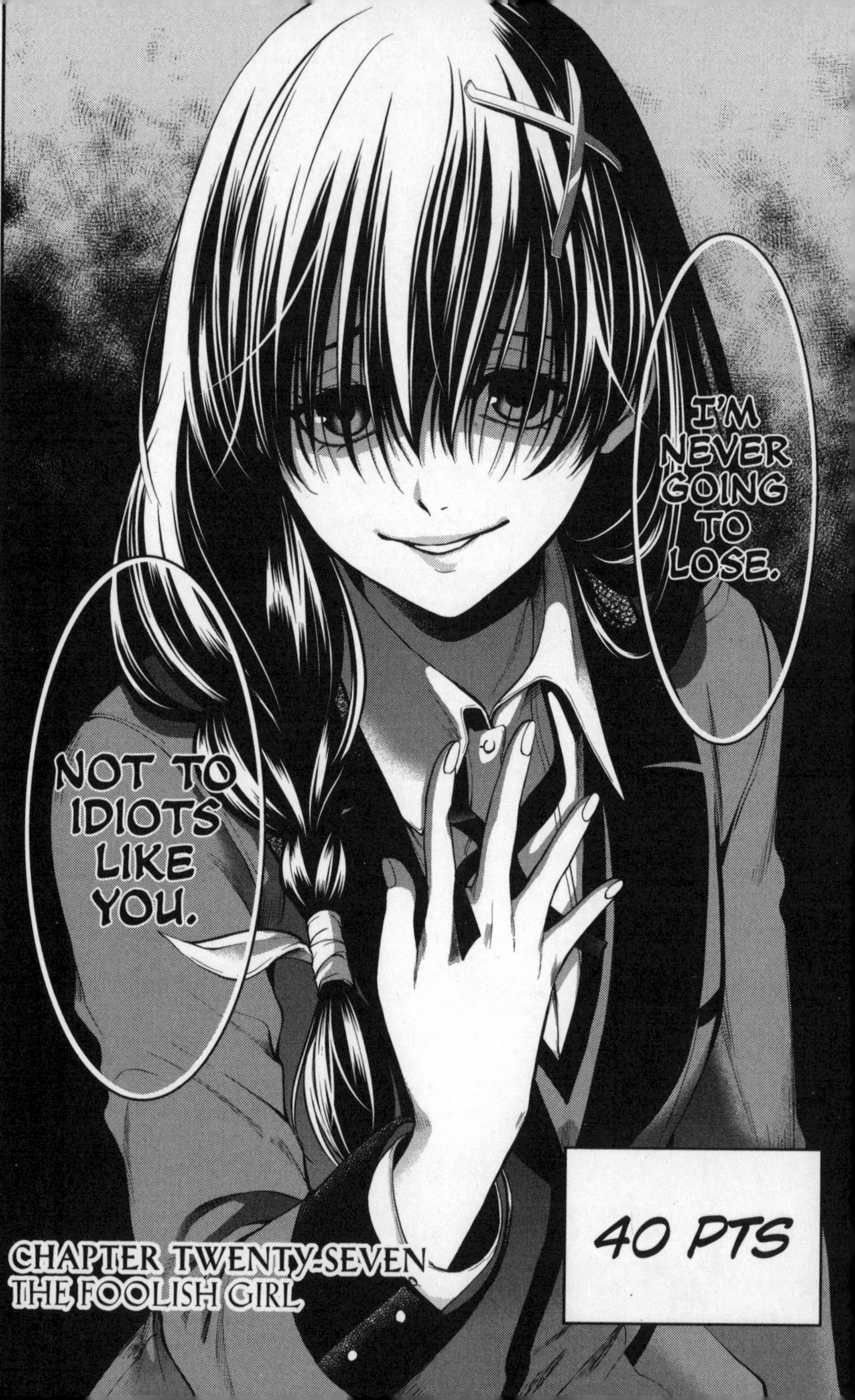
I'M NEVER GOING TO LOSE.
NOT TO IDIOTS LIKE YOU.
40 PTS
CHAPTER TWENTY-SEVEN
THE FOOLISH GIRL

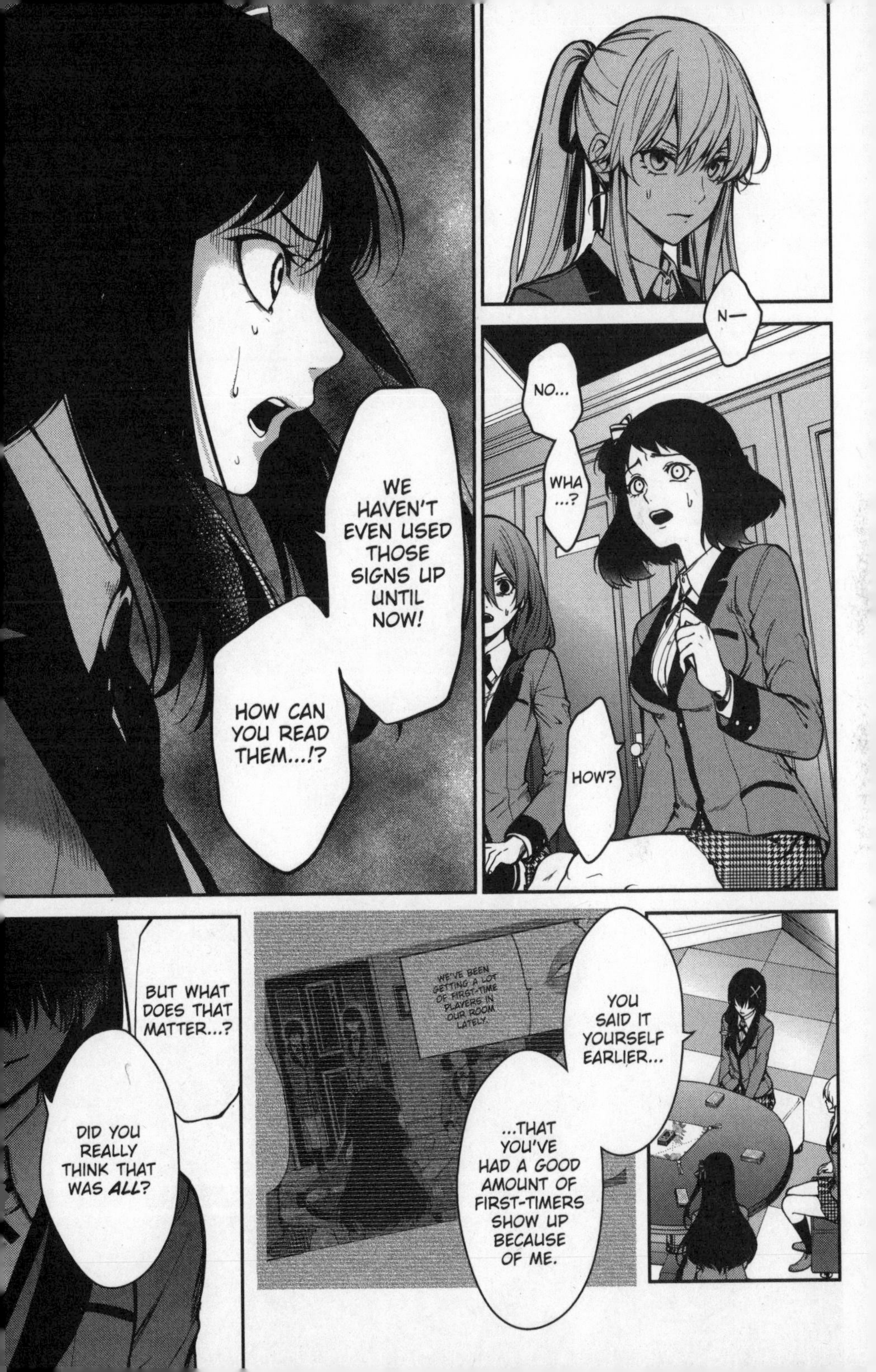
N—
NO...
WHA ...?
HOW?
WE HAVEN'T EVEN USED THOSE SIGNS UP UNTIL NOW!
HOW CAN YOU READ THEM...!?
YOU SAID IT YOURSELF EARLIER...
...THAT YOU'VE HAD A GOOD AMOUNT OF FIRST-TIMERS SHOW UP BECAUSE OF ME.
WE'VE BEEN GETTING A LOT OF FIRST-TIME PLAYERS IN OUR ROOM LATELY.
BUT WHAT DOES THAT MATTER...?
DID YOU REALLY THINK THAT WAS *ALL*?

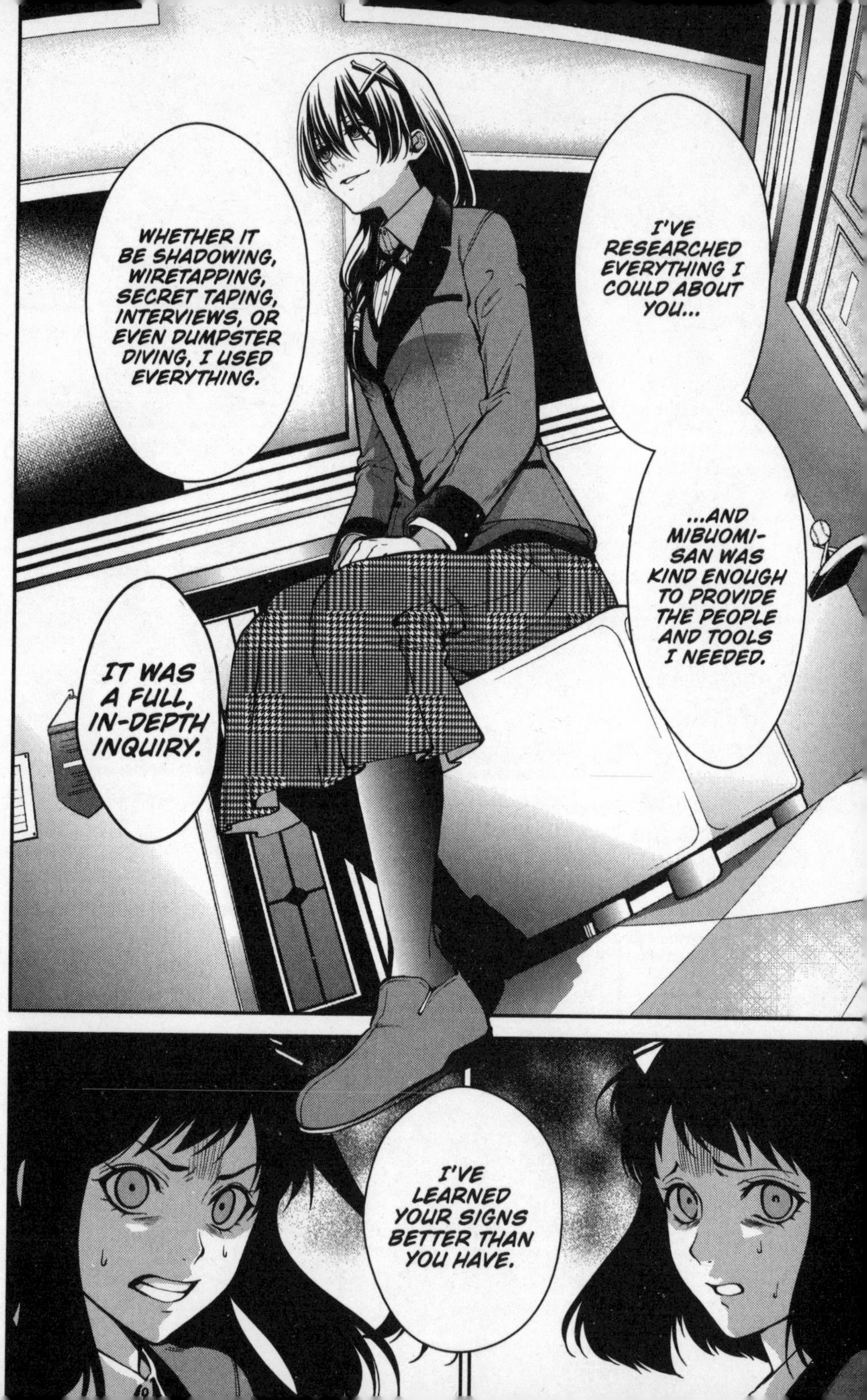
I'VE RESEARCHED EVERYTHING I COULD ABOUT YOU...
...AND MIBUOMI-SAN WAS KIND ENOUGH TO PROVIDE THE PEOPLE AND TOOLS I NEEDED.
WHETHER IT BE SHADOWING, WIRETAPPING, SECRET TAPING, INTERVIEWS, OR EVEN DUMPSTER DIVING, I USED EVERYTHING.
IT WAS A FULL, IN-DEPTH INQUIRY.
I'VE LEARNED YOUR SIGNS BETTER THAN YOU HAVE.

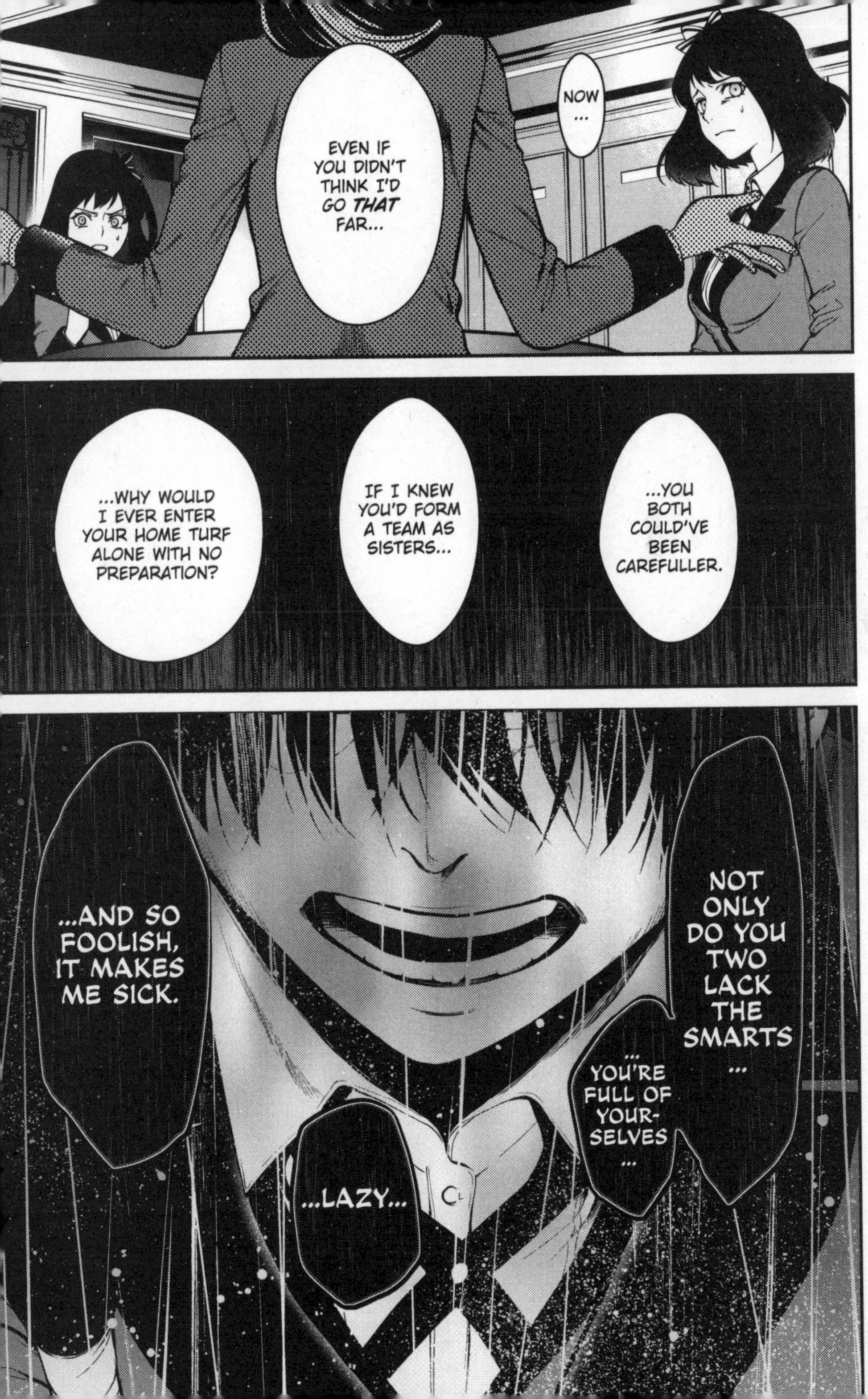
NOW ...
EVEN IF YOU DIDN'T THINK I'D GO *THAT* FAR...
...YOU BOTH COULD'VE BEEN CAREFULLER.
IF I KNEW YOU'D FORM A TEAM AS SISTERS...
...WHY WOULD I EVER ENTER YOUR HOME TURF ALONE WITH NO PREPARATION?
NOT ONLY DO YOU TWO LACK THE SMARTS ...
... YOU'RE FULL OF YOUR-SELVES ...
...LAZY...
...AND SO FOOLISH, IT MAKES ME SICK.

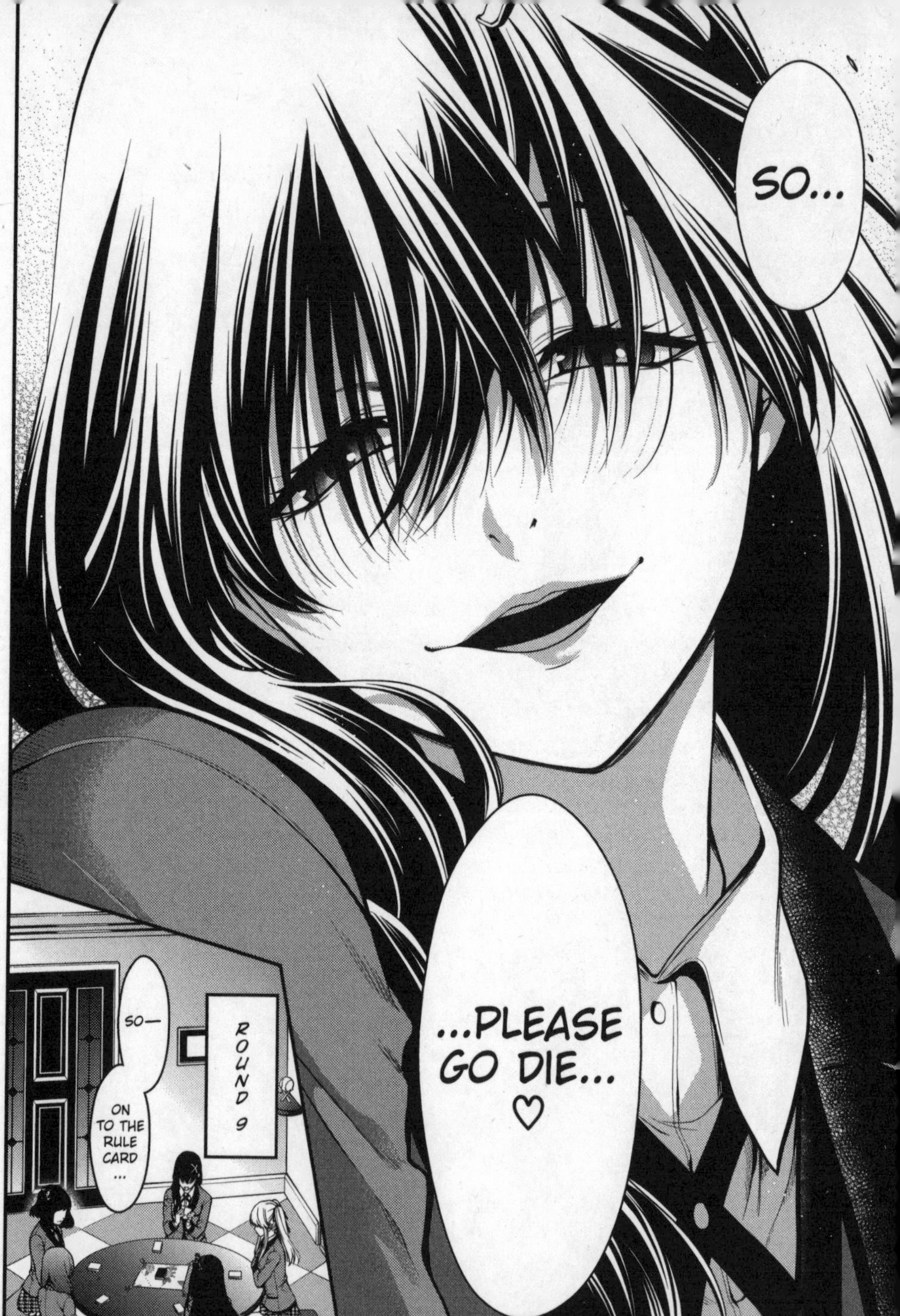
SO...
...PLEASE GO DIE... ♡
ROUND 9
SO—
ON TO THE RULE CARD...

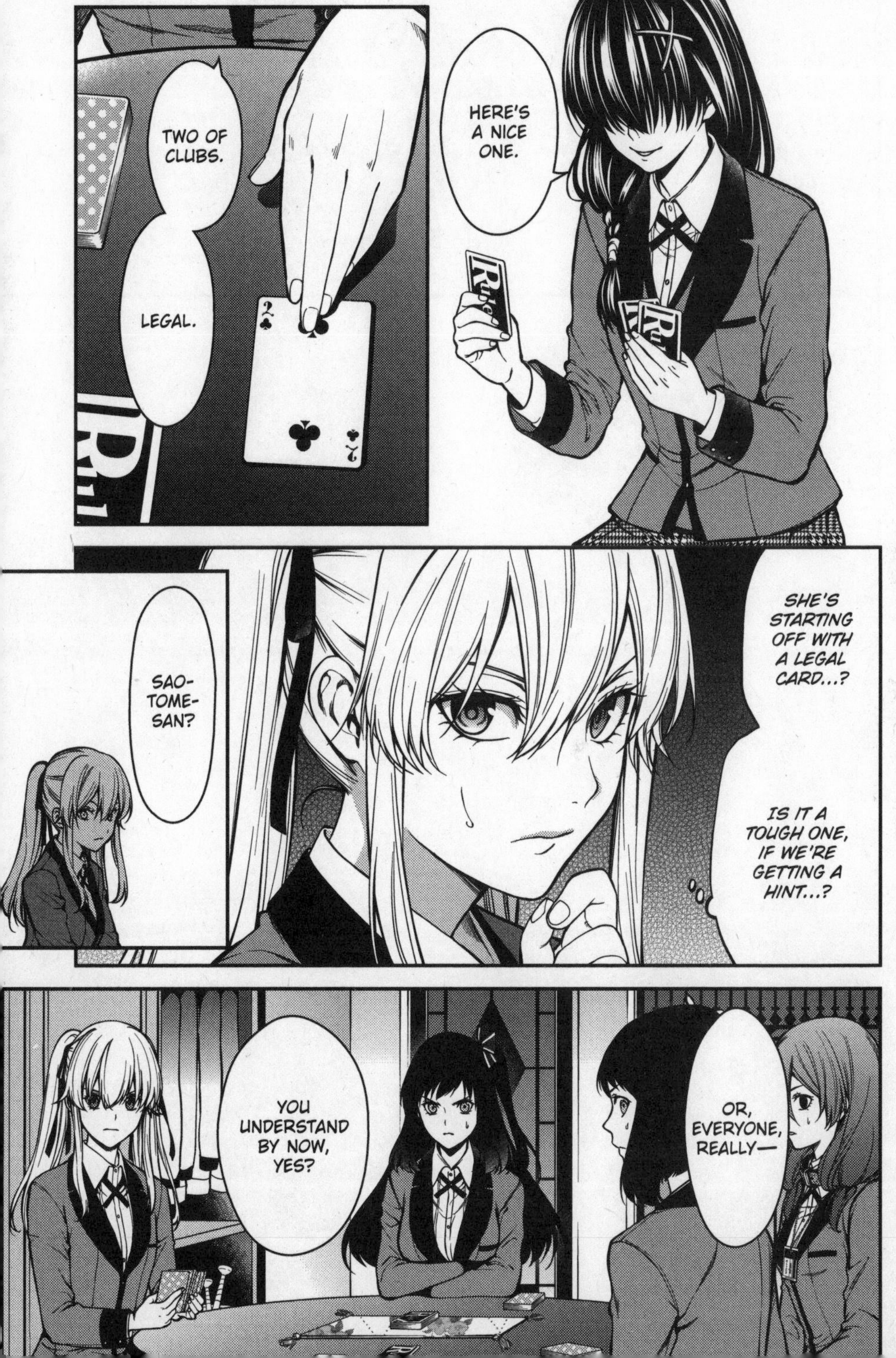
HERE'S A NICE ONE.
TWO OF CLUBS.
LEGAL.
SHE'S STARTING OFF WITH A LEGAL CARD...?
IS IT A TOUGH ONE, IF WE'RE GETTING A HINT...?
SAO-TOME-SAN?
OR, EVERYONE, REALLY—
YOU UNDERSTAND BY NOW, YES?

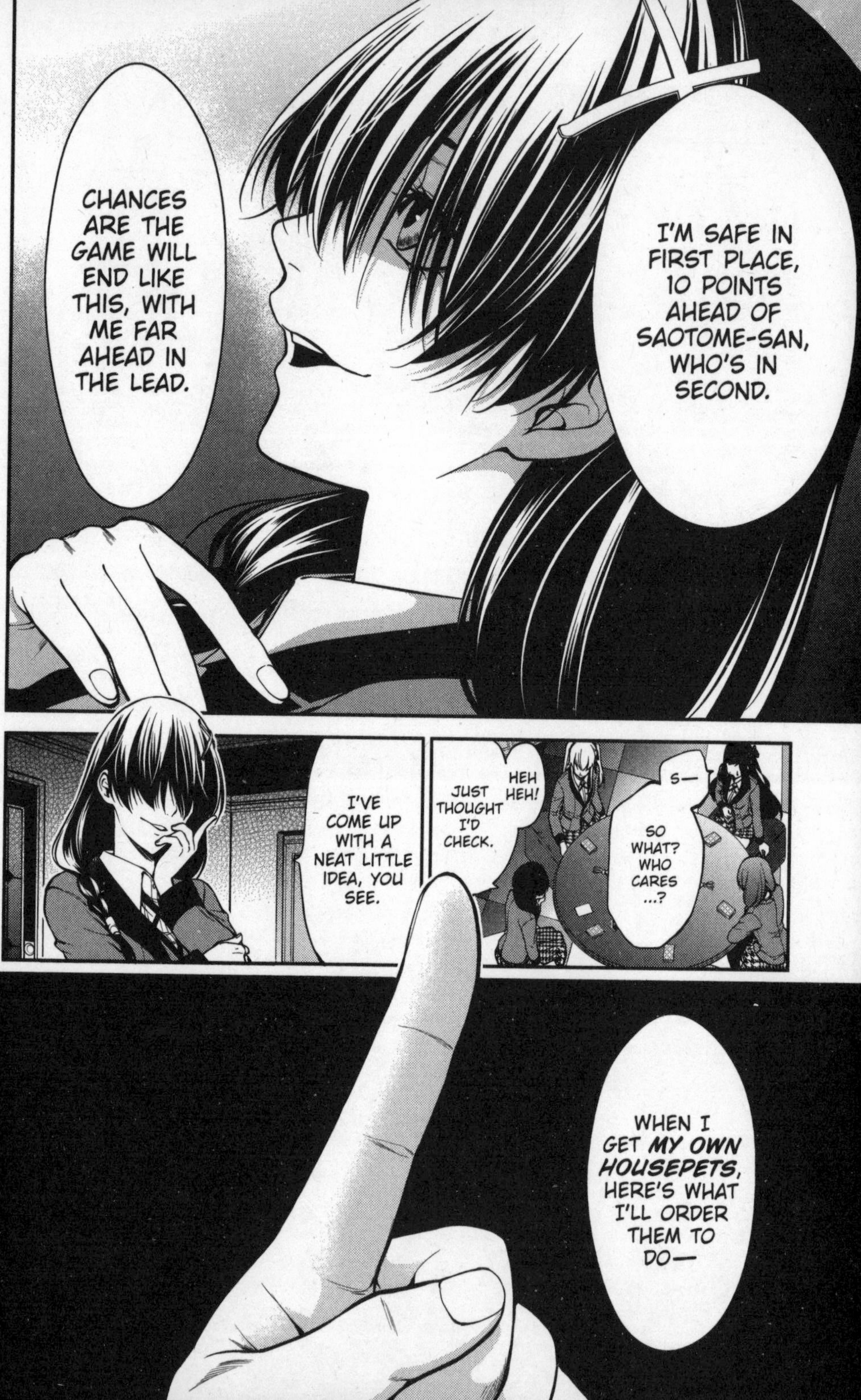
I'M SAFE IN FIRST PLACE, 10 POINTS AHEAD OF SAOTOME-SAN, WHO'S IN SECOND.
CHANCES ARE THE GAME WILL END LIKE THIS, WITH ME FAR AHEAD IN THE LEAD.
S—
SO WHAT? WHO CARES ...?
HEH HEH!
JUST THOUGHT I'D CHECK.
I'VE COME UP WITH A NEAT LITTLE IDEA, YOU SEE.
WHEN I GET ***MY OWN HOUSEPETS***, HERE'S WHAT I'LL ORDER THEM TO DO—

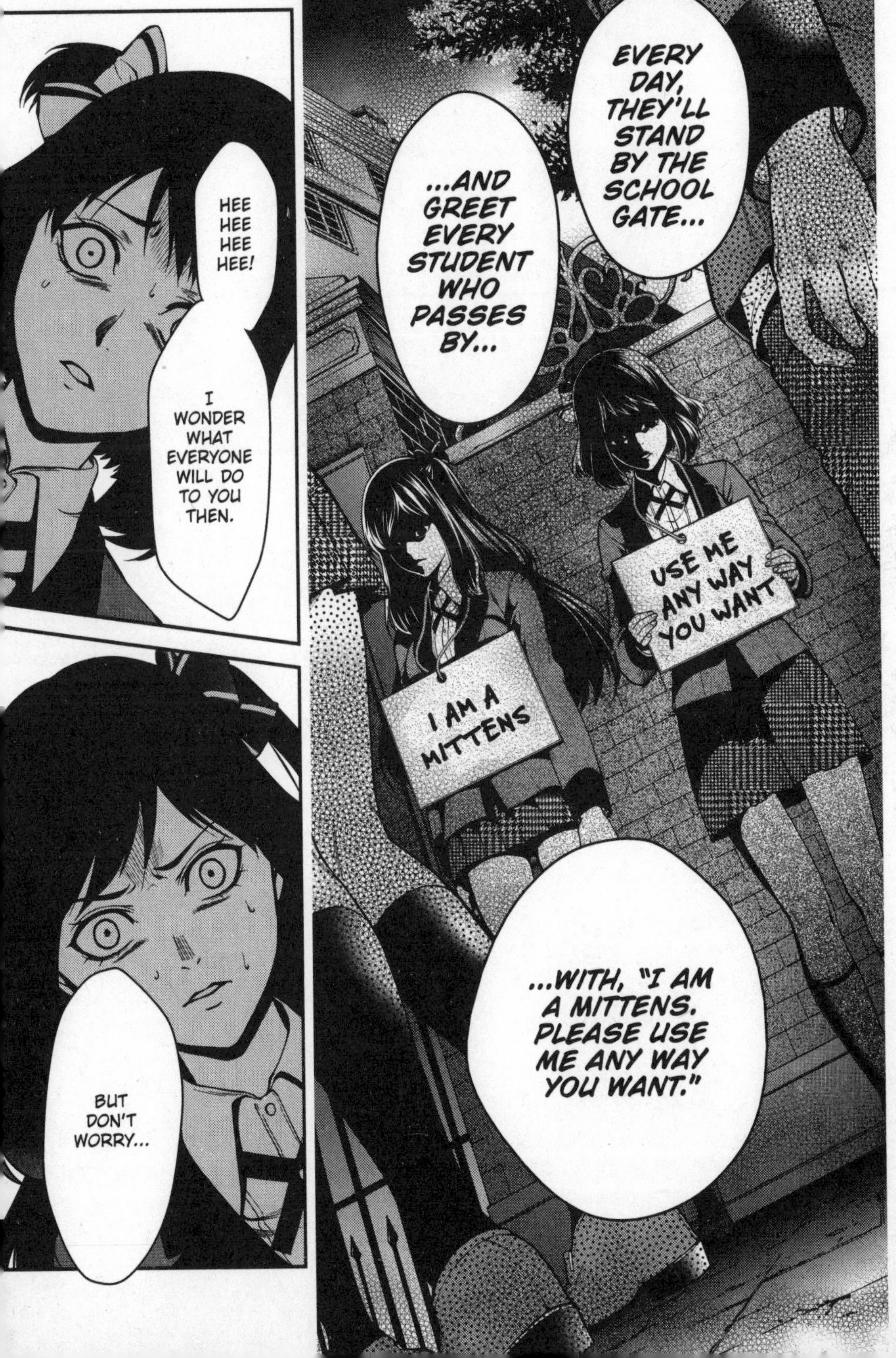
EVERY DAY, THEY'LL STAND BY THE SCHOOL GATE...
...AND GREET EVERY STUDENT WHO PASSES BY...
USE ME ANY WAY YOU WANT
I AM A MITTENS
...WITH, "I AM A MITTENS. PLEASE USE ME ANY WAY YOU WANT."
HEE HEE HEE HEE!
I WONDER WHAT EVERYONE WILL DO TO YOU THEN.
BUT DON'T WORRY...

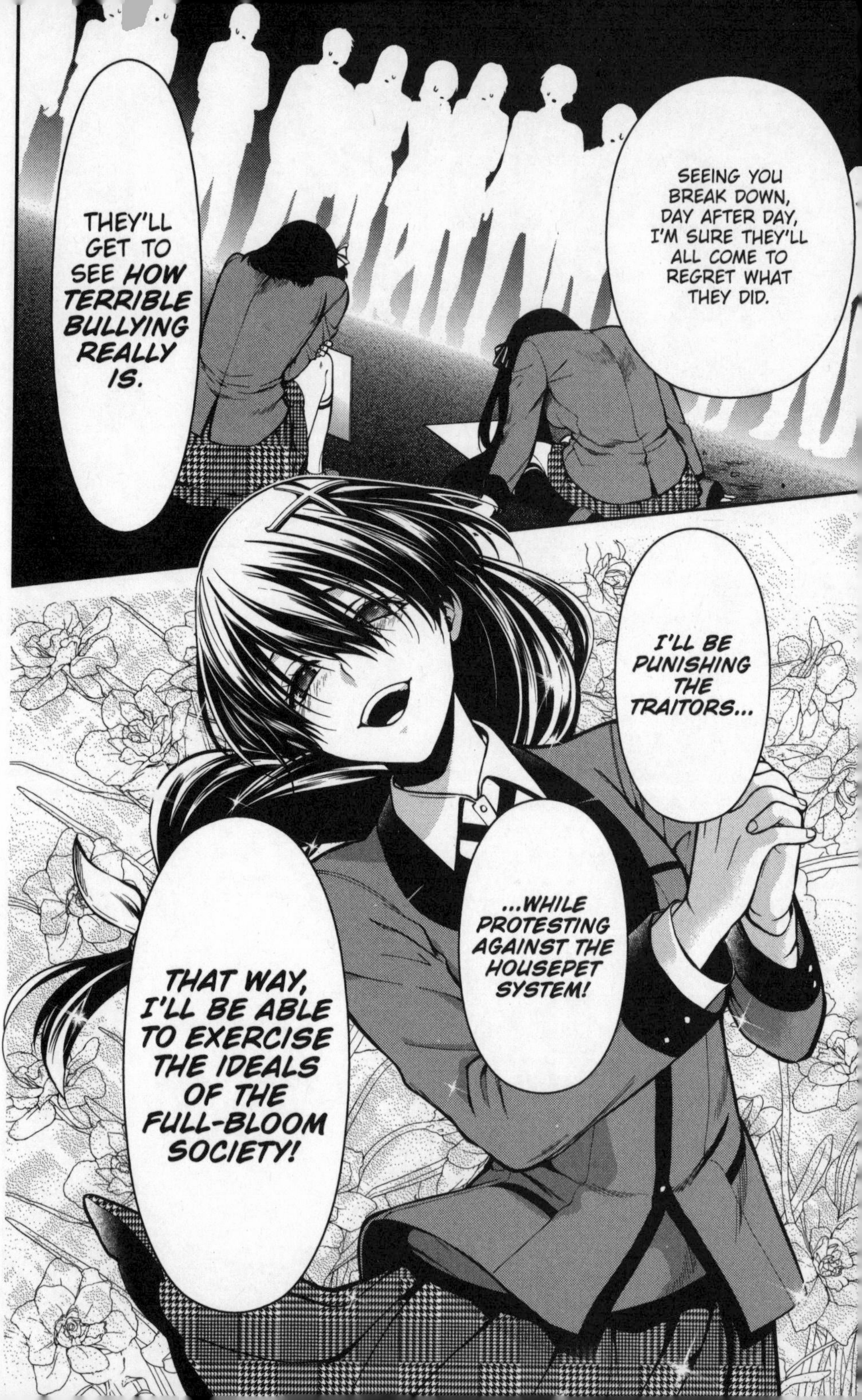
SEEING YOU BREAK DOWN, DAY AFTER DAY, I'M SURE THEY'LL ALL COME TO REGRET WHAT THEY DID.
THEY'LL GET TO SEE *HOW TERRIBLE BULLYING REALLY IS.*
I'LL BE PUNISHING THE TRAITORS...
...WHILE PROTESTING AGAINST THE HOUSEPET SYSTEM!
THAT WAY, I'LL BE ABLE TO EXERCISE THE IDEALS OF THE FULL-BLOOM SOCIETY!

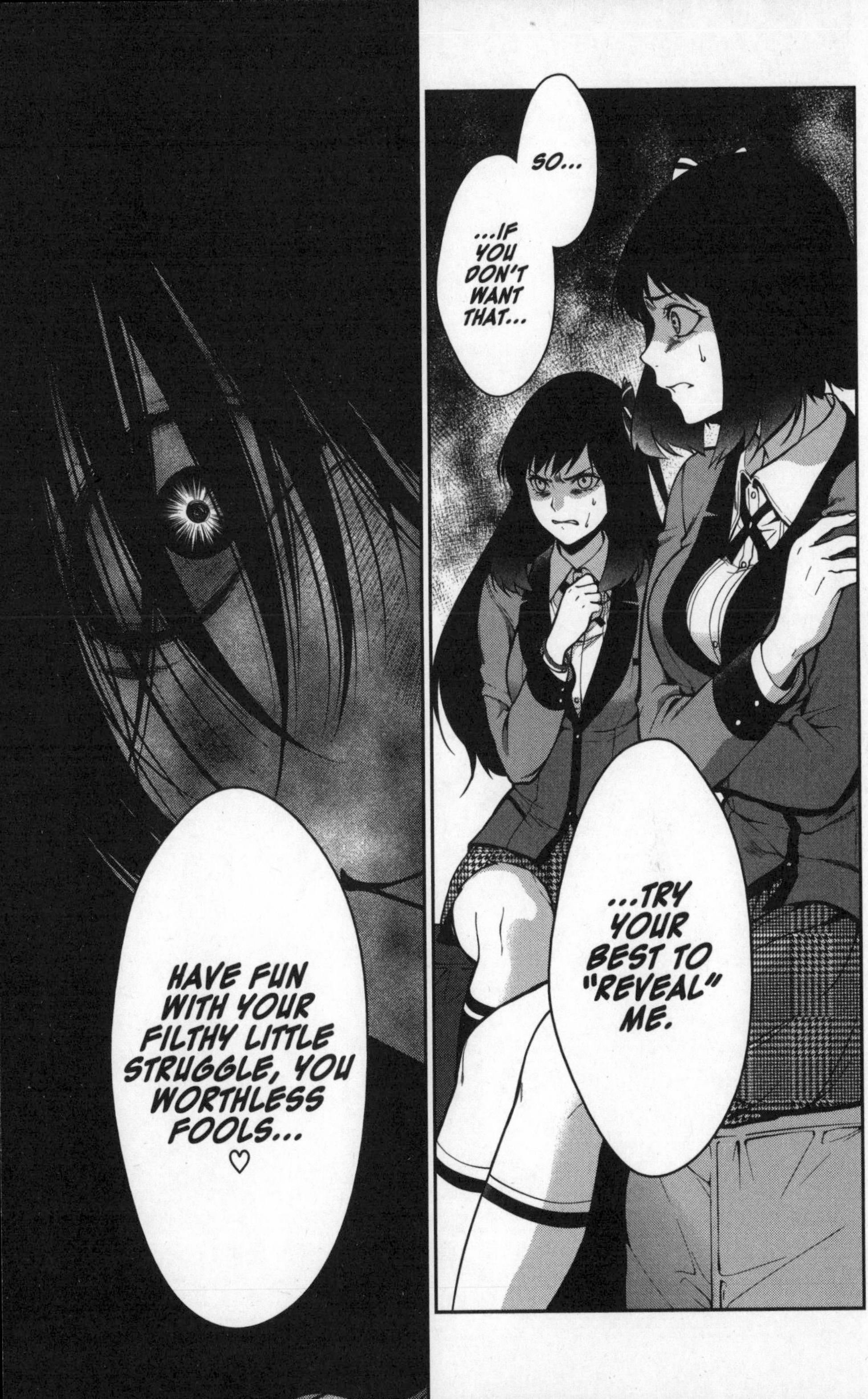
SO...
...IF YOU DON'T WANT THAT...
...TRY YOUR BEST TO "REVEAL" ME.
HAVE FUN WITH YOUR FILTHY LITTLE STRUGGLE, YOU WORTHLESS FOOLS... ♡

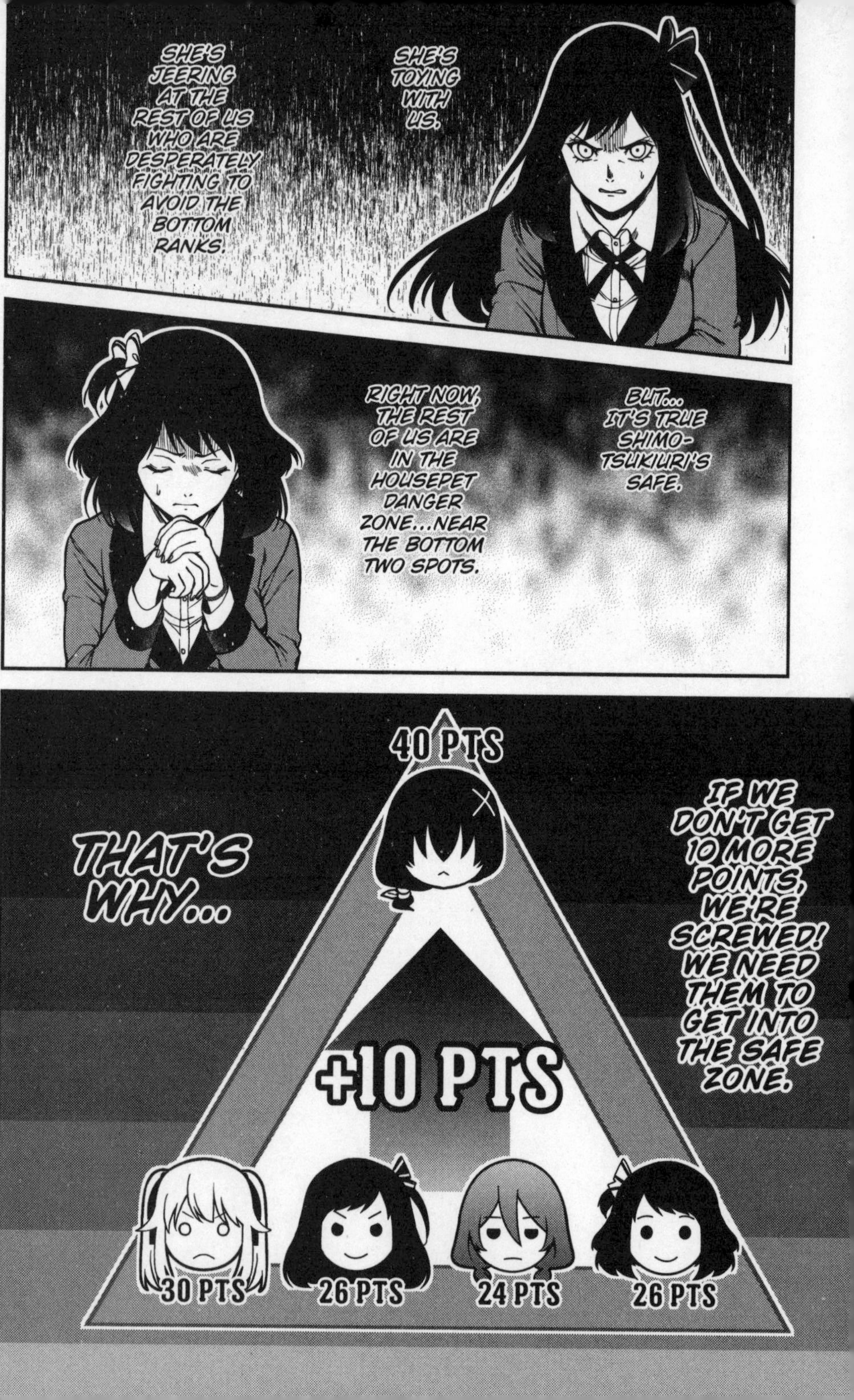
SHE'S TOYING WITH US.
SHE'S JEERING AT THE REST OF US WHO ARE DESPERATELY FIGHTING TO AVOID THE BOTTOM RANKS.
BUT... IT'S TRUE SHIMO-TSUKIURI'S SAFE.
RIGHT NOW, THE REST OF US ARE IN THE HOUSEPET DANGER ZONE...NEAR THE BOTTOM TWO SPOTS.
40 PTS
IF WE DON'T GET 10 MORE POINTS, WE'RE SCREWED! WE NEED THEM TO GET INTO THE SAFE ZONE.
THAT'S WHY...
+10 PTS
30 PTS
26 PTS
24 PTS
26 PTS

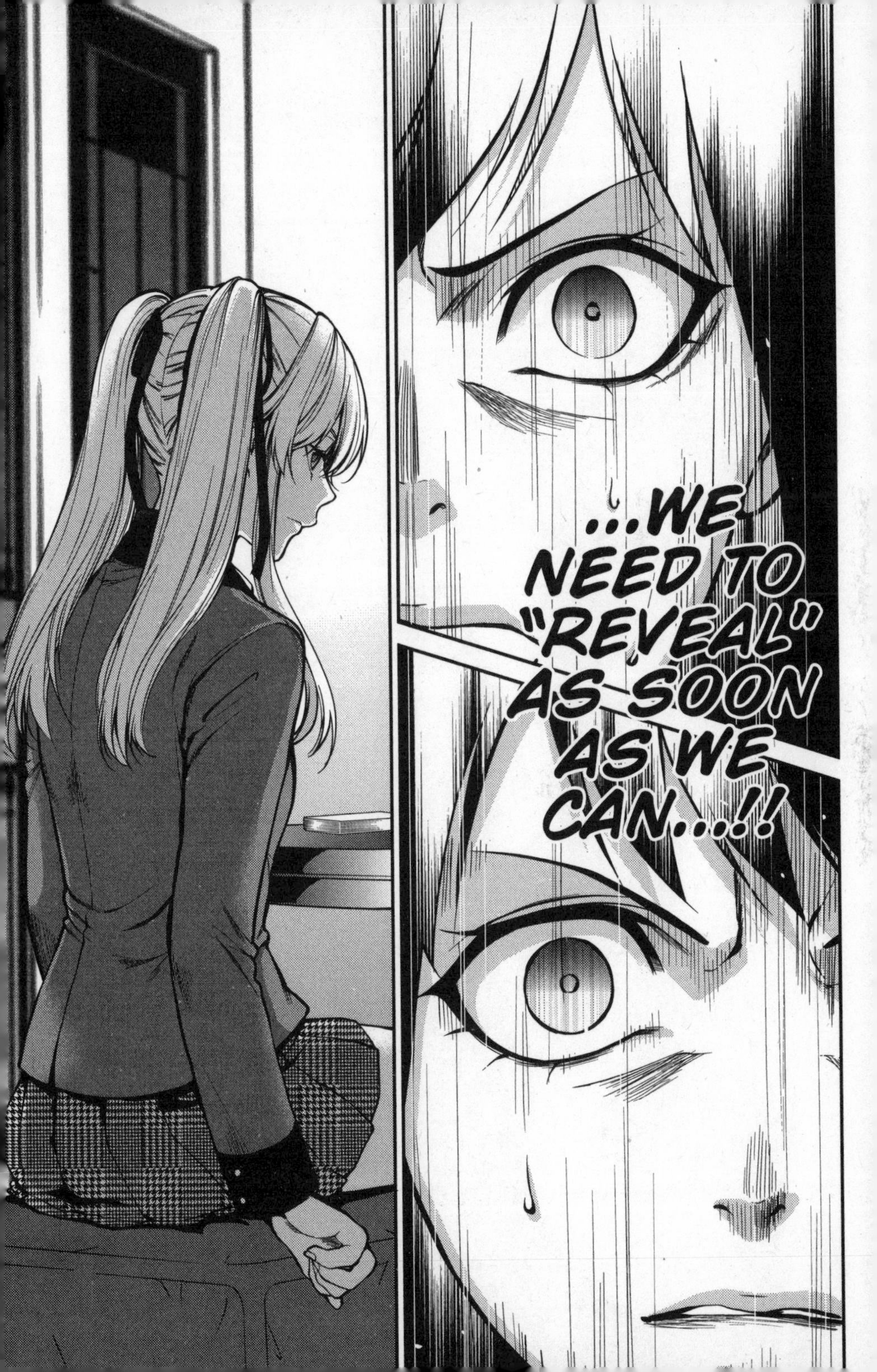
...WE NEED TO "REVEAL" AS SOON AS WE CAN...!!

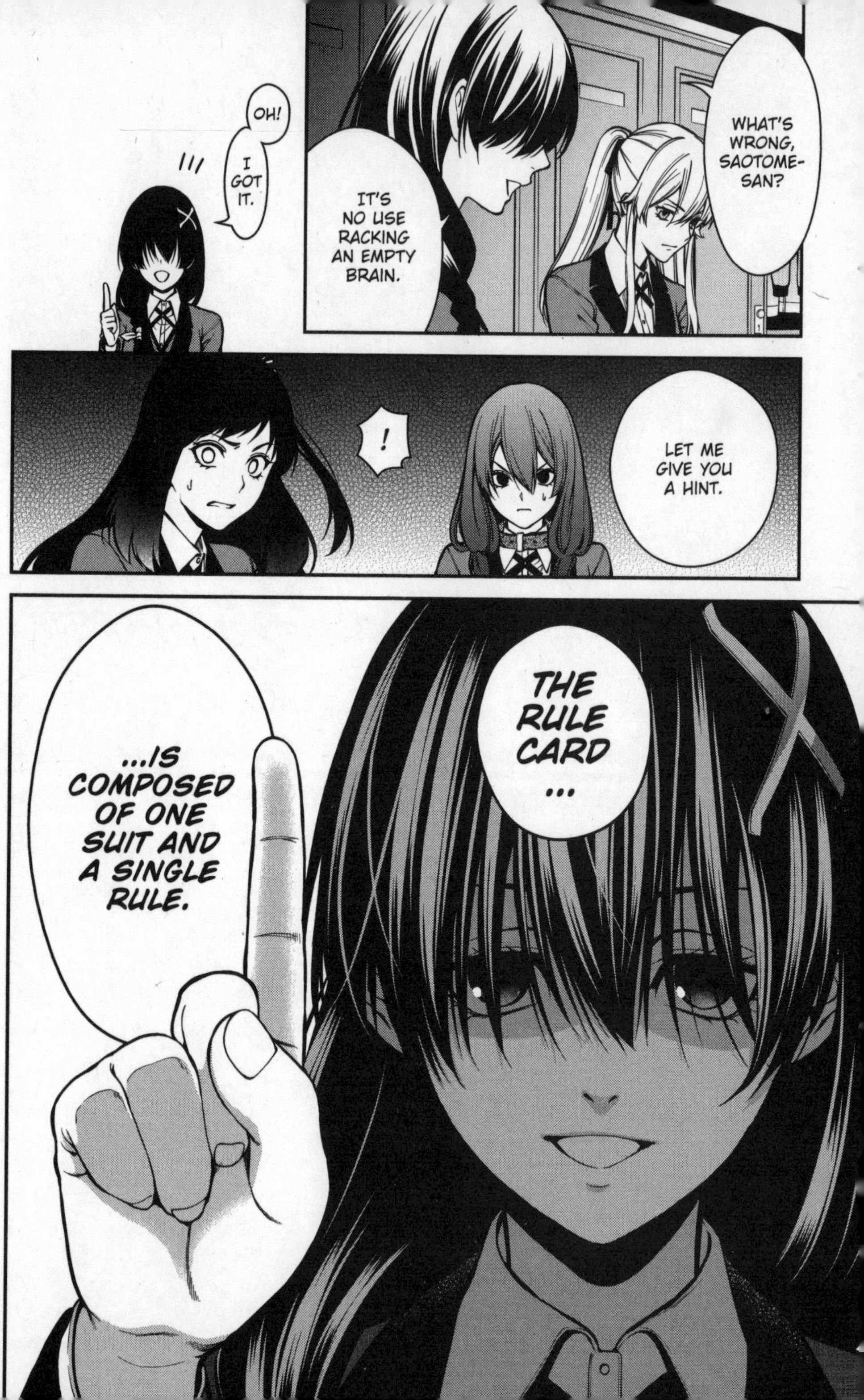
WHAT'S WRONG, SAOTOME-SAN?
IT'S NO USE RACKING AN EMPTY BRAIN.
OH!
I GOT IT.
///
LET ME GIVE YOU A HINT.
!
THE RULE CARD ...
...IS COMPOSED OF ONE SUIT AND A SINGLE RULE.

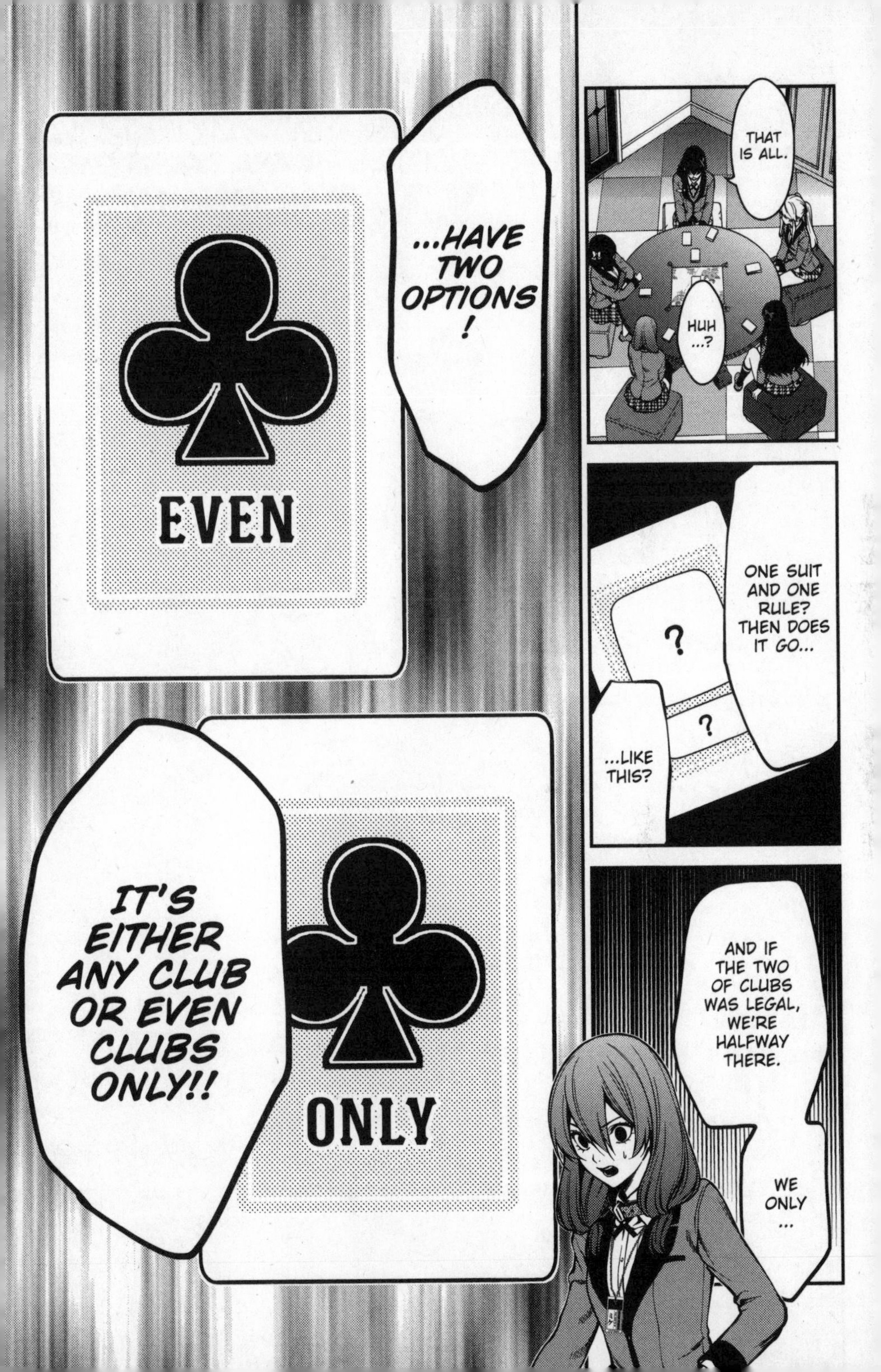
THAT IS ALL.
HUH ...?
ONE SUIT AND ONE RULE? THEN DOES IT GO...
?
?
...LIKE THIS?
AND IF THE TWO OF CLUBS WAS LEGAL, WE'RE HALFWAY THERE.
WE ONLY ...
...HAVE TWO OPTIONS!
EVEN
ONLY
IT'S EITHER ANY CLUB OR EVEN CLUBS ONLY!!

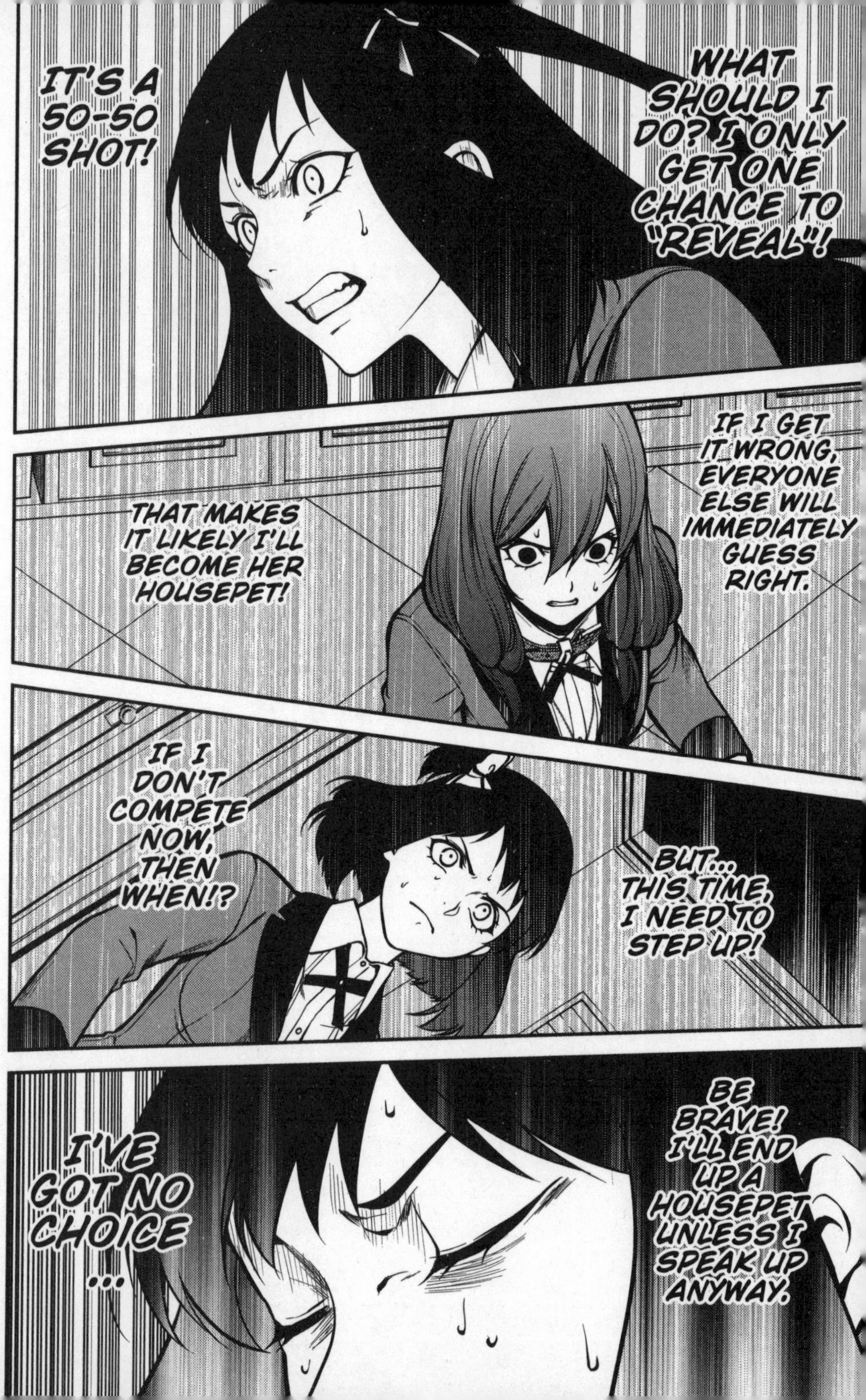
WHAT SHOULD I DO? I ONLY GET ONE CHANCE TO "REVEAL"!
IT'S A 50-50 SHOT!
IF I GET IT WRONG, EVERYONE ELSE WILL IMMEDIATELY GUESS RIGHT.
THAT MAKES IT LIKELY I'LL BECOME HER HOUSEPET!
BUT... THIS TIME, I NEED TO STEP UP!
IF I DON'T COMPETE NOW, THEN WHEN!?
BE BRAVE! I'LL END UP A HOUSEPET UNLESS I SPEAK UP ANYWAY.
I'VE GOT NO CHOICE ...

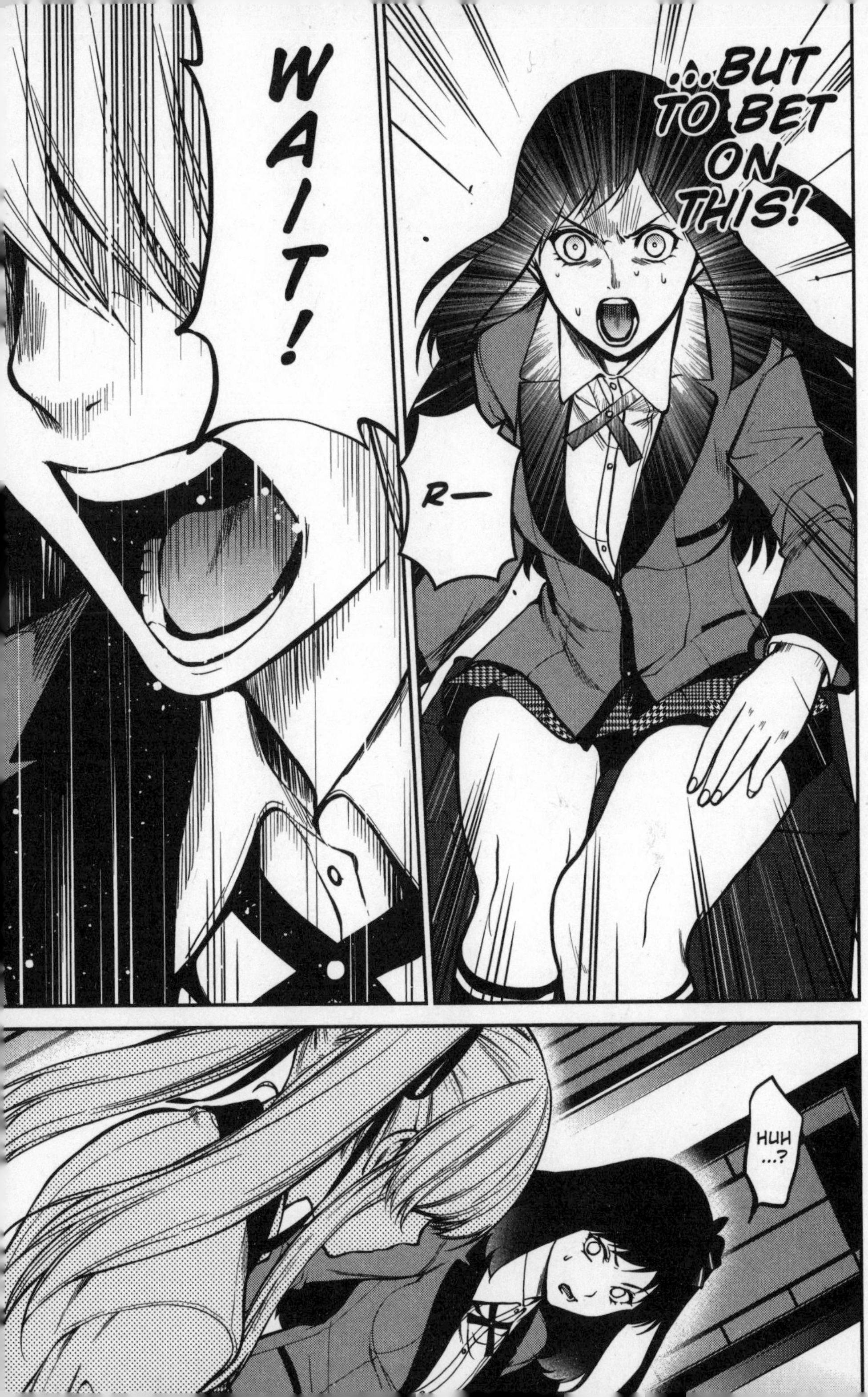
...BUT TO BET ON THIS!
R—
WAIT!
HUH ...?

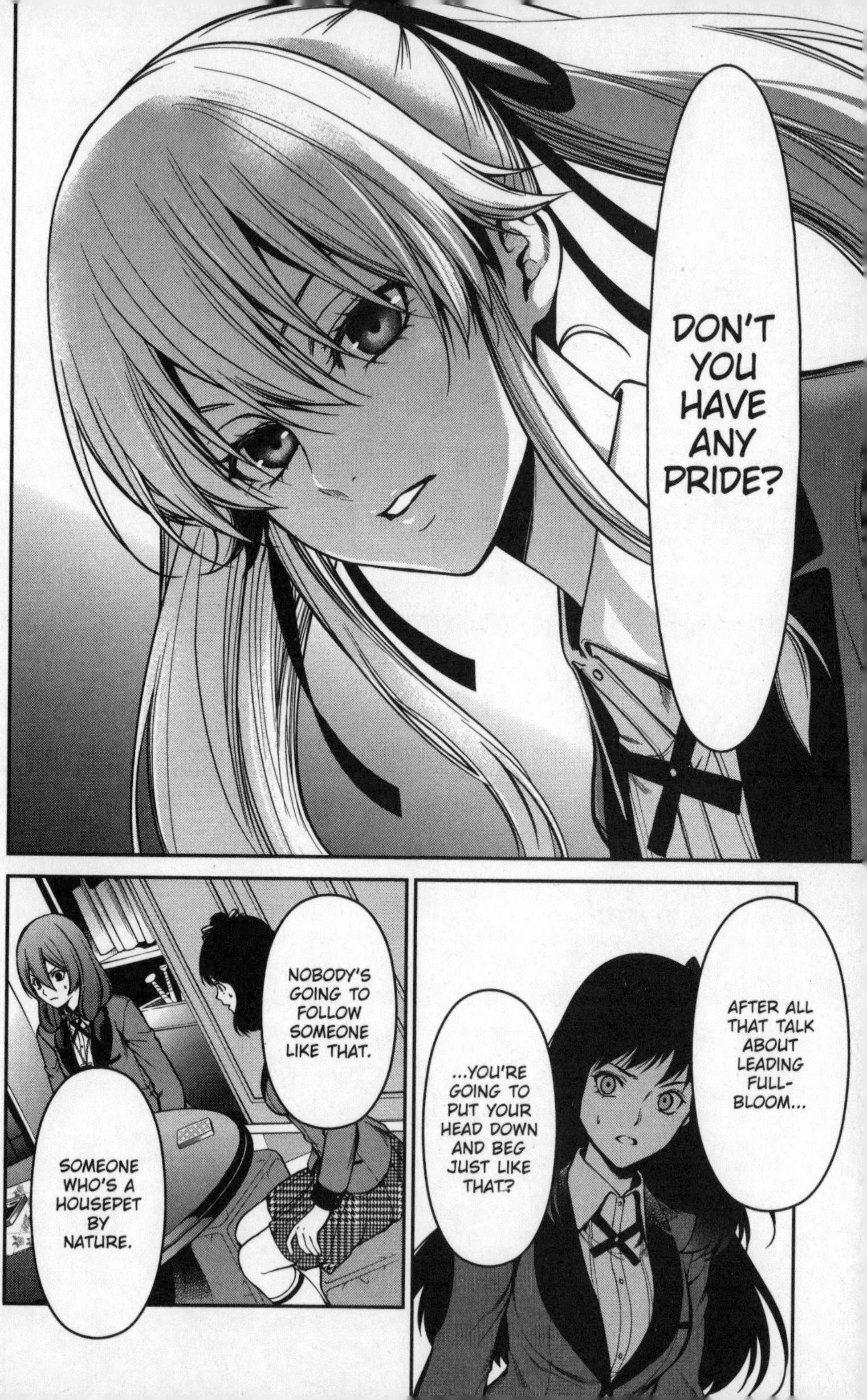
DON'T YOU HAVE ANY PRIDE?
AFTER ALL THAT TALK ABOUT LEADING FULL-BLOOM...
...YOU'RE GOING TO PUT YOUR HEAD DOWN AND BEG JUST LIKE THAT?
NOBODY'S GOING TO FOLLOW SOMEONE LIKE THAT.
SOMEONE WHO'S A HOUSEPET BY NATURE.

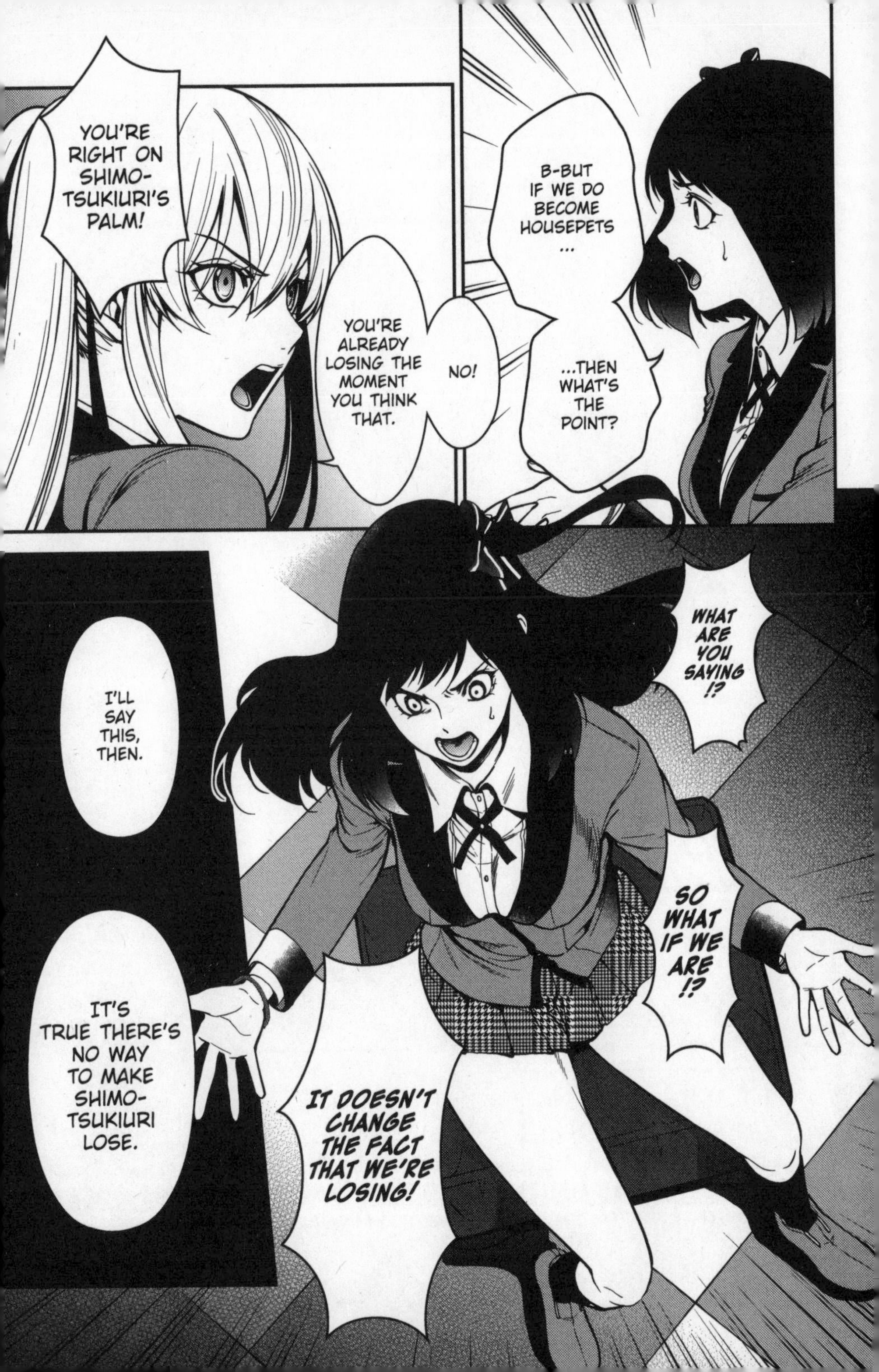
B-BUT IF WE DO BECOME HOUSEPETS ...
...THEN WHAT'S THE POINT?
NO!
YOU'RE ALREADY LOSING THE MOMENT YOU THINK THAT.
YOU'RE RIGHT ON SHIMO-TSUKIURI'S PALM!
WHAT ARE YOU SAYING !?
SO WHAT IF WE ARE !?
IT DOESN'T CHANGE THE FACT THAT WE'RE LOSING!
I'LL SAY THIS, THEN.
IT'S TRUE THERE'S NO WAY TO MAKE SHIMO-TSUKIURI LOSE.

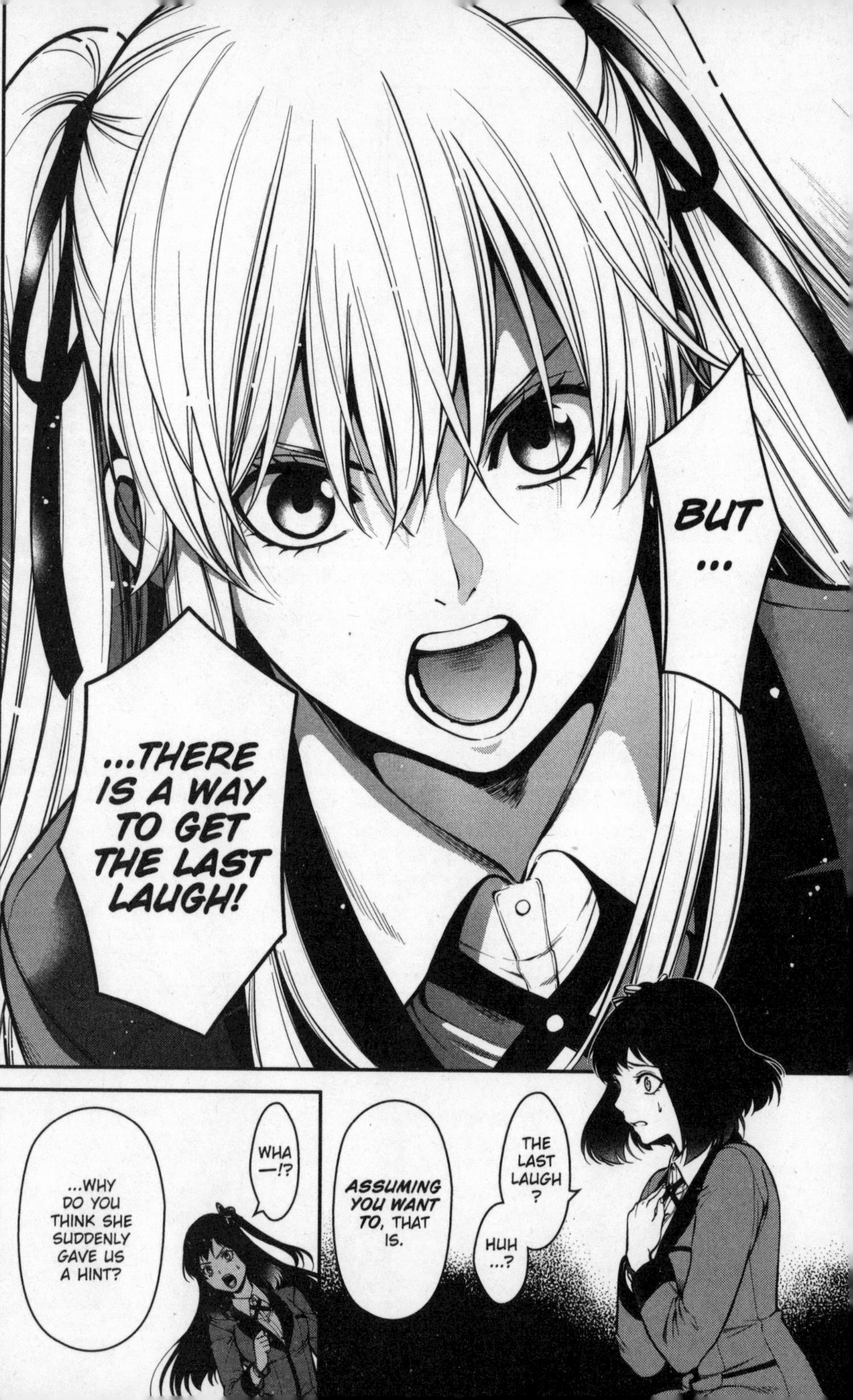
BUT ...
...THERE IS A WAY TO GET THE LAST LAUGH!
THE LAST LAUGH?
HUH ...?
ASSUMING YOU WANT TO, THAT IS.
WHA—!?
...WHY DO YOU THINK SHE SUDDENLY GAVE US A HINT?

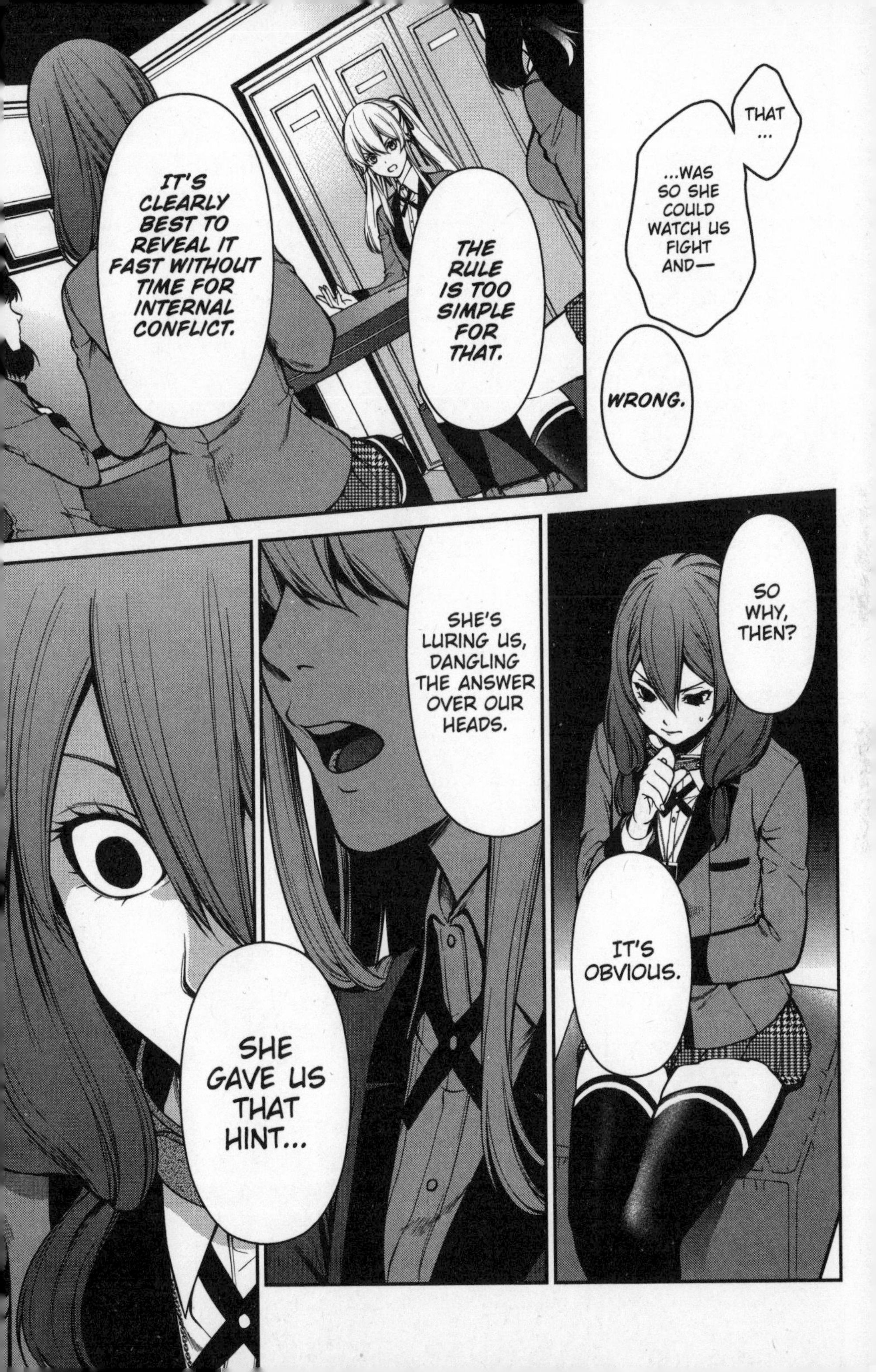
THAT ...
...WAS SO SHE COULD WATCH US FIGHT AND—
WRONG.
THE RULE IS TOO SIMPLE FOR THAT.
IT'S CLEARLY BEST TO REVEAL IT FAST WITHOUT TIME FOR INTERNAL CONFLICT.
SO WHY, THEN?
IT'S OBVIOUS.
SHE'S LURING US, DANGLING THE ANSWER OVER OUR HEADS.
SHE GAVE US THAT HINT...

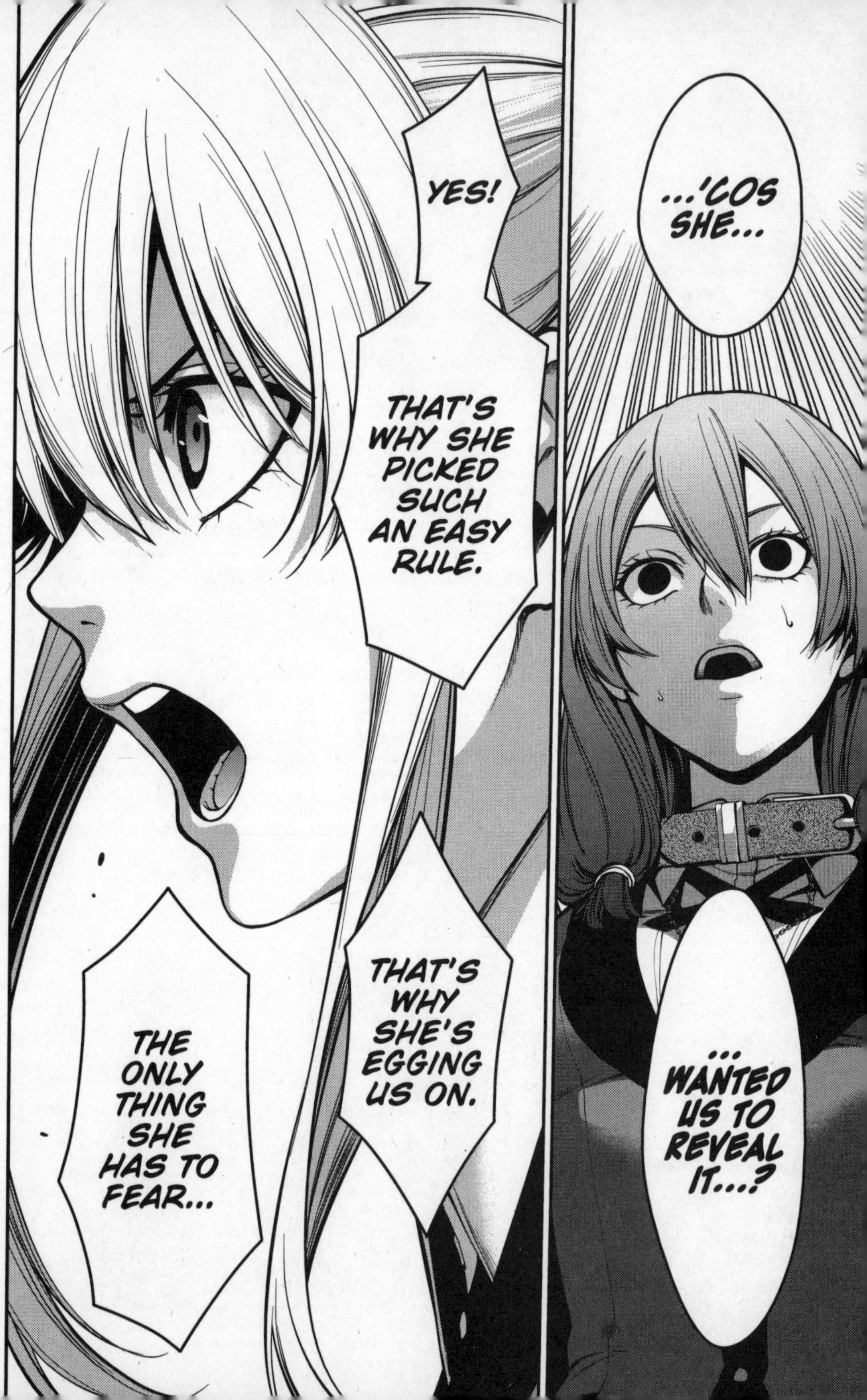
...'COS SHE...
...WANTED US TO REVEAL IT...?
YES!
THAT'S WHY SHE PICKED SUCH AN EASY RULE.
THAT'S WHY SHE'S EGGING US ON.
THE ONLY THING SHE HAS TO FEAR...

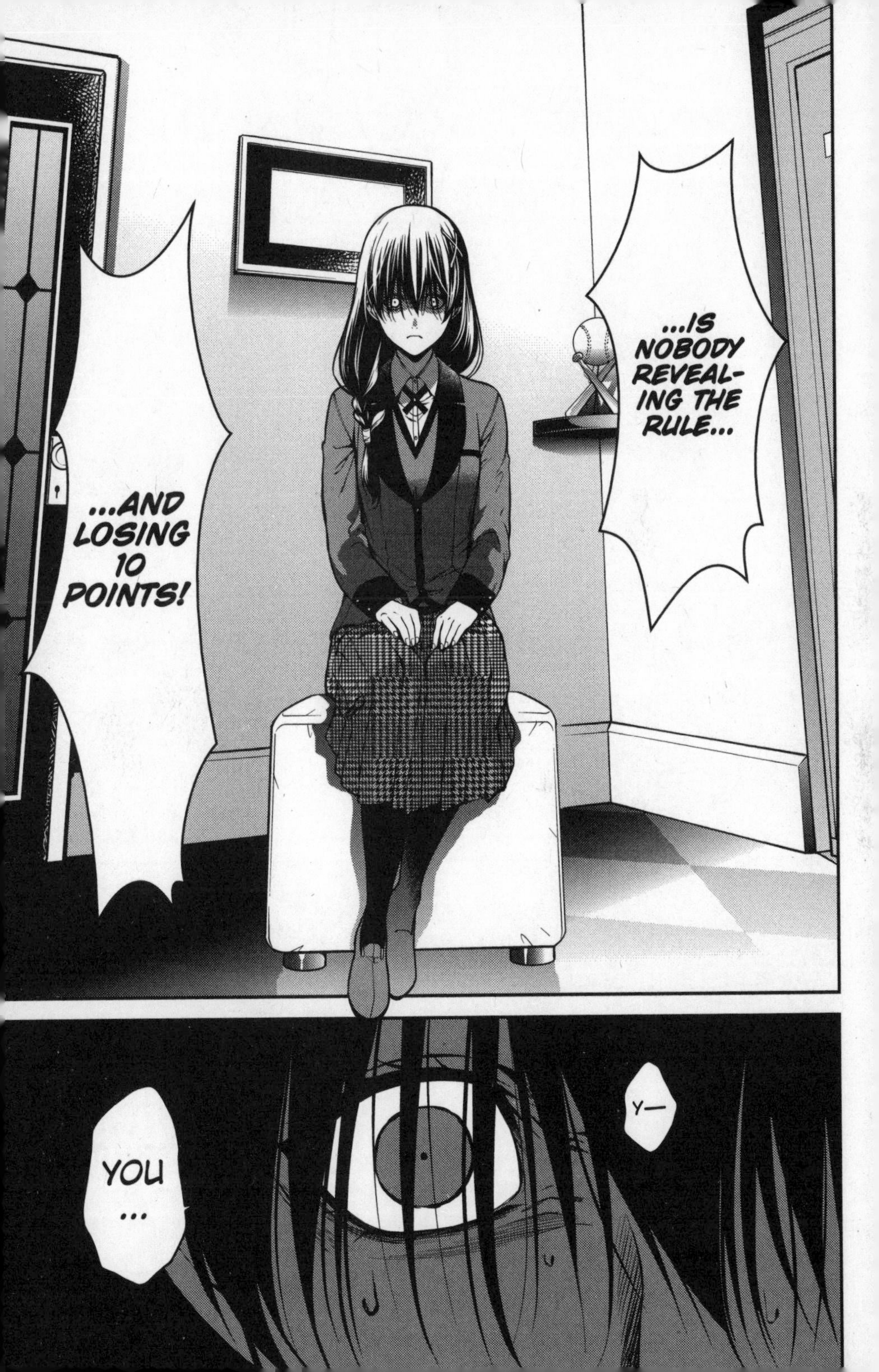
...IS NOBODY REVEALING THE RULE...
...AND LOSING 10 POINTS!
Y—
YOU ...

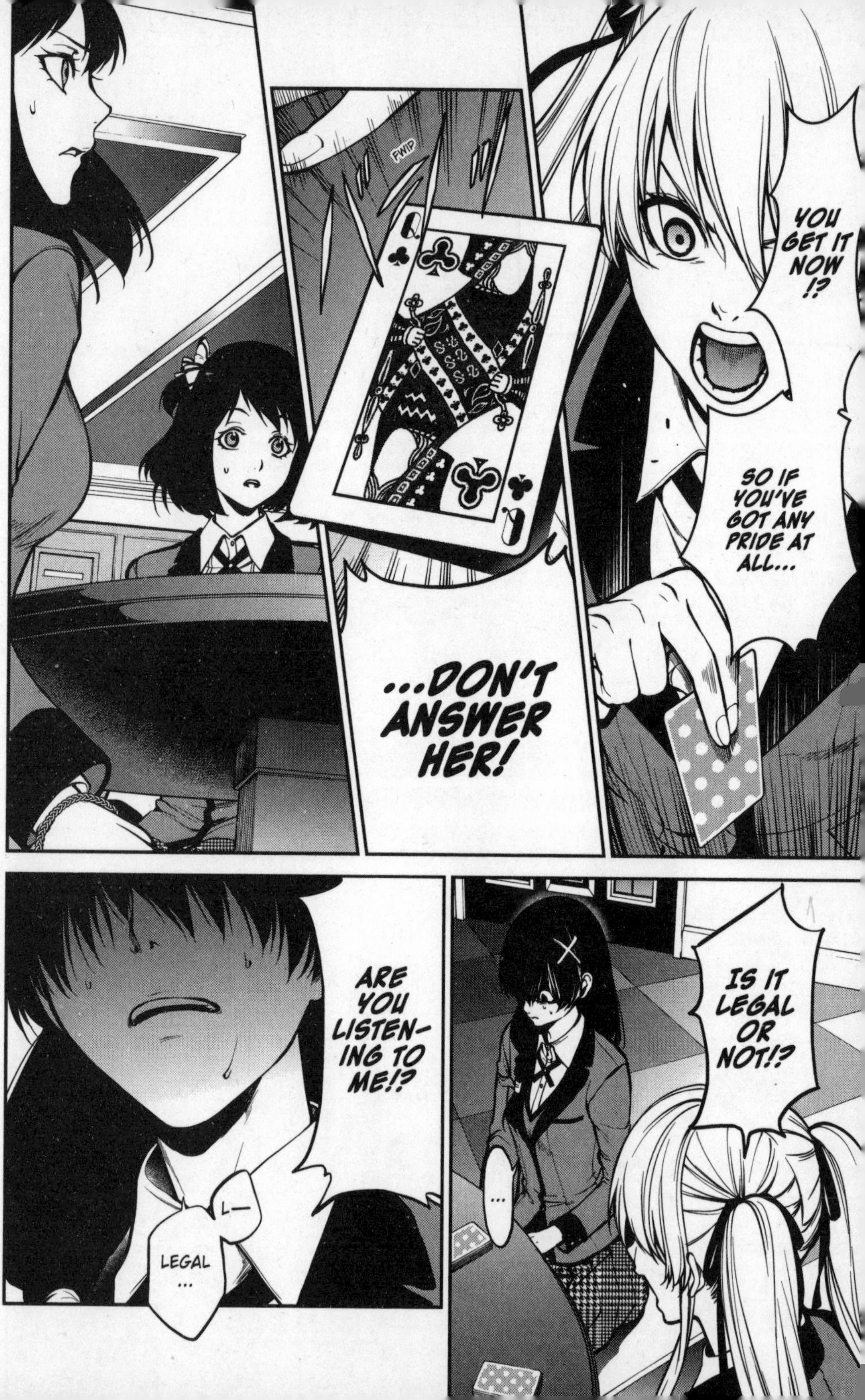
YOU GET IT NOW!?
SO IF YOU'VE GOT ANY PRIDE AT ALL...
FWIP
...DON'T ANSWER HER!
IS IT LEGAL OR NOT!?
...
ARE YOU LISTEN-ING TO ME!?
L—
LEGAL...

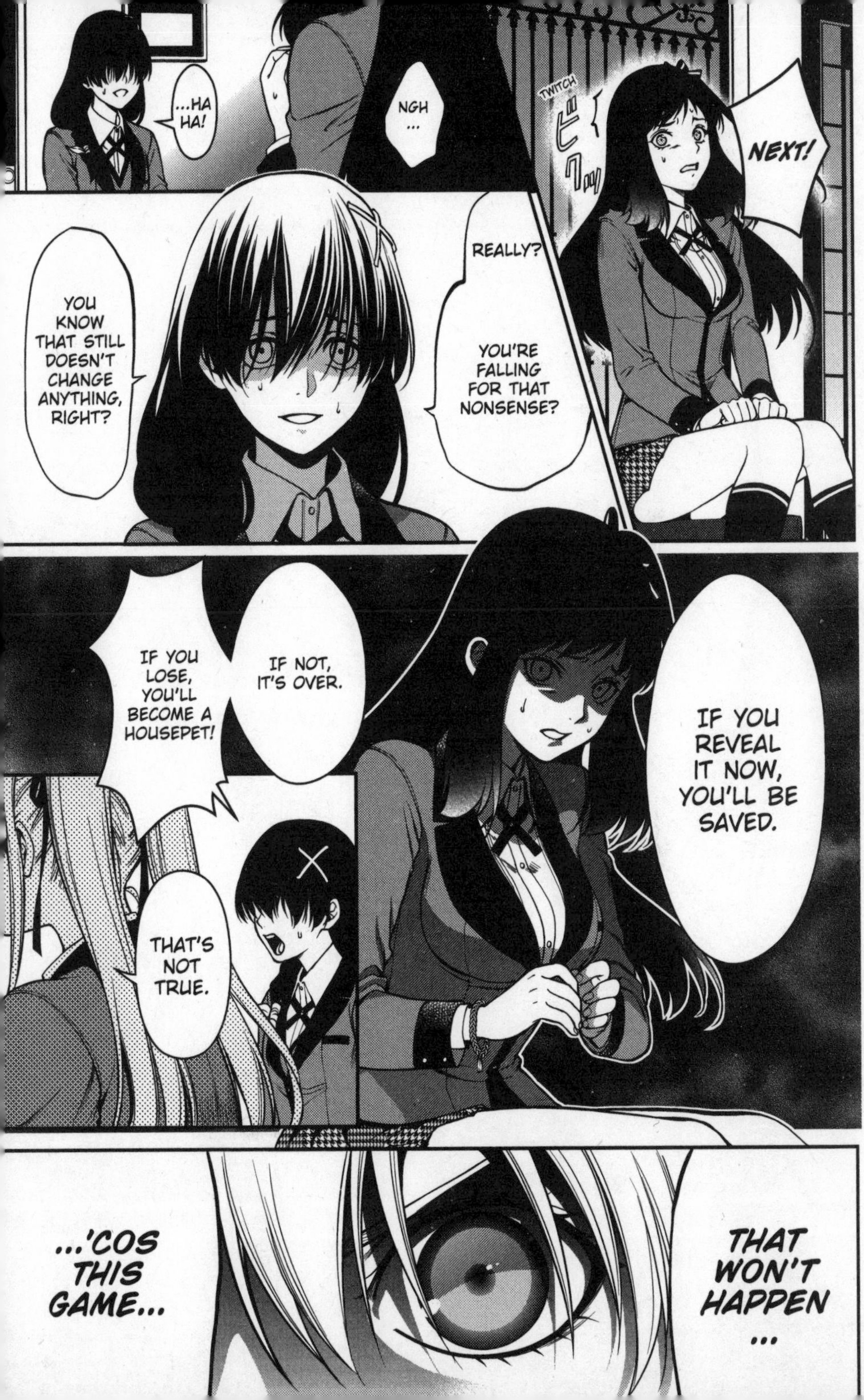
TWITCH
ビクッ
NEXT!
NGH ...
...HA HA!
REALLY?
YOU'RE FALLING FOR THAT NONSENSE?
YOU KNOW THAT STILL DOESN'T CHANGE ANYTHING, RIGHT?
IF YOU REVEAL IT NOW, YOU'LL BE SAVED.
IF NOT, IT'S OVER.
IF YOU LOSE, YOU'LL BECOME A HOUSEPET!
THAT'S NOT TRUE.
THAT WON'T HAPPEN ...
...'COS THIS GAME...

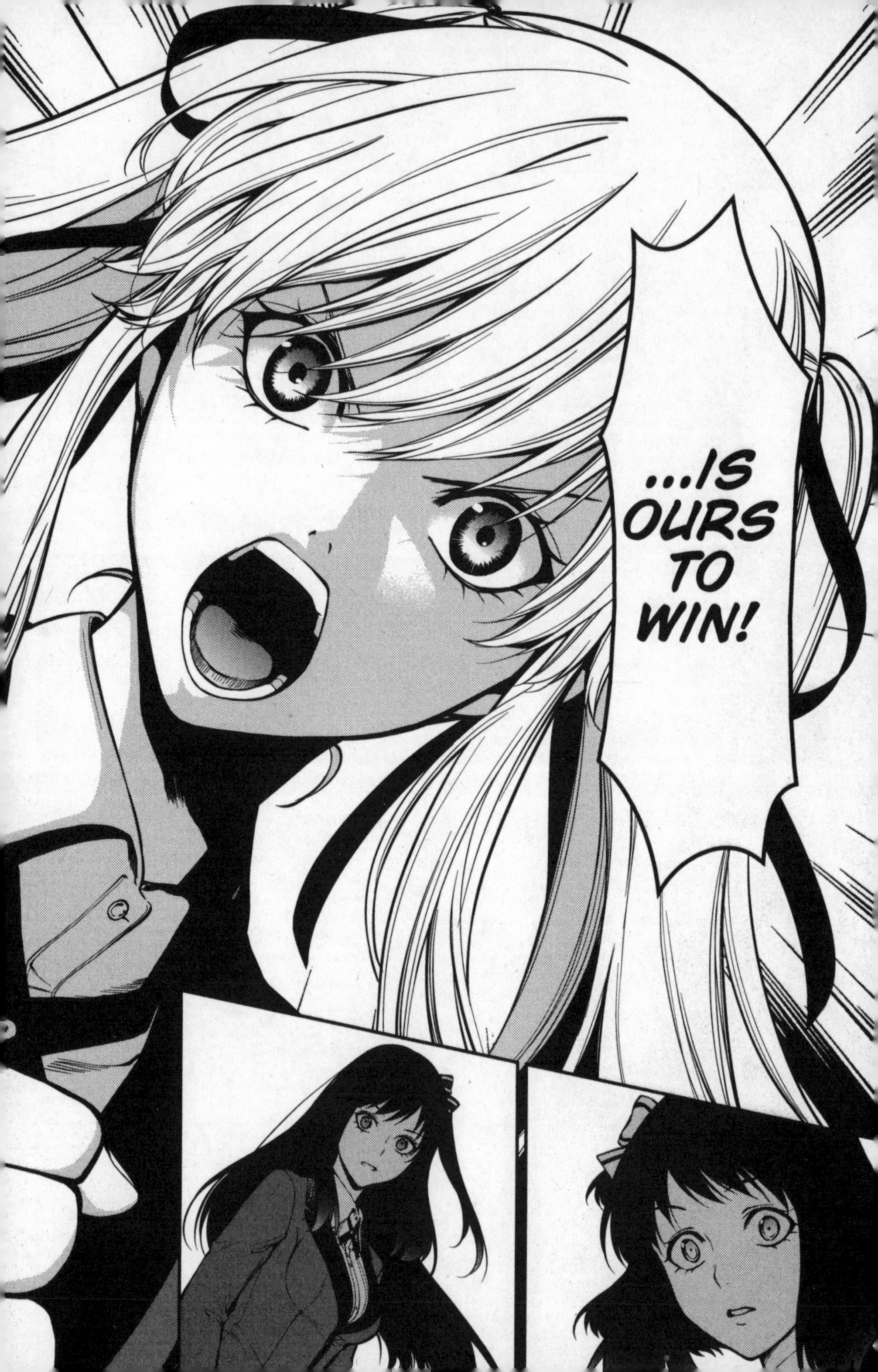
...IS OURS TO WIN!

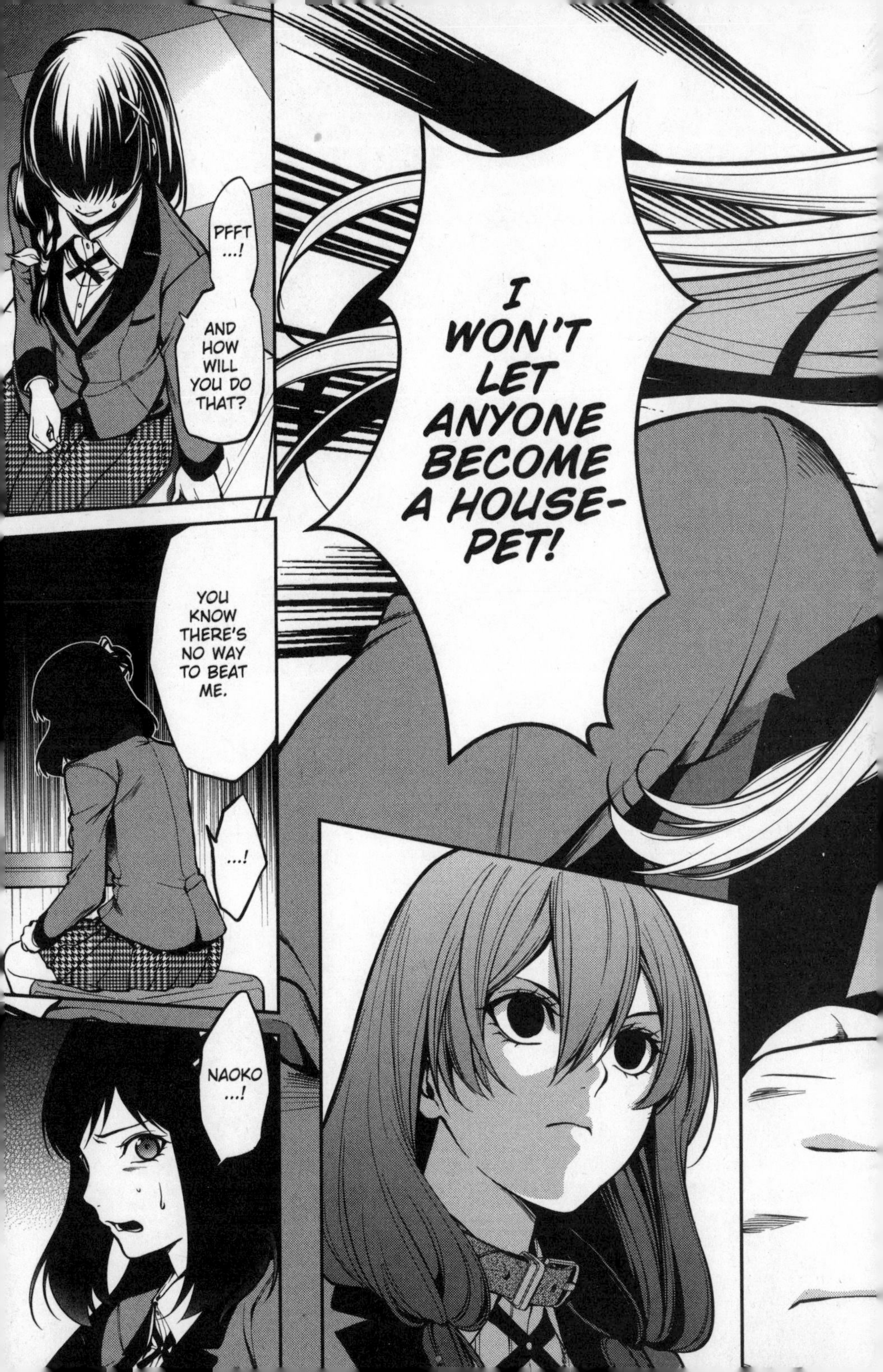
I WON'T LET ANYONE BECOME A HOUSE-PET!
PFFT ...!
AND HOW WILL YOU DO THAT?
YOU KNOW THERE'S NO WAY TO BEAT ME.
...!
NAOKO ...!

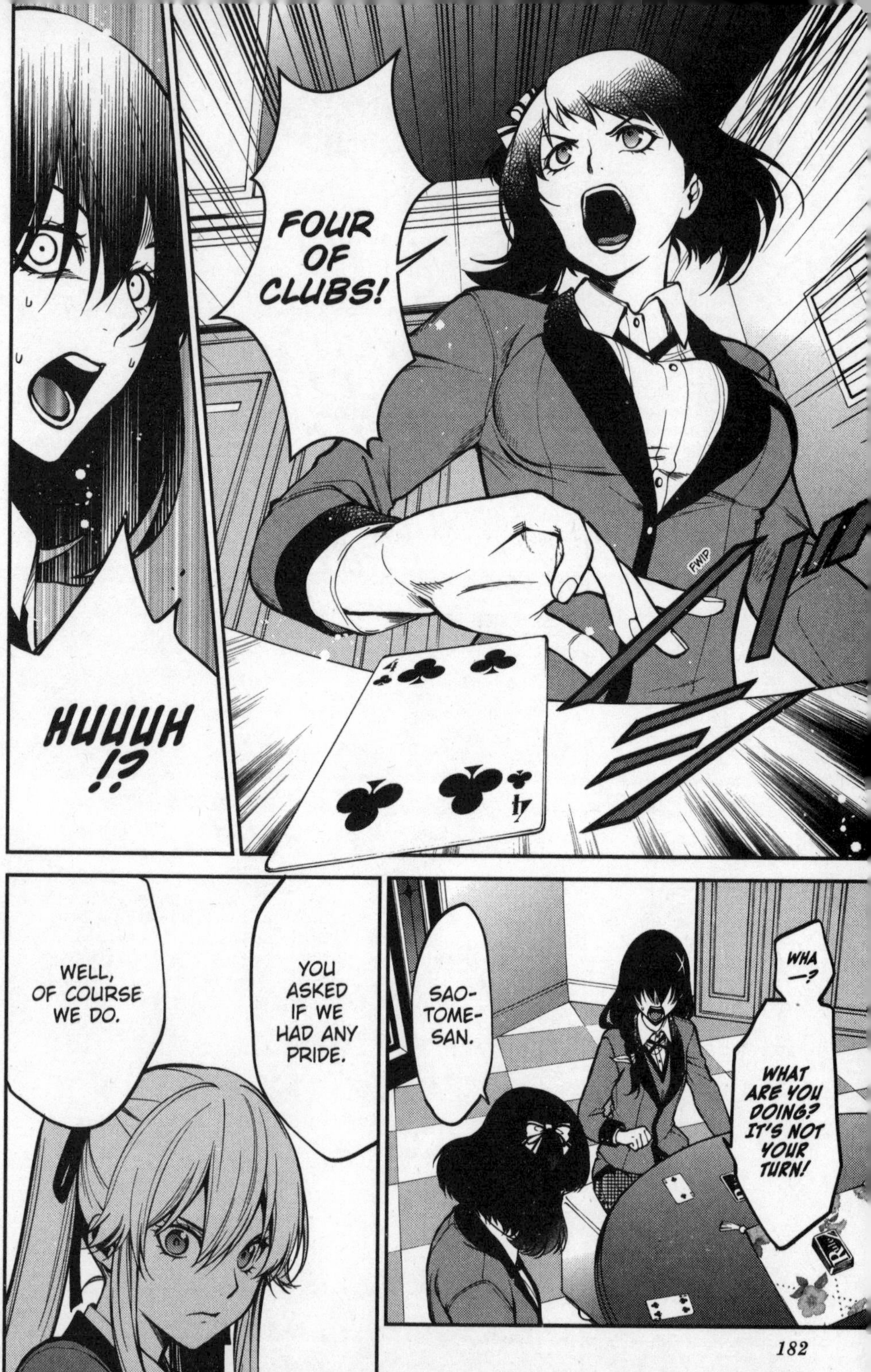
FOUR OF CLUBS!
FWIP
HUUUH!?
WHA—?
WHAT ARE YOU DOING? IT'S NOT YOUR TURN!
SAO-TOME-SAN.
YOU ASKED IF WE HAD ANY PRIDE.
WELL, OF COURSE WE DO.

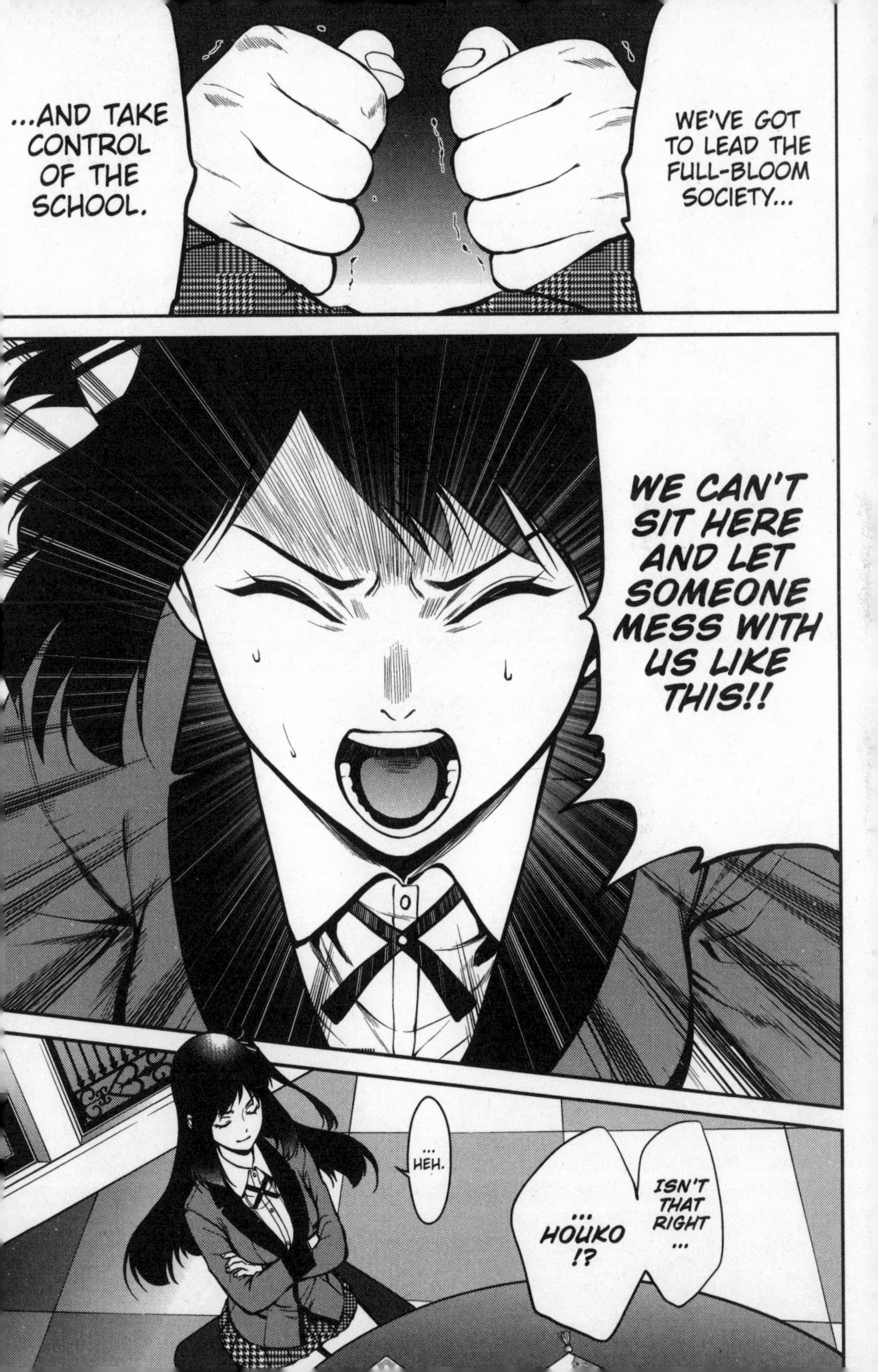
WE'VE GOT TO LEAD THE FULL-BLOOM SOCIETY...
...AND TAKE CONTROL OF THE SCHOOL.
WE CAN'T SIT HERE AND LET SOMEONE MESS WITH US LIKE THIS!!
ISN'T THAT RIGHT ...
... HÖUKO !?
... HEH.

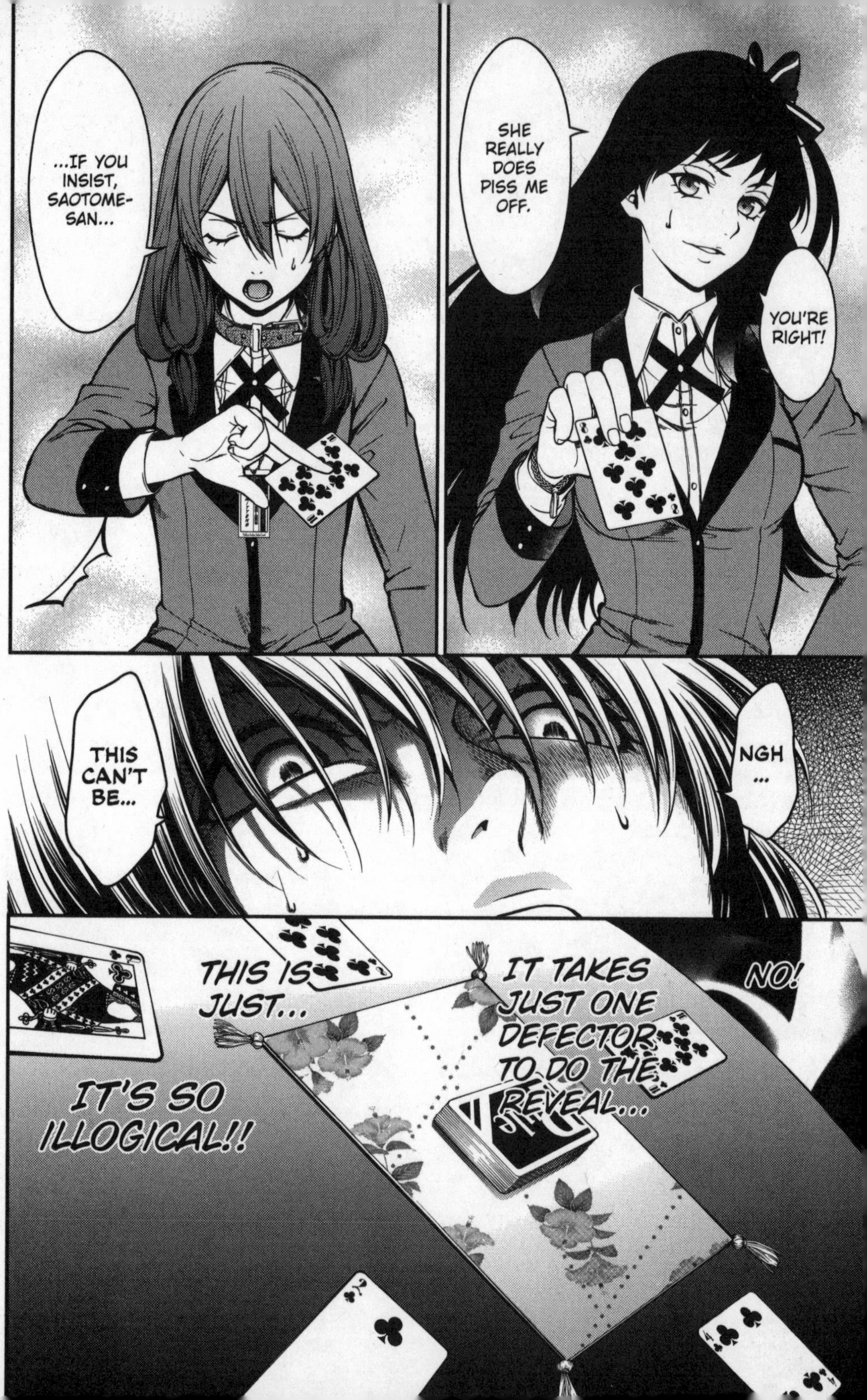
SHE REALLY DOES PISS ME OFF.
YOU'RE RIGHT!
...IF YOU INSIST, SAOTOME-SAN...
NGH...
THIS CAN'T BE...
NO!
IT TAKES JUST ONE DEFECTOR TO DO THE REVEAL...
THIS IS JUST...
IT'S SO ILLOGICAL!!

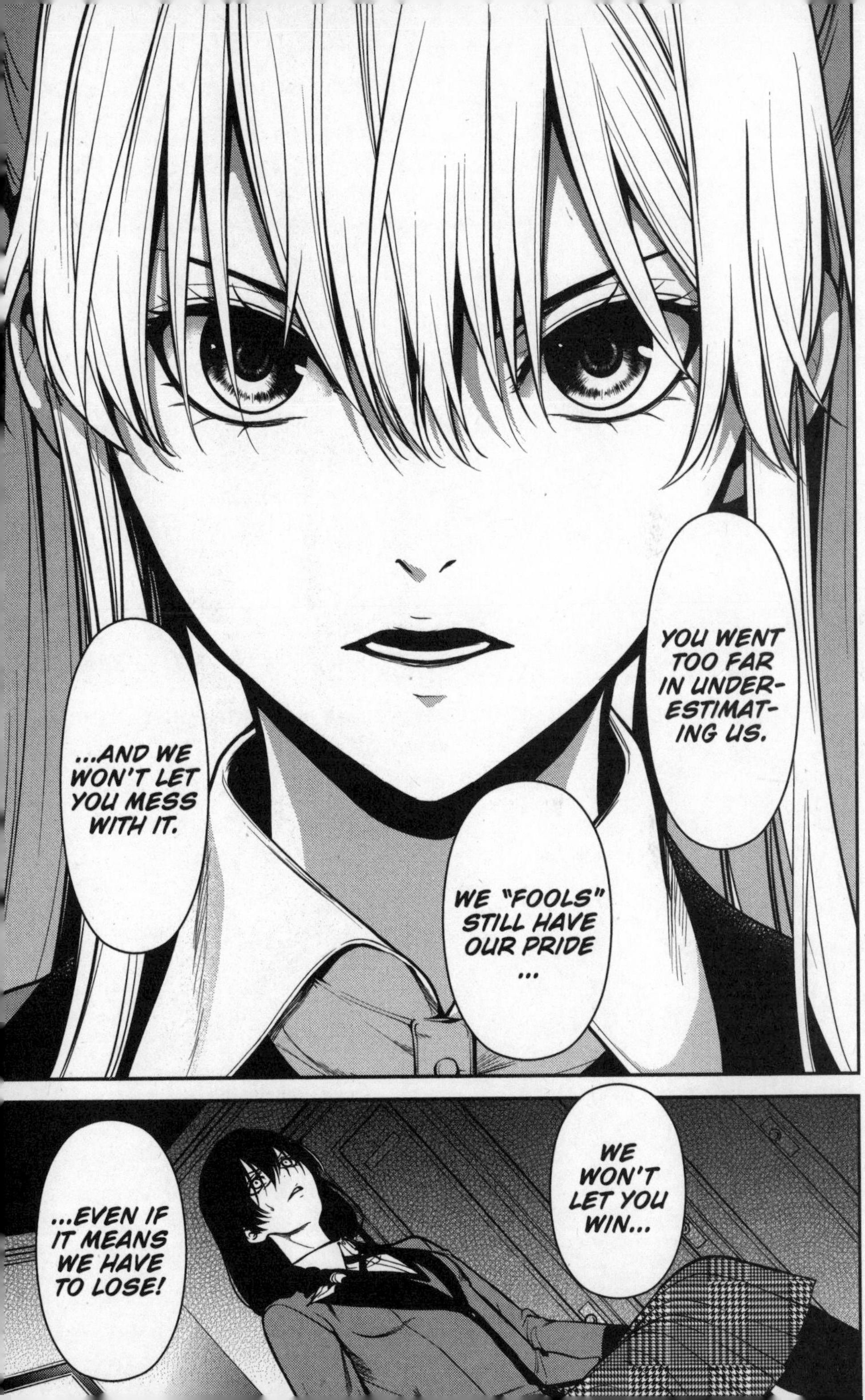
YOU WENT TOO FAR IN UNDER-ESTIMATING US.
WE "FOOLS" STILL HAVE OUR PRIDE ...
...AND WE WON'T LET YOU MESS WITH IT.
WE WON'T LET YOU WIN...
...EVEN IF IT MEANS WE HAVE TO LOSE!

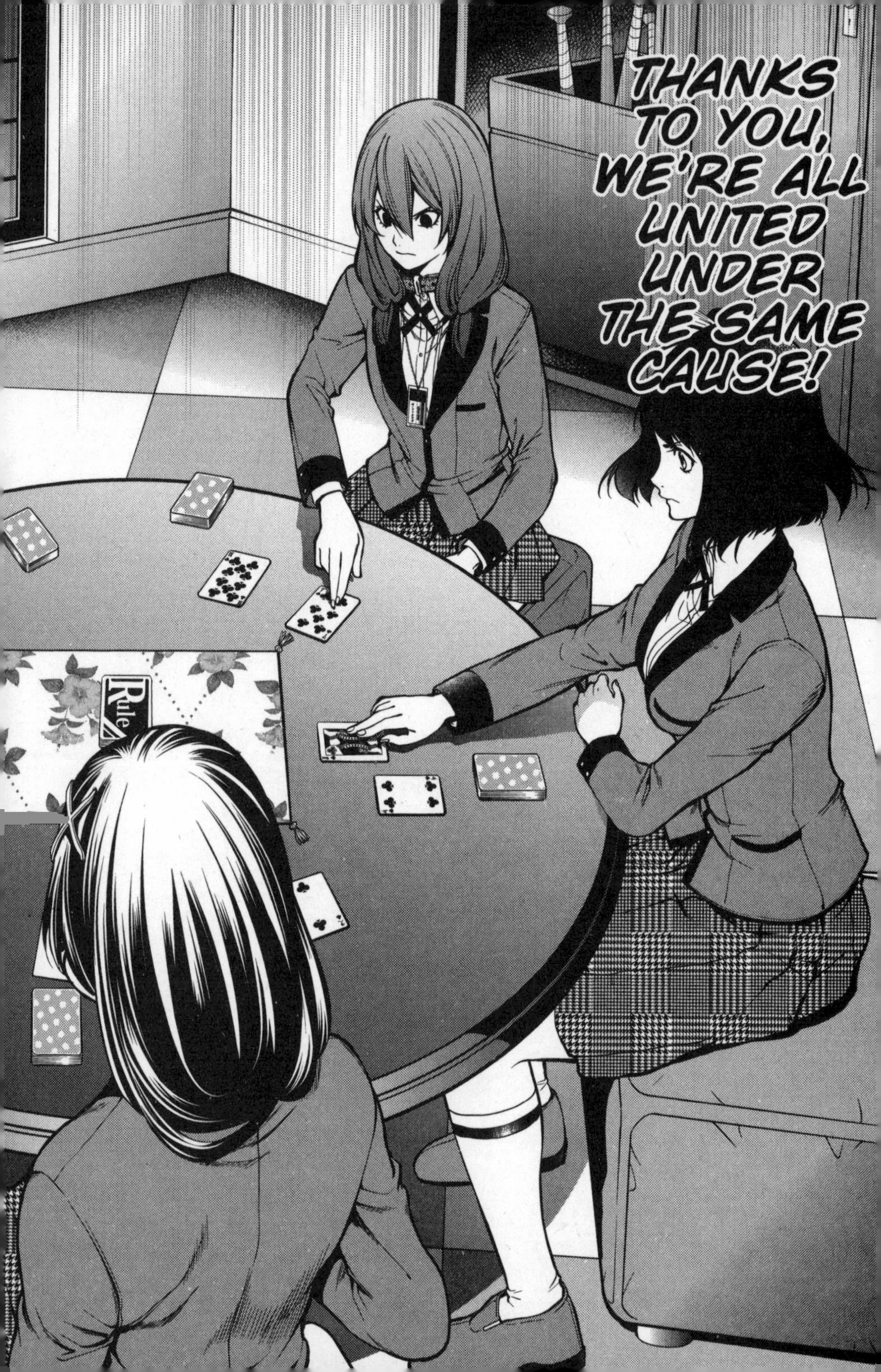
THANKS TO YOU, WE'RE ALL UNITED UNDER THE SAME CAUSE!

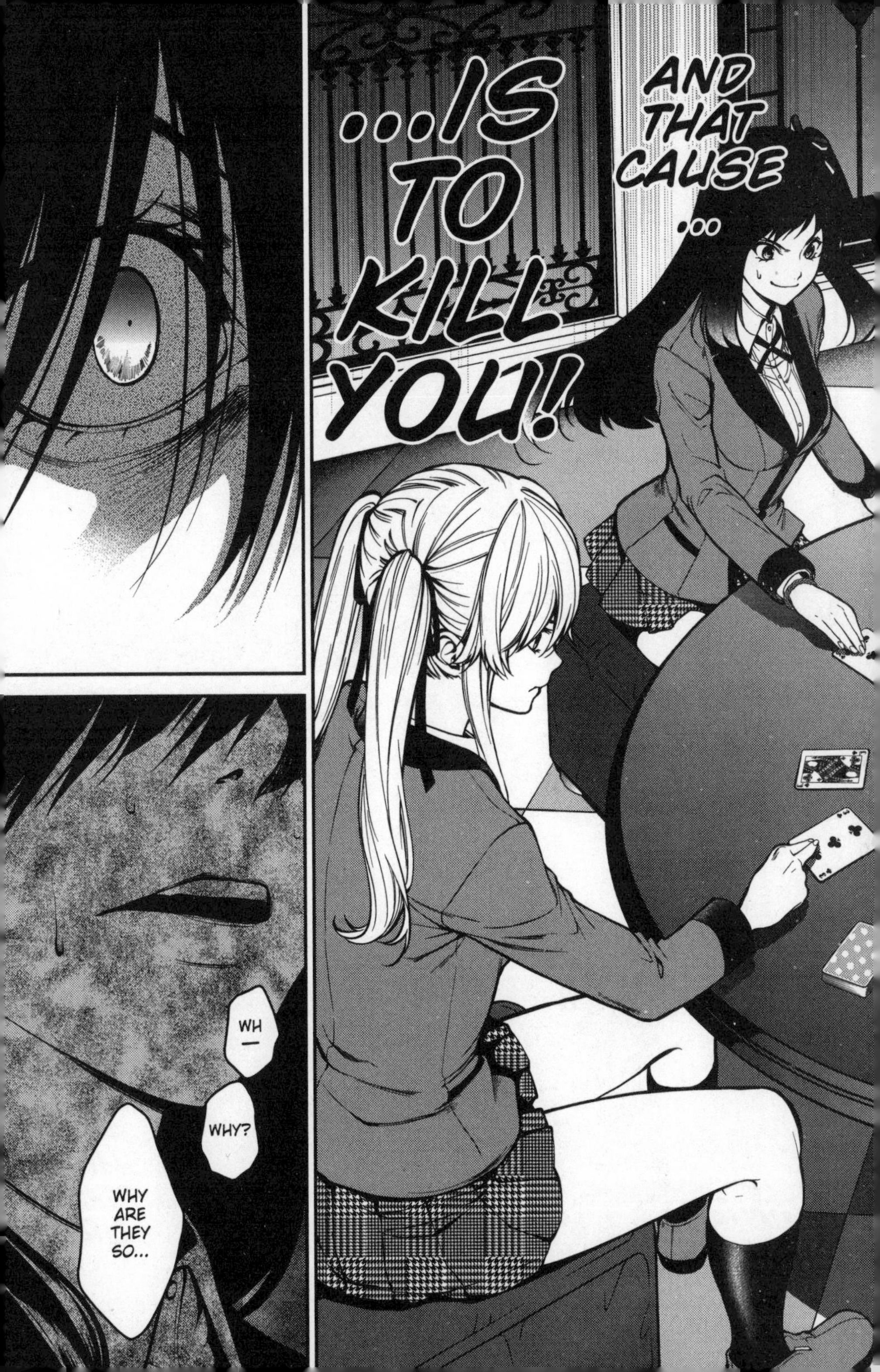
AND THAT CAUSE ...
...IS TO KILL YOU!!
WH—
WHY?
WHY ARE THEY SO...

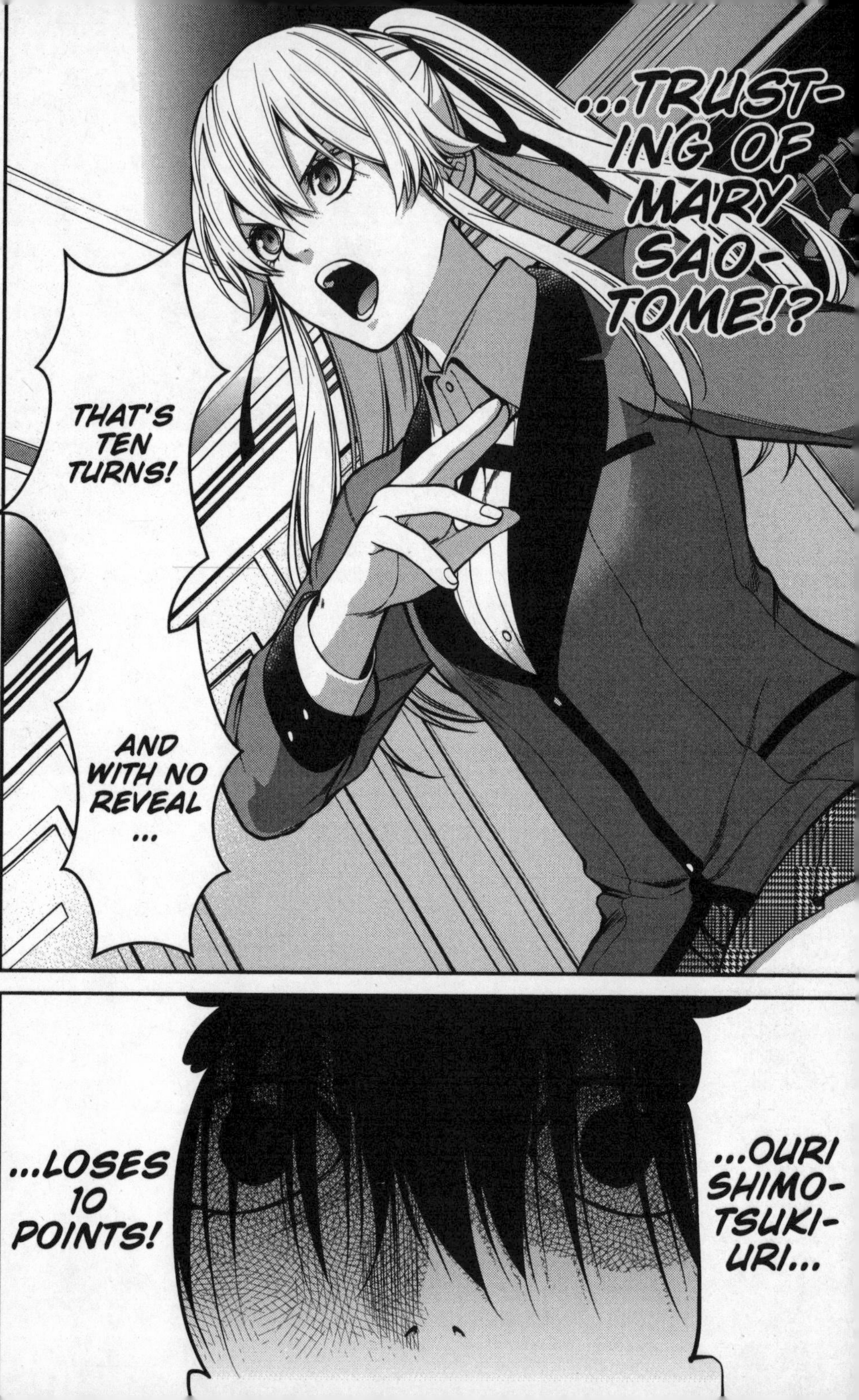
...TRUSTING OF MARY SAOTOME!?
THAT'S TEN TURNS!
AND WITH NO REVEAL ...
...OURI SHIMOTSUKIURI...
...LOSES 10 POINTS!

CHAPTER TWENTY-EIGHT
THE TRULY FOOLISH GIRL

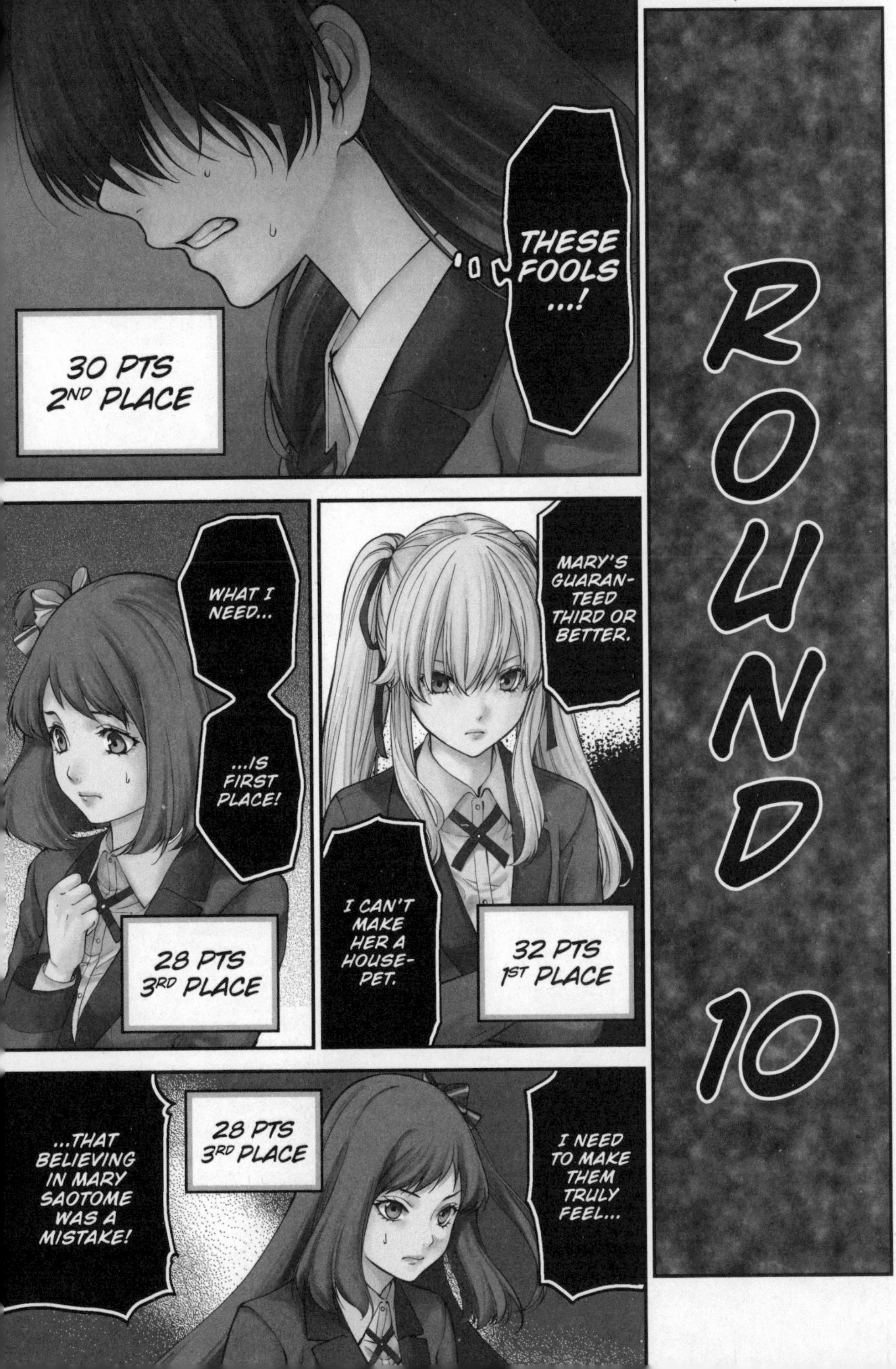

ROUND 10
THESE FOOLS ...!
30 PTS 2ND PLACE
MARY'S GUARAN-TEED THIRD OR BETTER.
I CAN'T MAKE HER A HOUSE-PET.
32 PTS 1ST PLACE
WHAT I NEED...
...IS FIRST PLACE!
28 PTS 3RD PLACE
I NEED TO MAKE THEM TRULY FEEL...
28 PTS 3RD PLACE
...THAT BELIEVING IN MARY SAOTOME WAS A MISTAKE!

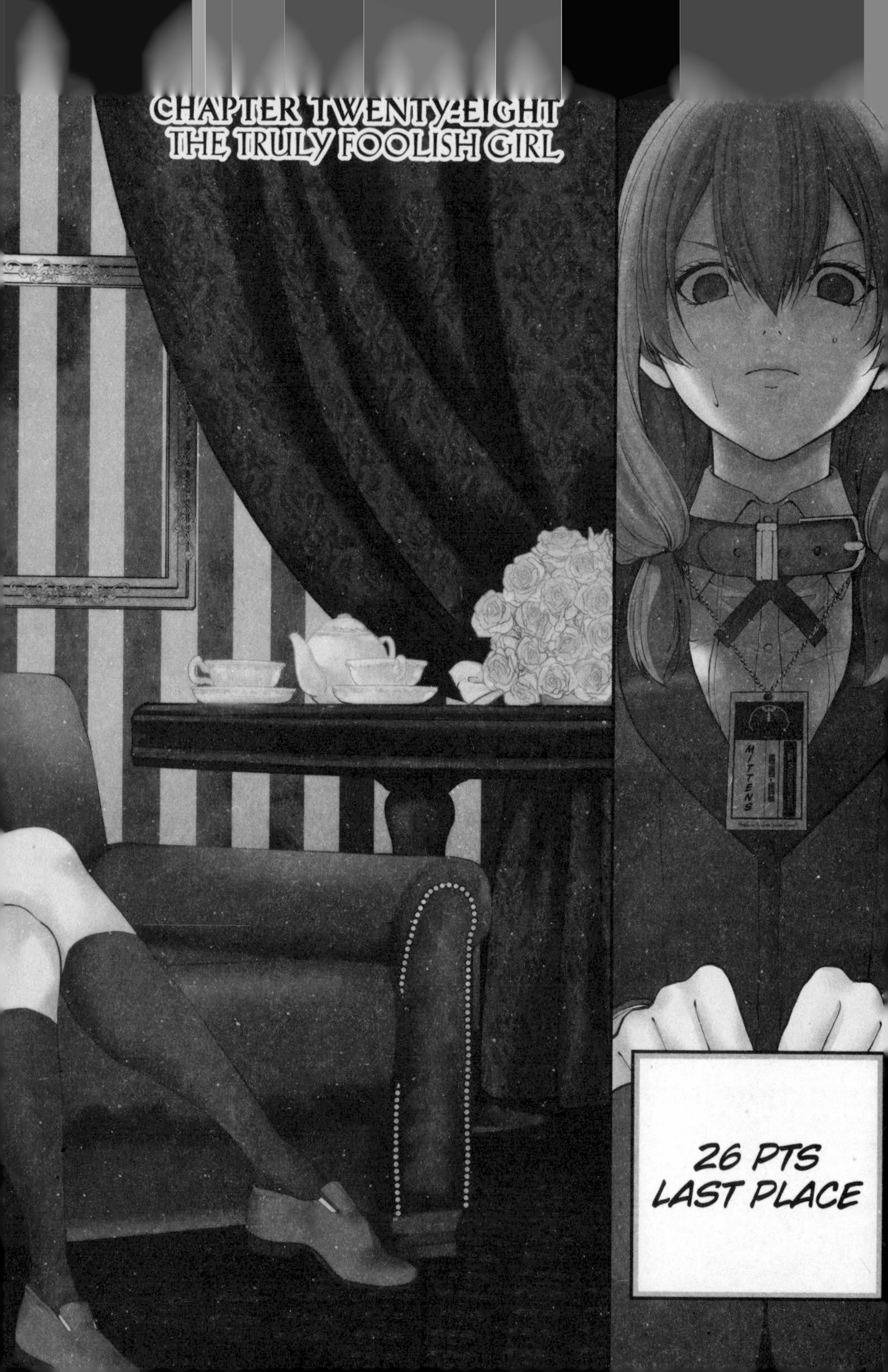
MITTENS
26 PTS
LAST PLACE
CHAPTER TWENTY-EIGHT
THE TRULY FOOLISH GIRL

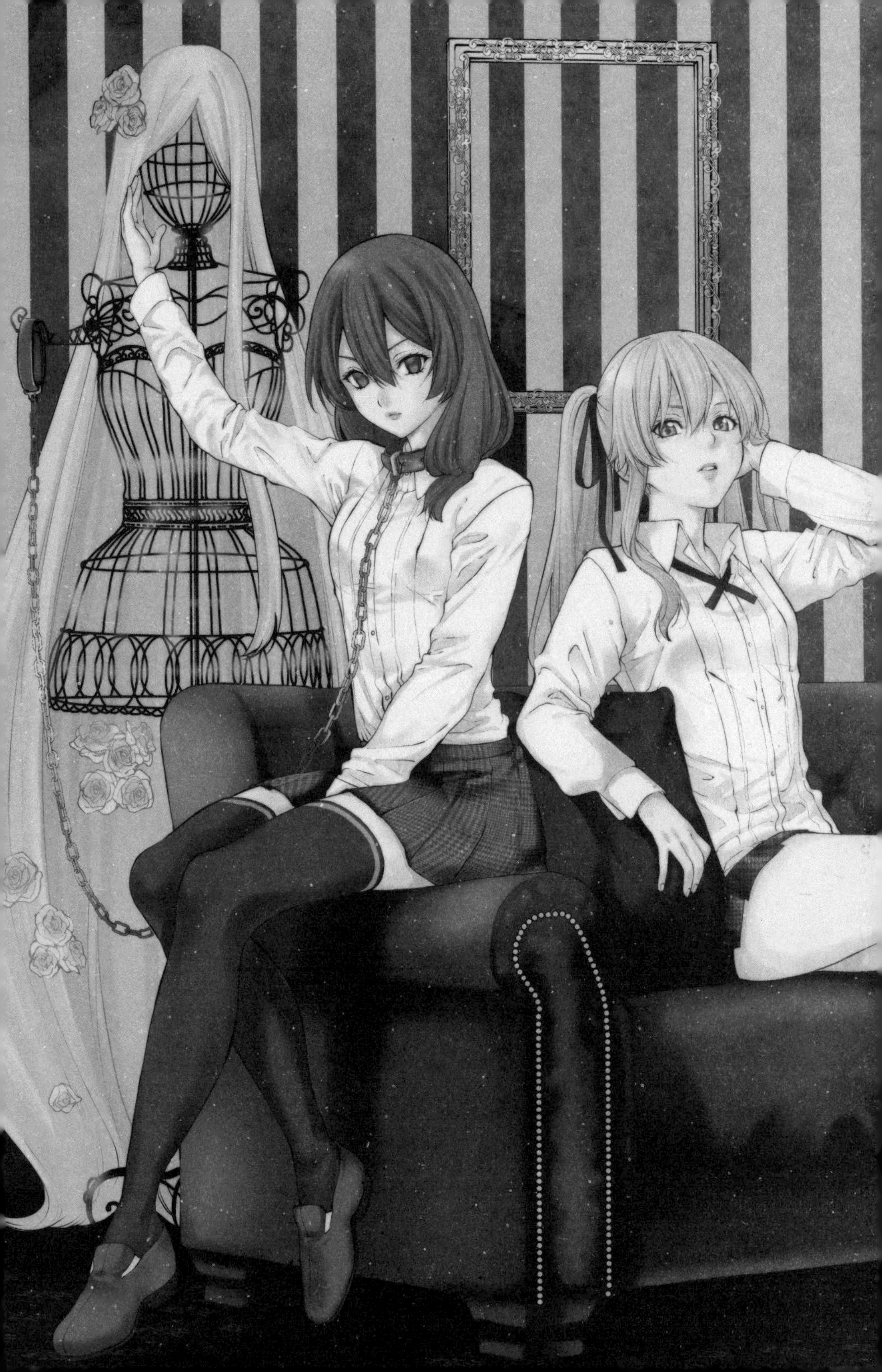

Kakegurui Twin

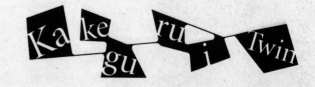

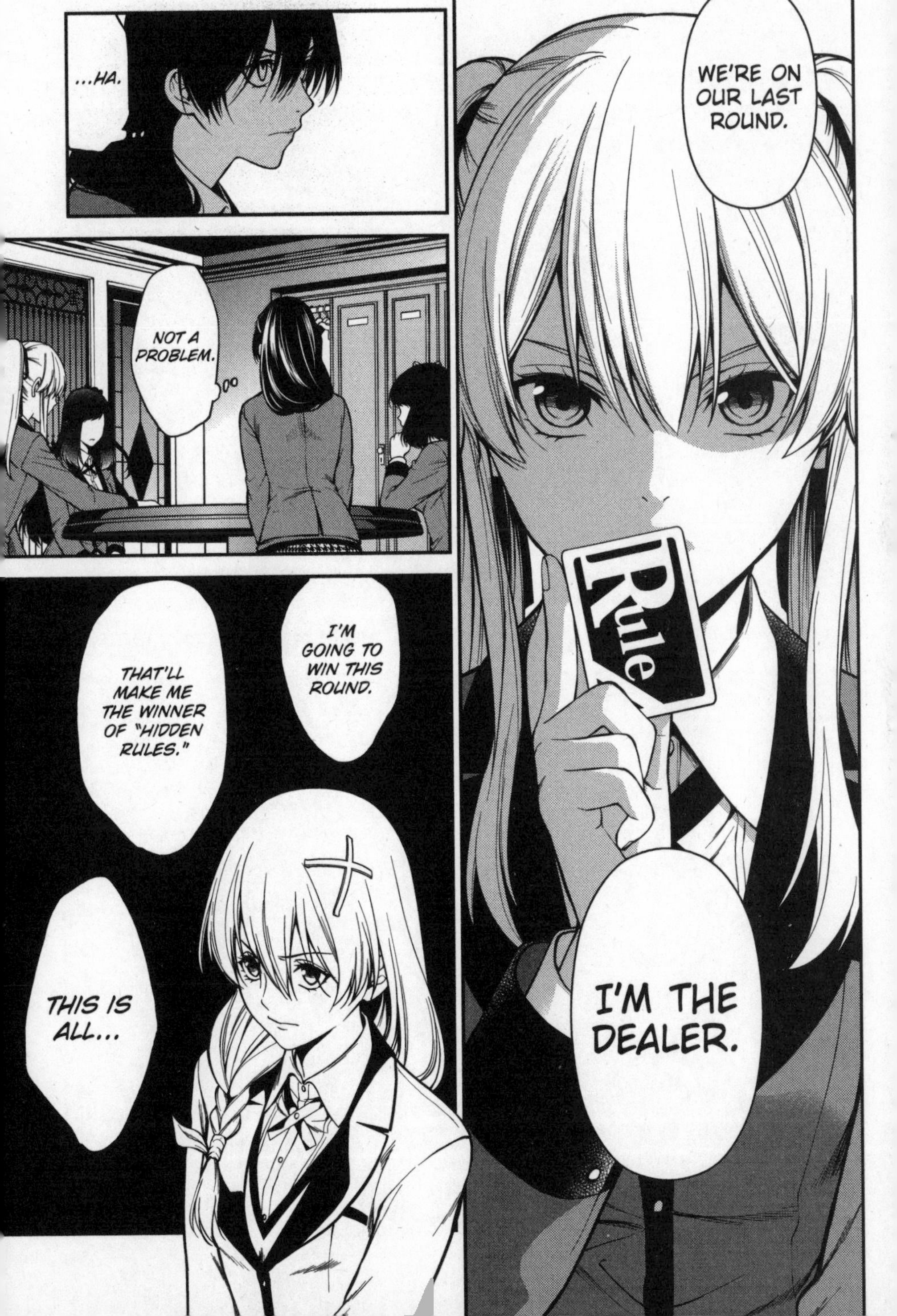
WE'RE ON OUR LAST ROUND.
Rule
I'M THE DEALER.
...HA.
NOT A PROBLEM.
I'M GOING TO WIN THIS ROUND.
THAT'LL MAKE ME THE WINNER OF "HIDDEN RULES."
THIS IS ALL...

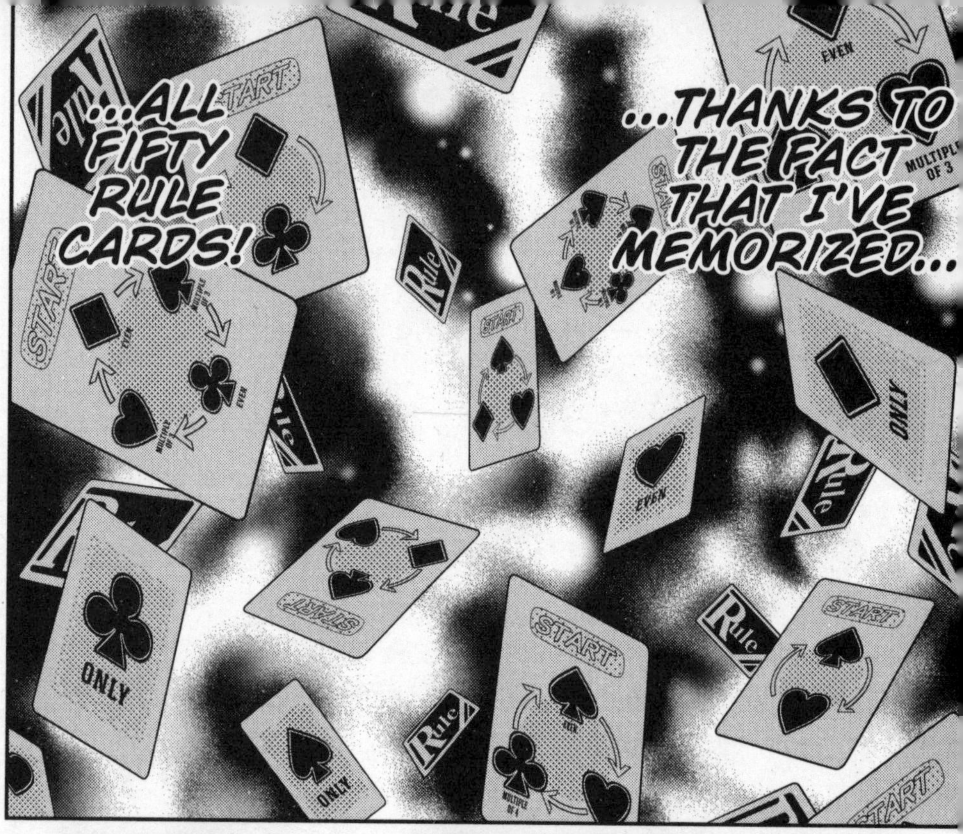
...THANKS TO THE FACT THAT I'VE MEMORIZED...
...ALL FIFTY RULE CARDS!

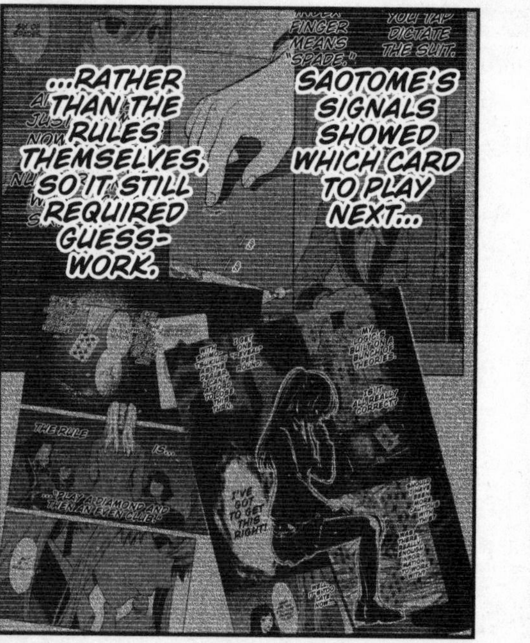
SAOTOME'S SIGNALS SHOWED WHICH CARD TO PLAY NEXT...
...RATHER THAN THE RULES THEMSELVES, SO IT STILL REQUIRED GUESS-WORK.
THE RULE IS...
..."PLAY A DIAMOND AND THEN AN EVEN CLUB."
I'VE GOT TO GET THIS RIGHT!!

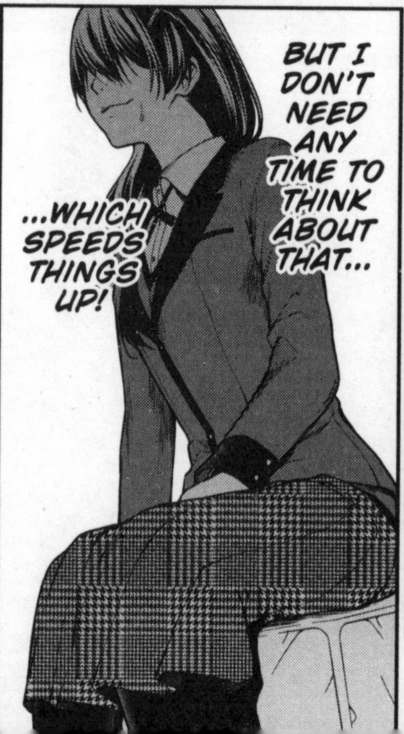
BUT I DON'T NEED ANY TIME TO THINK ABOUT THAT...
...WHICH SPEEDS THINGS UP!

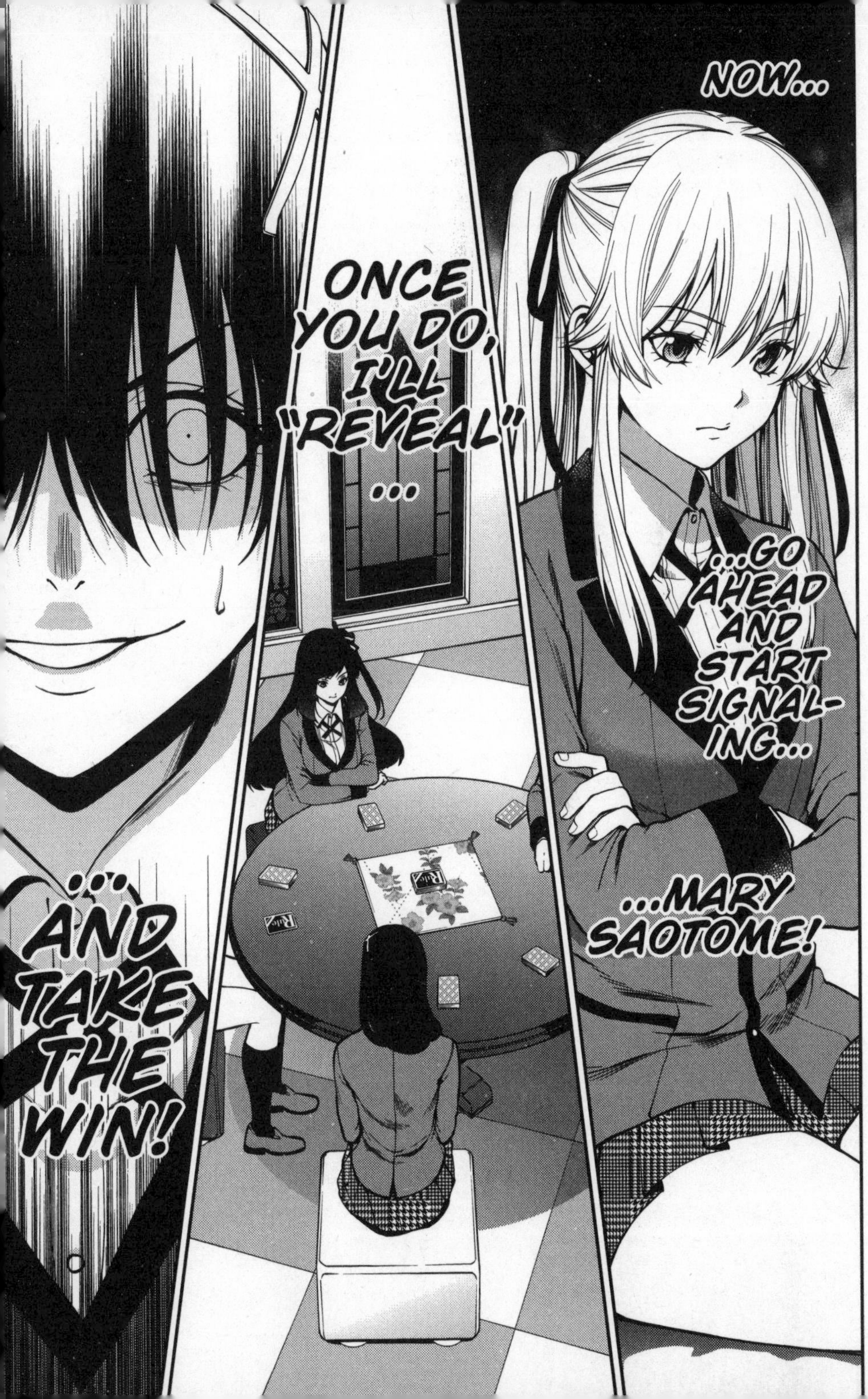
NOW...
...GO AHEAD AND START SIGNALING...
...MARY SAOTOME!
ONCE YOU DO, I'LL "REVEAL"
...
...
AND TAKE THE WIN!

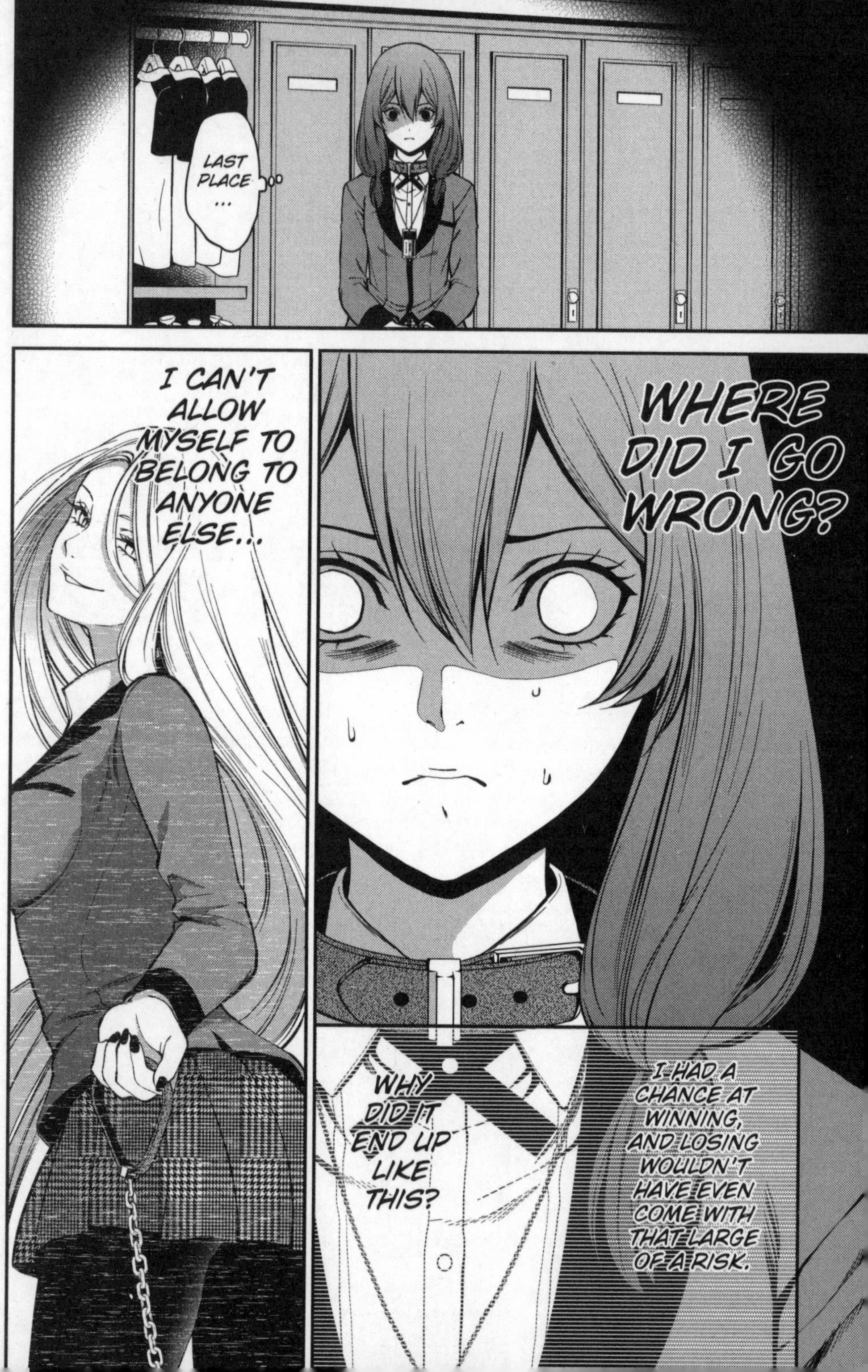
LAST PLACE ...
WHERE DID I GO WRONG?
I HAD A CHANCE AT WINNING, AND LOSING WOULDN'T HAVE EVEN COME WITH THAT LARGE OF A RISK.
WHY DID IT END UP LIKE THIS?
I CAN'T ALLOW MYSELF TO BELONG TO ANYONE ELSE...

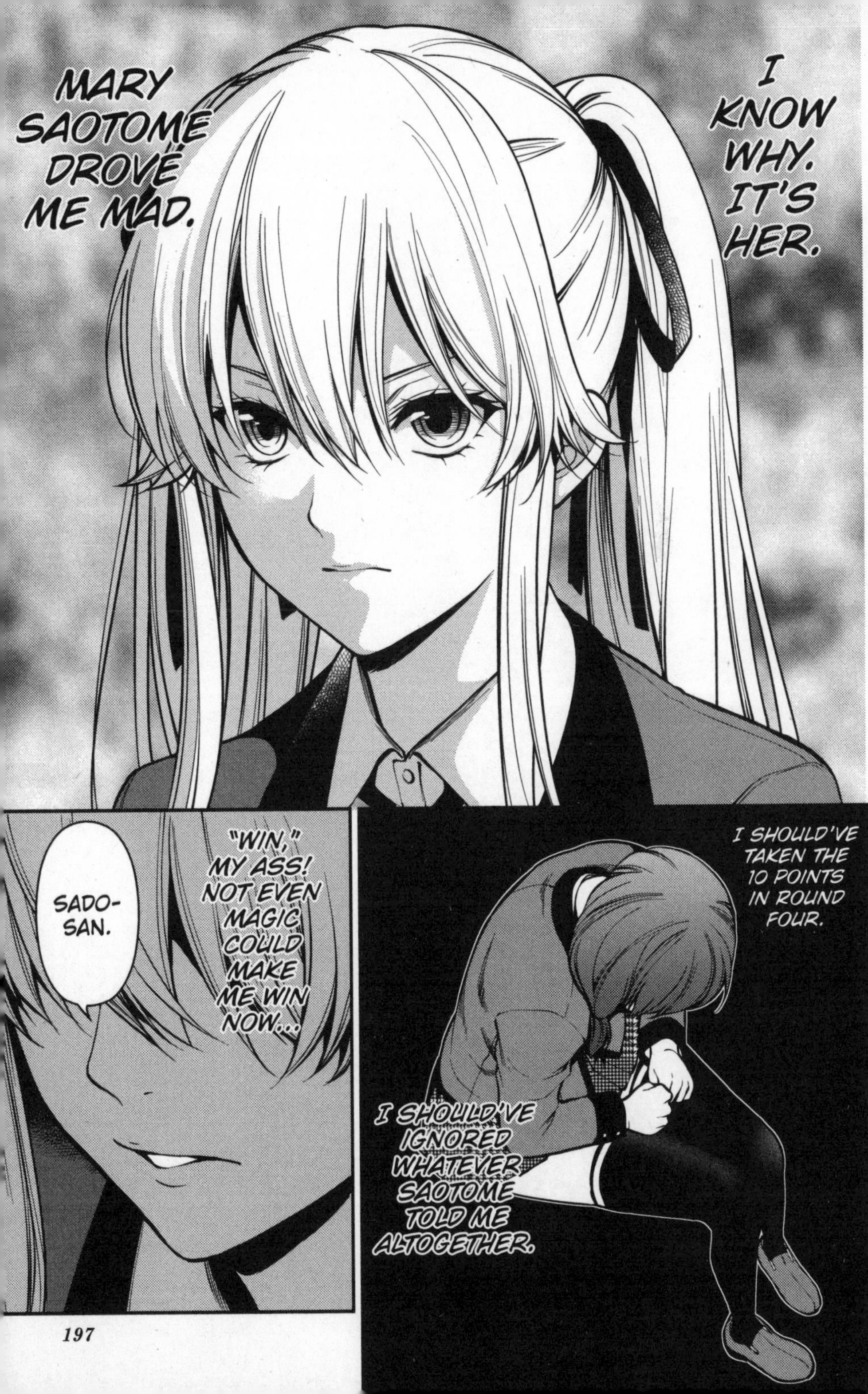
I KNOW WHY. IT'S HER.
MARY SAOTOME DROVE ME MAD.
I SHOULD'VE TAKEN THE 10 POINTS IN ROUND FOUR.
I SHOULD'VE IGNORED WHATEVER SAOTOME TOLD ME ALTOGETHER.
"WIN," MY ASS! NOT EVEN MAGIC COULD MAKE ME WIN NOW...
SADO-SAN.

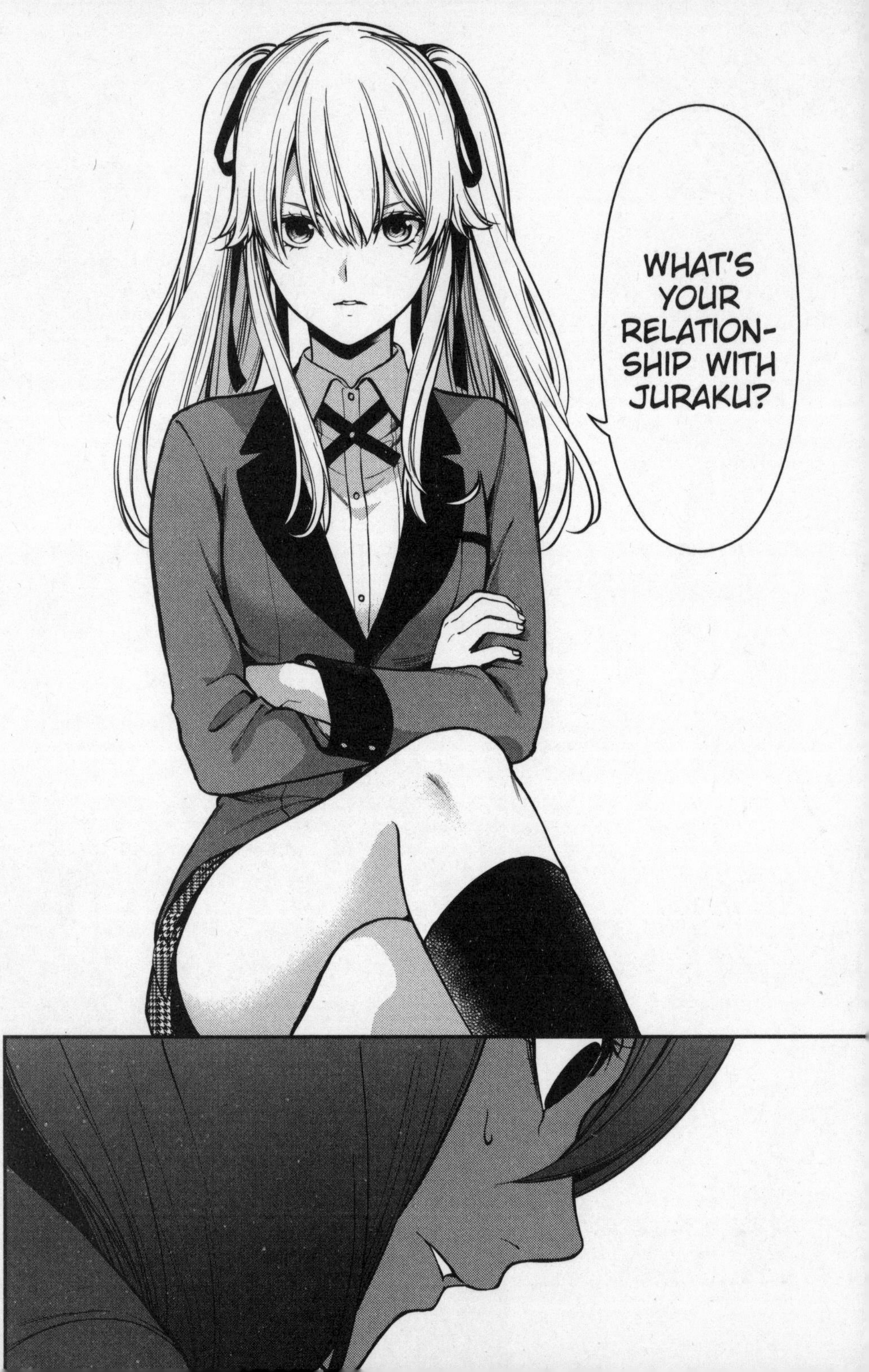
WHAT'S YOUR RELATION-SHIP WITH JURAKU?

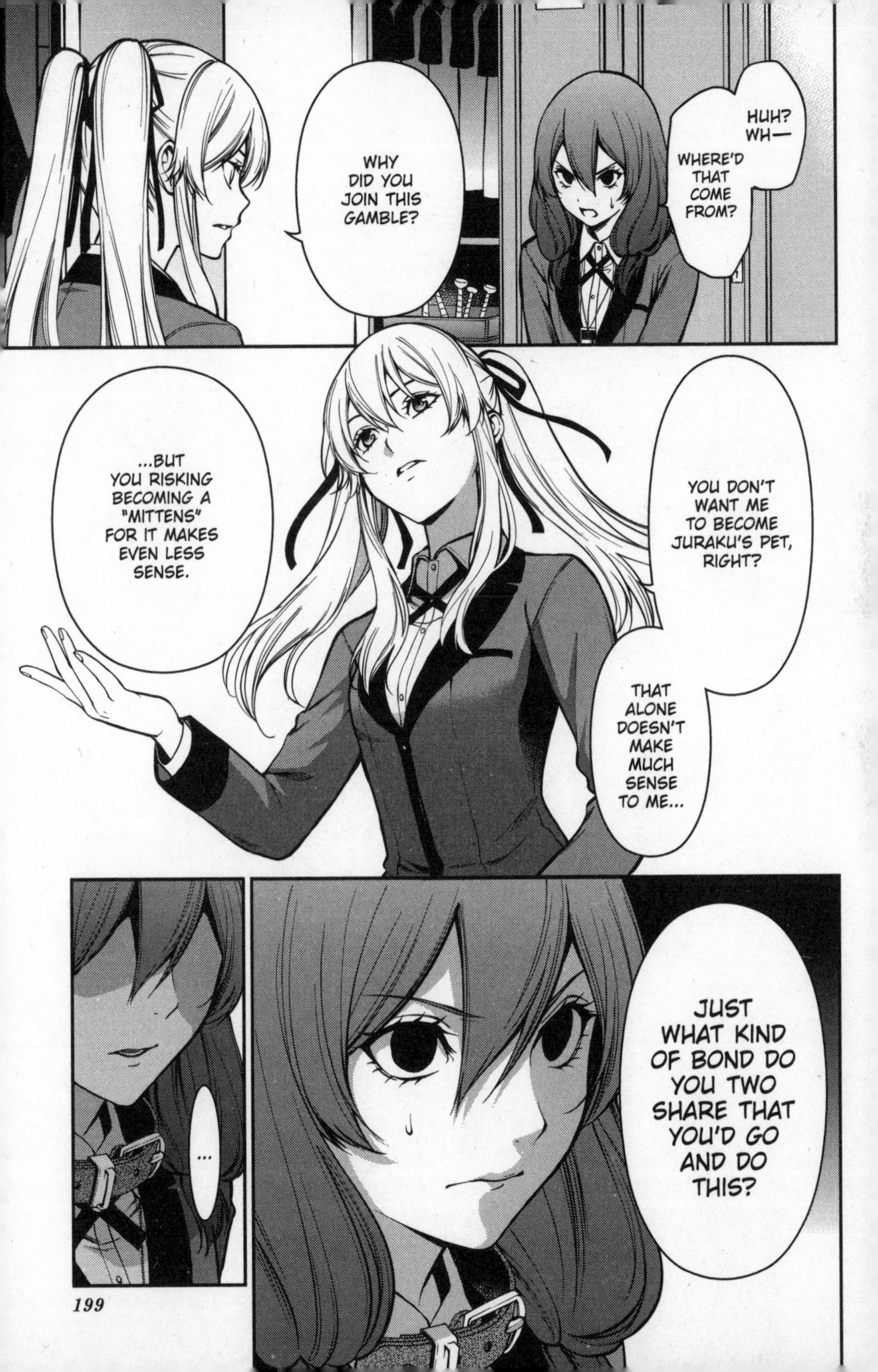
WHY DID YOU JOIN THIS GAMBLE?
HUH? WH—
WHERE'D THAT COME FROM?
YOU DON'T WANT ME TO BECOME JURAKU'S PET, RIGHT?
THAT ALONE DOESN'T MAKE MUCH SENSE TO ME...
...BUT YOU RISKING BECOMING A "MITTENS" FOR IT MAKES EVEN LESS SENSE.
JUST WHAT KIND OF BOND DO YOU TWO SHARE THAT YOU'D GO AND DO THIS?
...

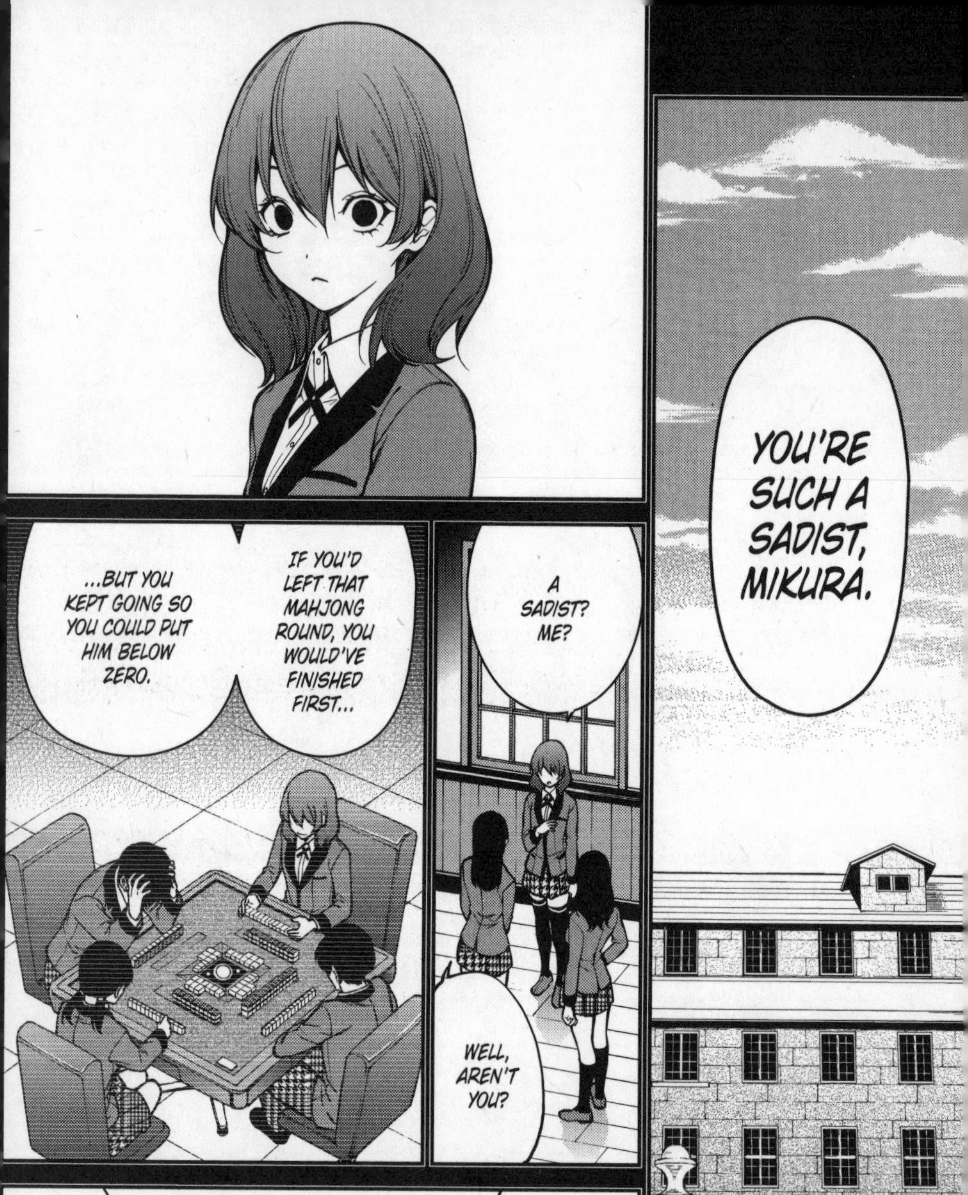
YOU'RE SUCH A SADIST, MIKURA.
A SADIST? ME?
WELL, AREN'T YOU?
IF YOU'D LEFT THAT MAHJONG ROUND, YOU WOULD'VE FINISHED FIRST...
...BUT YOU KEPT GOING SO YOU COULD PUT HIM BELOW ZERO.
YOU WANTED TO MAKE HIM A HOUSEPET, DIDN'T YOU?
HA!
THAT'S NONE OF MY BUSINESS.

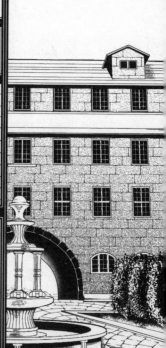

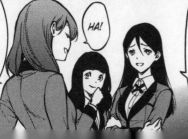

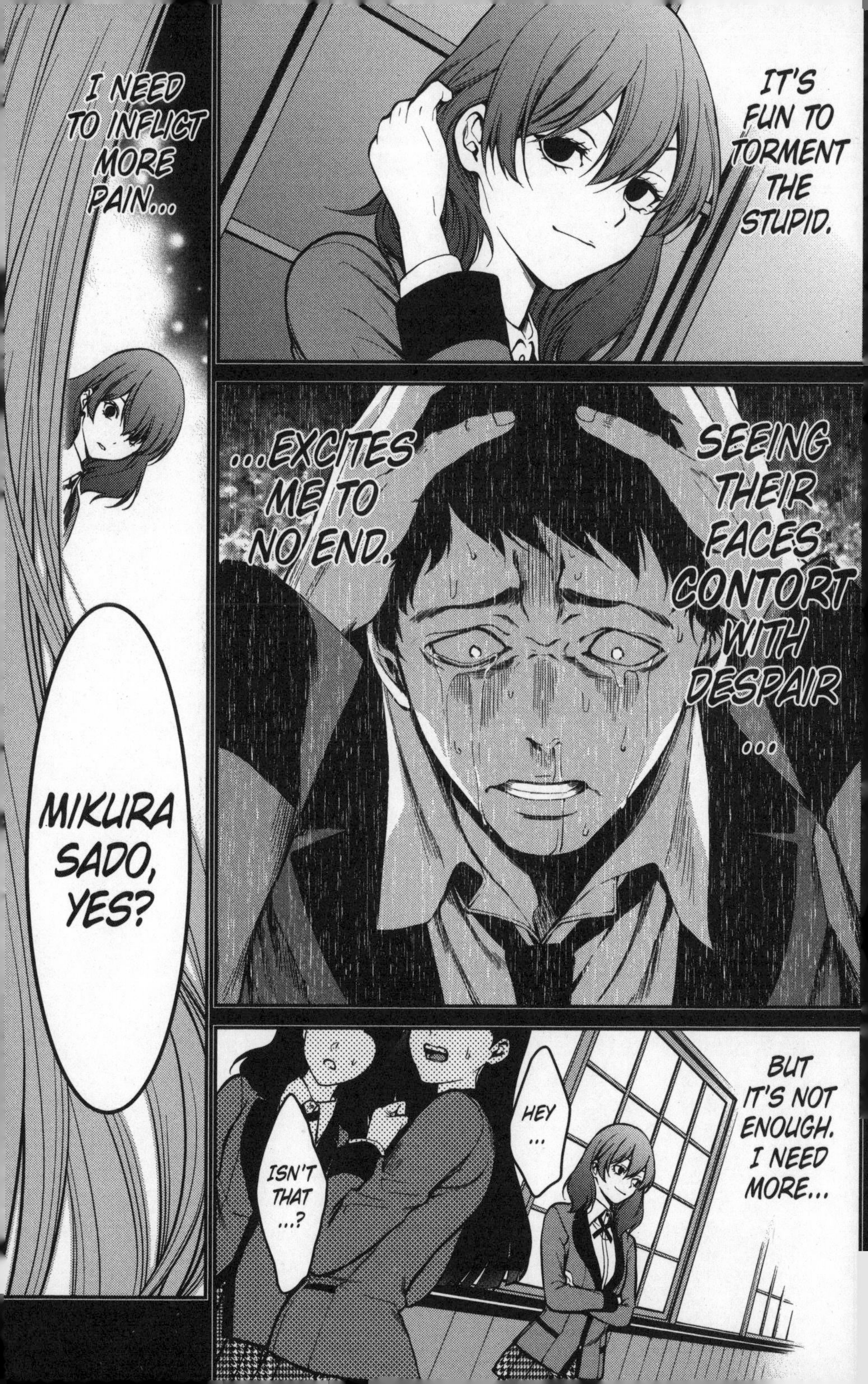
IT'S FUN TO TORMENT THE STUPID.
SEEING THEIR FACES CONTORT WITH DESPAIR ...
...EXCITES ME TO NO END.
BUT IT'S NOT ENOUGH. I NEED MORE...
HEY ...
ISN'T THAT ...?
I NEED TO INFLICT MORE PAIN...
MIKURA SADO, YES?

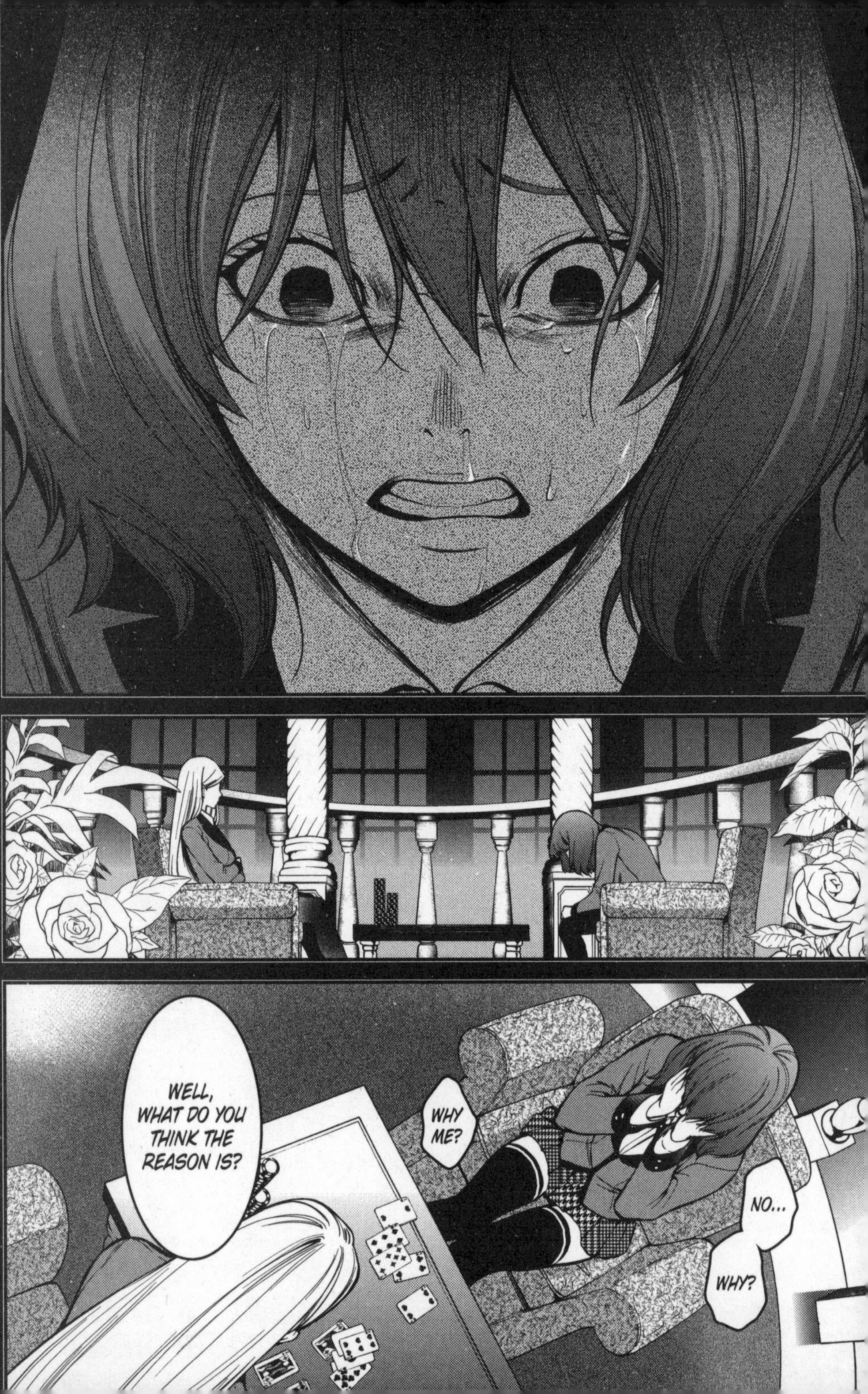
NO...
WHY?
WHY ME?
WELL, WHAT DO YOU THINK THE REASON IS?

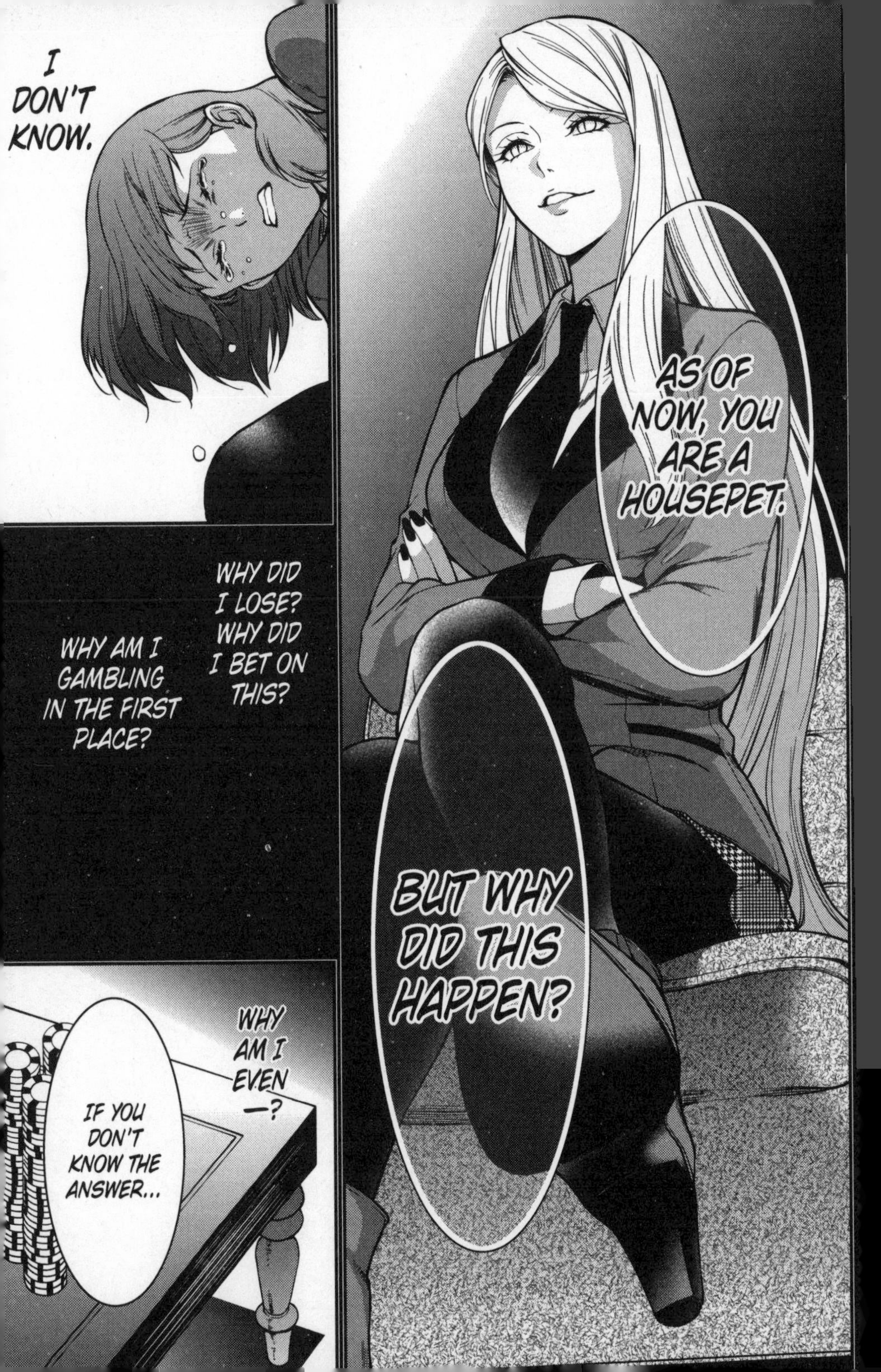

AS OF NOW, YOU ARE A HOUSEPET.
BUT WHY DID THIS HAPPEN?
I DON'T KNOW.
WHY DID I LOSE? WHY DID I BET ON THIS?
WHY AM I GAMBLING IN THE FIRST PLACE?
WHY AM I EVEN—?
IF YOU DON'T KNOW THE ANSWER...

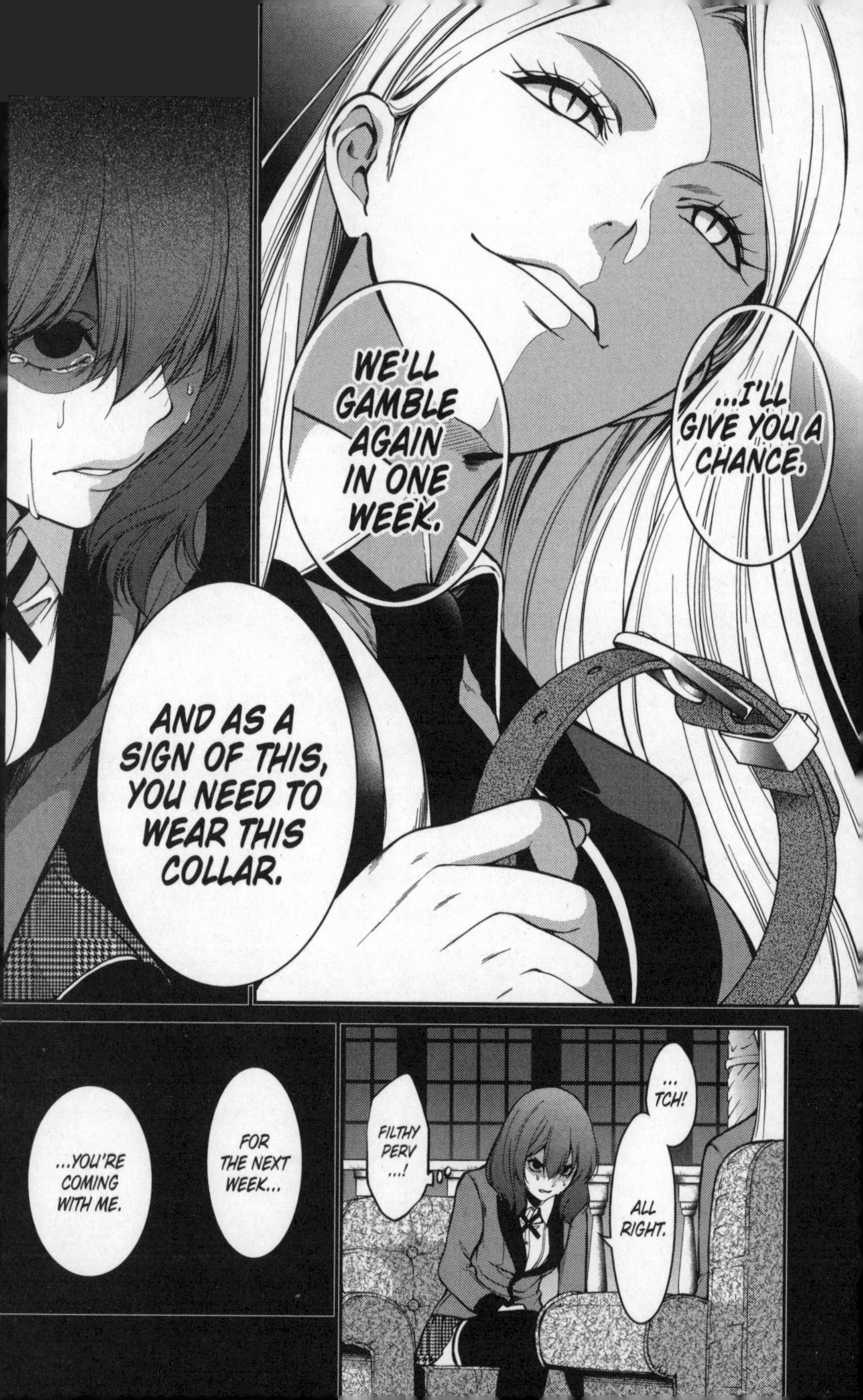
...I'LL GIVE YOU A CHANCE.
WE'LL GAMBLE AGAIN IN ONE WEEK.
AND AS A SIGN OF THIS, YOU NEED TO WEAR THIS COLLAR.
... TCH!
ALL RIGHT.
FILTHY PERV ...!
FOR THE NEXT WEEK...
...YOU'RE COMING WITH ME.

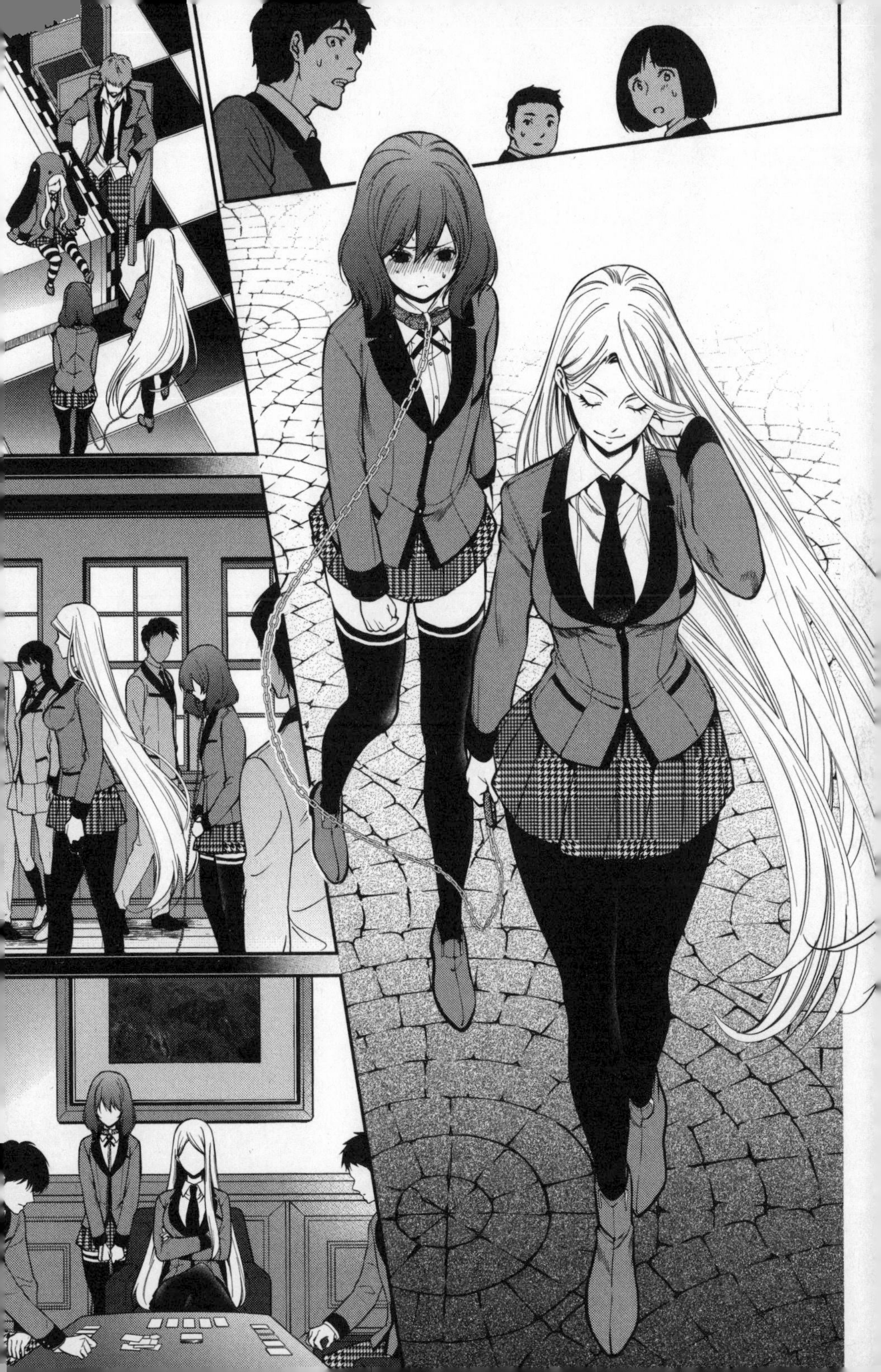

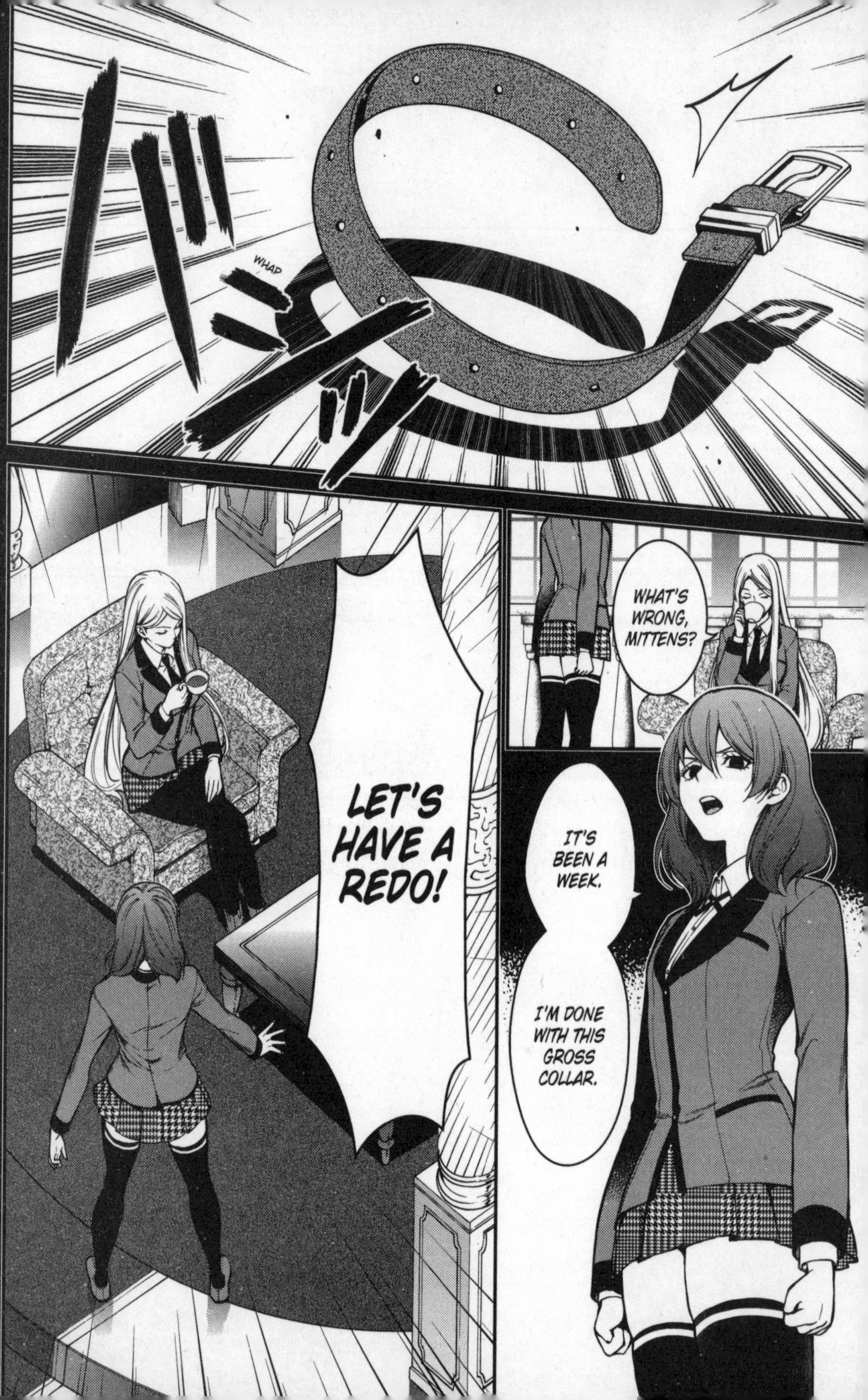
WHAP
WHAT'S WRONG, MITTENS?
IT'S BEEN A WEEK.
I'M DONE WITH THIS GROSS COLLAR.
LET'S HAVE A REDO!

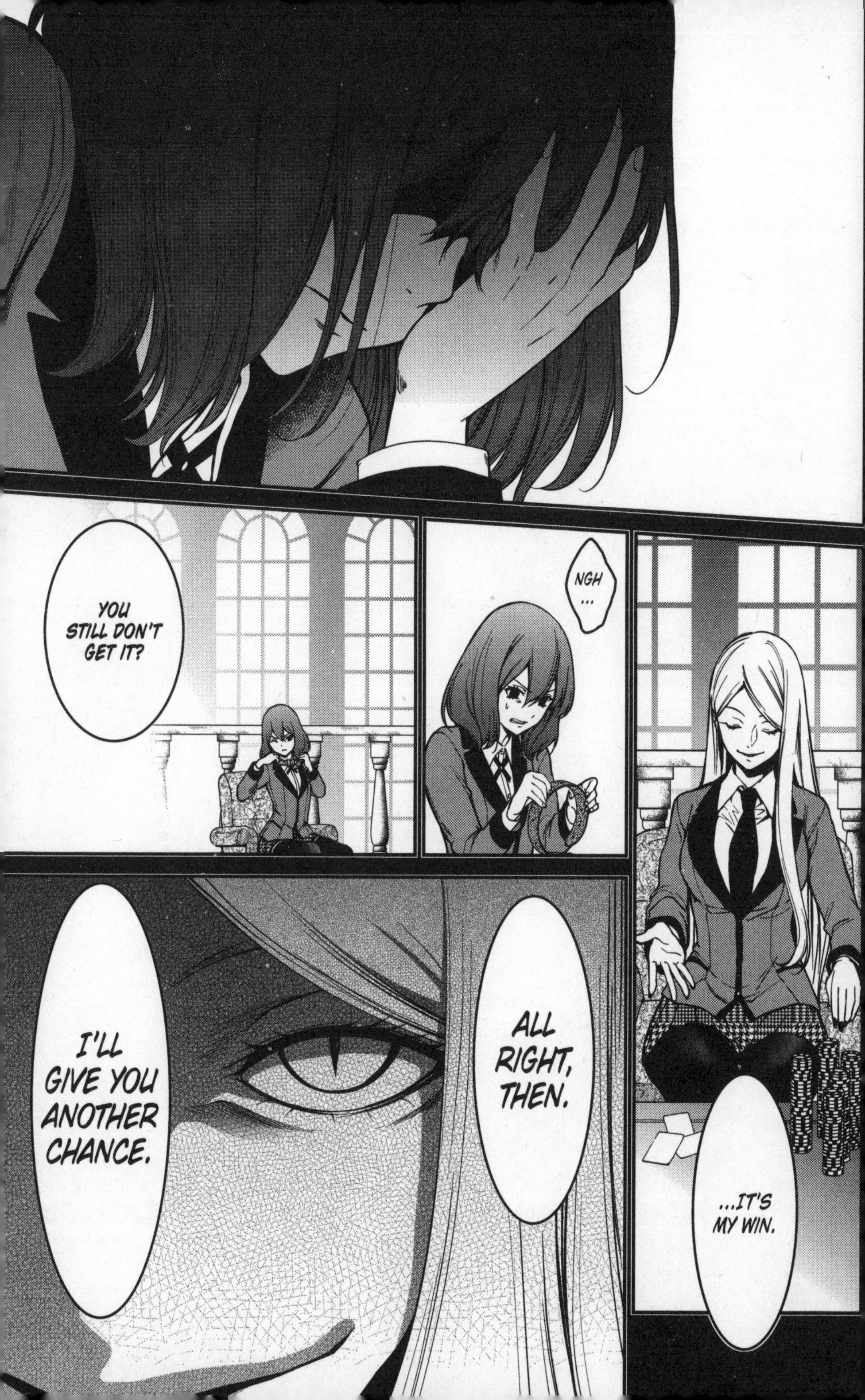
...IT'S MY WIN.
NGH ...
YOU STILL DON'T GET IT?
ALL RIGHT, THEN.
I'LL GIVE YOU ANOTHER CHANCE.

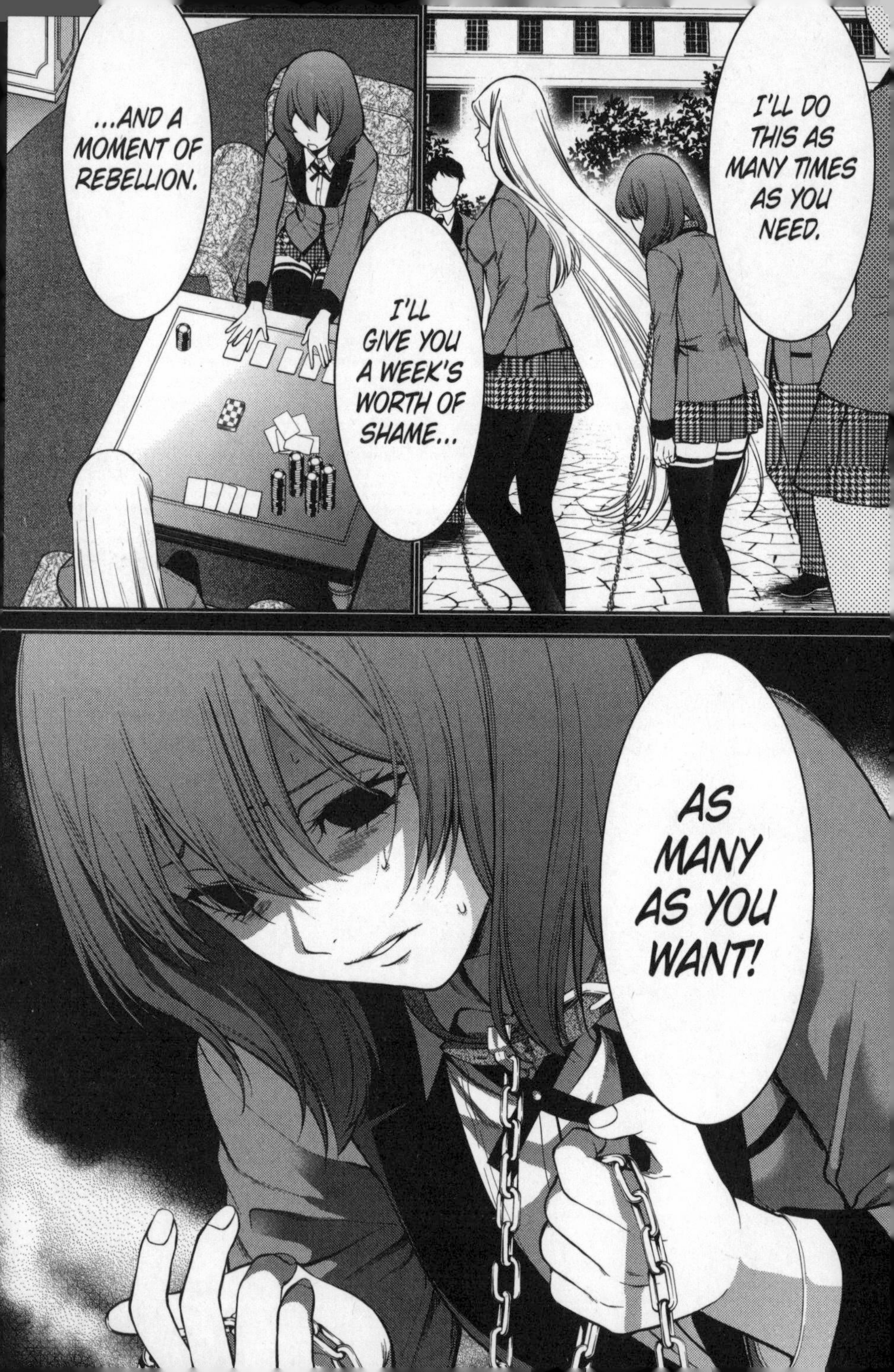
I'LL DO THIS AS MANY TIMES AS YOU NEED.
I'LL GIVE YOU A WEEK'S WORTH OF SHAME...
...AND A MOMENT OF REBELLION.
AS MANY AS YOU WANT!

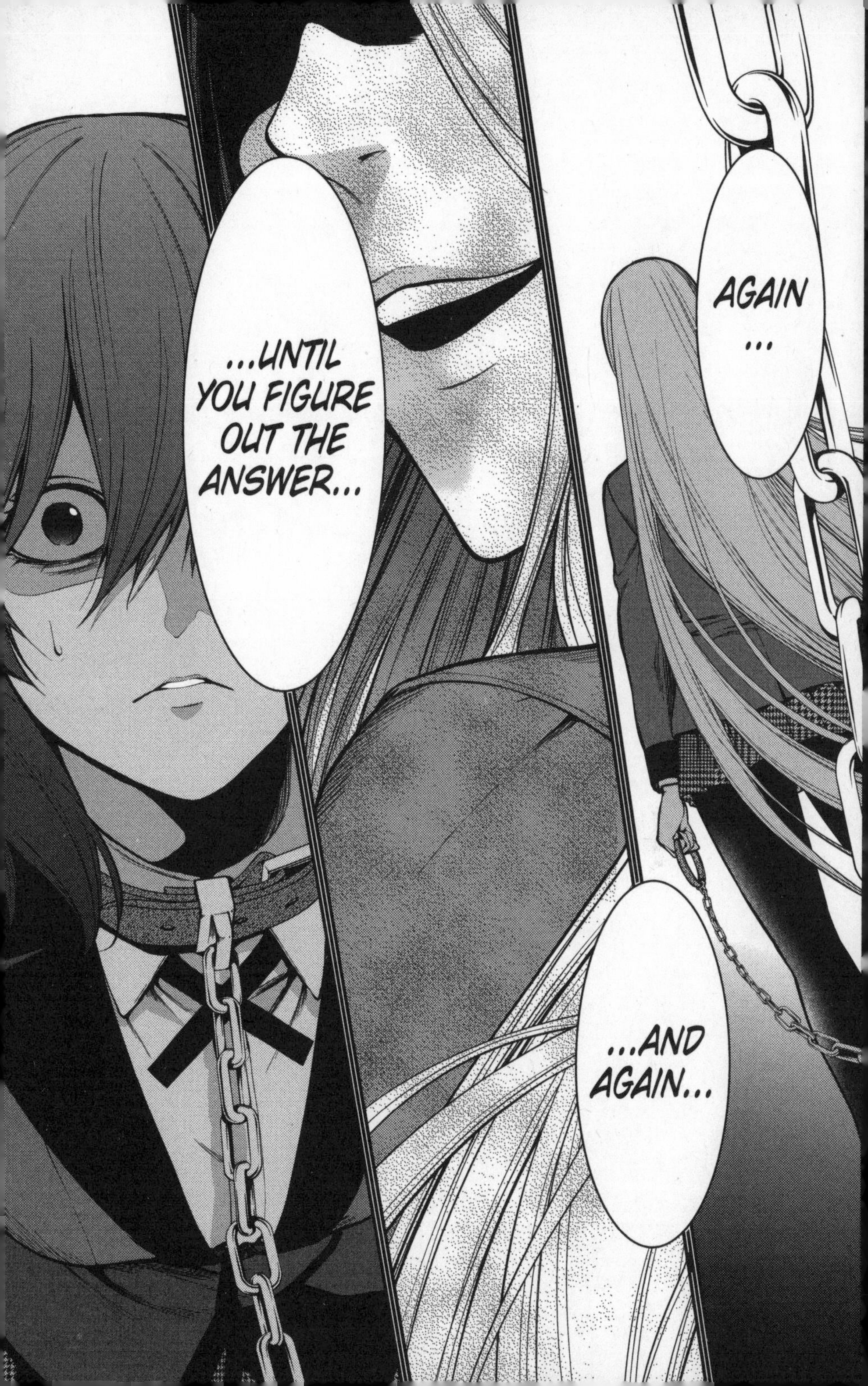
AGAIN ...
...AND AGAIN...
...UNTIL YOU FIGURE OUT THE ANSWER...

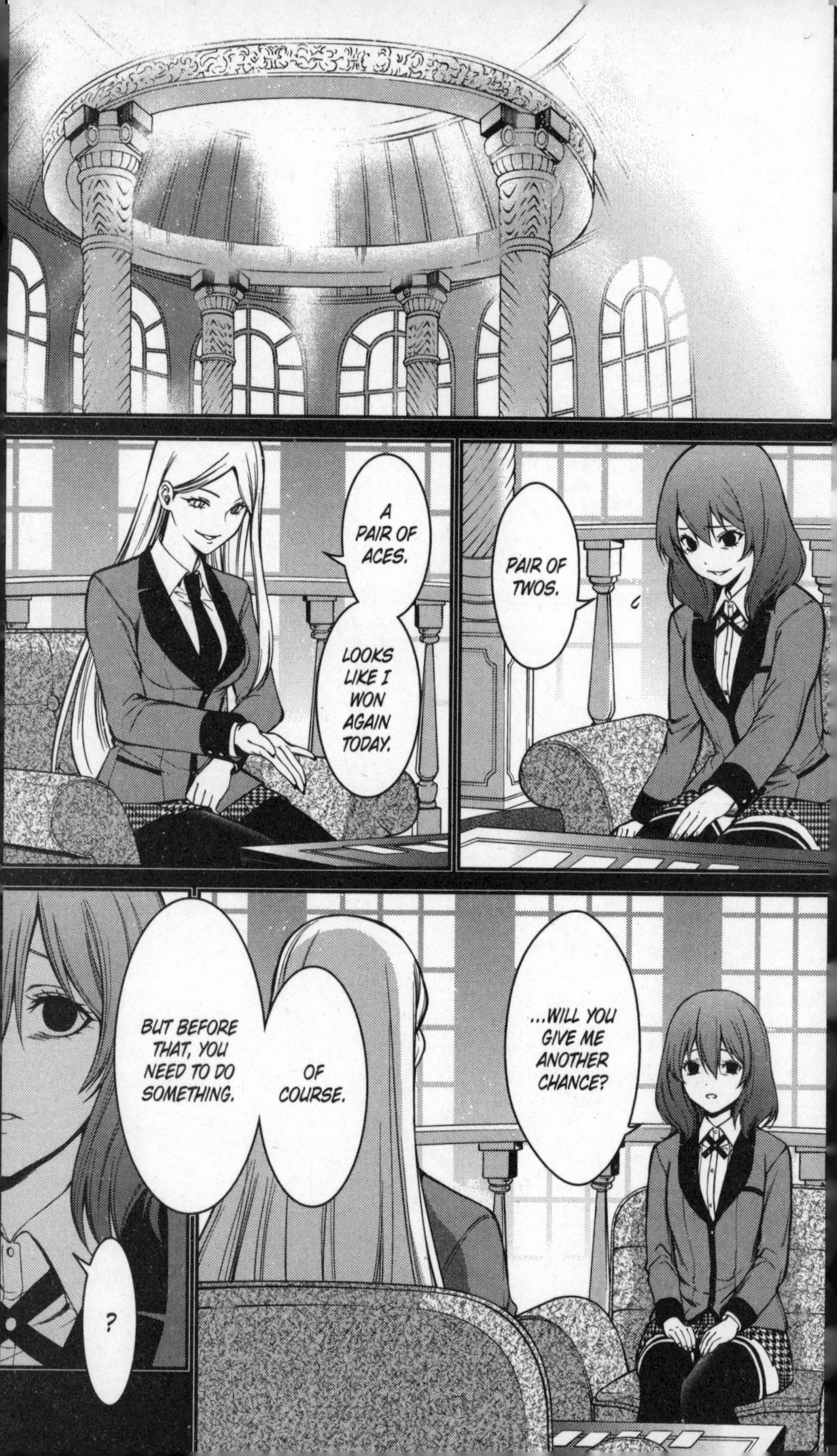
PAIR OF TWOS.
A PAIR OF ACES.
LOOKS LIKE I WON AGAIN TODAY.
...WILL YOU GIVE ME ANOTHER CHANCE?
OF COURSE.
BUT BEFORE THAT, YOU NEED TO DO SOMETHING.
?

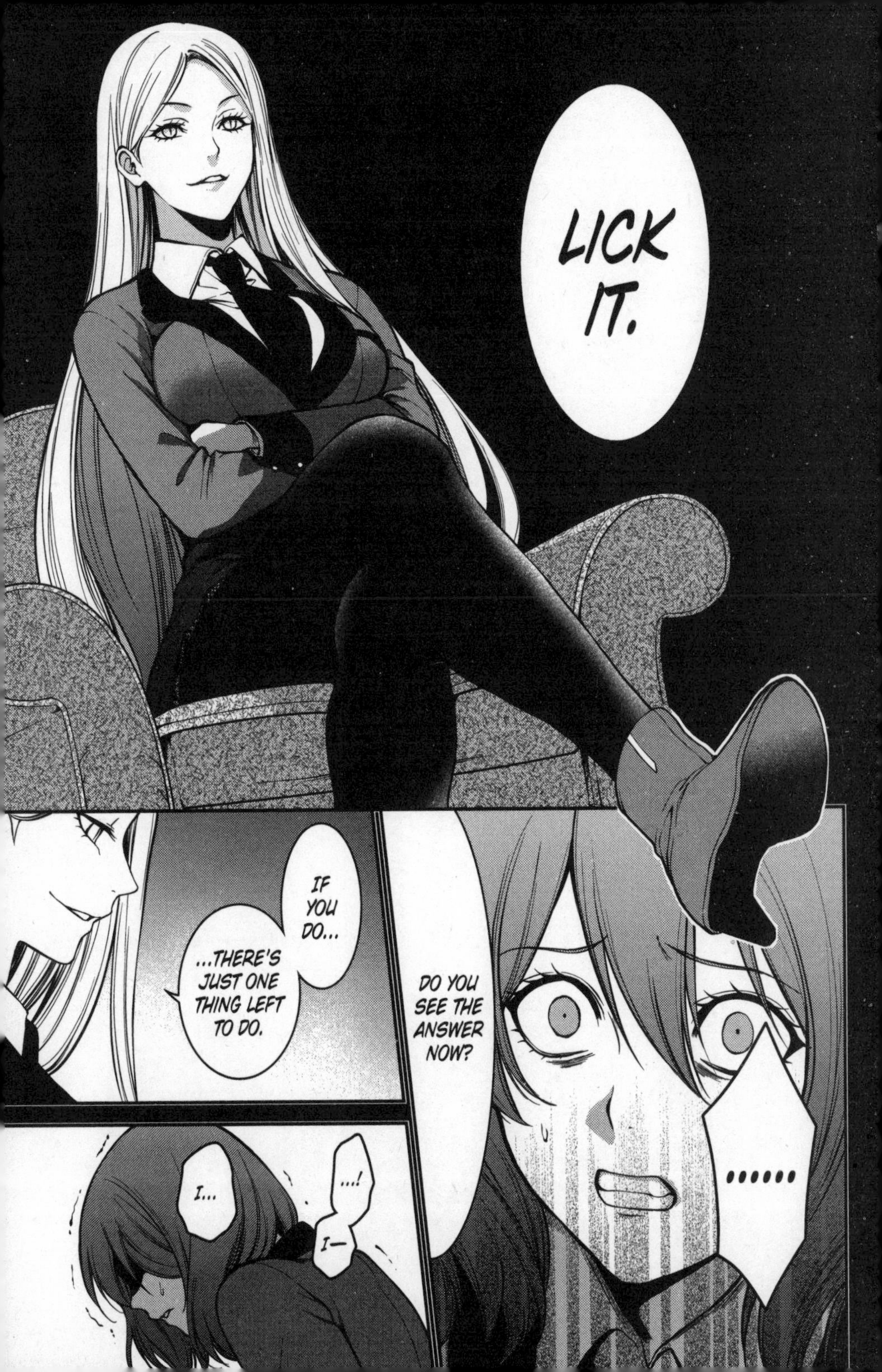

LICK IT.
DO YOU SEE THE ANSWER NOW?
......
IF YOU DO...
...THERE'S JUST ONE THING LEFT TO DO.
...!
I...
I—

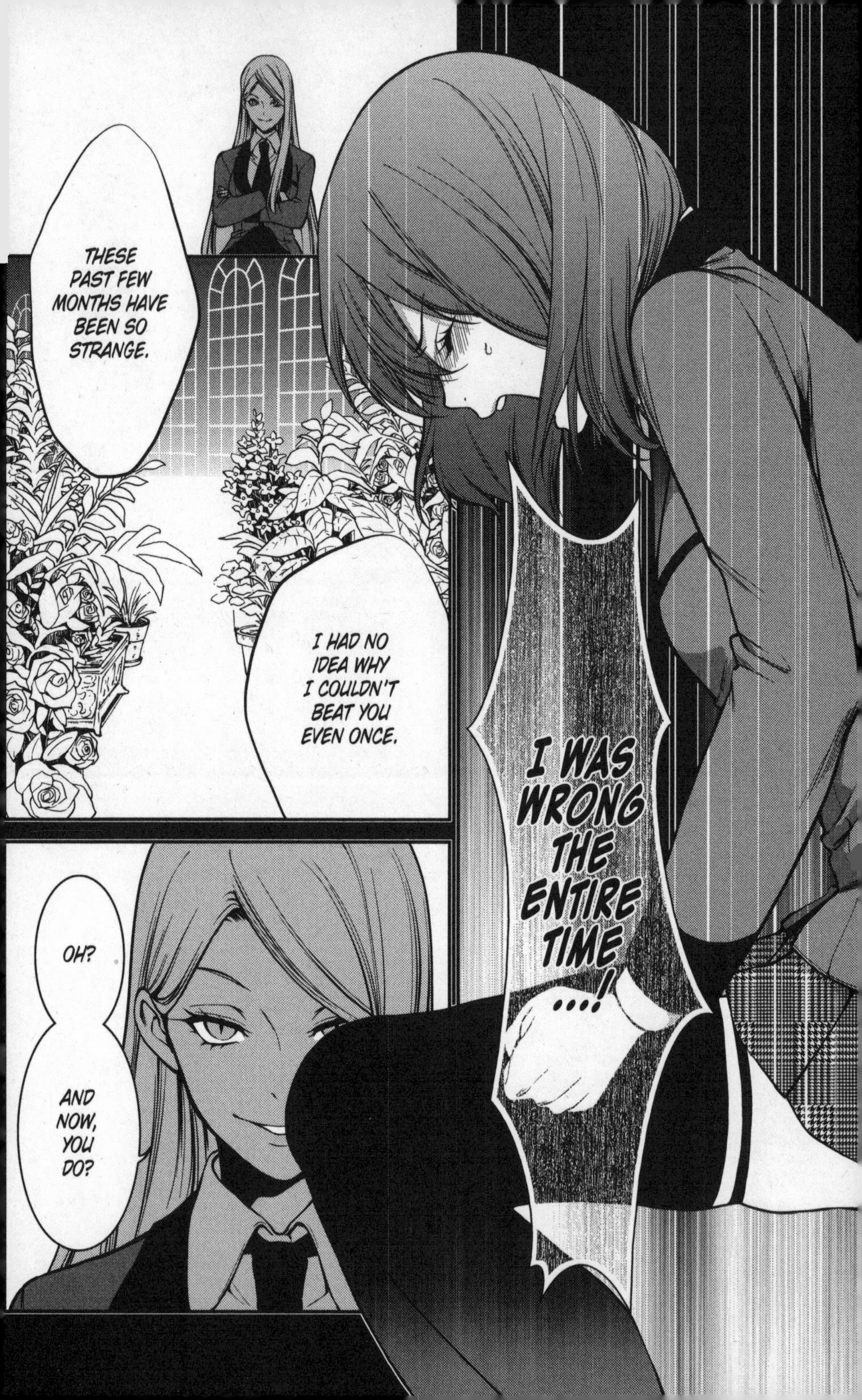
I WAS WRONG THE ENTIRE TIME...!
THESE PAST FEW MONTHS HAVE BEEN SO STRANGE.
I HAD NO IDEA WHY I COULDN'T BEAT YOU EVEN ONCE.
OH?
AND NOW, YOU DO?

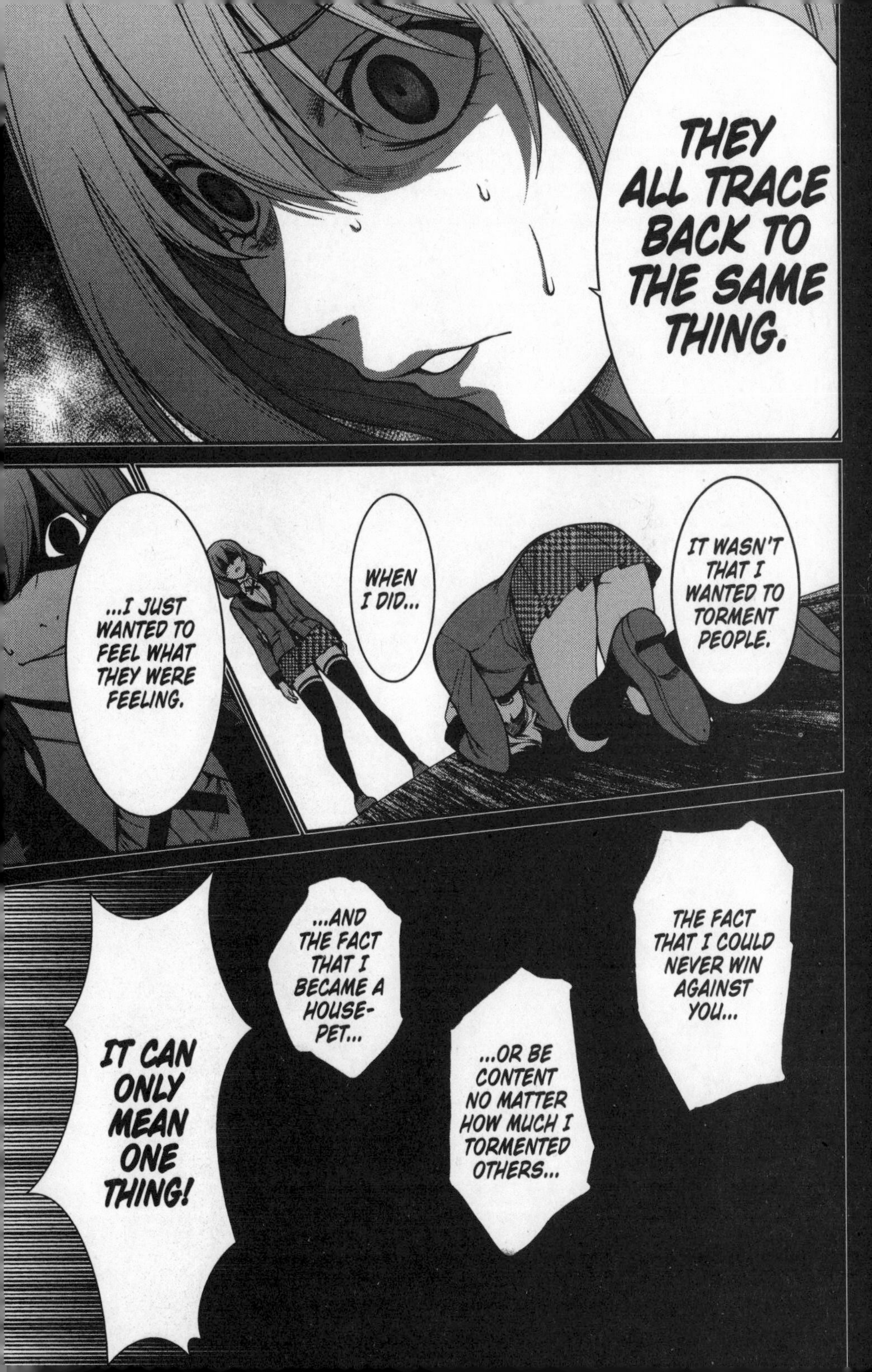
THEY ALL TRACE BACK TO THE SAME THING.
IT WASN'T THAT I WANTED TO TORMENT PEOPLE.
WHEN I DID...
...I JUST WANTED TO FEEL WHAT THEY WERE FEELING.
THE FACT THAT I COULD NEVER WIN AGAINST YOU...
...OR BE CONTENT NO MATTER HOW MUCH I TORMENTED OTHERS...
...AND THE FACT THAT I BECAME A HOUSE-PET...
IT CAN ONLY MEAN ONE THING!

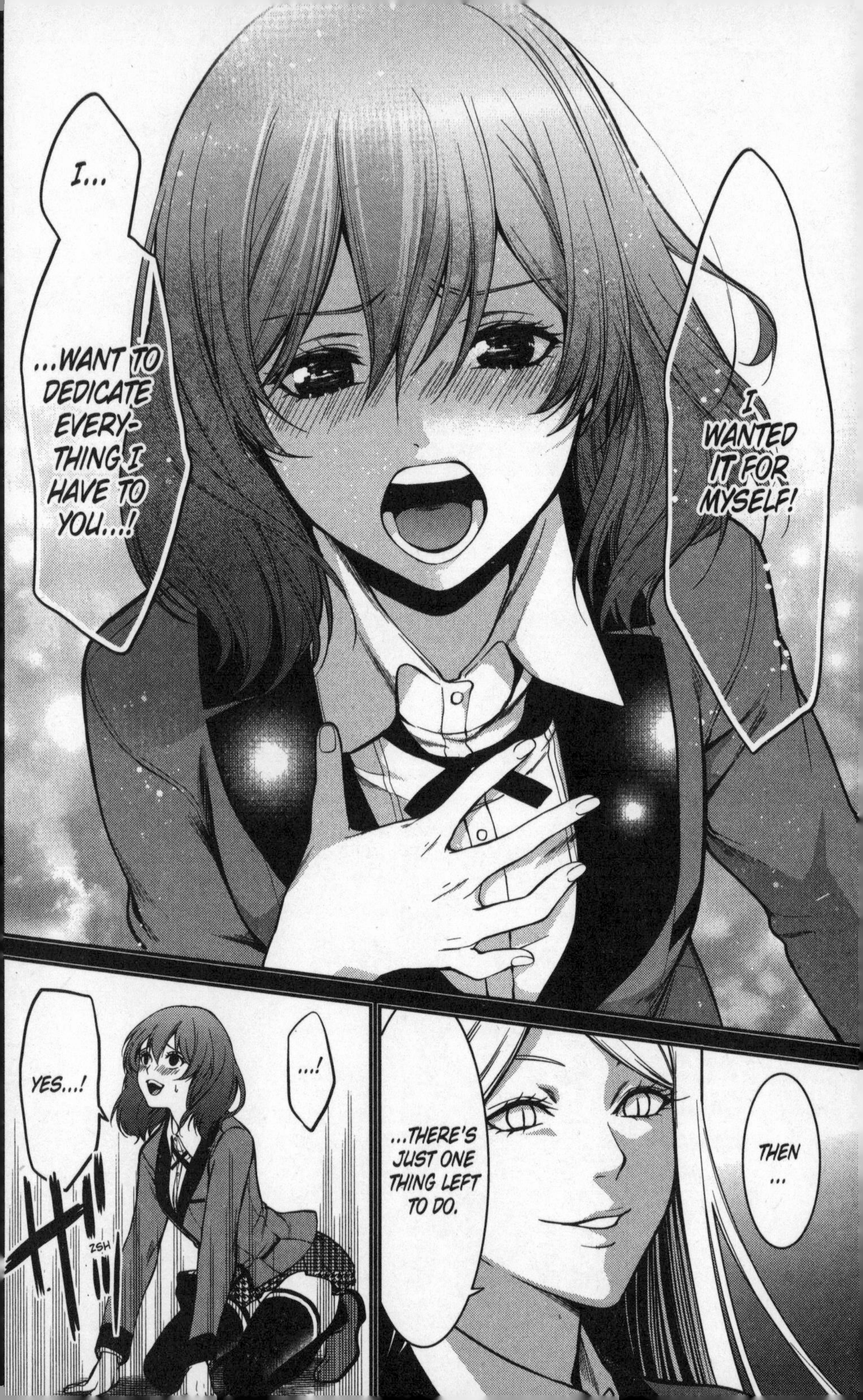
I...
...WANT TO DEDICATE EVERY-THING I HAVE TO YOU...!
I WANTED IT FOR MYSELF!
THEN ...
...THERE'S JUST ONE THING LEFT TO DO.
...!
YES...!
ZSH

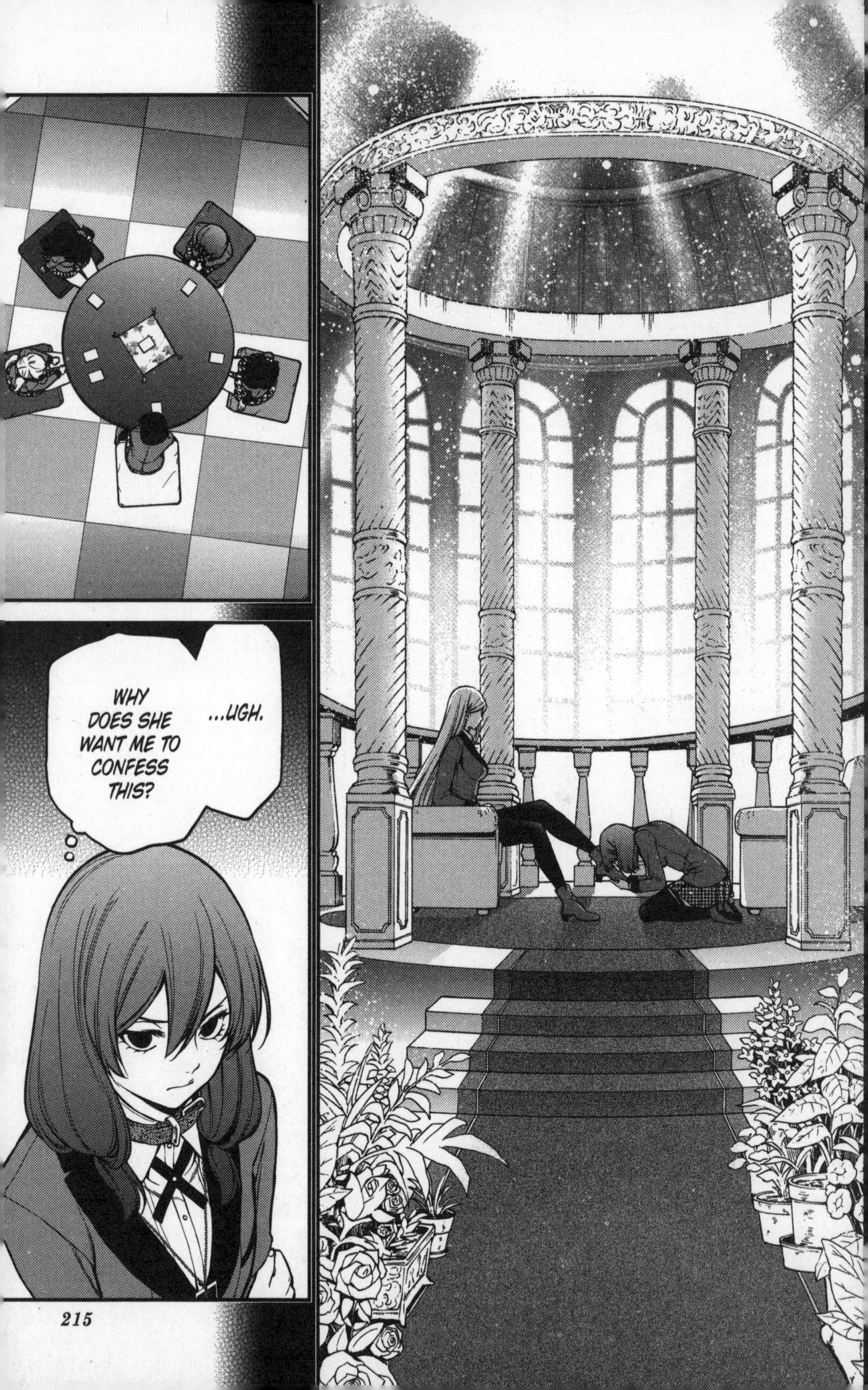
...UGH.
WHY DOES SHE WANT ME TO CONFESS THIS?

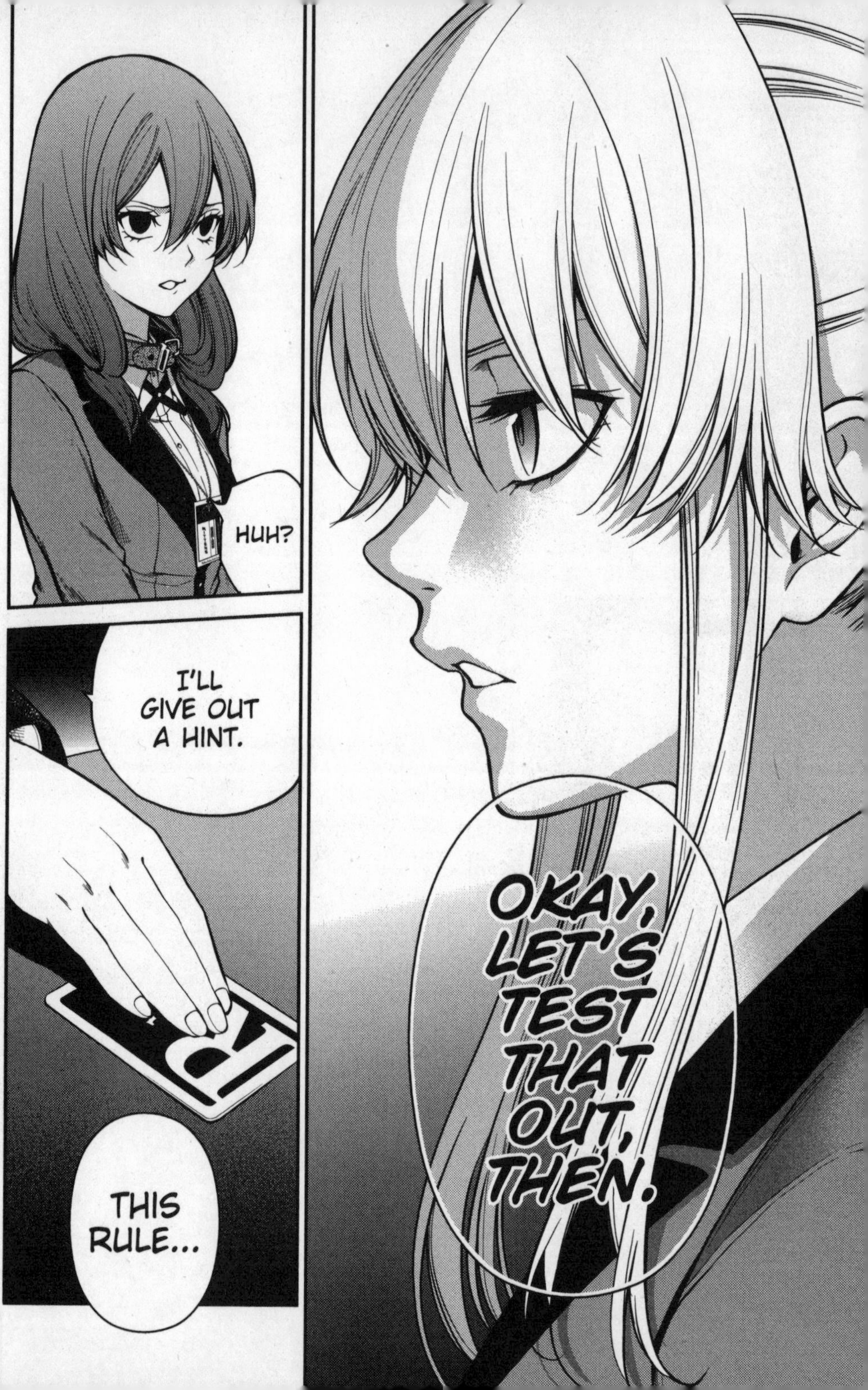
OKAY, LET'S TEST THAT OUT, THEN.
HUH?
I'LL GIVE OUT A HINT.
THIS RULE...

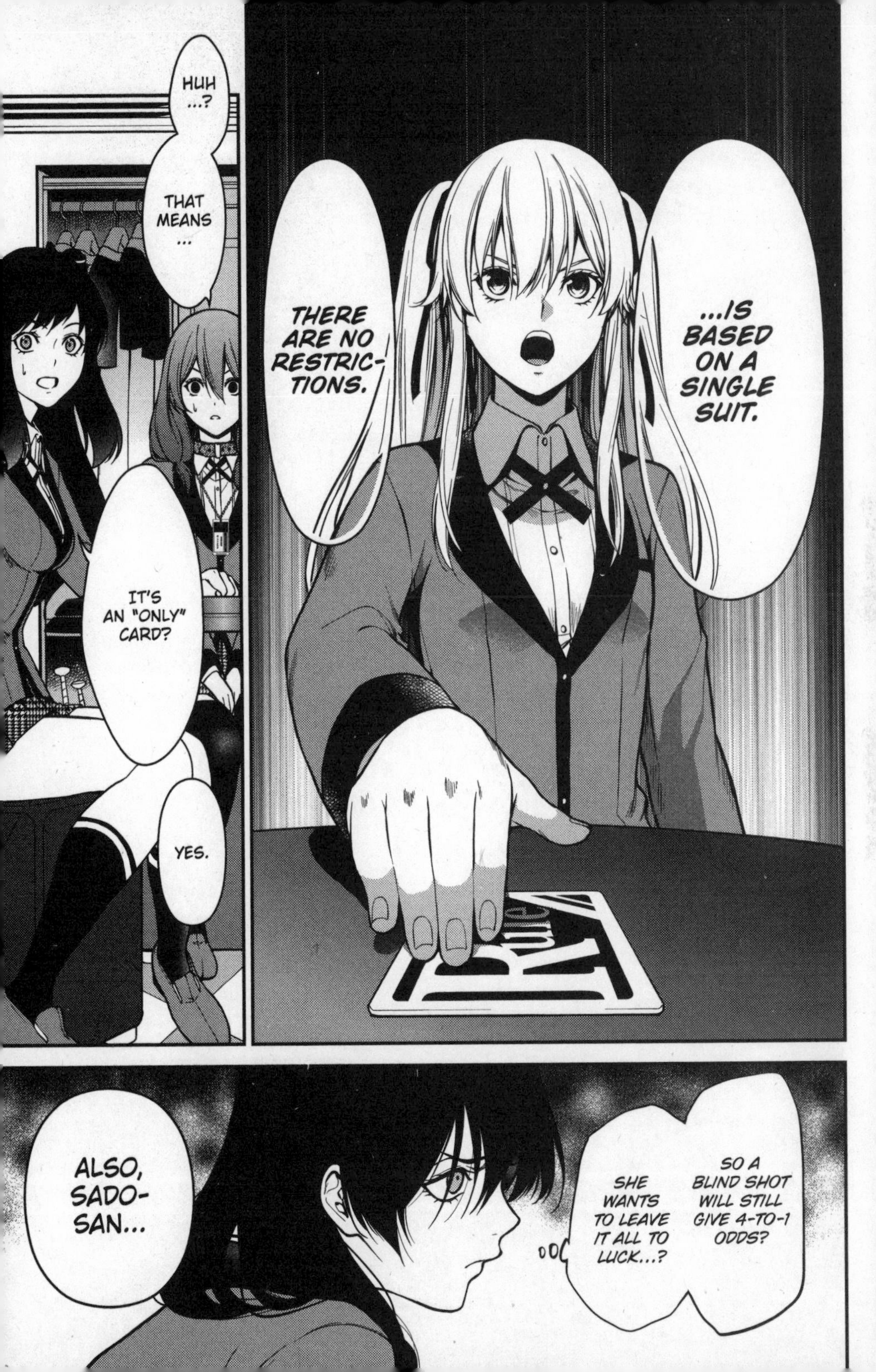
...IS BASED ON A SINGLE SUIT.
THERE ARE NO RESTRICTIONS.
HUH ...?
THAT MEANS ...
IT'S AN "ONLY" CARD?
YES.
SO A BLIND SHOT WILL STILL GIVE 4-TO-1 ODDS?
SHE WANTS TO LEAVE IT ALL TO LUCK...?
ALSO, SADO-SAN...

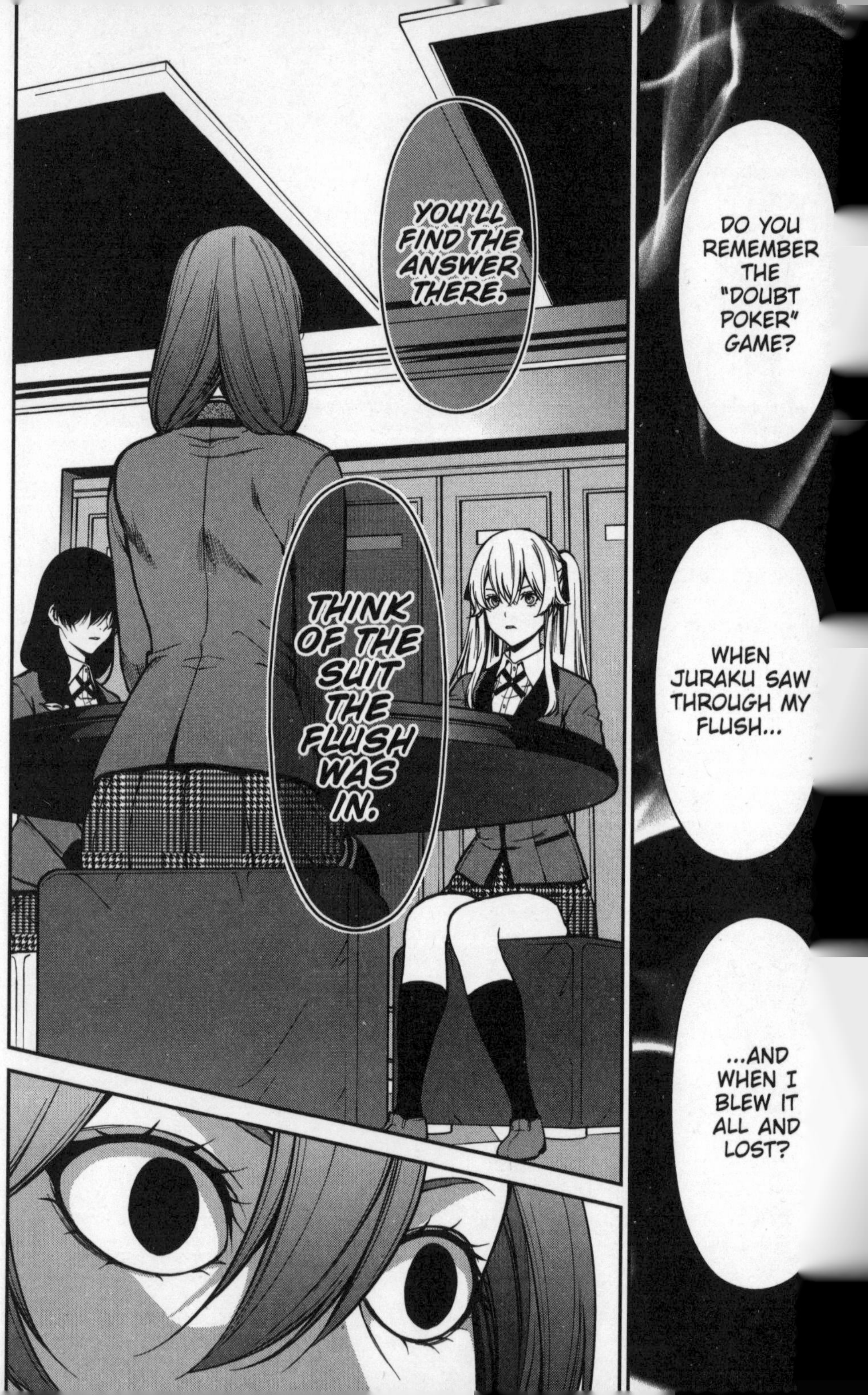
DO YOU REMEMBER THE "DOUBT POKER" GAME?
WHEN JURAKU SAW THROUGH MY FLUSH...
...AND WHEN I BLEW IT ALL AND LOST?
YOU'LL FIND THE ANSWER THERE.
THINK OF THE SUIT THE FLUSH WAS IN.

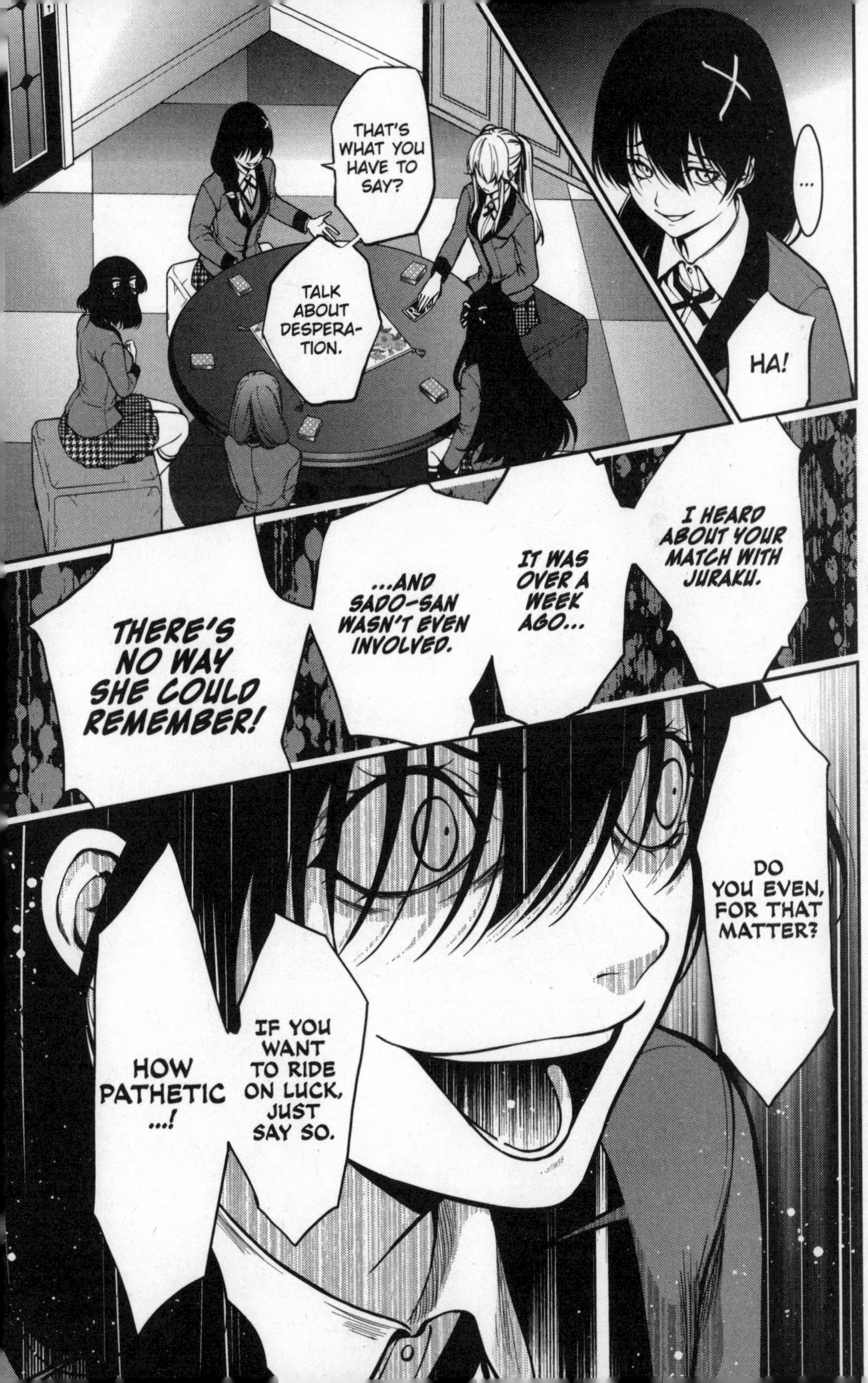
...
HA!
THAT'S WHAT YOU HAVE TO SAY?
TALK ABOUT DESPERA-TION.
I HEARD ABOUT YOUR MATCH WITH JURAKU.
IT WAS OVER A WEEK AGO...
...AND SADO-SAN WASN'T EVEN INVOLVED.
THERE'S NO WAY SHE COULD REMEMBER!
DO YOU EVEN, FOR THAT MATTER?
IF YOU WANT TO RIDE ON LUCK, JUST SAY SO.
HOW PATHETIC ...!

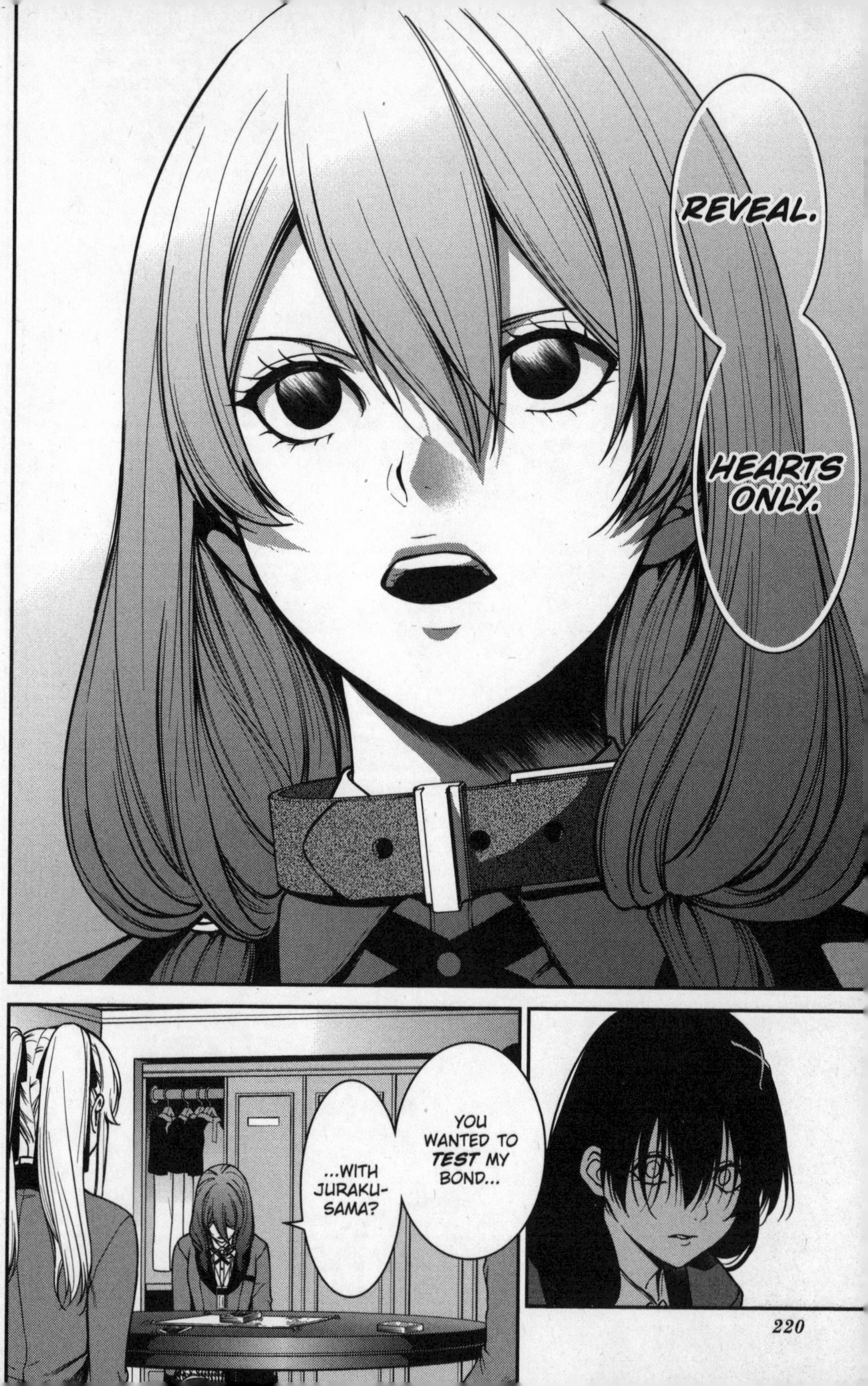
REVEAL.
HEARTS ONLY.
YOU WANTED TO TEST MY BOND...
...WITH JURAKU-SAMA?

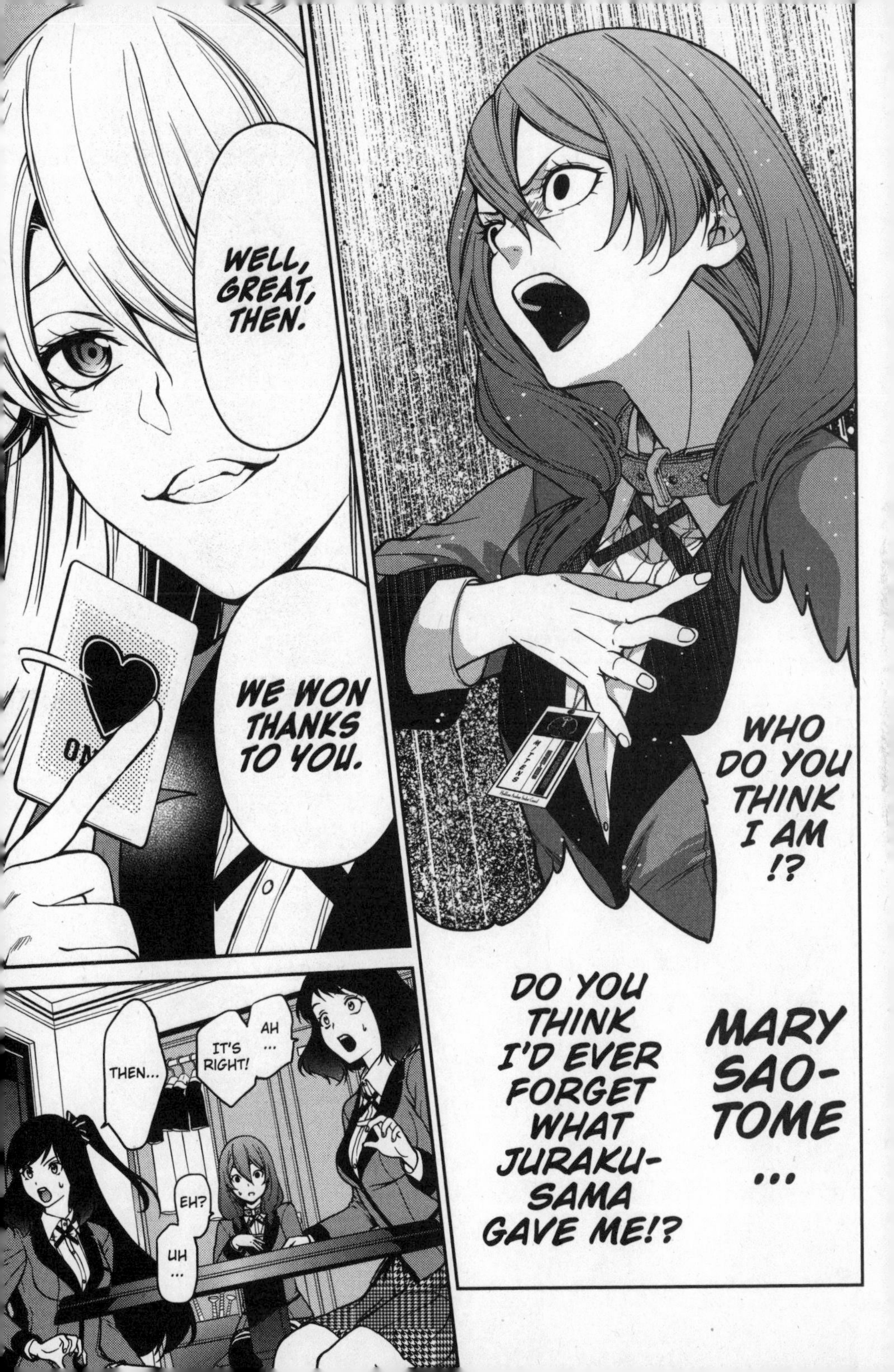
WHO DO YOU THINK I AM !?
MARY SAOTOME ...
DO YOU THINK I'D EVER FORGET WHAT JURAKU-SAMA GAVE ME!?
WELL, GREAT, THEN.
WE WON THANKS TO YOU.
AH ...
IT'S RIGHT!
THEN...
EH?
UH ...

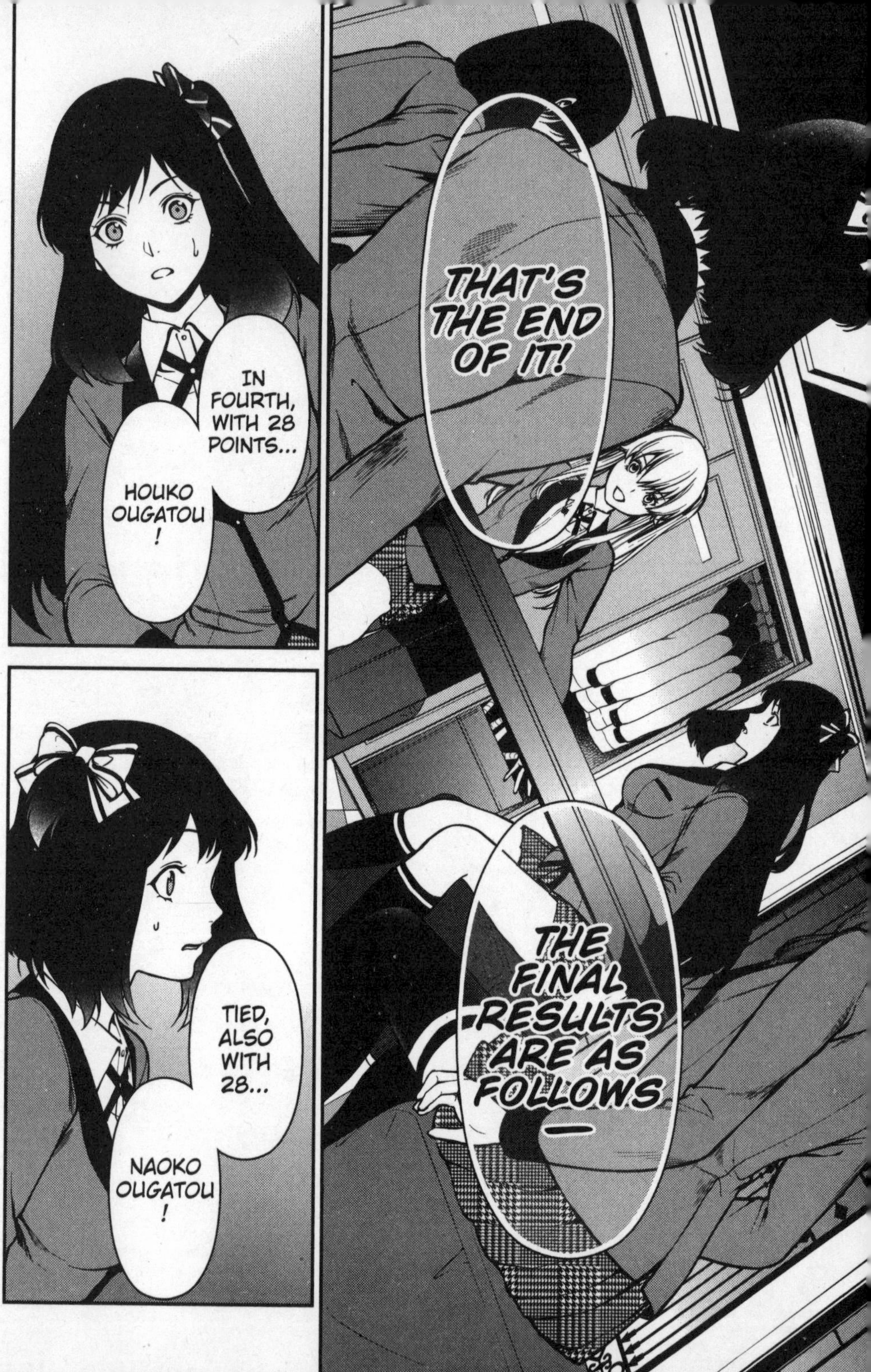
THAT'S THE END OF IT!
THE FINAL RESULTS ARE AS FOLLOWS—
IN FOURTH, WITH 28 POINTS...
HOUKO OUGATOU!
TIED, ALSO WITH 28...
NAOKO OUGATOU!

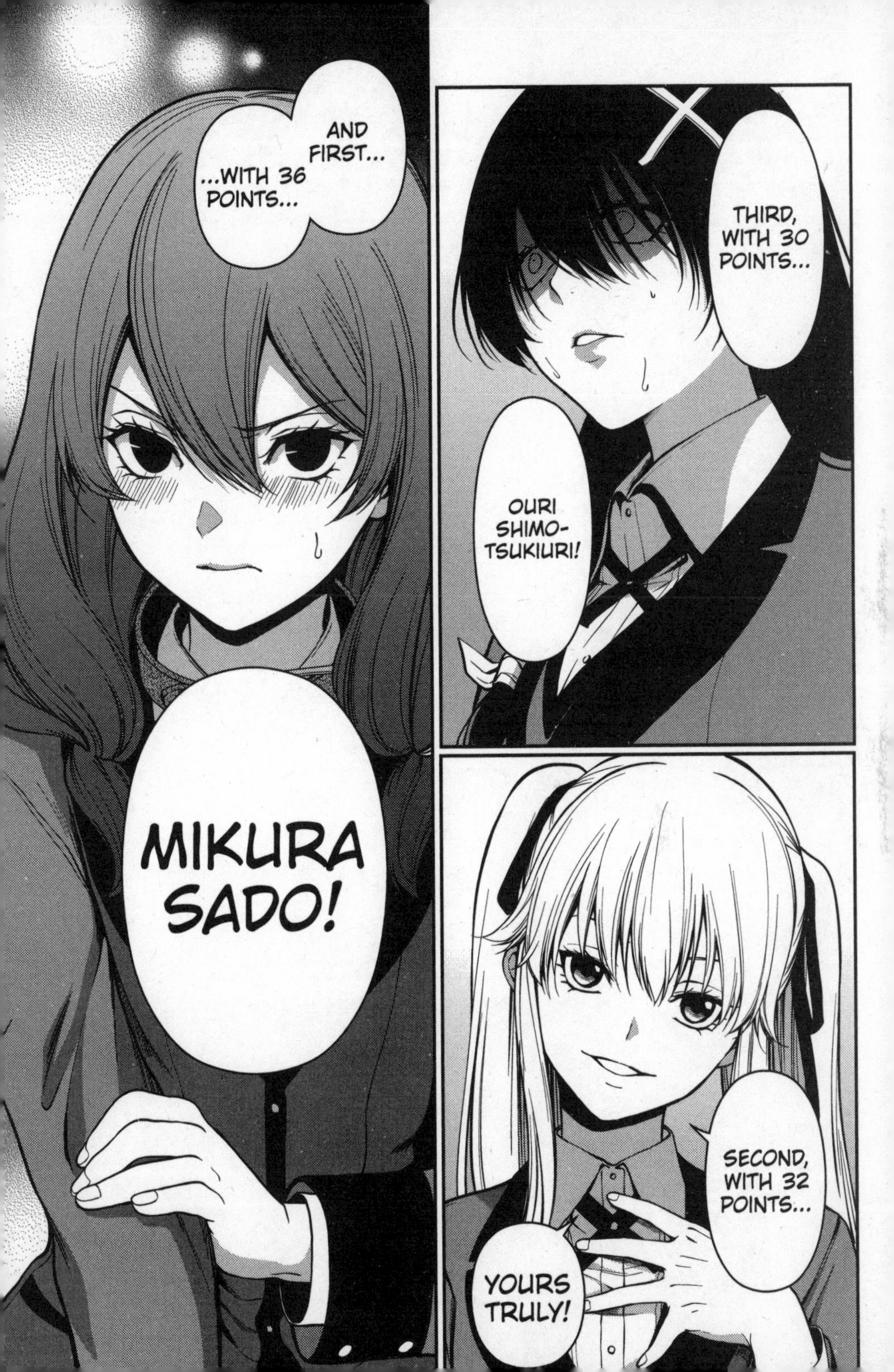
THIRD, WITH 30 POINTS...
OURI SHIMO-TSUKIURI!
SECOND, WITH 32 POINTS...
YOURS TRULY!
AND FIRST...
...WITH 36 POINTS...
MIKURA SADO!

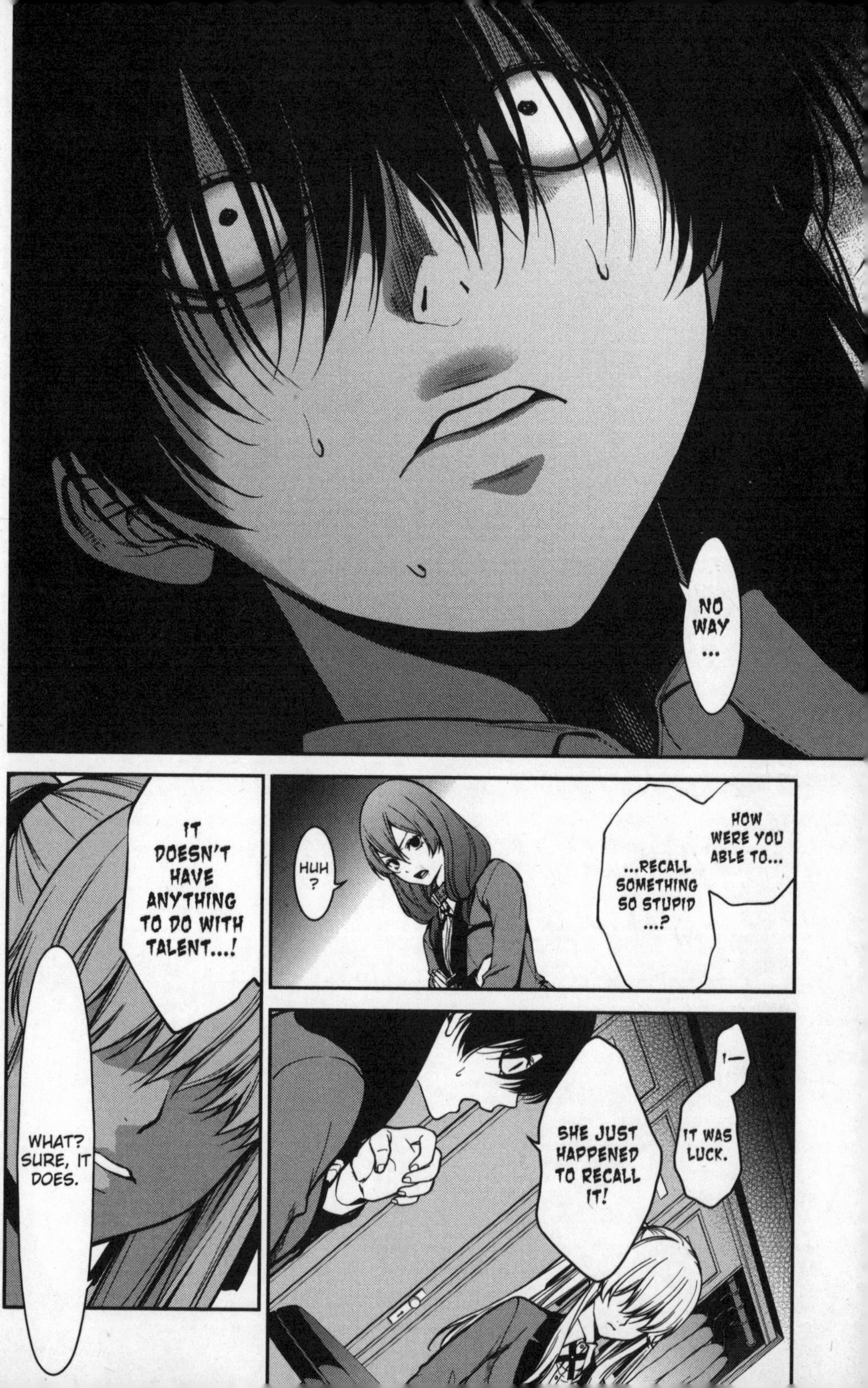
NO WAY ...
HOW WERE YOU ABLE TO...
...RECALL SOMETHING SO STUPID ...?
HUH?
I—
IT WAS LUCK.
SHE JUST HAPPENED TO RECALL IT!
IT DOESN'T HAVE ANYTHING TO DO WITH TALENT...!
WHAT? SURE, IT DOES.

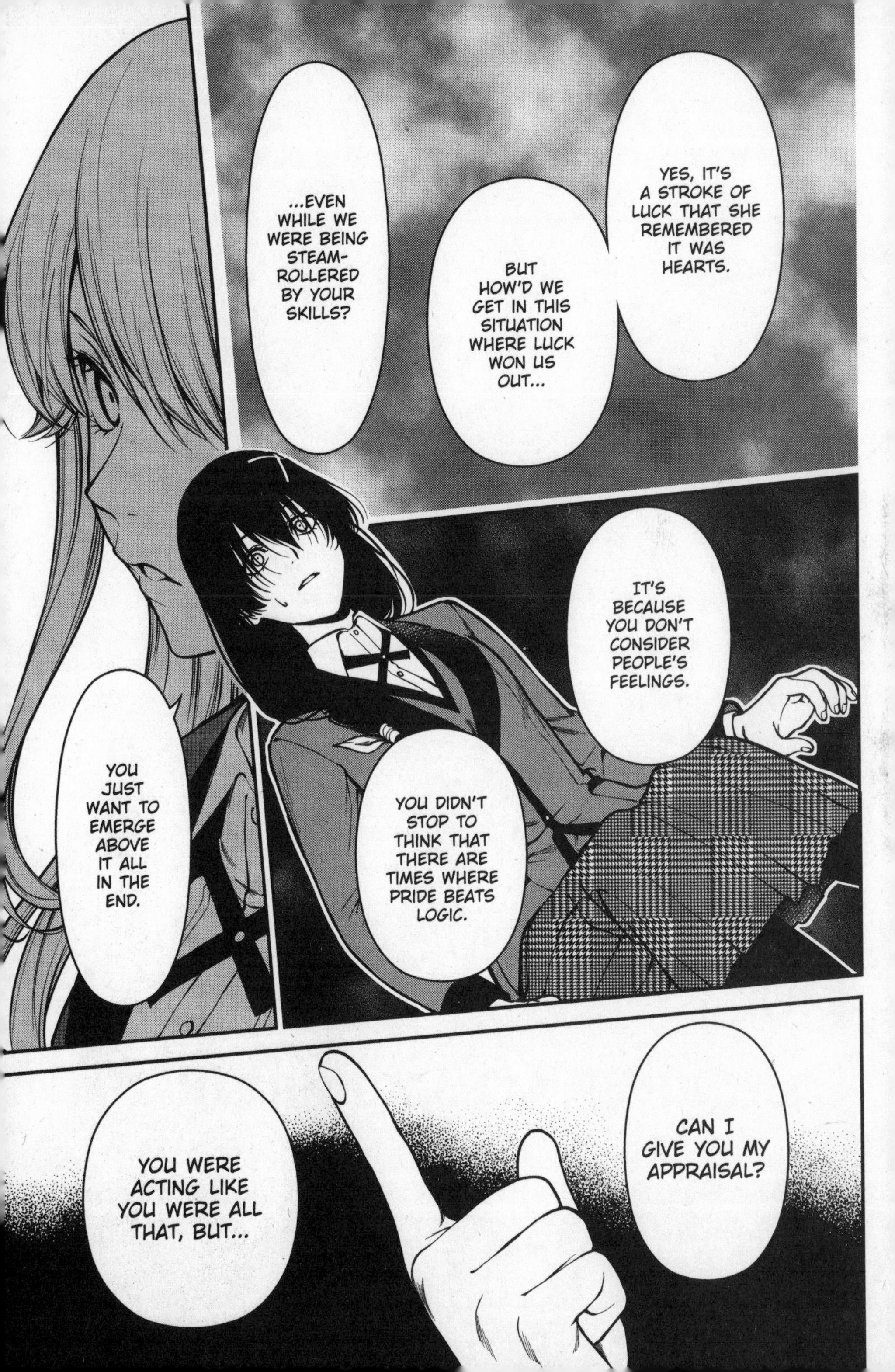
YES, IT'S A STROKE OF LUCK THAT SHE REMEMBERED IT WAS HEARTS.
BUT HOW'D WE GET IN THIS SITUATION WHERE LUCK WON US OUT...
...EVEN WHILE WE WERE BEING STEAM-ROLLERED BY YOUR SKILLS?
IT'S BECAUSE YOU DON'T CONSIDER PEOPLE'S FEELINGS.
YOU DIDN'T STOP TO THINK THAT THERE ARE TIMES WHERE PRIDE BEATS LOGIC.
YOU JUST WANT TO EMERGE ABOVE IT ALL IN THE END.
CAN I GIVE YOU MY APPRAISAL?
YOU WERE ACTING LIKE YOU WERE ALL THAT, BUT...

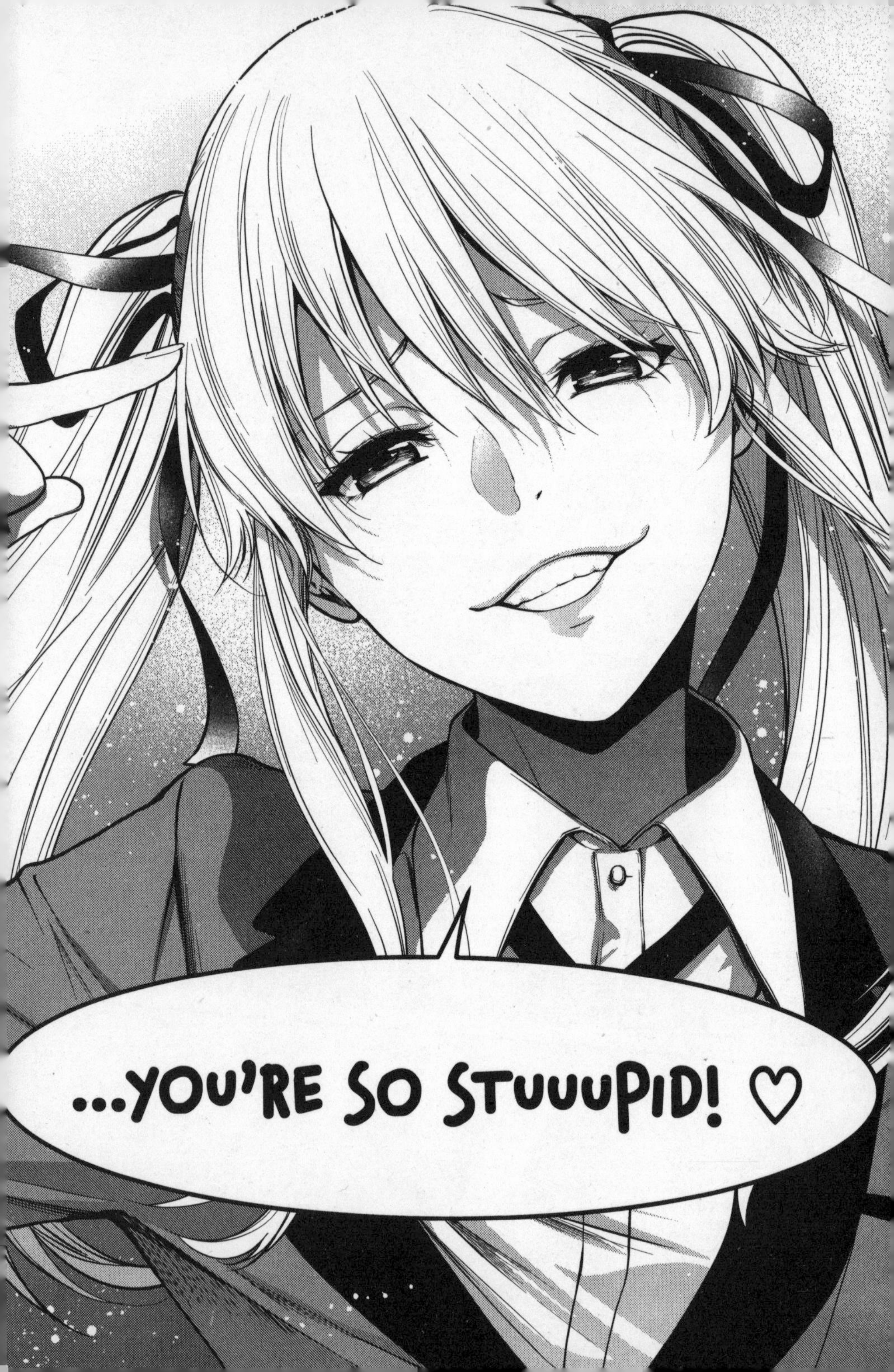
...YOU'RE SO STUUUPID! ♡

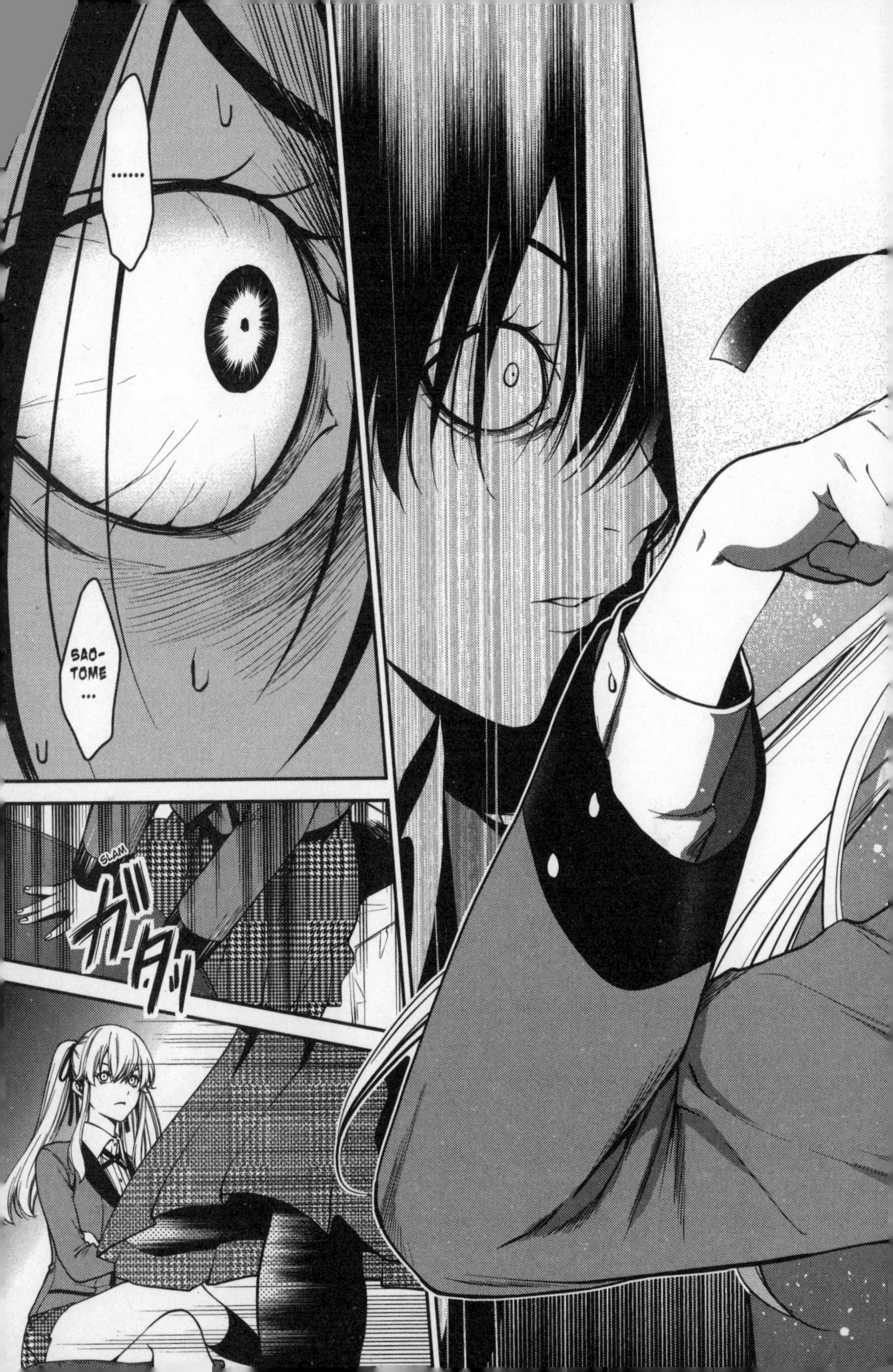
......
SAO-TOME ...
SLAM

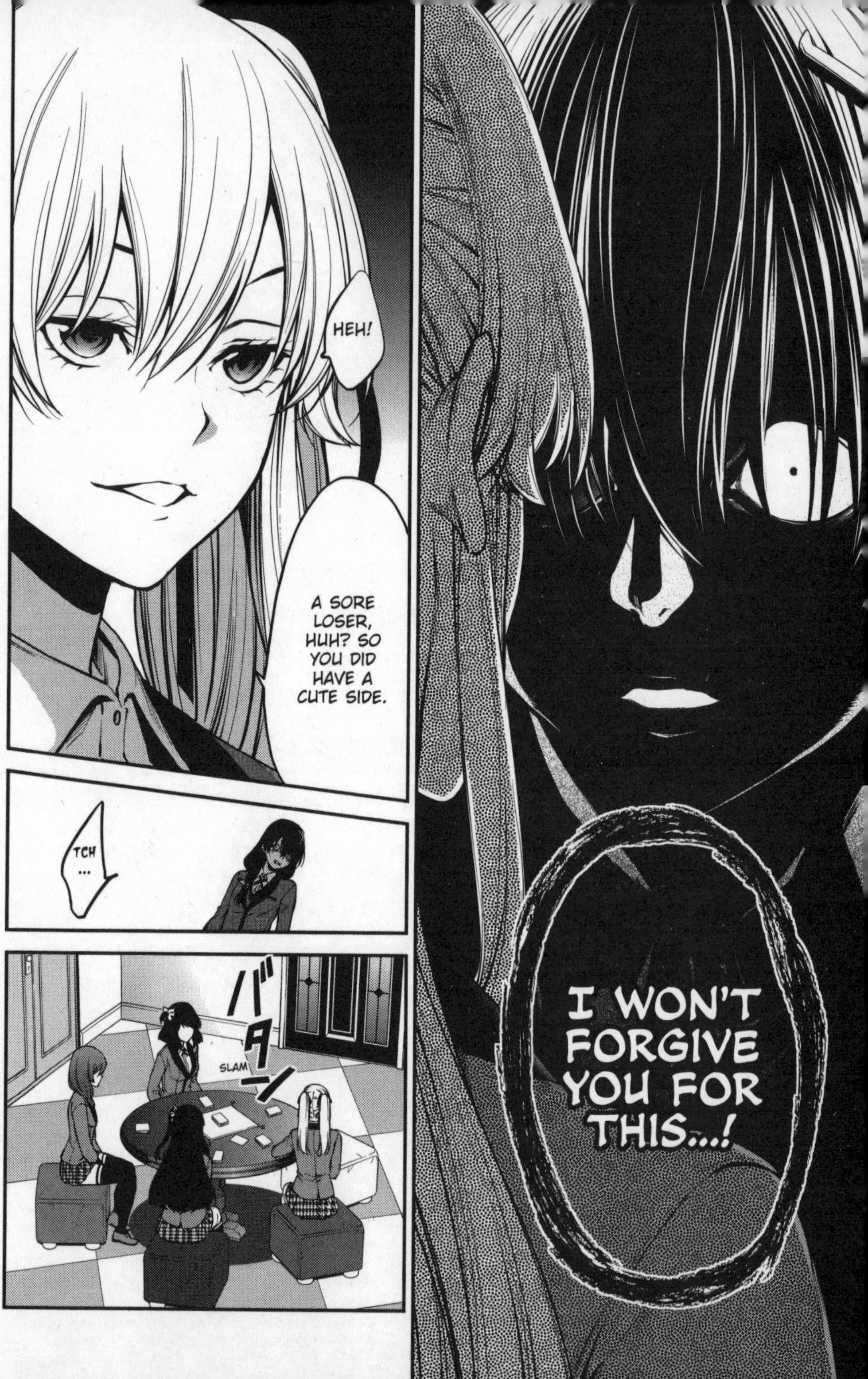
I WON'T FORGIVE YOU FOR THIS...!
HEH!
A SORE LOSER, HUH? SO YOU DID HAVE A CUTE SIDE.
TCH...
バターン
SLAM

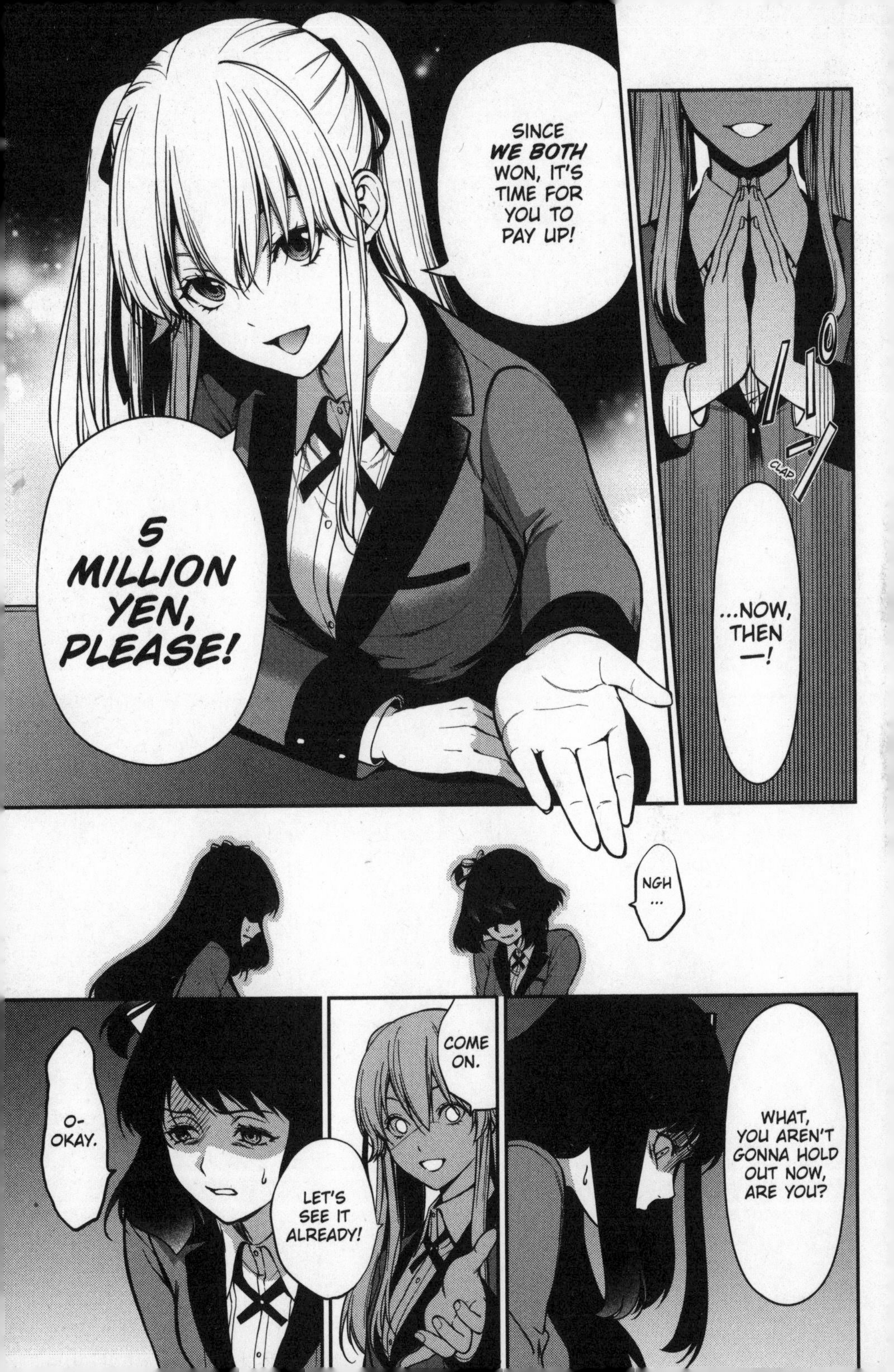
CLAP
...NOW, THEN—!
SINCE WE BOTH WON, IT'S TIME FOR YOU TO PAY UP!
5 MILLION YEN, PLEASE!
NGH...
WHAT, YOU AREN'T GONNA HOLD OUT NOW, ARE YOU?
COME ON.
LET'S SEE IT ALREADY!
O-OKAY.

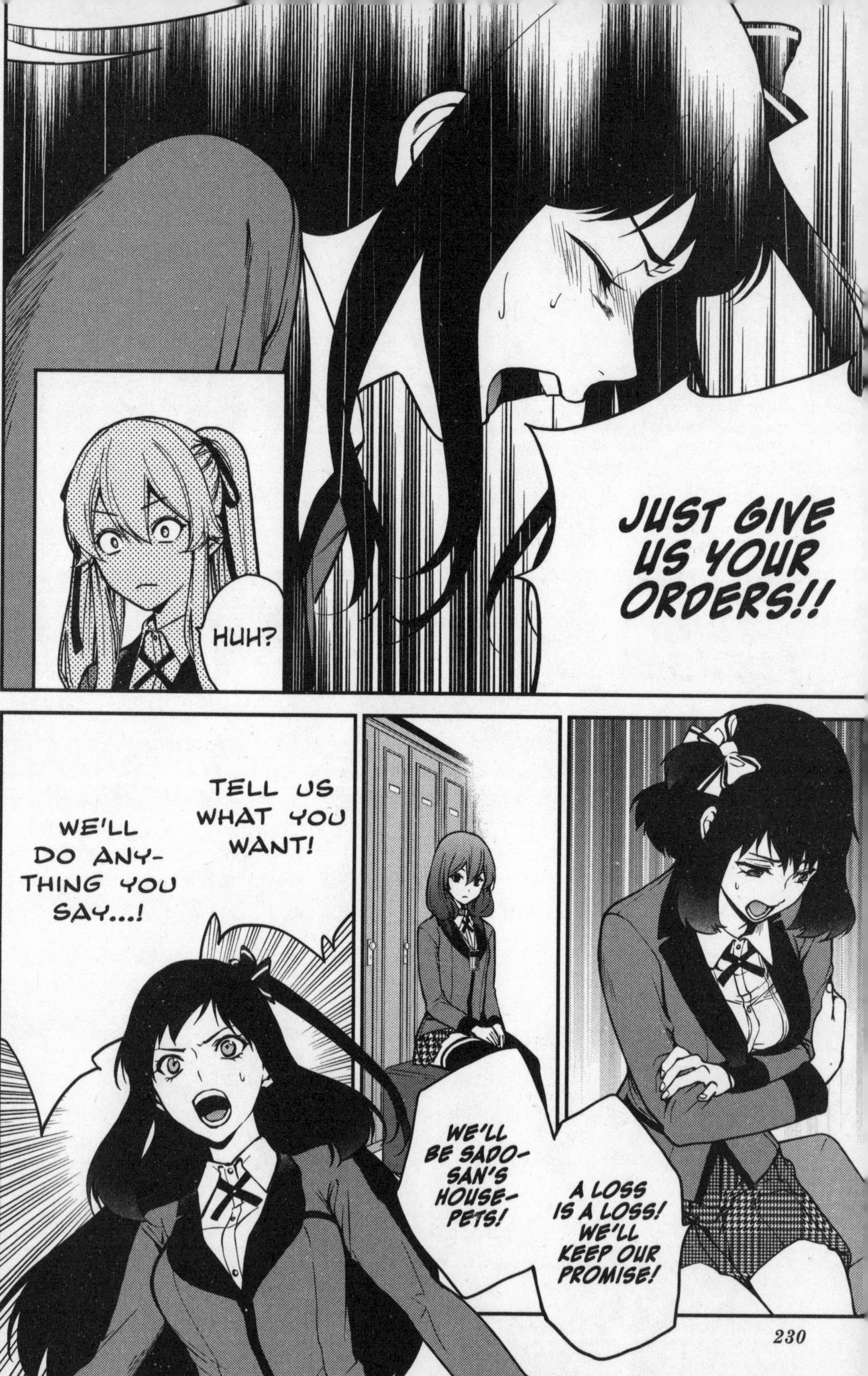
JUST GIVE US YOUR ORDERS!!
HUH?
A LOSS IS A LOSS! WE'LL KEEP OUR PROMISE!
TELL US WHAT YOU WANT!
WE'LL DO ANY-THING YOU SAY...!
WE'LL BE SADO-SAN'S HOUSE-PETS!

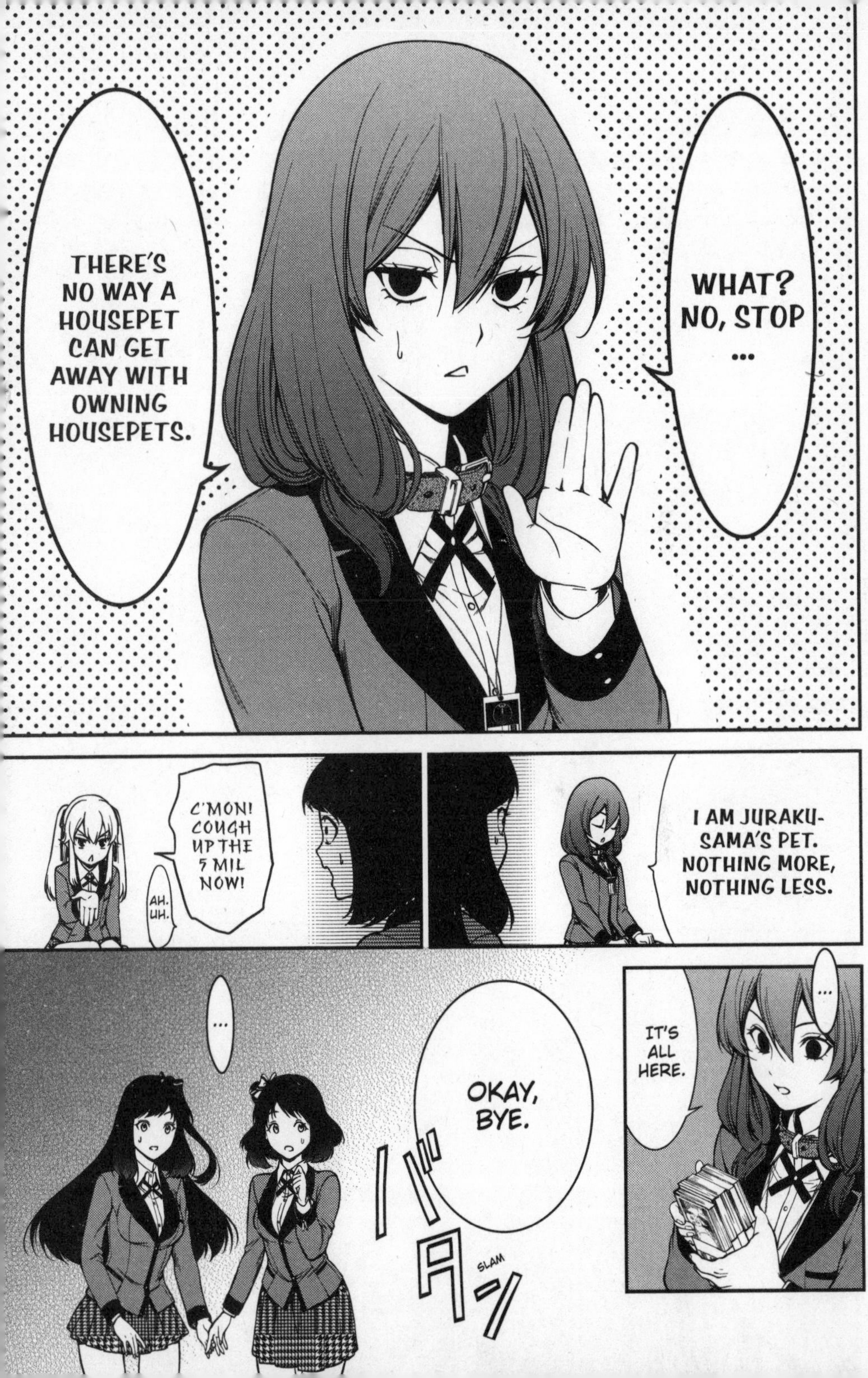
WHAT? NO, STOP ...
THERE'S NO WAY A HOUSEPET CAN GET AWAY WITH OWNING HOUSEPETS.
I AM JURAKU-SAMA'S PET. NOTHING MORE, NOTHING LESS.
C'MON! COUGH UP THE 5 MIL NOW!
AH. UH.
...
IT'S ALL HERE.
OKAY, BYE.
SLAM
...

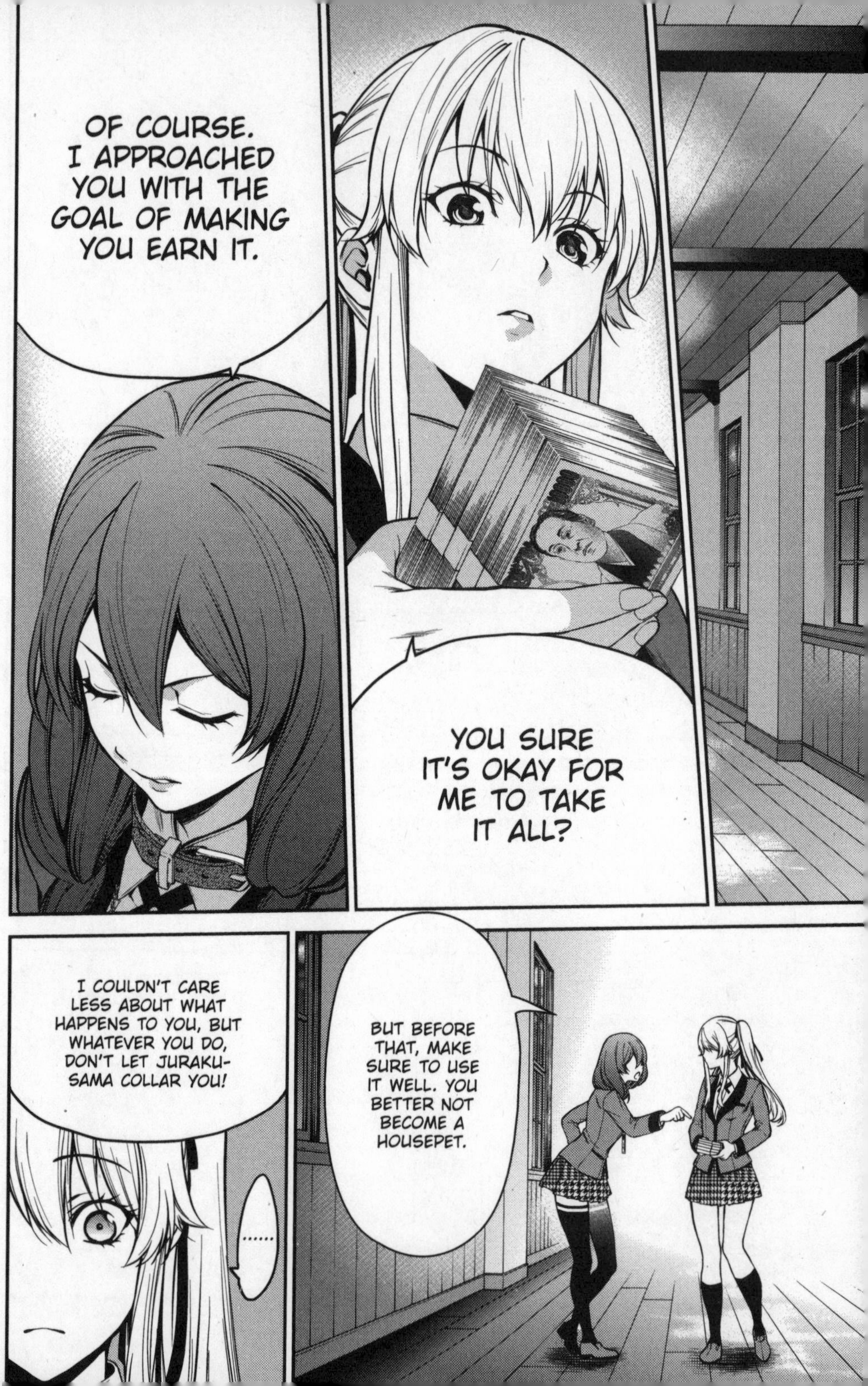
YOU SURE IT'S OKAY FOR ME TO TAKE IT ALL?
OF COURSE. I APPROACHED YOU WITH THE GOAL OF MAKING YOU EARN IT.
BUT BEFORE THAT, MAKE SURE TO USE IT WELL. YOU BETTER NOT BECOME A HOUSEPET.
I COULDN'T CARE LESS ABOUT WHAT HAPPENS TO YOU, BUT WHATEVER YOU DO, DON'T LET JURAKU-SAMA COLLAR YOU!
......

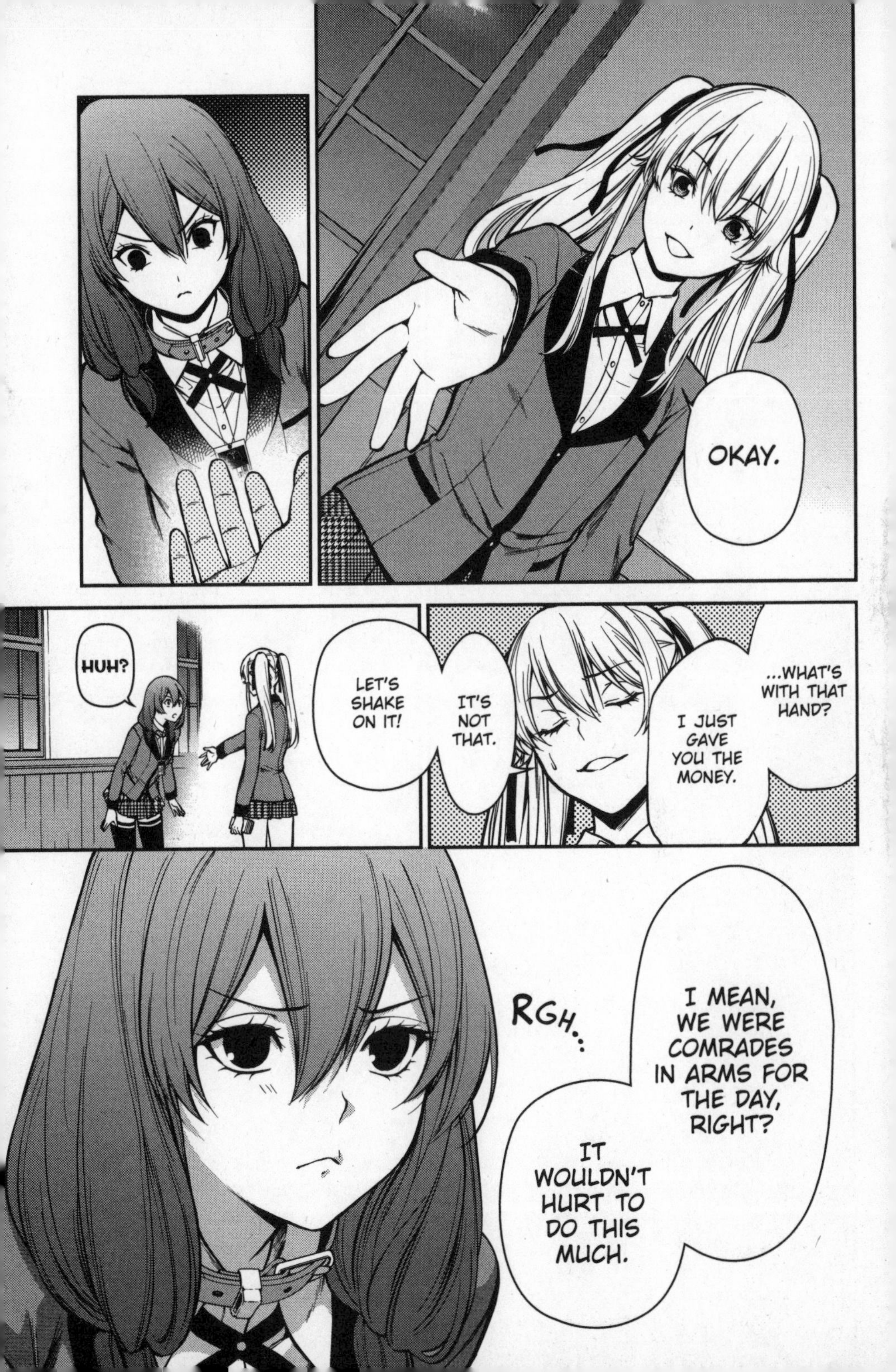
OKAY.
...WHAT'S WITH THAT HAND?
I JUST GAVE YOU THE MONEY.
IT'S NOT THAT.
LET'S SHAKE ON IT!
HUH?
I MEAN, WE WERE COMRADES IN ARMS FOR THE DAY, RIGHT?
RGH...
IT WOULDN'T HURT TO DO THIS MUCH.

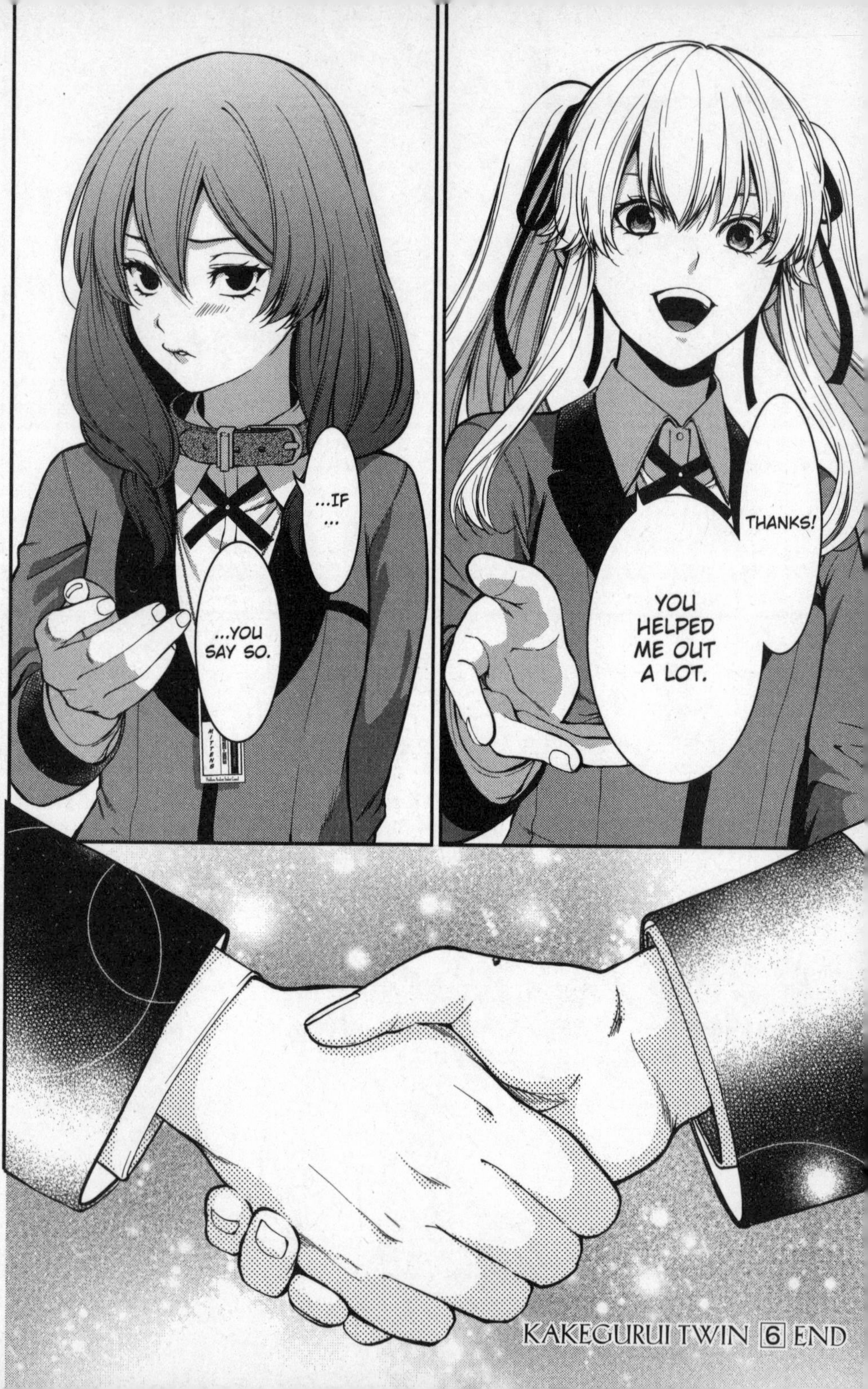
THANKS!
YOU HELPED ME OUT A LOT.
...IF ...
...YOU SAY SO.
KAKEGURUI TWIN 6 END

TIME FOR SOME END-OF-THE-VOLUME BONUS COMICS!

INSIDER KNOWLEDGE

* This has no relation to the actual story.

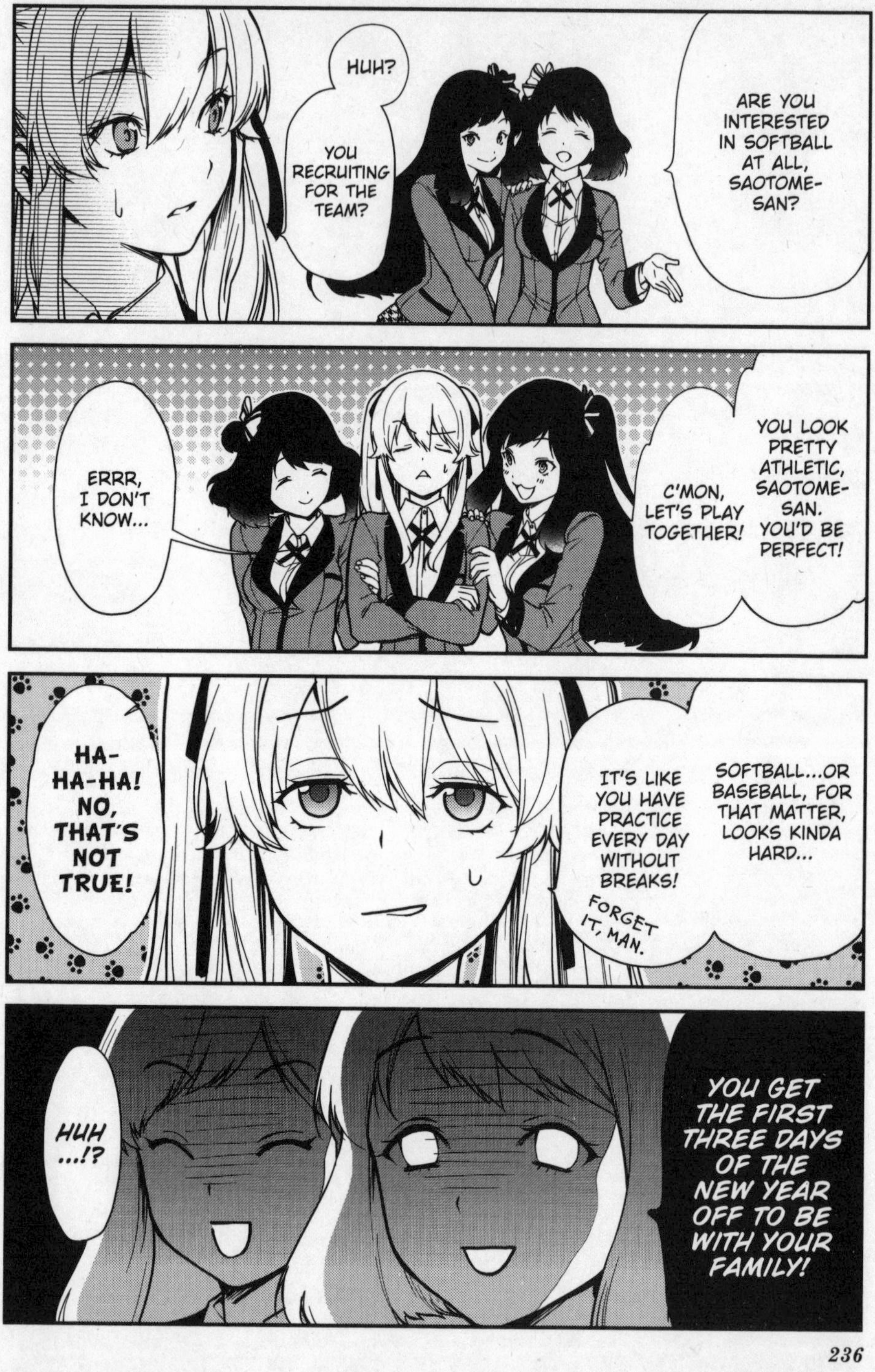
ARE YOU INTERESTED IN SOFTBALL AT ALL, SAOTOME-SAN?
HUH?
YOU RECRUITING FOR THE TEAM?
YOU LOOK PRETTY ATHLETIC, SAOTOME-SAN. YOU'D BE PERFECT!
C'MON, LET'S PLAY TOGETHER!
ERRR, I DON'T KNOW...
SOFTBALL...OR BASEBALL, FOR THAT MATTER, LOOKS KINDA HARD...
IT'S LIKE YOU HAVE PRACTICE EVERY DAY WITHOUT BREAKS!
FORGET IT, MAN.
HA-HA-HA! NO, THAT'S NOT TRUE!
YOU GET THE FIRST THREE DAYS OF THE NEW YEAR OFF TO BE WITH YOUR FAMILY!
HUH ...!?

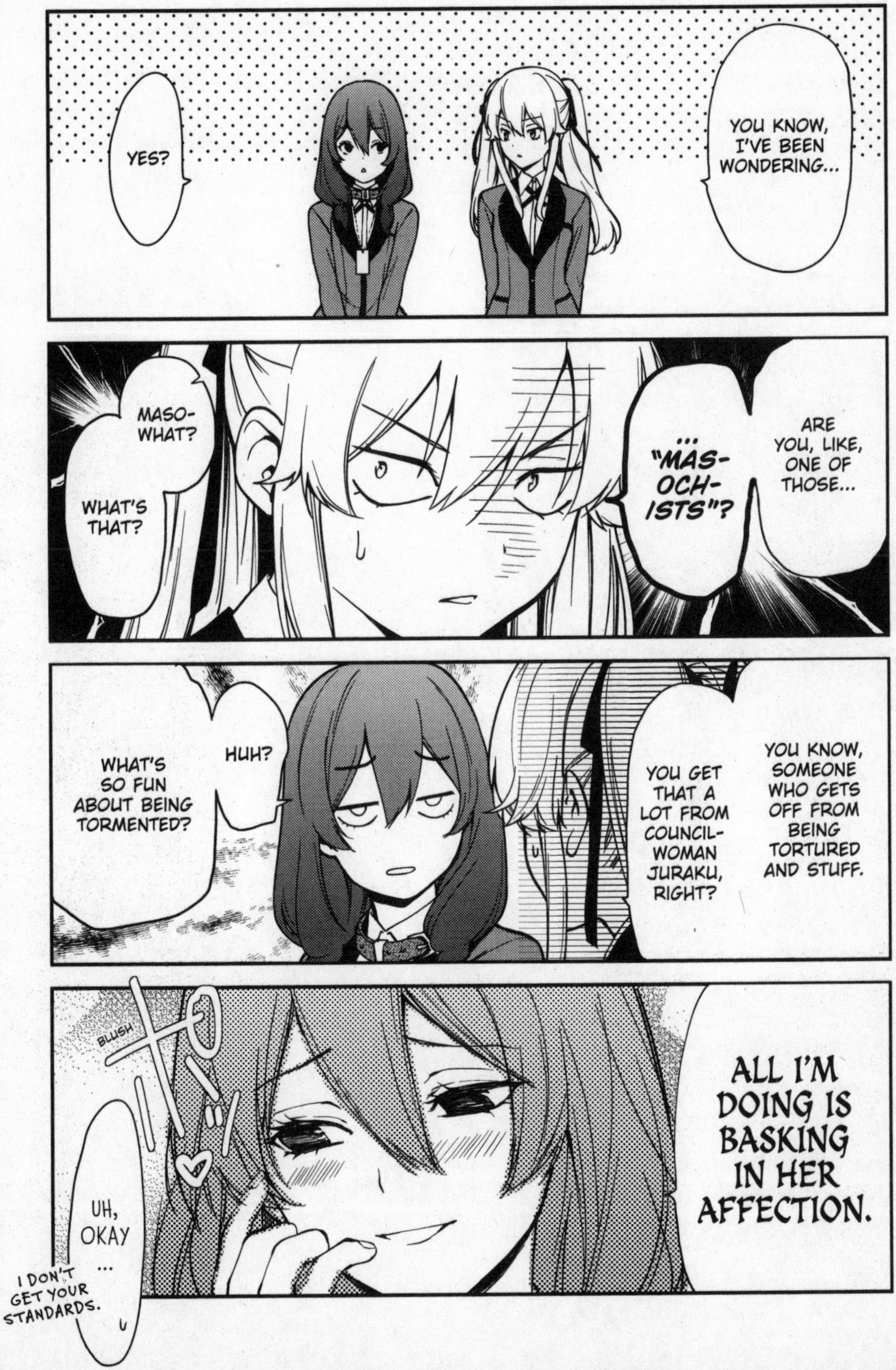
YOU KNOW, I'VE BEEN WONDERING...
YES?
ARE YOU, LIKE, ONE OF THOSE...
..."MAS-OCH-ISTS"?
MASO-WHAT?
WHAT'S THAT?
YOU KNOW, SOMEONE WHO GETS OFF FROM BEING TORTURED AND STUFF.
YOU GET THAT A LOT FROM COUNCIL-WOMAN JURAKU, RIGHT?
HUH?
WHAT'S SO FUN ABOUT BEING TORMENTED?
ALL I'M DOING IS BASKING IN HER AFFECTION.
BLUSH
UH, OKAY...
I DON'T GET YOUR STANDARDS.

GAMBLING, THAT IS MY RAISON D'ÊTRE.

Hidden Rules

This playing saw a lot of correct answers, thanks to the rampant cheating and people with superhuman memory skills involved, but I think it's a much harder game in real life. The Ougatou sisters would've been able to run away with it normally, so the fact that it turned out how it did for them indicates they messed with the wrong fellows. When looking for a match, choose your opponent carefully.

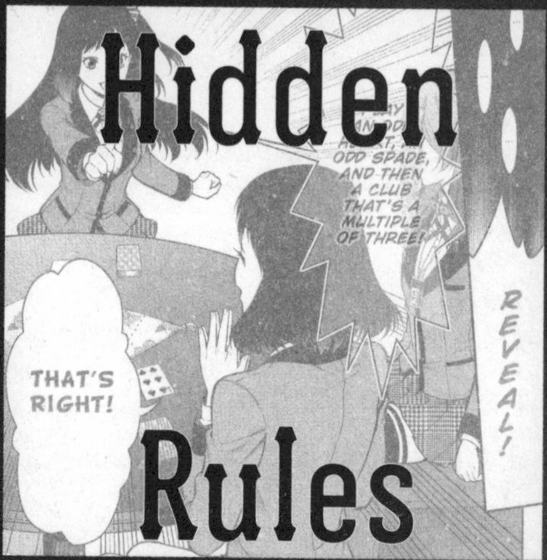
ODD SPADE, AND THEN A CLUB THAT'S A MULTIPLE OF THREE!
REVEAL!
THAT'S RIGHT!

Thank you for picking up the sixth volume of *Kakegurui Twin*.
When *Twin* first began running, I naturally had a general outline of how Mary's first year would begin, how it would end, and how it would connect to the main *Kakegurui* tale.
But as the series has unfolded, I feel like Mary has really grabbed the reins from me, taking the story in places I never thought it would go. As the writer, I can't wait to see where she's going to go next.
Now for some thanks. I'd like to thank Saiki-sensei and his assistants for their art, which continues to grow cuter and bolder over time. Also, I'd like to express my thanks to our story editors, Sasaki-sama and Yumoto-sama for putting up with our meetings when they go into the night. And of course, thanks to our readers.
It took the efforts of many people to bring Volume 6 into the world. I can't thank them all enough, and I hope we can keep working together.
See you all in Volume 7!

Homura Kawamoto

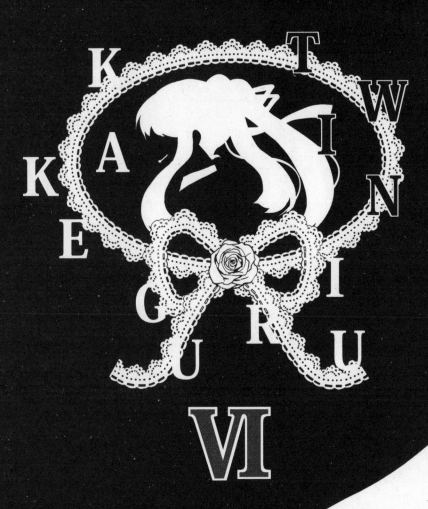

KAKEGURU TWIN VI

◆ Special Thanks ◆

My editors
Kawamoto-sama

Ken'ichi Sato-sama
Kozue Tachikawa-sama

Thank you for purchasing Volume 6.
Mary's sure bounced back from adversity,
hasn't she? What a strong, robust girl.
Between her fighting alongside Mikura,
those lovable twins, and Ouri's insanity,
this volume's really made me look forward
to the future!
Personally, I think it'd be nice if a little
friendship buds between Mary
and Mikura, but we'll see, huh?
See you in the next volume.

Kei Saiki

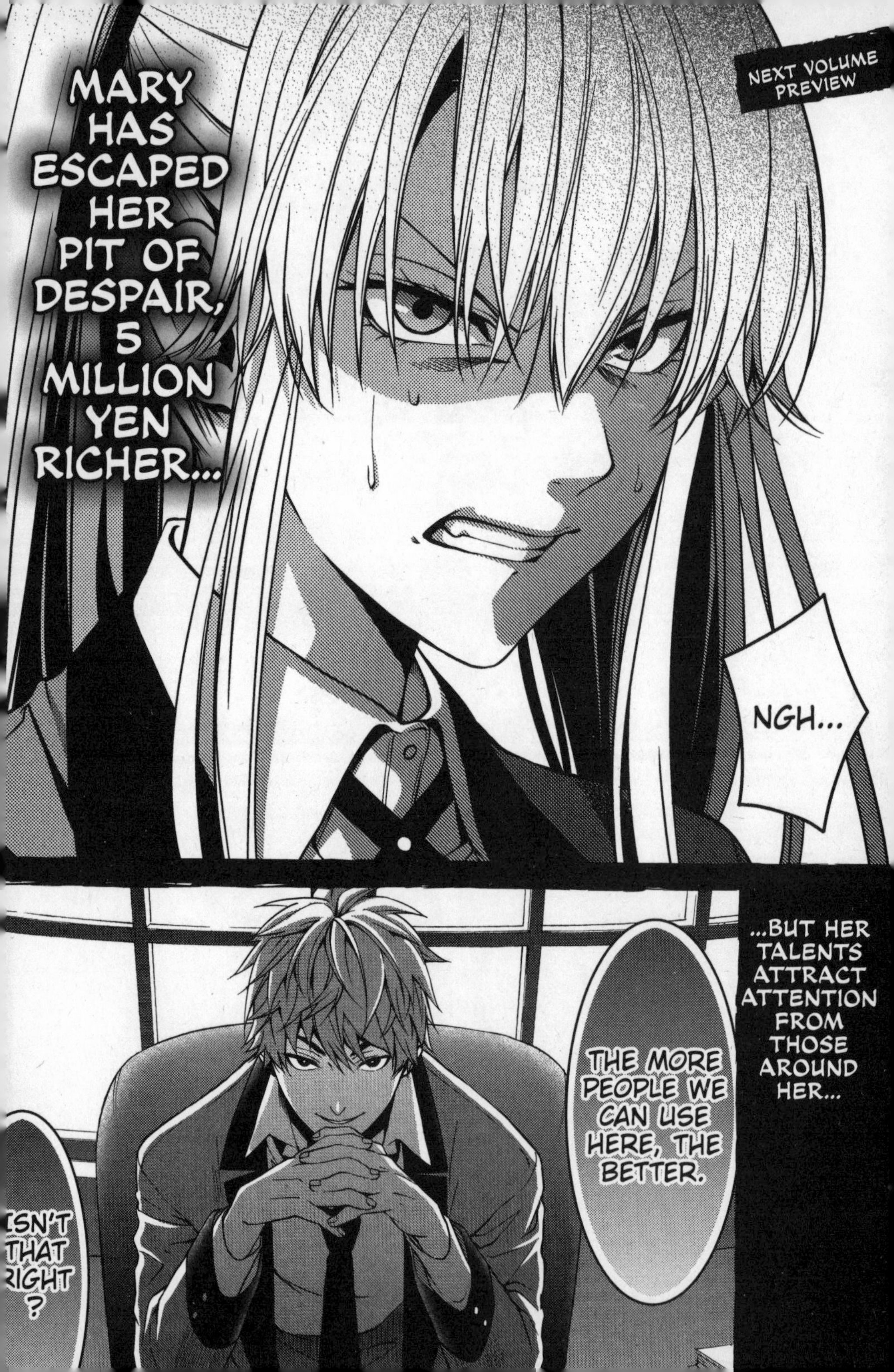
NEXT VOLUME PREVIEW
MARY HAS ESCAPED HER PIT OF DESPAIR, 5 MILLION YEN RICHER...
NGH...
...BUT HER TALENTS ATTRACT ATTENTION FROM THOSE AROUND HER...
THE MORE PEOPLE WE CAN USE HERE, THE BETTER.
ISN'T THAT RIGHT?

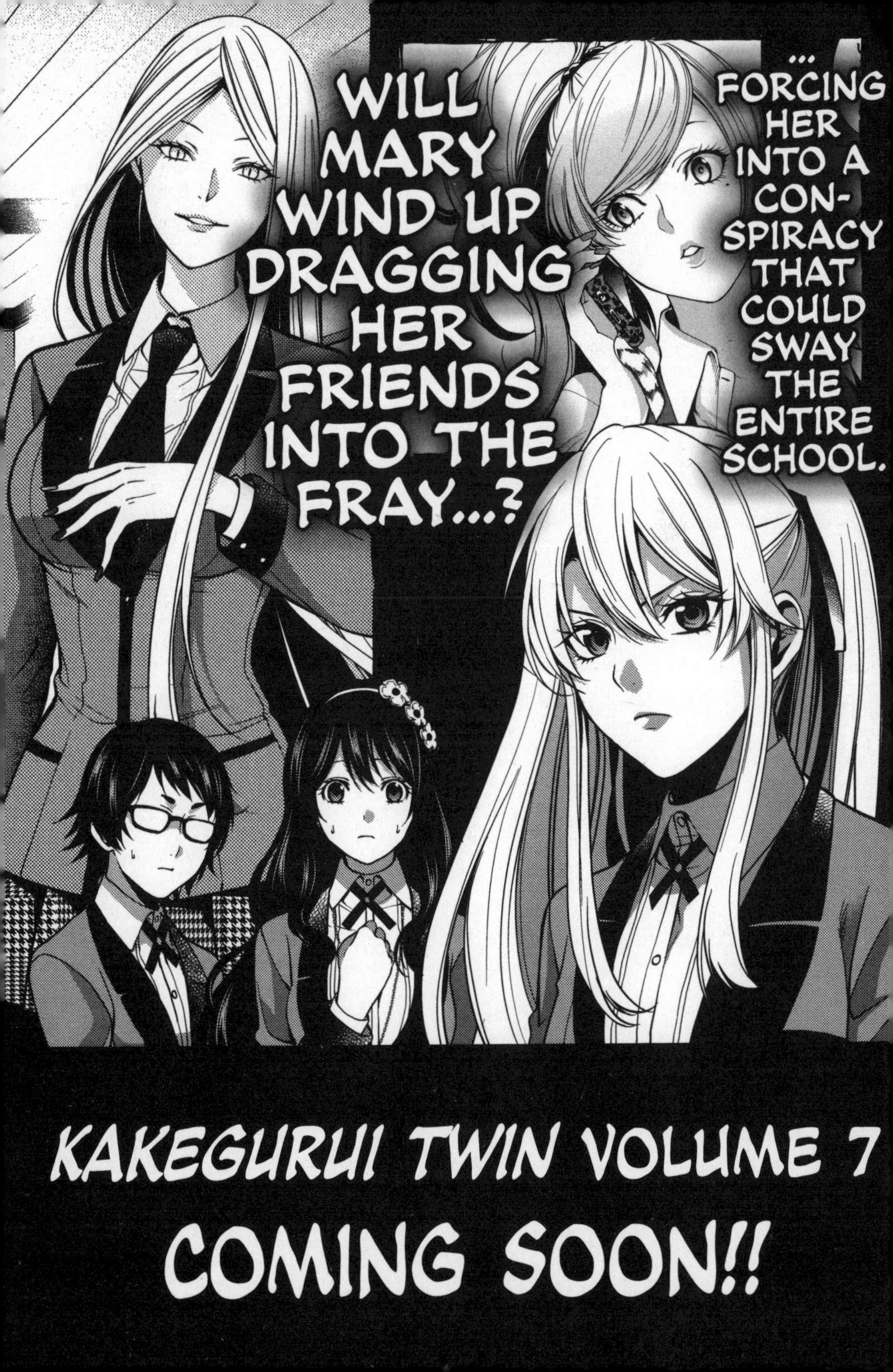
...FORCING HER INTO A CON-SPIRACY THAT COULD SWAY THE ENTIRE SCHOOL.
WILL MARY WIND UP DRAGGING HER FRIENDS INTO THE FRAY...?

KAKEGURUI TWIN VOLUME 7

COMING SOON!!

STORY: **Homura Kawamoto**   ART: **Kei Saiki**

Translation: Kevin Gifford   Lettering: Anthony Quintessenza

This book is a work of fiction. Names, characters, places, and incidents are the product of the author's imagination or are used fictitiously. Any resemblance to actual events, locales, or persons, living or dead, is coincidental.

KAKEGURUI TWIN Vol. 6 ©2018 Homura Kawamoto, Kei Saiki/
SQUARE ENIX CO., LTD.
First published in Japan in 2018 by SQUARE ENIX CO., LTD.
English translation rights arranged with SQUARE ENIX CO., LTD.
and Yen Press, LLC through Tuttle-Mori Agency, Inc.

English translation ©2020 by SQUARE ENIX CO., LTD.

Yen Press
150 West 30th Street, 19th Floor
New York, NY 10001

Visit us at yenpress.com
facebook.com/yenpress
twitter.com/yenpress
yenpress.tumblr.com
instagram.com/yenpress

First Yen Press Edition: May 2020

Yen Press is an imprint of Yen Press, LLC.
The Yen Press name and logo are trademarks of Yen Press, LLC.

The publisher is not responsible for websites (or their content) that are not owned by the publisher.

Library of Congress Control Number: 2018961911

ISBNs: 978-1-9753-0343-3 (paperback)
978-1-9753-0365-5 (ebook)

10 9 8 7 6 5 4 3 2 1

WOR

Printed in the United States of America